Warfare in H

GW00538556

INFANTRY WARFARE
—— IN THE ——
EARLY FOURTEENTH CENTURY

DISCIPLINE, TACTICS, AND TECHNOLOGY

This study departs from the conventional view of the dominance of cavalry in medieval warfare: its objective is to establish the often decisive importance of infantry. In pursuit of evidence, Kelly DeVries examines the role of the infantry, and the nature of infantry tactics, in nineteen battles fought in England and Europe between 1302 and 1347. In most of these battles it was the infantry which secured victory. Evidence from first-hand accounts of the battles – a major feature of this study – is employed to argue that victory came not because of superior technology, even when the longbow was used, but due to a solid and disciplined infantry line making a defensive stand able to withstand the attacks of opposing soldiers, whether cavalry or infantry.

KELLY DeVRIES teaches medieval history and the history of technology at Loyola College in Maryland.

Warfare in History
General Editor: Matthew Bennett
ISSN 1358–779X

The Battle of Hastings: Sources and Interpretations
edited and translated by Stephen Morillo

Infantry Warfare in the Early Fourteenth Century:
Discipline, Tactics, and Technology
Kelly DeVries

The Art of Warfare in Western Europe during the Middle Ages
from the Eighth Century to 1340
J.F. Verbruggen

Knights and Peasants:
The Hundred Years War in the French Countryside
Nicholas Wright

INFANTRY WARFARE
—— IN THE ——
EARLY FOURTEENTH CENTURY

DISCIPLINE, TACTICS, AND TECHNOLOGY

Kelly DeVries

THE BOYDELL PRESS

First published 1996
The Boydell Press, Woodbridge
Reprinted in paperback 1998

Transferred to digital printing

ISBN 978-0-85115-571-5

The Boydell Press is an imprint of Boydell & Brewer Ltd
PO Box 9, Woodbridge, Suffolk IP12 3DF, UK
and of Boydell & Brewer Inc.
668 Mt Hope Avenue, Rochester, NY 14620, USA
website: www.boydellandbrewer.com

A CiP catalogue record for this book is available
from the British Library

Library of Congress Catalog Card Number: 96-12439

This publication is printed on acid-free paper

CONTENTS

ACKNOWLEDGEMENTS

Upon completing my dissertation, *Perceptions of Victory and Defeat in the Southern Low Countries during the Fourteenth Century: A Historiographical Comparison*, at the University of Toronto's Centre for Medieval Studies in 1987, it was suggested that I should divide what I had written into two studies: one which discussed what was happening on the battlefield and another which analyzed how medieval writers rationalized military defeat. I will be forever grateful to my advisors, Professors Bert S. Hall and Michael R. Powicke, for their constant stewardship and friendship in the initial writing of my dissertation. Also owed thanks are Professors Joseph Goering, John Munro, and John Gilchrist who read and commented on that dissertation.

This book is the first result of that suggestion, discussing what occurred on the battlefields of Europe from 1302 to 1347. Three of the chapters, on the battles of Courtrai, Mons-en-Pévèle, and Cassel, are drawn directly from the research which I completed in that dissertation. The other chapters grew out of a desire to discover whether what was occurring in battles fought in the southern Low Countries during the early fourteenth century was also happening elsewhere throughout Europe. I quickly realized that it was, and the book from that time on simply 'wrote itself'.

I have been assisted in this endeavor primarily by a Junior Faculty Sabbatical awarded to me by Loyola College and funded by the Center for the Humanities there. Other funding came from a Loyola College Summer Research Grant and a Wilfrid Laurier University Research Initiation Grant. Assistance has also come from the Interlibrary Loan Departments at Loyola College and Wilfrid Laurier University Libraries.

I again must thank my wife, Barbara Middleton, for reading and editing this manuscript, and for many others who constantly urged me to complete it. I wish also to express my love and thanks to my children. Finally, I wish to thank the Little League Baseball teams which I have coached during the past three years. They have taught me that every team has sufficient offense to win, but that it is defense that ultimately decides victory.

ABBREVIATIONS

AHDG	*Archives historiques du département de la Gironde*
CCF	*Corpus chronicorum Flandriae*
CL	*Chroniques Liégeoises*
CRHB	Commission royale d'histoire de Belgique
CS	Camden Society
EETS	Early English Text Society
EHS	English Historical Society
FRG	*Fontes rerum Germanicarum*
HS	Historians of Scotland
MGH	*Monumenta Germaniae Historica*
MGH, SS	*Monumenta Germaniae Historica, Scriptores*
PG	*Patrologia Graeca*
RHF	*Recueil des historiens de la Gaule et de la France*
RS	Rolls Series
SHF	Société de l'histoire de France
SRI	*Scriptores rerum Italicarum*
WHGU	Werken uitgegeven door het Historisch Genootschap te Utrecht
WUVG	Werken uitgegeven door de Vereenigen Gelre

INTRODUCTION

THIS BOOK IS ABOUT medieval battles. Until only recently, up to the last forty years or so, the study of medieval battles had been an important scholarly endeavor. Historians writing large surveys of medieval military history in the late nineteenth and early twentieth centuries, such as G. Kohler, Sir Charles Oman, Hans Delbrück, E. Daniels, and W. Erben, all based their works on battle narrative, or what John Keegan would later call the 'battle piece.'[1] One need only take a cursory look at the table of contents in these works to see that chapters on other aspects of medieval warfare, most notably military technology, are almost completely ignored among those devoted to medieval battles. Also omitted is nearly all discussion of siege warfare, campaign strategy, logistics, military obligation and recruitment, booty, the laws of war, ethics and religious aspects of military conflict, military intelligence, the psychology of the medieval soldier, and the relationship between war, government, and society.

This tradition survived into the middle of this century. Ferdinand Lot's two-volume *L'art militaire et les armées au Moyen Age, en Europe et dans le Proche-Orient*, published in 1946, is nearly identical to Oman's or Delbrück's previous works in its approach to the subject, except that Lot dwells far more on the numbers of soldiers participating in medieval battles than do his predecessors.[2] A decade later, Lieutenant-Colonel Alfred H. Burne devoted two volumes to the study of the Hundred Years War which, although also addressing the siege warfare and campaign strategies of the conflict, used a 'battle piece' methodology to link it all together.[3]

Finally, perhaps the most important and certainly one of the most enduring studies of medieval battles appeared in 1954, although to a large extent its popularity was not realized until after a flawed English translation was published in 1977.[4] J.F.

---

[1] G. Kohler, *Die Entwicklung des Kriegswesens und der Kriegführung in der Ritterzeit von Mitte des 11. Jahrhunderts bis zu den Hussitenkriegen*, 3 vols. (Breslau, 1886); Sir Charles Oman, *A History of the Art of War: The Middle Ages from the Fourth to the Fourteenth Century* (London, 1898) and *A History of the Art of War in the Middle Ages*, 2 vols. (London, 1905); Hans Delbrück, *History of the Art of War Within the Framework of Political History*, vol. III: *Medieval Warfare*, trans. W.J. Renfroe, Jr. (Westport, 1984), originally *Geschichte der Kriegskunst im Rahmen des Politischen Geschichte*, vol. III: *Mittelalter*, 2nd ed. (Berlin, 1923); E. Daniels, *Geschichte des Kriegswesens*, vol. II: *Das mittelalterliche Kriegswesen*, 2nd ed. (Berlin, 1927); and W. Erben, *Kriegsgeschichte des Mittelalters* (Berlin, 1929). See also John Keegan, *The Face of Battle* (Harmondsworth, 1978).

[2] Ferdinand Lot, *L'art militaire et les armées au moyen âge en Europe et dans le proche orient*, 2 vols. (Paris, 1946).

[3] Alfred H. Burne, *The Crecy War: A Military History of the Hundred Years War from 1337 to the Peace of Bretigny, 1360* (London, 1955) and *The Agincourt War: A Military History of the Latter Part of the Hundred Years War from 1369 to 1453* (London, 1956).

[4] J.F. Verbruggen, *The Art of Warfare in Western Europe during the Middle Ages: From the Eighth Century to 1340*, trans. S. Willard and S.C.M. Southern (Amsterdam, 1977). This publication lacked notes or bibliography, abridges the first section by eliminating many of Verbruggen's examples, and

Verbruggen's *De krijgkunst in west-europa in de middeleeuwen (IXe tot XIVe eeuw)* uses several battle narratives to explain his theses on medieval strategy and tactics.[5] In presenting these theses Verbruggen disagrees with most other medieval military historians, including all mentioned above – although Lot, Verbruggen's mentor, receives his softest criticisms; these other historians, Verbruggen complains, frequently misread and thus misused original sources describing the battles on which they were writing. In particular, they disregarded vernacular sources, preferring to use Latin ones. They also often ignored battle eyewitnesses, despite the obvious superiority of such sources. Finally, and most importantly for Verbruggen, those authors he criticizes considered medieval warfare to be without an 'art': medieval soldiers did not fight with a strategy or tactic in mind, and generalship, by strict definition, did not exist. To Verbruggen, there definitely was an 'art' of medieval warfare. Both cavalry and infantry warriors fought with a tactical skill for which modern scholars have generally not given them credit. They fought as units of soldiers and not as individuals; these units fought with order and cohesion.

Cavalry soldiers, knights, were trained to fight in this way, as skilled in battlefield tactics as they were in the use of warhorses and weaponry. It was, as Verbruggen calls it, a 'psychology of fighting', which certainly did not disappear once they entered battle. Knights knew the tactical meaning of the standard, the importance of order in formations, the protection of the flanks, the place of the suppliers on the battlefield, and the regrouping of formations after contact. The 'psychology of fighting' also was aided by a strict obedience to commands and the use of banners and trumpets to increase communication. It resulted in difficult and learned battlefield maneuvers such as the feigned retreat.

But cavalry alone rarely won battles. Only when infantry was used to support the knights, and when archers were used to soften the enemy in preparation for cavalry charges, were great victories had in medieval battles. Verbruggen describes in detail seven battles in which the cavalry/infantry tactics show a planned order and an understanding of good military methods: Antioch (February 9 and June 28, 1098), Axpoel (June 21, 1128), Arsoef (September 7, 1191), the Steppes (October 13, 1213), Bouvines (July 27, 1214), and Woeringen (June 5, 1288).

While cavalry alone rarely won battles, infantry alone sometimes did. In what he describes as 'the miracle of the fourteenth century', Verbruggen cites the success of peasant infantry forces – the Swiss, Welsh, and Scots – and urban infantry forces – the Italian militias, the Flemings, and the Liégeois – as examples of infantry-based armies which were highly skilled in battlefield tactics. These led to several 'victories', although Verbruggen only recounts three: Courtrai (July 11, 1302), Arques (April 4, 1303), and Mons-en-Pévèle (August 18, 1304). (Even though Verbruggen does not characterize Mons-en-Pévèle as a victory, he does claim that the Flemish

---

excludes, inexplicably, the author's narrative on the battle of the Steppes. A new translation restoring these omissions is currently being prepared.

5 J.F. Verbruggen, *De krijgkunst in west-europa in de middeleeuwen (IXe tot XIVe eeuw)* (Brussels, 1954). See also J.F. Verbruggen, 'La tactique militaire des armées de chevaliers,' *Revue du nord* 29 (1947), 161–80.

infantry's adept knowledge of tactical maneuvers used there caused great slaughter among the much larger French cavalry-based force.)

Although challenging some of his infantry warfare theses, and also his battle narratives of Courtrai, Arques, and Mons-en-Pévèle, this study must consider Verbruggen's work as its scholarly grandfather.

It has been more than forty years since Verbruggen's work originally appeared and more than eighteen years since its English translation was published. Most historians have continued to praise it,[6] but few have followed its lead or tested its theses. The most popular surveys on medieval military history written after Verbruggen, Philippe Contamine's *War in the Middle Ages* and John Beeler's *Warfare in Feudal Europe*, have very little to say about medieval tactics.[7] The same holds true for works which survey shorter chronological periods.[8] Justifiably, medieval military historians have looked elsewhere to increase the knowledge of military topics. Good, lengthy works have recently been written on siege warfare, military organization and obligation, Just War and the Peace of God, military orders, chivalry, and military technology.[9]

---

[6] See, for example, Claude Gaier, 'Relire Verbruggen,' *Moyen Age* 85 (1979), 105–12 and Bryce Lyon, 'The Role of Cavalry in Medieval Warfare: Horses, Horses All Around and Not a One to Use,' *Mededelingen van de Koninklijke Academie voor Wetenschappen, Letteren en Schone Kunsten van België* 49 (1987), 77–90. Another article which draws upon Verbruggen for inspiration is Dennis E. Showalter, 'Caste, Skill, and Training: The Evolution of Cohesion in European Armies from the Middle Ages to the Sixteenth Century,' *Journal of Military History* 57 (1993), 407–30.

[7] Philippe Contamine, *War in the Middle Ages*, trans. M. Jones (London, 1984) and John Beeler, *Warfare in Feudal Europe, 730–1200* (Ithaca, 1971).

[8] See, for example, John Beeler, *Warfare in England, 1066–1189* (Ithaca, 1966); Stephen Morillo, *Warfare under the Anglo-Norman Kings, 1066–1135* (Woodbridge, 1994); R.C. Smail, *Crusading Warfare, 1097–1193* (Cambridge, 1956); Christopher Marshall, *Warfare in the Latin East, 1192–1291* (Cambridge, 1992); Christopher Allmand, *The Hundred Years War: England and France at War, c.1300–c.1450* (Cambridge, 1988); and Anne Curry, *The Hundred Years War* (Houndmills, 1993).

[9] For an excellent bibliography of medieval military topics (to 1983) see Philippe Contamine, *War in the Middle Ages*, pp. 309–60. The following include some of the book titles which have appeared since then. On siege warfare: Jim Bradbury, *The Medieval Siege* (Woodbridge, 1992); R. Rogers, *Latin Siege Warfare in the Twelfth Century* (Oxford, 1992); and Ivy A. Corfis and Michael Wolfe, eds., *The Medieval City Under Siege* (Woodbridge, 1995). On military obligation and organization: Richard P. Abels, *Lordship and Military Obligation in Anglo-Saxon England* (Berkeley, 1988); James F. Powers, *A Society Organized for War: The Iberian Municipal Militias in the Central Middle Ages, 1000–1284* (Berkeley, 1988); Mark C. Bartusis, *The Late Byzantine Army: Arms and Society, 1204–1453* (Philadelphia, 1992); and Andrew Ayton, *Knights and Warhorses: Military Service and the English Aristocracy under Edward III* (Woodbridge, 1994); On Just War and Peace of God: Thomas Head and Richard Landes, eds., *The Peace of God: Social Violence and Religious Response in France around the Year 1000* (Ithaca, 1992). On military orders: Alan Forey, *The Military Orders: From the Twelfth to the Fourteenth Century* (Toronto, 1992); Helen Nicholson, *Templars, Hospitallers and Teutonic Knights: Images of the Military Orders, 1128–1291* (Leicester, 1995); Peter Partner, *The Knights Templar and their Myth* (Oxford, 1981); and Malcolm Barber, *The New Knighthood: A History of the Order of the Temple* (Cambridge, 1994). On chivalry: Maurice Keen, *Chivalry* (New Haven, 1984); Juliet R.V. Barker, *The Tournament in England, 1100–1400* (Woodbridge, 1986); and Howell Chickering and Thomas H. Seiler, eds., *The Study of Chivalry: Resources and Approaches* (Kalamazoo, 1988). On military technology: Kelly DeVries, *Medieval Military Technology* (Peterborough, 1992); John R. Kenyon, *Medieval Fortifications* (New York, 1990); N.J.G. Pounds, *The Medieval Castle in England and Wales: A Social and Political History* (Cambridge, 1990); M.W. Thompson, *The Rise of the Castle* (Cambridge, 1991); M.W. Thompson, *The Decline of the Castle* (Cambridge, 1987); R.H.C.

A few good biographies on military leaders have also been published.[10]

However, battle narrative has all but disappeared, and despite Verbruggen's continued popularity, there still endures a nearly universal belief that medieval tactics were non-existent. Sir Charles Oman's characterization of medieval fighting skill, 'when mere courage takes place of skill and experience, tactics and strategy alike disappear' and '. . . it was impossible to combine the movements of many small bodies when the troops were neither disciplined nor accustomed to act together', still holds for most writing about medieval warfare.[11] For example, one of the most popular textbooks of military history, *Men in Arms*, describes medieval tactics:

> A feudal army in the field was an indescribably undisciplined force. Many tenants-in-chief would take orders only from their immediate overlord, the king; therefore an effective chain of command was impossible. There was a superabundance of courage, which tended to aggravate rather than to relieve the normal disorder. Long centuries of control of the art of war by one class, the exaggerated concentration upon cavalry warfare alone, and the absence of any provision for group training except in a restricted fashion in the reformed tournament meant that the study and practice of organized tactics had all but vanished . . . once the battle was joined, all semblance of order disappeared, and the struggle became nothing more than a confused melee of hundreds of individual encounters.[12]

Medieval military scholars are no different in their criticism of medieval tactics and tactical leadership. As Philippe Contamine writes:

Davis, *The Medieval Warhorse* (London, 1989); and John H. Pryor, *Geography, Technology, and War: Studies in the Maritime History of the Mediterranean, 649–1571* (Cambridge, 1988).

10 On Fulk Nerra see: Bernard S. Bachrach, *Fulk Nerra, the Neo-Roman Consul, 987–1040* (Berkeley, 1993). On William the Conqueror see: David C. Douglas, *William the Conqueror: The Norman Impact upon England* (Berkeley, 1964) and Frank Barlow, *William I and the Norman Conquest* (New York, 1965). On the Cid see: Richard Fletcher, *The Quest for El Cid* (Oxford, 1989). On Richard the Lionheart see: John Gillingham, *Richard the Lionheart* (London, 1978). On Saladin see: Malcolm Cameron Lyons and D.E.P. Jackson, *Saladin: The Politics of the Holy War* (Cambridge, 1982). On William Marshal see: Georges Duby, *William Marshal: The Flower of Chivalry*, trans. R. Howard (New York, 1985) and David Crouch, *William Marshal* (London, 1994). On Edward I see: Michael Prestwich, *Edward I* (Berkeley, 1988). On Robert Bruce see G.W.S. Barrow, *Robert Bruce and the Community of the Realm of Scotland*, 3rd ed. (Edinburgh, 1988) and Ronald McNair Scott, *Robert the Bruce: King of Scots* (New York, 1982). On Edward the Black Prince see: Richard Barber, *Edward, Prince of Wales and Aquitaine: A Biography of the Black Prince* (London, 1978). On Henry V see: Christopher Allmand, *Henry V* (Berkeley, 1992). On Charles VII see: M.G.A. Vale, *Charles VII* (Berkeley, 1974). On John Talbot see: Hugh Talbot, *The English Achilles: The Life and Campaigns of John Talbot, 1st Earl of Shrewsbury* (London, 1981) and A.J. Pollard, *John Talbot and the War in France, 1427–1453* (London, 1983). And on Joan of Arc, among many others, see: Marina Warner, *Joan of Arc: The Image of Female Heroism* (Harmondsworth, 1981) and Reginé Pernoud, *Joan of Arc: By Herself and Her Witnesses*, trans. E. Hyams (New York, 1964).

11 Sir Charles Oman, *The Art of War in the Middle Ages A.D. 378–1515*, ed. J.H. Beeler (Ithaca, 1953), pp. 58, 60. This is Oman's undergraduate essay, published in 1885, and should not be confused either with his 1898 version or his 1905 two volume revision.

12 Richard A. Preston, Alex Roland, and Sydney F. Wise, *Men at Arms*, 5th ed. (Fort Worth, 1991), pp. 69–70. See also John Keegan, *Face of Battle*, p. 336; Martin van Creveld, *Command in War* (Cambridge, 1985); and Archer Jones, *The Art of War in the Western World* (Oxford, 1989), pp. 144–45.

It should be agreed that medieval military history includes many battles which were nothing but hasty, instinctive and confused confrontations in which captains played the role of simple leaders of men, incorporated almost anonymously into the first line of battle, and where the warriors' chief concern was to find an adversary worthy of rank or valour, without any preoccupation for their companions in arms. They grappled on the battlefield with a sort of holy fury, free to flee precipitately as soon as things seemed to be going against them, and the individual search for booty and ransom was all-important.[13]

Even those who do give some plausibility to medieval tactical efficiency seem to 'damn with faint praise', as B.H. Liddell Hart illustrates:

In the West during the Middle Ages the spirit of feudal chivalry was inimical to military art, though the drab stupidity of its military course is lightened by a few bright gleams – no fewer perhaps, in proportion, than at any other period in history.[14]

This has led to an attempted determinism of battlefield victory that removes the soldier or his general as the cause of victory. Greater numbers, the presence of the mounted shock combat, and superior technology are more frequent determinants for victory in medieval battles. One example of this is the enduring belief that knightly cavalry continued to dominate the battlefield. These troops after all excelled in the tactics of mounted shock combat. Couching lances under their arms and using the force of their charging warhorses, they were able to deliver a blow with such an impact that few could defend against it. Those few infantry victories accorded by defenders of 'The Age of the Horse' are portrayed as temporary accidents.[15] Such a portrayal completely ignores the numerous infantry victories of the early fourteenth century, nineteen of which are recounted here.

Another good example of this, and one that is particularly pertinent to this work, is the 'tenacious myth' of the longbow. Since at least the sixteenth century many military historians have believed that the longbow significantly changed English strategy and tactics in the later Middle Ages, so much so that England was to gain many victories solely because of its use in warfare. In 1298, for example, Edward I took a troop of over 10,000 archers with him on his conquest of Scotland (a ratio of three archers to one mounted man-at-arms), an extremely large number in

---

[13] Contamine, *War in the Middle Ages*, p. 229.
[14] B.H. Liddell Hart, *Strategy: The Indirect Approach* (New York, 1954), p. 75. See also John Beeler, 'Towards a Re-Evaluation of Medieval English Leadership,' *Journal of British Studies* 3 (1963), 1–10.
[15] See Contamine, *War in the Middle Ages*, pp. 126–32; Bryce Lyon; Preston, Roland, and Wise, pp. 62–66; Michael Howard, *War in European History* (Oxford, 1976), pp. 1–19; Claude Gaier, 'La cavalerie lourde en Europe occidentale du XIIe au XVIe siècle,' *Revue internationale d'histoire militaire* 31 (1971), 385–96; and Robert Bartlett, 'Military Technology and Political Power,' in *The Making of Europe: Conquest, Colonization and Cultural Change, 950–1350* (Princeton, 1993), pp. 60–63. See also J.F. Verbruggen, 'La tactique de la chevalerie Française de 1340 à 1415,' *Publications de l'université de l'état à Elisabethville* 1 (1961), 39–48 and J.F. Verbruggen, 'De rol van de ruiterij in de middeleeuwse oorlogvoering,' *Revue Belge d'histoire militaire* 30 (1994), 389–418. Verbruggen insists in these articles that, although cavalry armies remained dominant until the end of the Middle Ages, they did adapt their tactics to counter the new tactics of infantry armies.

comparison with the numbers of archers included in English armies previous to this time. And he was victorious. Also victorious was the English army, again including a large contingent of archers, which faced the Scots at Dupplin Moor in 1332 and at Halidon Hill in 1333. Finally, English archers participated in the decisive victories over the French army at the battles of Sluys (1340), Morlaix (1342), Crécy (1346), Poitiers (1356) and Agincourt (1415).[16] Crediting the longbow with all of these victories, however, removes any recognition of the non-archery infantry soldiers which were also present among the English forces. Furthermore, it also devalues English generalship, determining that Edward III, the Black Prince, or Henry V did little more than take advantage of this 'invincible' technology. Finally, it also fails to explain the victories of non-English armies during the same period.

This book is about medieval battles. In particular, it is about nineteen battles which were fought in Europe between 1302 and 1347. This is not to say that medieval battles were the most important aspect of warfare during this period, or in fact during any period of medieval history, nor that any of the battles discussed here could be considered 'decisive' in the way that Sir Edward Creasy, Major General J.F.C. Fuller, or Joseph Dahmus would define the term.[17] Indeed, only in the battle of Kephissos, fought between the Catalan Company and the duke of Athens in 1311, was one side so defeated, the Athenians, that the other side immediately took over their previous land holdings and began to govern their previous subjects. Yet, this government lasted only for seventy years, hardly establishing the battle as 'decisive'.

In most other instances, the battles discussed here did not even decide the immediate future of the two sides, necessitating that further battles be fought. Thus the Scots fought with the English at Loudon Hill in 1307, at Bannockburn in 1314, at Dupplin Moor in 1332, at Halidon Hill in 1333, and at Neville's Cross in 1346; the English fought the French at Morlaix in 1342, at Auberoche in 1345, at Crécy in 1346, and at Le Roche-Derrien in 1347; and the Flemings fought the French at Courtrai in 1302, at Arques in 1303, at Mons-en-Pévèle in 1304, and at Cassel in 1328. (They also assisted the English against the French at Sluys and Tournai in 1340 and at Calais in 1346–47, conflicts not discussed in this work.) The threat of Flemish assistance to the English may even have been the determining factor in rushing the French attack at Crécy in 1346.

---

[16] T.H. McGuffie, 'The Long-bow as a Decisive Weapon,' *History Today* 5 (1955), 737–41; Jim Bradbury, *The Medieval Archer* (New York, 1985), 71–138; Robert Hardy, *Longbow: A Social and Military History*, 3rd ed. (London, 1992); Robert Hardy, 'The Longbow,' in *Arms, Armies and Fortifications in the Hundred Years War*, ed. A. Curry and M. Hughes (Woodbridge, 1994), pp. 161–82; Clifford J. Rogers, 'The Military Revolutions of the Hundred Years War,' *Journal of Military History* 57 (1993), 249–51; and Gareth Rees, 'The Longbow's Deadly Secrets,' *New Scientist* 138 (June 5, 1993), 24–25. Against the decisiveness of the longbow, see John Keegan, *Face of Battle*, pp. 78–116 and Claude Gaier, 'L'invincibilité anglaise et le grande arc après la guerre de cent ans: un mythe tenace,' *Tijdschrift voor gescheidenis* 91 (1978), 378–85. See also my discussion in *Medieval Military Technology*, pp. 37–39.

[17] Sir Edward Creasy, *The Fifteen Decisive Battles of the World*, 36th ed. (London, 1894); J.F.C. Fuller, *The Decisive Battles of the Western World and their Influence upon History*, 2nd ed., 2 vols. (London, 1970); and Joseph Dahmus, *Seven Decisive Battles of the Middle Ages* (Chicago, 1983).

Other battles may stand out as far as opponents are concerned, but they too cannot be considered 'decisive' in that the conflicts had very limited results. This is especially true in the battles which were fought against rebels, where independence, if gained at all by the battle, was generally fairly short in duration. This includes not only all of the Flemish/French battles, but also the battle of Morgarten, fought in 1315 between the duke of Austria and Swiss rebels; the battle of Boroughbridge, fought in 1322 between the army of King Edward II of England and the rebellious force of the duke of Lancaster; the battle of Staveren, fought in 1345 between the William, the count of Hainault, and his Frisian rebels; and the battle of Vottem, fought in 1346 between the prince-bishop of Liège and his rebellious subjects. Of these, only the battle of Morgarten brought some lasting independence for its victors. Finally, almost as an anomaly, the battle of Laupen was fought in 1339 between two neighboring Swiss towns; it also decided very little.

What all of these battles have in common, beyond the chronological similarity, is that large infantry forces participated in all of them; and in most instances they were victorious – the battles of Mons-en-Pévèle and Cassel being the only exceptions. Moreover, in each instance victory came not because of superior technology, even when the longbow was present, but because a solid, disciplined, and tactically proficient infantry line making a defensive stand was able to withstand the attacks of opposing soldiers, whether cavalry or infantry.

Although nineteen battles are detailed here, these certainly are not all of the battles of the early fourteenth century. The selection of these battles was made simply because original sources detailing the tactics on the battlefield were available. In some cases, notably the battles of Courtrai, Bannockburn, and Crécy, there were several sources which reported the battlefield action, while other battles had only one or two sources which discussed the tactics, namely Loudon Hill, Laupen, and Staveren. Even then, the number of early fourteenth-century battles which are mentioned in the sources without a discussion of tactics are numerous. This undoubtedly makes the early fourteenth century the most prolific period for battles in the entire Middle Ages, and certainly one of the reasons for the narrow focus of this study.

The chronological boundaries of this study are, hopefully, justified. The Black Death, which begins in Europe in 1347, changed the nature of warfare for the remainder of the Hundred Years War. Thus while there is surely some comparison between the battle of Poitiers, fought in 1356, and those battles which are discussed here, the difference in sizes of English and French forces at Poitiers and those at Crécy must be ascribed to the loss of population. The decision of 1302 as the beginning point of the study is perhaps more difficult to explain. In choosing to begin there, I have decided to follow Verbruggen's lead in recognizing the originality of the battle of Courtrai rather than moving the chronological time-frame back to the battles of Woeringen, Stirling Bridge, or Falkirk, despite some similarities between those battles and the ones which are included in this book.

Finally, in order to understand what this book is trying to say there is a need to define the word 'battle'. While most dictionaries may define 'battle' in a rather general way – Merriam-Webster defines it as 'a general military engagement' – only battles which saw two armies entirely assembled and ordered against each other are included for study here. That comprises all but three of the nineteen conflicts listed above, excluding the battles of Morgarten, Auberoche, and La Roche-Derrien, all of which are for the purposes here defined as 'ambushes'. (Details of these conflicts have been included in an appendix.)

I

THE BATTLE OF COURTRAI, 1302

IN 1302, PHILIP THE FAIR ruled France. Four years earlier, he had signed a truce with his enemy, Edward I of England, after a small war fought entirely on Flemish soil which resulted in Edward's loss and his expulsion from the continent. For his participation in the war, Guy of Dampierre, the count of Flanders and ally to Edward I, was imprisoned by Philip.[1] James of St. Pol became the royal governor of Flanders who enforced the king's laws with a large French army. (Indeed, it was the only standing army in Philip's France.) The independent towns of Flanders considered any intrusion by France into their affairs, especially occupation by a large fighting force, to be a breach of their political power. James of St. Pol recognized the hatred of the Flemish towns, especially Bruges, and on May 17, accompanied by Pierre Flote, the king's chief advisor and negotiator, he took his army into Bruges to negotiate a peace with the towns.

When they arrived at Bruges, most of the rebellious faction of the city had fled, and those who were left refused to negotiate with James. The French army harassed the townspeople, especially the families of those who had fled, and stories of mistreatment were conveyed to the rebels hiding outside the town. At sunrise on May 18, while the French army for the most part was asleep, the Brugeois rebels attacked, killing over 300 soldiers. James of St. Pol and Pierre Flote fled the city, James to the castle of Courtrai and Pierre to the city of Lille, where they informed the king of the rebellion and massacre.[2]

Knowing that this massacre would bring certain violent repercussions, the people of Bruges amassed their forces and sent representatives to the other Flemish towns asking for support. All but Ghent responded favorably. This army then moved to Oudenaarde, the nearest stronghold of the French. Guy of Namur and William of Jülich, the son and grandson of the imprisoned count, met the army at Oudenaarde and joined their small forces to it, becoming the leaders of the entire armed contingent. Oudenaarde fell within a few days, and the Flemish soldiers marched to

[1] An excellent study of Philip's relations with Flanders is Frantz Funck-Brentano, *Philippe le Bel en Flandre: Les origines de la guerre de cent ans* (Paris, 1896).

[2] Several sources detail the 'Matins' massacre of May 18, 1302 in Bruges. The most notable original source is the anonymous *Annales Gandenses*, ed. Hilda Johnstone (London, 1951), which is, however, partisan to the Brugeois rebels. The best secondary narratives are Funck-Brentano, *Philippe le Bel*, pp. 400–04, and J.F. Verbruggen, *De slag der guldensporen, bijdrage tot de gescheidenis van Vlaanderens vrijheidsoorlog, 1297–1305* (Antwerp, 1952), pp. 262–75.

the next fortress held by French troops, the castle of Courtrai, reaching it on June 26.[3] Philip the Fair was determined to avenge the Brugeois massacre, and he responded by sending a large French army, composed mainly of mounted knights and led by Robert, the count of Artois, against the rebels.[4] On July 11, the two armies met in battle outside the town and castle of Courtrai.

By evening, the Flemings had achieved the greatest victory in the county's history. The French had fled from the battlefield with the Flemings chasing them for as many as seven miles. The bodies of the dead were stripped, and from five to seven hundred golden spurs, spurs given for victory in tournaments, were collected by the Flemings and hung in the Cathedral of the Virgin at Courtrai. (This in turn gives the battle its modern name: the Battle of the Golden Spurs.) The list of French dead was long and contained a number of important French nobles. Dead were Robert of Artois, the leader of the French force, the count of Eu, the count of Aubermarle, Godfrey of Brabant, Jean of Hainault, Raoul de Neele (the constable of France), James of St. Pol, Henry of Luxembourg, Pierre Flote and many more.

News of the victory spread quickly throughout Europe. The pope, Boniface VIII, who had had previous difficulties with Philip, received by letter a detailed account of the battle and rejoiced in the news.[5] The victory was also reported in England, Holland, Austria and Switzerland.

The Flemings were exuberant; they paved the streets of Bruges with flowers, dragging the fleur-de-lys through the mud and shouting, 'On with the lion, and down with the lily.' Lodewijk van Velthem, a contemporary Flemish chronicler, writes: 'Never did we hear such sounds from the trumpet. The victors paraded up and down the town.'[6] Another contemporary writer, the Florentine Giovanni Villiani, adds: 'So proud and bold the Flemings have become through their victory at Courtrai, that one Fleming with his goededag would dare invite a battle against two French knights on horse.'[7]

To these and other contemporary chroniclers, the battle of Courtrai was the most important battle of their age, and indeed more fourteenth-century writers comment on it than on any other battle of the century including those fought at Crécy and at Poitiers. To many commentators the Flemish victory compared with the greatest victories in history: with the Greeks over the Trojans,[8] with the Israelites under David

---

[3] See Verbruggen, *Slag*, pp. 262–75, for a discussion of the Flemish army movements between May 18 and July 11, 1302.

[4] For Philip's reaction to the Matins massacre and his efforts to mobilize an army see Funck-Brentano, *Philippe le Bel*, p. 405. For a discussion of the size of this force see nos. 23–24 below.

[5] See Gilles li Muisit, *Chronicon*, in *Corpus chronicorum Flandriae*, ii, ed. J.J. de Smet (Brussels, 1841), p. 196.

[6] See Lodewijk van Velthem, *Voortzetting van de Spiegel historiael (1284–1316)*, ed. H. Vander Linden et al, Commission royale d'histoire de Belgique (Brussels, 1922), II:338.

[7] Giovanni Villani, *Istorie Fiorentine*, in *Scriptores rerum Italicarum*, xiii, ed. L. Muratori (Rome, 1728), c.338: '. . . per queste vittorie salirono in tanta superbia & ardire, che uno Fiamingo a pie con uno Godendac in mano harebbe atteso due cavaglieri Franceschi a cavallo.'

[8] See Jan de Klerk, *Brabantse yeesten of rijmkroniek van Braband*, ed. J.F. Willems and J.H. Bormans (Brussels, 1839), I:426.

at Gilboa[9] and with the Romans under Scipio Africanus against the Carthaginians.[10] To others the French defeat echoed Roland's loss at Roncesvalles.[11] In fact, the story of the battle of Courtrai became so well known that by the time the Dutchman Melis Stoke wrote (c.1305) he refused to give the details of the battle itself saying: 'I will not tell what happened there, for it is well known.'[12]

Although none of these contemporary or near contemporary sources claims to be an eyewitness to the battle, several contain extensive accounts of what occurred there. As well, there exists a contemporary historiography which presents both a French and a Flemish version of what occurred at the battle. For the Flemings there is the *Annales Gandenses*, written c.1310 by an anonymous Franciscan monk living in Ghent, Lodewijk van Velthem's *Spiegel historiael*, written c.1316 by a Flemish ecclesiastic, the *Chronicon comitum Flandriae*, the first part of which was written in 1329 by a monk living in the abbey of Clairmarais in St. Omer, the *Ancienne chronique de Flandre* and the *Chronique de Flandre*, which may be two redactions of the same mid-fourteenth century chronicle written in St. Omer, and the early fifteenth century *Rijmkroniek van Vlaenderen*. There is also the famous Oxford Chest, carved by a Flemish sculptor shortly after the battle, which depicts the events of the conflict. For the French there is the *Chronique Artésienne*, written c.1304 by an anonymous writer who was probably from Arras, Guillaume Guiart's historical poem, the *Branche des royaux lignages*, which was written by a French soldier who served in the Franco-Flemish war but probably did not fight at Courtrai, Geoffroi de Paris' *Chronique rimée*, written between 1314 and 1317 by a bourgeois writer living in Paris, Gilles le Muisit's *Chronicon*, written by the abbot of St. Martin's in Tournai between 1346 and 1348, the *Récits d'un bourgeois de Valenciennes*, written c.1366, two continuators of Guillaume de Nangis' *Chronicon*, the first who wrote in 1303 and the second in 1316, the *Grandes chroniques de France*, written continually throughout the fourteenth century at the Abbey of St. Denis in Paris and intended to be the official chronicles of France, and the *Chronographia regum Francorum*, written in the early fifteenth century by an anonymous author possibly also writing at St. Denis in Paris. As well, there are four significant accounts of the battle written by 'foreign' authors, men who undoubtedly spent much time in the wealthy southern Low Countries and there heard the story of the battle: Ottokar von Stiermarken's *Oesterreichische reimkroniek*, written by an official, perhaps a diplomat, of the court

---

[9] See the poem appended to the manuscript of Johannes Thilrode, *Chronicon*, in *Monumenta Germanica historiae, scriptores* (hereafter *MGH, SS*), xxv, ed. G.H. Pertz (Hannover, 1880), p. 583 and Otto von Stiermarken, *Oesterreichische reimkroniek*, in *MGH, Deutschen Chroniken*, v, ed. J. Seemuller (Hannover, 1893), II:858.

[10] See Ottokar von Stiermarken, p. 858.

[11] See Geoffroi de Paris, *Chronique rimée*, in *Recueil des historiens de la Gaule et de la France* (hereafter *RHF*), xxii, ed. Guignant and de Wailly (Paris, n.d.), ll. 1364–66; Jean de Winterthur, *Chronicon*, in *MGH, SS* (nova series), iii, ed. F. Baethegen (Hannover, 1924), p. 65; Willem Procurator, *Chronicon*, ed. Pijnacker Hardwijk, Werken uitgegeven door het Historisch Genootschap te Utrecht, 3rd ser., 20 (Amsterdam, 1904), p. 65; and Jan de Klerk, *Brabantse yeesten*, I:421.

[12] Melis Stoke, *Rijmkroniek van Holland*, ed. W.G. Brill, Werken uitgegeven door het Historisch Genootshcap te Utrecht, n.s. xl and xlii (Utrecht, 1885), p. 183: 'Te telne, wat hem daer na gheval:/ Wat si daden, weet men wel.'

of Otto von Lichtenstein c.1309, Jean de Winterthur's *Chronicon*, written in the mid-fourteenth century by a Swiss Franciscan, Willem Procurator's *Chronicon*, written by the abbot of the Benedictine monastery of Egmond in the county of Holland c.1332, and Giovanni Villani's *Istorie Fiorentine*, written c.1340 by an ambassador from Florence who frequently visited Flanders during this period.[13] From these sources a good picture of what happened at the battle of Courtrai emerges.

The Flemish army arrived at Courtrai first, on June 26, planning to besiege the town's castle which held a small garrison of French troops. The Flemish army was quite large, having been drawn from many towns and villages in the county. Lodewijk van Velthem records their numbers at 13,000, while the *Annales Gandenses* claims a total of 60,000.[14] Modern historians are not as generous in their calculations, although the number they give also indicates a sizable force, between 7,378 and 11,000.[15] Most of these were infantry soldiers, clothed with very little armor and equipped only with a popular local weapon known as a 'goededag.'[16] There were

---

[13] *Annales Gandenses*, pp. 27–33; Lodewijk van Velthem, II:285–342; *Chronicon comitum Flandriae*, in *Corpus chronicorum Flandriae*, i, ed. J.J. de Smet (Brussels, 1837), pp. 168–71; *Chronique de Flandre*, in *Istore et croniques de Flandres*, ed. Kervyn de Lettenhove (Brussels, 1879), I:476–79; *Ancienne chronique de Flandre*, in *RHF*, xxii, ed. Guignant and de Wailly (Paris, n.d.), pp. 378–79; *Rijmkroniek van Vlaenderen*, in *Corpus chronicorum Flandriae*, iv, ed. J.J. de Smet (Brussels, 1865), 797–801; *Chronique Artésienne et chronique Tournaisienne*, ed. F. Funck-Brentano (Paris, 1898), pp. 44–52; Guillaume Guiart, *Branche des royaux lignages*, in *RHF*, xxii, ed. Guignant and de Wailly (Paris, n.d.), pp. 232–240; Geoffroi de Paris, pp. 92–105; Gilles le Muisit, pp. 194–97; *Récits d'un bourgeois de Valenciennes*, ed. Kervyn de Lettenhove (Brussels, 1877), pp. 113–16; Guillaume de Nangis, *Chronicon et continuationes*, ed. H. Geraud, Société d'histoire de France (Paris, 1843), pp. 317–24; *Les grandes chroniques de France*, ed. J. Viard, Société d'histoire de France (Paris, 1934), IX:203–09; *Chronographia regum Francorum*, ed. H. Moranville (Paris, 1891), I:104–12: Ottokar von Stiermarken, pp. 846–54; Jean de Winterthur, pp. 31–32; Willem Procurator, pp. 63–65; and Giovanni Villani (ed. Muratori), cols. 387–88. A good description of the Oxford Chest is Charles ffoulkes, 'A Carved Flemish Chest at New College, Oxford,' *Archaeologia*, 2nd ser., 15 (1914), 113–28.

Henri Pirenne is the earliest historian to remark on the existence of a varying Flemish and French version of the events at the battle of Courtrai. In an article entitled 'La version flamande et la version française de la bataille de Courtrai, note historiographie de XIVe siècle' (*Bulletin de la commission royale d'histoire* 4th ser., 17 (1890), 11–50), and a later 'Note supplémentaire' (*Bulletin de la commission royale d'histoire* 5th ser., 2 (1892), 85–123), which was written in response to questions which arose in Franz Funck-Brentano's work, *Mémoire sur la bataille de Courtrai (1302, 11 juillet) et les chroniqueurs qui en ont traité, pour servir à l'historiographie du règne de Philippe le Bel* (Paris, 1891), Pirenne argued that by studying the earliest and most complete sources commenting on the battle of Courtrai it was possible to see two divergent versions of the battle based on national origin of the commentator. For a comment on Pirenne's thesis and a discussion of all the sources on Courtrai see Verbruggen, *Slag* and Verbruggen, 'De historiografie van de guldensporenslag,' *De leiegouw* (1977), 245–72.

[14] Lodewijk van Velthem, II:289 and *Annales Gandenses*, pp. 28–29.

[15] For an estimation of the number of Flemish soldiers at Courtrai see J.F. Verbruggen, *Slag*, pp. 199–237; Joseph de Smet, 'Les effectifs Brugeois à la bataille de Courtrai en 1302,' *Revue Belge de philologie et d'histoire* 12 (1933), 631–36; and Ferdinand Lot, *L'art militaire et les armées au moyen âge en Europe et dans le proche orient* (Paris, 1946), I:263–64.

[16] That the Flemings were mostly, if not all, infantry soldiers is remarked on by several of the sources. See, for example, the *Annales Gandenses*, p. 29; the *Chronique de Flandre*, I:477; and Gilles le Muisit, p. 195. The use of the 'goededag' is also of interest to many, among them the *Grandes chroniques* (VIII:204). The 'goededag' seems to have been Flemish in origin and to have been used there almost

also a few crossbowmen and a few knights, although the numbers of these troops were quite small.[17] Of the knights, few had military experience, and these – among them Guy of Namur, William of Jülich, John of Renesce, Henry of Loncin, Gossuin of Godenshoven, Dietrich of Hondeschoote, Robert of Leewergem and Baldwin of Popperorde – took up positions of leadership on the field. Pieter de Coninck, the leader of the massacre at Bruges, was also present and may have had some leadership responsibilities.[18]

The Flemings surrounded the castle and began the siege. At the same time, perhaps recognizing the probability of a battle there, they began to dig a number of ditches in the fields beyond their besieging forces. These ditches would play an important role in the battle which was to follow. Many of them were connected to the Lys river and thus filled with water; others were hidden by dirt and branches.[19] A later account, that of the *Kronyk van Vlaenderen*, written c.1477, claims that fog on the battlefield further hid the ditches.[20]

While the Flemings were besieging the castle at Courtrai, Philip the Fair had begun to gather an army. The response to the massacre of French troops at Bruges was impressive. The large size of the French army is noted in almost every account of the battle. Some of these sources, such as the *Grandes Chroniques* report only that the army contained 'many great French knights and a large multitude of infantry,'[21] while the *Chronicon comitum Flandriae* compares the force with its 'multitude' to the Flemish army 'with few men.'[22] Several sources give specific numbers for these troops ranging from a low number of 7,024 given by Lodewijk van Velthem to a high of 20,000 mentioned in the *Chronique Artésienne* and in the *Chronicon comitum*

---

exclusively. Its chief function was to bring down a knight from his horse. The best contemporary illustration of this weapon appears on a side panel of the famous Oxford Chest, carved by a Flemish sculptor shortly after the battle to celebrate the victory. (For a discussion of the Oxford Chest see Charles ffoulkes, 'A Carved Flemish Chest at New College, Oxford,' *Archaeologia* 2nd ser. 15 (1914), 113–28.) J.F. Verbruggen has written an excellent article on this weapon entitled 'De goededag,' *Militaria Belgica* 1977, 65–70.

[17] Both Lodewijk van Velthem and the anonymous author of the *Annales Gandenses* mention crossbowmen among the Flemish troops at Courtrai. They are also shown on the Oxford Chest. Their number, however, is not mentioned. Verbruggen has determined that there were fewer than 500 crossbowmen present in the Flemish army at Courtrai (*Slag*, pp. 210–11). The number of knights present offers even a more difficult calculation. While several authors note their presence, and the fact that they dismounted to fight with the infantry, no firm estimate has been given. Even Verbruggen seems hesitant to guess, again giving a total of under 500 (*Slag*, p. 211).

[18] Few sources record the names of the Flemish leaders, except for Guy of Namur, William of Jülich and John of Renesse (who may have had the chief military command). It is only the *Annales Gandenses* which provides the list above (p. 29).

[19] Almost all of the contemporary sources mention the ditches. Those who mention their construction and concealment include Otto von Stiermarken, p. 852; Geoffroi de Paris, p. 148; Jean de Winterthur, p. 22; and the *Chronographia*, I:105. The strategy of digging ditches to disrupt the charge of an opponent was not new, having been used since the sixth century, if not earlier. See R.H.C. Davis, *The Medieval Warhorse* (London, 1989), p. 14.

[20] *Kronyk van Vlaenderen van 580 tot 1467*, ed. P. Blommaert and C.P. Serrière (Ghent, 1839), I:159. Although this is not mentioned by more contemporary sources, it is a possible occurrence as this part of modern Belgium suffers frequent patches of quite thick fog during the summer months.

[21] *Grandes chroniques*, VIII:204.

[22] *Chronicon comitum Flandriae*, p. 168.

Flandriae.[23] Modern historians have reduced the latter number significantly, estimating a total of 3,000 knights and 4,000–5,000 infantry in the French army.[24] Still, by medieval military standards, the French force was quite large.

Moreover, while the Flemish soldiers fought on foot, the main and most impressive part of the French army was the cavalry. All the great and proud knights of France were present at Courtrai, clothed impressively with expensive armor and equipped with lances and swords. Many had won golden spurs at tournaments, and these symbols, together with the large number of heraldic banners, represented a force of soldiers considered by some to be the 'flower of French chivalry.'[25] At their head was the militarily experienced and distinguished Robert of Artois.

The French arrived at Courtrai on July 8. For three days the French army surveyed the situation and planned for their attack. The Flemish army had chosen the site and had prepared the field for battle. The French in turn jockeyed for a strong position from which to attack them and raise the siege of the castle.[26]

Little is known about the military activity which occurred during this period. Both the *Annales Gandenses* and Lodewijk van Velthem claim that some pre-battle skirmishing took place between the two armies, although this seems to have resulted in little actual combat.[27] Some fighting may have taken place around the site of a destroyed bridge across a 'river' running in front of the castle. Two French sources, the first continuator of Guillaume de Nangis' *Chronicon* and the *Grandes chroniques*, claim that during the days preceding the battle, the French troops attempted to repair the bridge which had been destroyed by the Flemings during their preparation of the battlefield. However, every attempt was thwarted, with the Flemings 'always attacking the French and disturbing whatever work they attempted.'[28] This may be an incorrect report, however, as it is not mentioned by any of the Flemish sources, despite the fact that such an occurrence should have elicited some comment. If it did occur, and the river referred to is the Lys River, this could represent an attempt by the French army to surround the Flemings and to attack them from the rear.

The *Annales Gandenses* also claims that Robert of Artois allowed his army to pillage the Flemish countryside around Courtrai. According to this Flemish

---

[23] Lodewijk van Velthem, II:302, 311; *Chronique Artésienne*, p. 40; and *Chronicon comitum Flandriae*, p. 168.

[24] For modern historical estimates of the French army size see Verbruggen, *Slag*, 237–50 and Lot, I:261–62.

[25] Many sources note the large number of knights in the French army, especially in comparison to the few knights who fought alongside the Flemings. Some, like the *Chronique Artésienne*, even list the names and titles of the most prominent French knights (pp. 44–45). See also *Annales Gandenses*, pp. 27–28; Willem Procurator, p. 63; *Ancienne chronique*, p. 378; and *La chronique Liégeoise de 1402*, ed. E. Bacha (Brussels, 1900), p. 246. The pride of these troops is acknowledged in the *Chronographia*, I:110.

[26] See the *Chronique de Flandre*, I:476.

[27] *Annales Gandenses*, p. 29 and Lodewijk van Velthem, II:302.

[28] *Continuatio chronici* of Guillaume de Nangis, I:318: 'Ultra enim transire non poterant propter pontem quem Brugenses fregerant super aquam fluminis prope Corteriacum decurrentis. Ubi dum reparationi pontis gens Francorum intenderet, Brugenses saepius aciebus dispositis occurrentes, et opus quantum poterant disturbantes, [quotidie] ad bellum Francigenas provocabant.' See also *Grandes chroniques*, VIII:143.

chronicle, the French killed women, children and the sick and decapitated and defaced church statues in order 'to show their ferocity and terrorize the Flemings.' That this did not have the desired effect for the French is attested to by the anonymous author's further comment: 'However, such doings did not terrorize the Flemings, but stimulated and provoked them to still greater indignation and rage and violent fighting.'[29]

Robert of Artois was also busy gathering intelligence about the Flemish troops and their preparation of the battlefield. In particular, according to his register of expenses, he purchased a map of the ditches made on the battlefield. This was bought from a man known only as Pierre l'Orrible (perhaps a pseudonym) for the exorbitant amount of *xiii lb. x s. x d. par.*[30]

Because they anticipated an attack at any time after the arrival of the French, the Flemish army must have ordered their position and held that order until the battle was fought. They knew that they held the best ground, with their backs to the river and the ditches in front of them. With the exception of Gilles le Muisit, who writes that the Flemings initially did not exhibit a strong spirit,[31] almost every account of the battle describes their high morale.[32] They certainly were frightened, as is attested to by Lodewijk van Velthem, not knowing whether they would live or die; but they believed that God was on their side, and they believed that He would lead them to victory.[33] Ultimately they were, in the words of Jean de Brusthem, 'rejoicing and excited, roaring in the manner of lions.'[34]

The Flemings were also well led. It was these leaders who ordered their troops in a single line as a shield wall against the Lys river, in a win-or-die formation.[35] It was they who also ordered the dismounting of knights and nobles to fight as infantry alongside the non-noble soldiers. And it was they who kept the morale of the Flemish army high. Many contemporary sources report that before going into battle the leaders of the Flemings addressed their troops. John of Renesse took the lead, telling the soldiers of the oncoming attack and asking them neither to flee nor to retreat. He asked the troops to attack the horses with their weapons and to push them into the ditches. He requested that they 'fight strongly for their wives and their children, for

---

[29] *Annales Gandenses*, p. 28: 'Franci autem Flandriam intrantes Flamingantem, ut ostenderent ferocitatem animi sui, et Flandrenses terrere volentes, non parcebant mulieribus, nec infantibus, nec decrepitis, quin eos occiderent quos invenire poterant; imo et imagines sanctorum in ecclesiis, ac si homines fuissent vivi, decapitaverunt, alia eis etiam membra amputantes. Hoc autem factum Flandrenses non terruit, sed magis ad iram et furorem et ad crudeliter pugnandum animavit et provocavit.'
[30] Robert of Artois' register of expenses is found in Funck-Brentano, *Mémoire*, pp. 79–85. The purchase of the map is found on p. 80.
[31] Gilles li Muisit, p. 195.
[32] See, for example, the description of the Flemings in the *Grandes chroniques*, VIII:204 and in the *Rijmkroniek van Vlaenderen*, p. 800.
[33] Lodewijk van Velthem, II:303. See also the *Récits d'un bourgeois de Valenciennes*, pp. 114–15.
[34] Jean de Brusthem, *Chronique*, in *Chroniques Liégeoises*, ii, ed. C.S. Balau (Liège, 1931), p. 60: 'Quo gaudentes et animati Flandrenses, more leonum rugientes et viriliter decertantes, tandem Francos bello vicerunt.' This chronicle, essentially an abridgement of Jean de Hocsem's *Chronicle*, was written in the early sixteenth century. This passage is not found in Hocsem's work.
[35] A number of sources characterize the Flemish formation as a shield wall. These include: Lodewijk van Velthem, p. 303; *Chronographia*, I:106; and *Chronique de Flandre*, I:477.

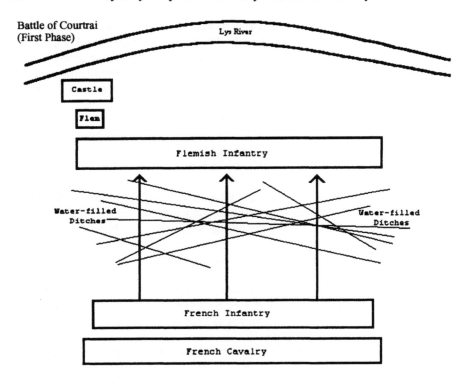

the laws and liberty of their homeland.' He promised the troops that if they resisted pride, putting their faith in God, that 'He would be merciful to those who were humble, giving consolation and victory to them.'[36] It was only the leaders, according to the *Chronicon comitum Flandriae*, who kept the Flemings from fleeing at the sight of the French army.[37]

On the French side a different picture is given. Most sources report that the French

---

[36] There are two different versions of this oration. The *Chronicon comitum Flandriae* (p. 168) does not mention who gave the speech, but records it as:

> Estote, inquit, viri fortes et viriliter pugnate pro uxoribus et liberis vestris ac pro legibus ac libertatis patriae vestrae, quia nisi praestiteritis, non remanebit de vobis neque de genere vestro mingens ad parietem, quin omnes gladio perfodiantur. Quicumque autem fugerit vel retroc- esserit, vel ad spolia se inclinaverit usque post bellum perfossus pereat. Equos invadite primo cum lanceis et baculis, et equo perfosso, miles subito superatur.

The second version of the battlefield oration, found in Willem Procurator's *Chronicon* (p. 64), is given by John of Renesse and is entirely different:

> O fortissimi et divites, patriam et filios defendentes! Non turbetur cor vestrum neque formidet; nam vos animas vestras pro justitia ponitis et Deus justus suam pro vobis semel positam adhuc minus subtrahit, si ejus pietati et misercordie spem et fiduciam tribuatis. Ecce, vos humiliter proponitis vestrum defendere et ipsi in superbia et abusione alienum tollere. Unde qui superbis resistit, ipsis deficiet, et qui humilibus dat gratiam, ipse vos consolatione et victoria decorabit.

See also Lodewijk van Velthem, II:305–06 and *Kronyk van Vlaenderen*, I:158. On the praise for the Flemish leaders see Lodewijk van Velthem, II:305–06, 313.

[37] *Chronicon comitum Flandriae*, p. 169.

were haughty, believing that they could defeat the Flemings at will.[38] Certainly Robert of Artois held this opinion. When he called a council on the day of battle, the *Chronographia regum Francorum* notes, he ignored the advice of many of his nobles who did not want to attack the Flemings,[39] and shortly before noon, with trumpets blaring he ordered his troops in three lines and began to attack the Flemish army.[40]

The battle began with an exchange of crossbow fire. Because there were so few archers on either side this attack was largely ineffectual.[41] The French infantry then began their approach, making their way across the ditch-filled field quite easily it seems, until they began to attack the Flemings. So effective was this attack that, in the words of Gilles le Muisit, 'they were almost at the point of victory.'[42] But the infantry attack was halted by Robert of Artois who insisted that the knights be granted the victory. As the *Ancienne chronique de Flandre* reports the incident, a French knight seeing that the infantry was about to defeat the Flemings approached Robert of Artois and asked him: 'Lord, why do you wait any longer? Our infantry . . . advances so that they will have victory here, and we will obtain no honor.' Robert responded by recalling the infantry and charging his knights across the field.[43]

The French cavalry charge was disastrous. The knights charged 'pompously and without order' passing over the ditches and hitting a solid, impenetrable Flemish line. The French charge was halted; unable to pierce the infantry shield wall, the French horses stopped and the knights were pushed into ditches behind them.[44] Ensuing cavalry charges did not help, as these knights and their horses became further enmeshed in the ditches and the confusion. Nor did a desperate charge from the castle provide relief for the fallen French cavalry, for it was easily turned back by a Flemish contingent placed there to prevent such a charge.[45] In the words of a Middle English poem written to celebrate the victory, the French knights were like a 'hare' caught

---

[38] See the *Chronique Artésienne*, p. 48.

[39] *Chronographia*, I:107. On the battle council see also the *Chronique de Flandre*, I:477 and the *Récits d'un bourgeois de Valenciennes*, p. 114.

[40] On the order of the French lines see the *Annales Gandenses*, pp. 29–30; the *Chronicon comitum Flandriae*, p. 169 and the Oxford Chest (ffoulkes, pl. I). On the time of the battle see the *Annales Gandenses*, p. 30.

[41] See the *Chronographia*, I:107; the Oxford Chest (ffoulkes, pl. I; and Jean Desnouelles, *Chronique*, in *RHF*, xxi, ed. Guignant and de Wailly (Paris, 1855), p. 90.

[42] Gilles li Muisit, p. 195: '. . . et pedites dicti comitis Flandrenses superare, et esse quasi sub puncto habendi victoriam.' See also the *Chronographia*, I:107.

[43] *Ancienne chronique de Flandre*, p. 378: ' "Sire, que attendez vous plus? Noz gens de pié, quy de pres nous sièuent, s'avanceront tellement, que ilz en auront la victoire, et nous ne y acquerrons point d'honneur." ' See also the *Chronographia*, I:107 and the *Chronique de Flandre*, I:476–77. The *Chronique de Flandre* insists, however, that the French knights charged onto the battlefield only because they thought that the Flemings were fleeing from it (I:476–77).

[44] On the disastrous French charge see the *Annales Gandenses*, p. 30; Lodewijk van Velthem, II:307–19; the *Chronicon comitum Flandriae*, p. 169; the *Grandes chroniques*, VIII:204–05; Giovanni Villani (ed. Muratori), col. 387; the *Kronyk van Vlaenderen*, I:161; Thomas Gray, *Scalachronicon*, ed. J. Stevenson (Edinburgh, 1836), pp. 127–28; and Ives, *Pars ultima chronicon*, in *RHF*, xxi, ed. Guignant and de Wailly (Paris, 1855), p. 204.

[45] The castle attack is mentioned only in the *Annales Gandenses*, p. 30, but it is also shown on the Oxford Chest (ffoulkes, pl. I).

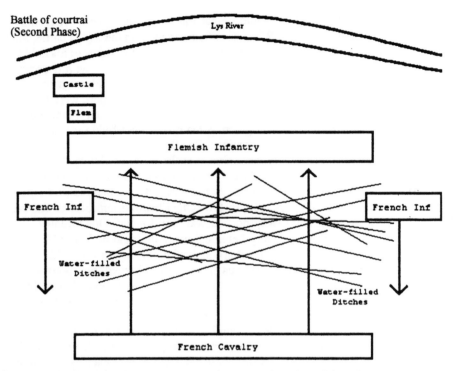

in a 'trap.'[46] Jean de Hocsem uses another metaphor describing the knights falling into the ditches as 'oxen slaughtered as a sacrifice without defense.'[47]

With victory at hand, the Flemish infantry marched forward across the field. They took no prisoners, killing any French knight not yet slain or drowned.[48] Among those yet to die was Robert of Artois. According to several sources he had lost his horse in a ditch, but had not fallen in himself. Unhorsed and defeated, in a scene reminiscent of Shakespeare's *Richard III*, he tried to save himself by pleading for his life. But his pleas went unheeded as he was killed.[49]

---

[46] There are several editions of this poem. The one I have used is edited by Rossell Hope Robbins in his collection, *Historical Poems of the XIVth and XVth Centuries* (New York, 1959), pp. 9–13. Other editions can be found in *Political Songs of England*, Camden Society, vi, ed. T. Wright (London, 1839), pp. 187–195 and *Chants historique de la Flandre, 400–1650*, ed. L. de Baecker (Lille, 1855), pp. 161–72. The above reference can be found in Robbins, pp. 192–93.

[47] Jean de Hocsem, *La chronique de Jean de Hocsem*, ed. G. Kurth (Brussels, 1927), p. 105: '. . . et apud Curtracum commisso prelio Francigenis ruentibus in fossatis sicut boves ad victimam sine defensione.' The *Annales St. Jacobi Leodensis* (in *MGH, SS*, xvi, ed. G.H. Pertz (Hannover, 1850), p. 653), in copying Hocsem's account, dropped the 'b' from *boves* to describe the knights as sheep, giving the phrase its more accustomed proverbial nature but losing the bulky image which Hocsem had probably intended initially: 'Fuit bellum apud Curtracum, ubi Francigenis in fossatum ruentibus, sicut oves sine defensione mactantur.'

[48] See the *Annales Gandenses*, p. 31 and the third continuation of the *Gesta abbatum St. Trudoniensum*, in *MGH, SS*, x, ed. G.H. Pertz (Hannover, 1851), p. 409.

[49] On the death of Robert of Artois see Lodewijk van Velthem, II:321–22; the *Récits d'un bourgeois de Valenciennes*, p. 115; and the Middle English poem (Robbins, pp. 192–93). All portray Robert

There were many French dead strewn across the field and filling the ditches. The Flemings gathered their booty, among which were the golden spurs to be hung in the Courtrai church. Then they retired from the field, leaving the bodies of their dead foes to putrefy.[50]

All of the chroniclers of the battle are impressed by the heavy casualties. Many French sources even record the names of the knights killed in lists which often surpass in length the account of the battle itself.[51] Modern historians too are impressed by the large numbers of knights killed, estimating that between forty and fifty percent of the French cavalry were lost.[52]

Why did the Flemings defeat the French knights? Modern historians disagree on their answer to this question. Sir Charles Oman claims that the victory was a 'mere accident' and that the French nobility 'comforted themselves with the reflection that it was the morass and not the Flemish infantry which won the battle.'[53] Henri Nowé blames the French loss on the battlefield ditches hidden deceptively by the Flemings.[54] Several other historians point to the ineptitude of Robert of Artois as a military leader. Indeed, no less a historical figure than Napoleon III remarks on the inane charge of the French cavalry over their own infantry, an event which does not seem to have occurred, the infantry having left the battlefield without incident. Yet, others echo his complaint. Georges Digard blames Robert for sending his knights 'blind' over a ditch-filled field, and Joseph Strayer sees a certain victory if the infantry had been allowed to continue.[55] But, it is Henri Pirenne who levels the

pleading unsuccessfully for his life. Only Gilles li Muisit differs with this picture, claiming instead that Robert chose to die rather than live in humiliation after the defeat of his troops (p. 319).

[50] For a reference to the rotting and putrification of the French corpses see the continuator of Guillaume de Nangis' *Chronicon*, pp. 319–20 and the Oxford Chest (ffoulkes, pl. I). This image is also a central theme in the ribald Flemish 'Gospel,' the *Passio Francorum secundum Flemingos*, written after the battle and edited in Paul Lehmann, *Die Parodie im Mittelalter* (Stuttgart, 1963), pp. 30–31. (Another edition and extended study of this source is J.M. de Smet, 'Passio francorum secundum flemyngos,' *De leiegouw* (1977), 289–319. See also Verbruggen, 'Historiografie,' pp. 246–47.) Contemporary sources report that none of the fallen soldiers was buried on the battlefield; however, the *Chronographia* (I:112–14) does note that angels saved the body of Robert of Artois from mutilation by sneaking it off to the safety of a nearby monastery.

[51] See, for example, the lengthy death lists found in the *Chronique Artésienne*, pp. 49–51; the *Chronicon comitum Flandriae*, p. 170; the *Chronographia*, I:110–12; the *Chronique de Flandre*, I:478–79; the *Grandes chroniques*, VIII:207–08; the third continuation of the *Gesta abbatum St. Trudoniensum*, p. 409; the *Chronique Normande de xiv siècle*, ed. A. and E. Molinier (Paris, 1882), pp. 18–19; and the *Chronique des Pays-Bas, de France, d'Angleterre et de Tournai*, in *Corpus chronicorum Flandriae*, iii, ed. J.J. de Smet (Brussels, 1856), pp. 123–24.

[52] Philippe Contamine in his *War in the Middle Ages* (trans. M. Jones (London, 1984), p. 258) puts the loss at forty percent of the French knights while both Verbruggen (*De krijgkunst in west-europa in de middeleeuwen (IXe tot XIVe eeuw)* (Brussels, 1954), p. 318) and Funck-Brentano (*Philippe le Bel*, p. 415) select the larger, fifty percent figure.

[53] Sir Charles Oman, *A History of the Art of War: The Middle Ages from the Fourth to the Fourteenth Century* (London, 1898), pp. 592–93. It should be noted that Oman himself changed his mind on the importance of the battle of Courtrai in his two volume revision of this work. However, on the issue of whether the defeat of the knights was an 'accident' or not, Oman does not alter his conclusions. See *A History of the Art of War in the Middle Ages* (London, 1905), II:118.

[54] Henri Nowé, *La bataille des éperons d'or* (Brussels, 1945), p. 80. See a similar argument used by R.H.C. Davis, p. 27.

[55] Napoleon III and I. Favé, *Du passé et l'avenir de l'artillerie* (Paris, 1856), I:33–34; Georges Digard,

harshest accusations against Robert of Artois calling him 'imprudent' and claiming that 'a charge of cavalry against a numerous infantry, formed in compact mass, solid and immobile as a wall, on a marsh plain and intersected by ditches is unable to end in anything but disaster.'[56]

Three historians, Frantz Funck-Brentano, Ferdinand Lot and J.F. Verbruggen, all credit the infantry tactics for providing the victory at Courtrai; it was the first victory of infantry over cavalry in a line of many later successes. Funck-Brentano is almost poetic in his discourse on the subject:

> Jacques de Châtillon and Robert of Artois were both representatives of the old world, of chivalry, of a feudal society. They had power, simple character and grandeur. But in Flanders they found themselves to be in the presence of a new world, where thought was stronger than force, a modern world by which they were conquered. Robert of Artois was the hero of chivalric wars where grand strokes of the sword decided the victory on an equal terrain between adversaries of equal arms. To strike a horse on the head was a felony at least if you were not fighting heretics. A whole other war awaited them, all the strategy and ambushes wherein the chivalry of France was to fall in one glorious catastrophe; what a fateful day for the cause they were defending.[57]

In looking at the contemporary accounts of the battle, one cannot help but agree with this trio of distinguished modern historians. Surely the battle of Courtrai shows that infantry was capable of defeating knights if they thoughtfully chose and prepared their terrain and if they stood their ground fighting a defensive rather than an offensive battle. It is too easy simply to blame the defeat on the ineptitude of Robert of Artois. Certainly he was a proud man, as were his knights who considered the Flemings to be 'poor and unarmed *rusticos*' in comparison to their expertise in warfare.[58] Perhaps he was also incautious and should have heeded the advice of his councilors who warned him not to attack the Flemish army that day. But we are not

---

Philippe le Bel et le Saint Siège de 1285 à 1304 (Paris, 1936), II:118; and Joseph Strayer, *The Reign of Philip the Fair* (Princeton, 1980), p. 334.

[56] Henri Pirenne, 'Note supplementaire,' pp. 89–90: 'Une charge de cavalerie contre une infantrie nombreuse, formée en masse compacte, solide et immobile comme un mur, dans une plaine marécageuse et coupée de fosses, ne pouvait qu'aboutir à un désastre.'

[57] Funck-Brentano, *Philippe le Bel*, pp. 405–06: 'Jacq. de Châtillon et Rob. d'Artois étaient tous deux les représentants d'un monde vielli, de la chevalerie, de la société féodale; ils en avient la force, le caractère simple et la grandeur: mais en Flandre ils devaient se trouver en présence d'un monde nouveau, où la réflexion avait plus d'action que la force, le monde moderne, par lequel ils devaient être vaincus. Rob. d'Artois était le héros des guerres chevalereques où les grands coups d'épée décidaient de la victoire sur un terrain égal, entre adversaires également armés. Frapper les chevaux à la tête était félonie, à moins que l'on ne combattit contre les hérétiques. Une toute autre guerre l'attenfait, toute de strategie et d'embûches, où la chevalerie française allait s'écrouler en une catastrophe glorieuse, mais néfaste à la cause qu'elle défendait. See also Lot, I:252 and Verbruggen *Krijgkunst*, p. 245.

[58] The description of the Flemings as '*rusticos*' is found in Jean de Paris, *Memoriale temporum*, in *RHF*, xxi, ed. Guignant and de Wailly (Paris, 1855), p. 638 and the *Continuatio chronici* of Guillaume de Franchet, in *RHF*, xx, ed. Guignant and de Wailly (Paris, 1840), p. 20. For the pride of the French army see also the *Chronographia*, I:110 and the *Continuatio chronici* of Guillaume de Nangis, I:331. The *Chronographia* also claims that the French army was infelicitous and corrupt (I:110).

told why these nobles did not want to fight: whether they actually perceived the danger in fighting an infantry army on a battlefield filled with ditches, or whether they had some other reason, perhaps not so prophetic, for desiring not to fight. In any case, a general's incaution in fighting against medieval infantry forces before this time had rarely meant defeat.

Nor can we attribute the Flemish victory only to the presence of the ditches on the battlefield. Despite the fact that these ditches are almost always mentioned by contemporary chroniclers, with some calling them 'treasonous,' 'evil' or 'mischievous,' and others claiming that the French 'trembled' when recounting them, there are many reasons why they cannot be recognized as the single cause of the French cavalry's defeat.[59] For one thing, few Flemish sources accord them any importance in determining the outcome of the battle. They are not portrayed on the Oxford Chest nor are they mentioned in the *Annales Gandenses*, and while they are discussed briefly in Lodewijk van Velthem's *Spiegel historiael*, he is not impressed by their destructive presence.

Second, those Flemish sources which do mention the ditches and the role they played in the defeat see their presence only as a secondary cause of defeat. For example, the *Chronicon comitum Flandriae* claims that the Flemings did not expect what eventually occurred; they were surprised that the ditches were so effective.[60] As well, the *Ancienne chronique de Flandre* and the third continuation of the *Gesta abbatum St. Trudoniensum* insist that the French knights did not encounter the ditches until after they had passed them. Only after being pushed back by the Flemish infantry into the ditches were they a factor in the defeat.[61]

Third, it was not the ditches themselves which caused the deaths of so many of the French knights. As Geffroi de Paris points out, it was the fact that they were filled with water and mud which seemed to have marked the end for so many heavily armored soldiers, especially if in being pushed back by the infantry line the knight's horse fell on top of him trapping him in the mud and under the water.[62]

Finally, despite the fervent belief of Giovanni Villani and others that the French knights did not know about the ditches on the battlefield,[63] other sources attest that they were indeed aware of their presence. For not only does the *Ancienne chronique de Flandre* report this knowledge, especially concerning a large ditch nearest the Flemish lines which the anonymous writer of this chronicle describes as 'very large and very deep,'[64] but the mere fact that the French infantry, visible to their cavalry

---

[59] These descriptions of the ditches can be found in the *Chronique anonymé Française finissant en MCCCLVI*, in *RHF*, xxi, ed. Guignant and de Wailly (Paris, 1855), p. 139; the *Chronique Artésienne*, p. 48; Guillaume Guiart, l. 6478; and Geoffroi de Paris, ll. 1488–90.

[60] *Chronicon comitum Flandriae*, p. 169.

[61] *Ancienne chronique de Flandre*, p. 378 and the third continuation of the *Gesta abbatum St. Trudoniensum*, p. 409.

[62] Geoffroi de Paris, ll. 6086–89.

[63] Giovanni Villani (ed. Muratori), col. 387.

[64] *Ancienne chronique de Flandre*, p. 378. See also the *Récits d'un bourgeois de Valenciennes*, p. 115; the third continuation of the *Gesta abbatum St. Trudoniensum*, p. 409; and the *Chronique de Flandre*, I:476.

cohorts, would also have needed to cross over them is evidence enough to support the knowledge of their presence. Ultimately, perhaps the best evidence to support the French knowledge of the Courtrai ditches is that Robert of Artois, as shown in his expense ledger, had purchased a map from a spy showing him where the ditches were on the battlefield.

The Flemings had dug the ditches there only to disrupt the charge of the French knights so that it might be weakened by the time it came into contact with the infantry line. It was the infantry line then which was the cause of victory at Courtrai. As was promised by their leaders, and because they had no place to flee with their backs to the river, the Flemish infantry did not break from their line. They stood bravely awaiting the charge of the French knights who rode with lance couched, clothed in expensive and impressive armor, and atop large warhorses. Their bravery should not be understated, for they could not have anticipated what would happen next. Unable to find a path through the Flemish line, and unwilling by nature to run over a man, the horses stopped.[65] The knights were unable to fight as accustomed, and the Flemings were able to advance without hindrance, pushing their horsed opponents into the ditches which they had just ridden over. A reinforcing assault by another French cavalry line would not only meet with the same result, but it would also run into its own first line, a situation which occurred at Courtrai.

An infantry force could and did defeat an experienced cavalry army. At Courtrai the Flemish infantry chose their field of battle, selecting a good defensive position from which to fight. They prepared the field for battle by digging ditches in an attempt to hinder and perhaps also to narrow any orderly attack against them, especially a cavalry charge. Finally, they chose to fight a defensive battle, ordered in a solid line, unbroken by flight or retreat. And in the end the cavalry opposing them was unable to defeat them, suffering humiliation and a heavy loss of life. It was, in the words of the anonymous author of the *Chronicon Rotomagensi*, 'as if the whole flower of French knighthood had disappeared.'[66]

There is an interesting postscript to the battle of Courtrai. Writing nearly one hundred years after the battle and chronicling a French victory at the same town in 1382, Jean Froissart reports that the French remembered that it was there that 'the count of Artois and all the flower of French nobility were slain.' To avenge this loss, the French burned the city and confiscated the golden spurs which still hung in the Cathedral of the Virgin.[67]

---

[65] For a convincing discussion of this phenonemon at the battle of Agincourt see John Keegan, *The Face of Battle* (Harmondsworth, 1978), pp. 94–96.

[66] *Chronicon Rotomagensi*, in *RHF*, xxiii, ed. de Wailly, Delisle and Jourdain (Paris, n.d.), p. 236: '...quasi totus flos militiae galicanae decedit, non quidem virtute hostium, sed incautela pugnantium, cadentium in fossata quae adversarii antea fecerant et cooperverant fradulenter.' See also Bernard Gui, *Flos chronicorum necnon e chronico regum Francorum*, in *RHF*, xxi, ed. Guignant and de Wailly (Paris, 1855), p. 713.

[67] Jean Froissart, *Chroniques*, in *Oeuvres de Froissart*, ed. Kervyn de Lettenhove (Brussels, 1870), XIII:177–78: 'Là y ot de rechief grant ochission et persécution faite, aval la ville, des Flamens qui y estoient repus, ne on n'en prendoit nul à merchy; car li François haioient la ville durement pour une bataille qui fu devant Courtray, où li contes d'Artois et toute la fleur de France fu jadis morte.'

II

THE BATTLE OF ARQUES, 1303

ALL OF THE COUNTY OF FLANDERS joined in the celebrations which followed the important, and unexpected, victory over the French at the battle of Courtrai. Towns, like Ghent, which had neglected to join the rebellion before the battle quickly federated themselves with the victorious rebels; support for the rebellion also came from the rural areas of Flanders. Guy of Namur and William of Jülich were heralded as heroes and assigned the task of governing the newly independent county. For administrative and military assistance in this task, Guy sent for his brothers, John and Henry of Namur and Philip of Chieti.

There was little doubt that the king of France, Philip IV, would attempt to retake his northern county. Flanders was far too wealthy a possession for Philip to allow it to be independent from the French realm.[1] Moreover, a secession of one of France's fiefs might encourage other unstable provinces, such as Bordeaux, Picardy, or Gascony, to seek their own independence.[2] So the sons and grandsons of Guy of Dampierre, still imprisoned by Philip IV, prepared for another French attack by strengthening the defenses of the major towns and building new fortresses which would hinder a French assault of their county.

The Flemings did not concern themselves solely with defensive matters, however, as they took advantage of the French confusion following Courtrai to secure their territory and to make new conquests. Within days of this victory, the castles of Courtrai and Cassel fell to the rebels, and their defeat was followed closely by the surrender of the towns of Lille, Douai, and Termonde; only Termonde resisted the Flemish attacks.[3]

There was no celebration held in France after the loss at Courtrai. A stunned Philip the Fair was forced to gather new funds and a new army to try to regain his lost territories. In addition to this, on November 18, perhaps instigated by the Flemish

---

[1] The two best discussions, despite their age, concerning the events between the battles of Courtrai and Arques can be found in Pirenne, *Histoire de Belgique*, I:392–95 and Funck-Brentano, *Philip le Bel et Flandre*, pp. 430–71. As for Philip the Fair's realization of the economic consequences of losing Flanders, see the *Chronicon comitum Flandriae*, p. 173.
[2] Both the first and second continuations of Guillaume de Nangis's *Chronicon* (I:324, 334) describe a rebellion which erupted in Bordeaux inspired by the success of the Flemish rebellion. As well, the *Chronographia regum Francorum* (I:119) reports that in 1303 some of the French nobles approached Philip IV asking him to raise an army to put down the Flemish rebellion as they feared that his inaction might encourage their own lands to rebel against them.
[3] See the *Annales Gandenses*, pp. 34–35.

victory, Philip's old foe, Pope Boniface VIII, issued his famous bull *Unam sanctam*. *Unam sanctam* reinforced the pope's earlier decretal, *Clericos laicos*, forbidding the use of church subsidies by lay rulers unless consented to by the Pope himself. There is no doubt that this bull was directed at Philip's situation.[4]

The French king, it seemed, had been defeated on two fronts, and yet he held his church and people together.[5] Moreover, Philip ably kept the English from seizing the opportunity to attack a weak and militarily unprepared French realm by negotiating an alliance with his potential enemy based on the cession of Gascony to England.[6] Philip could now concentrate on the recovery of the county of Flanders. However, it would be nearly two years before France was capable of attacking the rebels. Philip did gather an army before the end of 1302 and marched as far north as Vitry, two miles south of the Flemish town of Douai. But after a stay of five to six weeks, this army ran out of food and was forced to return to France, a return described as 'inglorious' by at least one contemporary French author.[7]

The Flemings did not wait for the French army's recovery, and before 1302 had ended, rebel armies attacked the counties of Holland and Hainault, lands to the north and southeast of the county of Flanders but controlled by the same lord, Count Jan I. Essentially the Flemish army had split into two parts, with William of Jülich leading a force south to Tournai and Guy of Namur leading another army north into Zeeland.[8] William's goal initially was much larger than Guy's; he besieged the French-partisan town of Tournai.

Tournai did not fall to the Flemings. Indeed, the impatient rebels only besieged the town for three days before they became fatigued and moved on to 'easier' targets. The anonymous author of the *Annales Gandenses* writes:

> The Flemings . . . besieged Tournai for three days, and did much damage to the city and the neighbourhood. They could not have taken it, however, unless by a long siege. So, being weary of the tumult of war and already burdened with heavy expense all through the summer, they left it and returned to their tents.[9]

William of Jülich's Flemings moved on to the supposedly easier siege of Lessines.

---

4 On the effect of *Unam sanctam* on Philip the Fair see Strayer, pp. 272–76.
5 It seems somewhat amazing that Philip, in the wake of military and ecclesiastical defeat, was able to keep his church together in support of him. But by a brilliant use of propaganda, through letters sent to his bishops and read aloud as 'sermones' before his people, Philip was indeed successful in uniting his kingdom in the wake of this defeat. See, for example, the original sources contained in Digard, II:122; Funck-Brentano, *Mémoire sur la bataille de Courtrai*, pp. 85–88; and Jean Leclerq, 'Un sermon prononcé pendant la guerre de Flandre sous Philippe le Bel,' *Revue du moyen âge latin* 1 (1945), 165–72.
6 See F.M. Powicke, pp. 653–54.
7 See, for example, the second continuator of Guillaume de Nangis, I:337.
8 See *Chronographia regum Francorum*, I:118, for a description of the Flemish attack of Zeeland.
9 *Annales Gandenses*, p. 37: 'Flandrenses . . . Tornacum tribus diebus obsederunt, damna plurima dicte civitati circumquaque inferentes. Ipsam tamen, nisi longiori tempore sedissent circa eam, non poterant obtinere; unde bellico tumultu lassati ac expensis maximis per totam estatem pregravati, eam reliquerunt, in tabernacula sua revertentes.'

By 1303, William of Hainault, the son of Jan I, decided that he could no longer wait until a French army would save his two counties from destruction at the hands of the Flemish rebels. He gathered an army from his counties and proceeded against the Flemings at Lessines.[10] The onslaught was successful; the rebels, unaccustomed to military opposition, were forced to give up their siege and retreat north. Concurrent with this minor defeat, and maybe because of it, Guy of Namur increased his attack against Holland, assaulting Zeeland from the land and sea in a concerted effort to take the town of Middleburg. William of Hainault was forced to march his small army north to defend the county of Holland.[11]

This maneuver lessened the pressure on William of Jülich's force, and he again moved south. First, he attacked and captured Lessines, now made vulnerable with the Hainaulter army in Holland. His next target was the French-garrisoned town of St. Omer. The French soldiers inside the town, among them the constable of France, Gaucher of Châtillon, responded by mounting a small attack on the rebel armies at the village of Arques, a short distance from St. Omer. On April 4, 1303, the battle of Arques was fought; by the end of the day, the French had retreated to the town, leaving the battlefield to the Flemings. But it was a costly 'victory' for the Flemings, as they had lost many, and on the following day, after burying their fallen troops and those of the French in a large mass grave, they too retreated from the site of the battle.[12]

The original sources for the battle of Arques are the same as those for Courtrai and Mons-en-Pévèle, with the *Annales Gandenses*, the *Chronique de Flandre*, and Guillaume Guiart, a combatant on the French side, as the most complete narratives.[13]

The battle of Arques is really a play in three acts. The first act begins with the travel of William of Jülich with his rebellious Flemish troops from the town of Lessines to St. Omer. Lessines, held by a garrison of German mercenaries according to the *Annales Gandenses*, had been attacked forcefully, 'with machines of war and daily assaults,' by the Flemings. They had taken it, but in the end their victory was somewhat hollow; the whole town was burned, with the gates, towers, and walls destroyed.[14]

Why William of Jülich chose to go to St. Omer after his victory at Lessines is a question left unanswered by the original sources. Only a few months prior to William's journey, an army of Flemings had tried to raid the county of Artois by traveling past St. Omer. Just outside the town they met Eudes of Burgundy whose large force put an end to the invasion by massacring most of the raiders.[15] Perhaps

---

[10] See *Annales Gandenses*, pp. 37, 42.
[11] For a description of the Flemish military activities in Zeeland see *Annales Gandenses*, pp. 42–48.
[12] There are few modern descriptions of the battle of Arques. The longest is Verbruggen, *De krijgkunst*, pp. 319–25. See also Funck-Brentano, *Philippe le Bel et Flandre*, pp. 437–41 and Nowé, pp. 85–86.
[13] In their narratives of the battle of Arques, unlike their accounts of Courtrai and Mons-en-Pévèle, the *Chronographia regum Francorum* is a Latin translation of the *Chronique de Flandre*.
[14] *Annales Gandenses*, p. 39.
[15] See *Chronique Artésienne*, pp. 58–59; *Chronique de Flandre*, I:259–60; *Chronographia regum Francorum*, I:123–24; *Récits d'un bourgeois de Valenciennes*, pp. 117–18; *Chronique Normande*, p. 23; *Ancienne chronique de Flandre*, p. 384; and *Rijmkroniek van Vlaenderen*, p. 806. Jean Desnouelles also mentions the defeat of the Flemings in Artois, but interchanges it with the 1303 battle of Arques (p. 193).

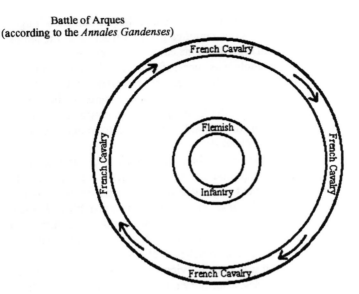

Battle of Arques
(according to the *Annales Gandenses*)

in response to this victory, or perhaps to guard against further invasions, Philip IV placed a large garrison of troops in St. Omer – 'mercenaries' the *Annales Gandenses* calls them – under the command of Jacques of Bayonne and Gaucher of Châtillon.[16] Thus such a target seems to have been an unwise selection by the young Flemish military leader. Why attack it then? The *Chronique de Flandre* claims that William merely wanted to retrieve the body of an unnamed brother killed in Eudes' massacre, while the *Annales Gandenses*, not a fan of this Flemish warrior, uses the words 'foolish' and 'indiscreet' to describe William's decision to go against St. Omer.[17]

But the explanation may also be one of more rationale military strategy. William of Jülich, brash of character and already many times victorious against the French, wished merely to use his large force to defeat the only sizeable army which Philip IV could employ to oppose the complete independence of Flanders. Victory would also in all likelihood cause a withdrawal by William of Hainault from his fight against the Flemings in Zeeland. However, to accept this explanation for William's move, we must agree with the claim of most original sources that the Flemish army was far larger than the numbers of troops garrisoned in the town. Numbers ranging from 10,000 to 50,000 may well be exaggerations, but they are always recorded in comparison to much smaller numbers of French soldiers.[18] Also in acceptance of this

---

16 *Annales Gandenses*, p. 48. Gaucher succeeded Raoul de Nesle as constable after the latter's death at the battle of Courtrai.
17 *Chronique de Flandre*, I:261; *Chronographia regum Francorum*, I:128; and *Annales Gandenses*, p. 39. See also the *Chronique des Pays-Bas*, p. 126.
18 The Flemish numbers are recorded as: 10,000 (*Chronique Artésienne*, p. 59); 30,000 (Jean Desnouelles, p. 193 and *Chronique des Pays-Bas*, p. 126); and 50,000 (*Chronique Normande*, p. 23). Other sources which describe the large size of the Flemish force without indicating a numerical figure include: *Chronique de Flandre*, I:261; *Chronographia regum Francorum*, I:128; *Chronicon comitum Flandriae*, p. 172; *Rijmkroniek van Vlaenderen*, p. 808; and Giovanni Villani (ed. Muratori), col. 409.

explanation we must note the numerous accounts of Flemish destruction around St. Omer in an effort to draw out the French troops from the town.[19]

Immediately on reaching the outskirts of St. Omer, William of Jülich divided his force into three parts. The first division, made up of troops from Ypres and recognizable with their red insignia, was ordered closest to the town. The second, men from St. Winoksbergen, was ordered behind the Yprois, 'a good league distant' according to the *Annales Gandenses*. It also contained the supply train. And the third contingent, the largest Flemish force, composed primarily of troops from Furnes and Cassel and led by William himself, was camped in the rear.[20] Why William ordered his troops in this manner rather than keeping everyone together cannot be determined from the sources.

The Yprois contingent met the French first at the small town of Arques. There they encountered sixty French soldiers, called bidauts in the *Chronique Artésienne*. The *Chronique Artésienne* claims that these were killed, the *Annales Gandenses* that they were put to flight.[21] At least some of them must have escaped to report the news to St. Omer, however, as in consequence of this attack, Jacques of Bayonne called his troops together and prepared to march out of the town to confront the Flemings.[22]

The approach of the Flemings frightened their French counterparts. Recognizing their much smaller numbers and undoubtedly remembering the Flemish victory at Courtrai, the *Chronique de Flandre* remarks that the French soldiers all 'expected certain death,' preparing for this by taking absolution from priests inside the town.[23] Still, there were many lords and knights among the French troops in St. Omer, and also many Flemings who had stayed loyal to the French, known as *Leliaerts*; they were not willing to hide behind the walls of a town while relief could be achieved by defeating the 'lesser' individuals outside.[24] They were also encouraged by a short speech given by Jacques of Bayonne promising them honor and victory.[25] The French,

French numbers are recorded as: 1,300 (Guillaume Guiart, l. 15461); 4,000 (Giovanni Villani (ed. Muratori), col. 409); and 20,000 (*Chronique des Pays-Bas*, p. 126).

[19] Arques and the suburbs of St. Omer were burned. See *Annales Gandenses*, p. 40; *Chronicon comitum Flandriae*, p. 172; *Récits d'un bourgeois de Valenciennes*, p. 119; *Chronique des Pays-Bas*, p. 126; and Giovanni Villani (ed. Muratori), col. 409. The *Annales Gandenses* claims, however, that Arques was burned by French troops fleeing from the Flemings into St. Omer.

[20] *Annales Gandenses*, p. 40; *Chronique de Flandre*, I: 262; and *Chronographia regum Francorum*, I:129–30. J.F. Verbruggen counts five divisions of Flemings, one from Ypres, two from St. Winoksbergen, and one each from Cassel and Furnes (*De krijgkunst*, p. 320). How he arrived at this number is a mystery, as it appears nowhere in the original sources.

[21] *Chronique Artésienne*, p. 60; *Annales Gandenses*, p. 40; and Guillaume Guiart, p. 249.

[22] Guillaume Guiart, p. 243; *Chronique de Flandre*, I:262; and *Chronographia regum Francorum*, I:131.

[23] *Chronique de Flandre*, I: 262; *Chronographia regum Francorum*, I:129; and Guillaume Guiart, p. 243.

[24] On the named French knights see Guillaume Guiart, p. 244; *Chronique de Flandre*, I:262; *Chronographia regum Francorum*, I:129; Gilles li Muisit, p. 199; *Rijmkroniek van Vlaenderen*, p. 805; and 'Une chronique Valenciennoise inedité,' p. 53.

[25] Guillaume Guiart, p. 243.

with banners flying and trumpets sounding, marched from St. Omer to do battle with their enemy.[26]

The first force they confronted was the same Yprois who had been successful at Arques. The Yprois seem not to have anticipated this fight, but they had time to form a solid line, identified as a 'grosse bataille' by the *Chronique de Flandre*, and this seems to have kept the French from attacking them. Jacques of Bayonne left his infantry behind to keep the Yprois from advancing on the town, and his cavalry, numbering some 800, rode toward the remaining Flemish force.[27] The curtain had fallen, with relatively little violence, on act one.

Act two was very short and much more violent. Only a brief time after their encounter with the Yprois, the French cavalry rode into the St. Winoksbergen soldiers. This Flemish contingent was 'unprepared for battle and in loose order,' according to the *Annales Gandenses*; nevertheless they fought valiantly, 'like a whole group of Rolands,' wrote the author of the *Chronique de Flandre*. Eventually, however, they were defeated and scattered. The supply train was also attacked and plundered. The number of Yprois killed was large and included many 'grooms and drivers.'[28]

Flushed with victory, the French cavalry moved on, and the third act began. By some unknown means, William of Jülich had learned of the attacks on his forward contingents, and he now took a defensive posture, dismounting all of his troops and ordering them to stand against a French cavalry charge. Goededags and pikes were put forward. This formation was not a line, as the Flemings had formed at Courtrai, but was, as the *Annales Gandenses* describes it, 'a circle like a bowl or a crown with [William] in the center.'[29] It was an impenetrable defensive formation which did not necessitate the use of terrain to be effective.

On this all of the original sources are in agreement. But what happened after William ordered his formation is in dispute. The *Annales Gandenses* claims that the French cavalry, recognizing the futility of attacking such a formation, rode 'cunningly' around it, looking for a weak spot. Deaths occurred only when a French soldier moved too closely to the Flemings, or when a Fleming broke from his protective formation. The annalist describes the scene:

> And thus they remained for nearly two hours, the king's mercenaries doing some little harm to the Flemings and *vice versa*. For after the battle of Courtrai the French, whether horse or foot, never ventured to launch their whole army against the Flemings, who always fought on foot, but always, riding round them if possible,

---

26 Guillaume Guiart, p. 243.

27 *Chronique de Flandre*, I:262; *Chronographia regum Francorum*, I:130; and *Annales Gandenses*, p. 40. The number 800 comes from the *Annales Gandenses*.

28 *Annales Gandenses*, p. 40; *Chronique de Flandre*, I:262–63; Guillaume Guiart, pp. 243–44; and *Chronique Artésienne*, p. 60.

29 *Annales Gandenses*, p. 40: 'Hoc audiens Wilhelmus velocius quo potuit suis in adjutorium venit, vidensque se paucos habere equites et hostes multos, appropinquans eis equos suos reliquit, et omnem exercitum suum pedes pugnare volens, aciem magnam rotundam ad modum cupe et corone ordinans, ipseque in medio ejus existens, hostes ad pugnam provocavit.' See also Guillaume Guiart, p. 246 and *Chronique Artésienne*, p. 60.

Battle of Arques
(according to Other Sources)

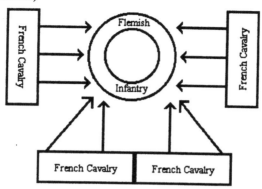

attacked them by threes and fours at a time, swiftly withdrawing with their horses, to entice them away from their own line, so that the others might then by a charge overthrow them.[30]

The Flemings never did break from their formation, and with the arrival of reinforcements from the Yprois and St. Winoksbergen divisions, the French fled from the field to St. Omer. Several met their death in the flight, but most reached St. Omer in safety.[31]

The other original sources, including that of eyewitness Guillaume Guiart, differ considerably from this account. They claim that in coming onto the Flemish formation, Jacques of Bayonne met with his troops and set his tactics. He divided his army into four lines: two lines would attack the front of the formation (at least that part of the formation directly in front of the French) with one line attacking the left flank and one the right. A small number of soldiers were left in reserve to prevent a reinforcing assault from the other Flemish contingents.[32] It was a 'bad plan' reports the *Chronique Artésienne*; despite pushing the Flemings back some distance, the French cavalry continually failed to penetrate the defensive formation. Charge upon charge proved futile.[33]

Finally, after a long battle with many killed on both sides and with night falling, Jacques of Bayonne sounded the call to retreat, and the fatigued French attempted to make their way back to St. Omer. Their retreat was orderly, with the Flemings in fierce pursuit. Several times the French turned as if to renew their attacks against the

---

[30] *Annales Gandenses*, pp. 40–41: 'Sicque stabant fere per duas horas stipendiarii regis Flandrensibus in modico nocentes et e contrario. Post bellum enim Curtracense numquam Franci ausi sunt, nec eques nec pedes, Flamingos semper pedes pugnantes insimul cum tota acie impugnare, sed semper eos circumequitantes quando poterant, per tres vel quatuor eorum aliquantulum invadebant, cito cum equis ab eis resilientes, ut ipsos de acie sua extraherent, et tunc alii ipsos cum impetu ad terram prosternerent.'
[31] *Annales Gandenses*, p. 41.
[32] Guillaume Guiart, p. 245.
[33] *Chronique Artésienne*, p. 60. See also Guillaume Guiart, pp. 245–47.

Flemings, and on each occasion the Flemings stopped and prepared for the charge. Even though some in the French leadership wanted to attack their pursuers, no charge came, but the pattern was repeated five or six times. Ultimately, the French reached the protective walls of St. Omer.[34]

The French had lost the battle of Arques, at least they had been forced to retreat from the battlefield. But to give the Flemings the victory is perhaps too generous, for they could not attack St. Omer, perhaps because of the losses they had taken in the battle, nor did they occupy the battlefield for long. Indeed, according to the *Chronique de Flandre*, on the day following the battle Jacques of Bayonne sent Aury the German to the Flemings in an attempt to bury French dead. Aury found no Flemings on the battlefield; the dead of both sides, some 15,000 according to this author, had been buried together in one large burial pit.[35] The play had ended.

Arques is a difficult battle to analyze, for although there are more than sufficient numbers of original sources, the fact that they differ on what occurred when the two main armies met each other has given rise to confusion and misunderstanding. J.F. Verbruggen, for example, has tried to accomodate both the account of what happened as recorded in the *Annales Gandenses* and that reported by the other original sources.[36] This simply cannot be done and begs the question of original source credibility. The *Annales Gandenses* has generally been seen as accurate in its account of the Flemish rebellion of 1302–1305,[37] but its details of the battles of Arques and Mons-en-Pévèle (seen in the following chapter) are often unreliable.

Still, even without discounting the *Annales Gandenses* narrative, the battle of Arques ably represents the tactics of infantry warfare that were prevalent everywhere in Europe during the early fourteenth century. William of Jülich may well have been presumptious in seeking to fight against the French garrison at St. Omer. At least that is what the *Chronique des Pays-Bas* reports the other Flemish leaders accused him of after the battle.[38] Moreover, the division of his force certainly displays a lack of wisdom that defies the unwritten strategy of 'not dividing one's forces.' But the fact remains that William's army was large enough to fight against the French even when so divided.

The Flemish leader also seems to have made no effort to select and prepare the site of battle, a tactic which had led to success at Courtrai and which would be repeated by most victorious infantry armies during this half century. Perhaps he was seeking to find a suitable spot for battle, and that is why he separated his troops into three divisions. It might also explain why his supply train was not with the largest

---

34 *Chronique de Flandre*, I:263–64; *Chronographia regum Francorum*, I:132; and Guillaume Guiart, p. 247. See also *Annales Gandenses*, p. 41 on the retreat.
35 *Chronique de Flandre*, I: 264 and *Chronographia regum Francorum*, I:132. Other death tallies include: 2,000 (*Chronique Normande*, p. 24); 12,000 (Jean Desnouelles, p. 193 and *Récits d'un bourgeois de Valenciennes*, p. 119); 15,000 (Guillaume de Franchet, p. 21); 16,000 Flemings killed (*Chronique Artésienne*, p. 60); and 24,000 Flemings killed (*Chronique des Pays-Bas*, p. 126).
36 Verbruggen, *De krijgkunst*, pp. 319–25.
37 Verbruggen, Funck-Brentano, and Pirenne all accept the *Annales Gandenses* without question.
38 *Chronique des Pays-Bas*, p. 126. See also *Annales Gandenses*, pp. 39–41 and *Rijmkroniek van Vlaenderen*, p. 805.

contigent of troops at the rear, but instead was with the smallest force, from St. Winoksbergen, in the middle. However, without more information from the original sources concerning this, such a conclusion would be weak conjecture at best.

Yet, once in battle and despite being somewhat surprised at encountering their foe, the Flemings performed the tactics that were necessary to provide victory over an experienced and noble cavalry army. With the exception of the second contingent, described as being 'in unprepared and loose order,' which was easily defeated by a cavalry charge, neither the Yprois division nor the main Flemish force fell victim to the French attacks. Both of these contingents, the Yprois seemingly containing no cavalry and the main force dismounting, ordered themselves in a defensive formation and prepared for a French cavalry assault. This alone seems to have discouraged the enemy. The French chose not to deliver a charge against the solid Yprois line, nor – if we trust the *Annales Gandenses* – against the main army's 'bowl or crown.' Even when the more credible version of the third act of the battle is accepted, that the French cavalry did indeed charge against William of Jülich's circle, perhaps many times, the defensive formation remains the significant feature leading to victory. For it could not be penetrated, and those manning it did not break under the pressure of constant cavalry onslaught. Ultimately, whether because of fatigue or because of approaching night, and undoubtedly having suffered numerous casualties from Flemish goededags and pikes, the French were forced to retreat and leave the battlefield to the Flemings.

Even then, with the French marching away from them, William of Jülich's army did not veer from their tactical plan. Each time the French turned around as if to mount another charge against them, some five or six times according to the *Chronique de Flandre*, the Flemings reordered their defensive formation and stood ready to fight. The French could do nothing except continue their retreat.

William may have won the battle of Arques, but he could not take advantage of the victory. He had lost many men, if only from the huge number of casualties suffered by the St. Winoksbergen contingent. More importantly, he had not been able to defeat the French decisively enough to prompt the surrender of St. Omer. Further military efforts against the town would necessitate a siege, and his army had already shown that they had no patience for such a military endeavor. So William of Jülich abandoned the field on which he had achieved such a hard-fought victory and also marched away. This provoked the harsh but perhaps justified comment by the annalist from Ghent following his description of the battle of Arques: 'Wherefore it seems that it was by the just judgment of God that he [William of Jülich] never, after the battle of Courtrai, was fortunate in any battle or other business.'[39]

---

[39] *Annales Gandenses*, p. 41: 'unde, ut videtur justo Dei judicio, numquam post bellum Curtracense in aliquo bello vel negotio bene prosperabatur.' To justify this statement the *Annales Gandenses* claims that William had extorted and lavishly spent money, cavorted with magicians and enchanters, and consulted evil spirits.

III

THE BATTLE OF MONS-EN-PEVELE, 1304

AFTER THE VICTORY AT the battle of Arques, William of Jülich's army again moved against Tournai. Still the town did not fall, although the Flemings were able to destroy its suburbs, and even at times to breach the gates.[1] From there the army traveled to the borders of Hainault and began undertaking raids and chevauchées into this neighboring county.

Philip the Fair could no longer remain inactive. It was clear that his loyal noble, Count William of Hainault and Holland, needed royal assistance if he were to keep his lands from the rebels. However, Philip was not yet prepared to send a large army against the Flemings so he resorted to other, more diplomatic means to stop the Flemish conquest of Hainault and Holland. Truces were negotiated and peace was sought. The king even permitted the imprisoned count of Flanders, Guy of Dampierre, to be released so that he might aid in this peace process.[2]

Ultimately, these measures failed. The truces were not kept by the rebels and peace was not attained by Guy of Dampierre who, bound by his chivalric code of honor, returned to prison. However, the time spent negotiating these peace measures did allow Philip's taxes to be collected and his army to regroup. By the beginning of 1304, the French king was ready to attack the Flemish rebels. While the French army, led by the king himself, marched north to attack William of Jülich's force, the French navy sailed to Zeeland to unite with the army of Hainault and Holland. It was this combined northern force in Zeeland which struck the first blow on May 11, 1304 when it soundly defeated Guy of Namur's army and navy at Zierkzee; Guy was captured and the Flemish conquest of Holland was halted.[3]

However, the main Flemish force was still active in the south. Philip the Fair had moved into the county and was waiting at Mons-en-Pévèle for word on the outcome

---

[1] For contemporary accounts of this siege see *Annales Gandenses*, p. 49, Gilles li Muisit, p. 198; and *Chronographia regum Francorum*, I:125–26.

[2] See Pirenne, *Histoire de Belgique*, I:396.

[3] The best contemporary French accounts of the battle of Zierkzee are found in *Chronographia regum Francorum*, I:148–49; *Continuatio chronici* of Guillaume de Nangis, I:340; and Etienne Delcambre, ed., 'Une chronique Valenciennoise inedité,' *Bulletin de la commission royale d'histoire de Belgique* 94 (1930), 57. The best Dutch sources are Melis Stoke, pp. 184–89; Jan Beke, *Chronographia Johannis de Beke*, ed. H. Bruch ('s Gravenhage, 1973), pp. 257–67; and Willem Procurator, pp. 70–74. And the best Flemish source for this battle is *Annales Gandenses*, pp. 58–63. This battle was fought almost entirely on shipboard; it has been wholly neglected by modern military or naval historians despite the large number of contemporary sources for it.

of the battle of Zierkzee. William of Jülich, desiring a battle with the French king, advanced on his position. Here he was joined by his uncles, John of Namur and Philip of Chieti, with their smaller levies. Another uncle, Henry of Namur, would also arrive at Mons-en-Pévèle with his force, but not until the day of the battle.[4] On August 18 the long and bloody battle of Mons-en-Pévèle took place. By the end of the day, the Flemings had fled from the battlefield, leaving Philip in possession of it. Casualties were high on both sides; modern historians estimate that the Flemings lost between seven and eight thousand men including their capable young general, William of Jülich, and that French losses were nearly as high.[5]

The defeat at Mons-en-Pévèle marked the end of this Flemish independence movement, for although Philip the Fair still encountered a large rebel army when he traveled to Lille, the Flemish morale had been broken, and they feared the destruction of their own homes and towns.[6] The remaining Flemish leaders, led by Philip of Chieti, readily agreed to a truce and signed the Treaty of Marquette at Lille in September 1304.[7] This time the truce would not be broken, and finally, in June 1305, after months of continual negotiations, a conclusive treaty of peace was signed at Athis-sur-Orge.[8] The conditions of this treaty were exceptionally harsh and not entirely conclusive but, for the moment at least, the Flemish independence movement had been halted.

The battle of Mons-en-Pévèle is one of the most difficult medieval battles to describe. This is not because of the paucity of contemporary sources on the battle. On the contrary, there is quite a large number of sources which recount the battlefield events, including most of the authors who wrote on the battle of Courtrai. Moreover, one of these sources, Guillaume Guiart, describes the battle from memory, having served with the French army there. His description thus ought to be the most reliable contemporary account, and in most cases it can be used with little scrutiny. However, Guiart's narration does not report one important battlefield event which every other source recounts – a Flemish attack which reached the French king nearly killing him. This might indicate an account which should be questioned more carefully, but it probably suggests only that as a relatively unimportant member of the French army, Guiart was not near the king when the Flemish attack against him was made.

But this is not the only problem that exists among the contemporary sources recounting the battle. The generally reliable *Annales Gandenses*, which provides the most descriptive account of the Flemish rebellion of 1302–05, including perhaps the most detailed narration of the battle of Mons-en-Pévèle from either the Flemish or French side, accords the victory not to the French but to the Flemings. This naturally presents many problems to the modern historian attempting to reconstruct what

---

[4] See *Chronographia regum Francorum*, I:156.
[5] See Verbruggen, *Krijgkunst*, p. 335 and Funck-Brentano, *Philippe le Bel*, pp. 476–77.
[6] For a description of the siege of Lille see *Chronographia regum Francorum*, I:162–65.
[7] On the treaty of Marquette see Franz Funck-Brentano, 'Le traité de Marquette (Septembre 1304),' in *Melanges Julien Havet* (1895; rpt. Geneva, 1972), pp. 749–58.
[8] On the treaty of Athis-sur-Orge see Funck-Brentano, *Philippe le Bel*, pp. 485–560; Strayer, pp. 336–37; and Hans van Werveke, 'Les charges financières de traité d'Athis (1305),' *Revue du Nord* 22 (1950), 81–93.

occurred in the battle; it may also be the cause of the doubt of several prominent historians, including Henri Pirenne, Henry Stephen Lucas, Ferdinand Lot, and Hans Delbrück, as to the conclusivity of the French victory there.[9] Still there seems to be little doubt that Philip the Fair's army did defeat the Flemings at Mons-en-Pévèle, although at a fairly high cost. And, while the report of the battle found in the *Annales Gandenses* should be used, the problems which it presents by claiming a Flemish victory should not be discounted.

All sources agree that it was the French army which first arrived at Mons-en-Pévèle and set up camp there.[10] This appears to have been a conscious decision of Philip the Fair, and most accounts insist that he chose this place to fight the Flemings. Only the *Annales Gandenses* claims otherwise, contending that Philip chose this place not as one of battle but as one of defence until he learned of the outcome of the northern battle of Zierkzee.[11]

All sources also agree on the large size of the French force. Most of these are impressed with the size of this army using simple phrases such as 'copiosa multitudo' and 'grand puissance' to describe it, while others actually attempt to tally the numbers usually counting a total in excess of 100,000 men.[12] Modern historians picture a much smaller force, although one quite sizeable for the time, totaling no more than 3,000 knights and 10,000 infantry.[13] It was this large number of knights which was most impressive to contemporary authors, and also to the Flemings who would face them. Indeed, Guillaume Guiart describes the French knights as a 'very noble race' which God had given primarily to defeat the rebellious Flemings, a foreboding which was undoubtedly felt by the smaller numbered rebels themselves.[14]

Also present with the French army were a number of artillery pieces, some trebuchets and mounted crossbows. It is, however, difficult to determine the number, size or capabilities of these machines from the sources reporting their presence. The *Chronique Artésienne*, for example, reports that five 'engiens' plus some 'espringales' were at Mons-en-Pévèle, while Guillaume Guiart mentions the presence of

9 Pirenne, *Histoire de Belgique*, I:396; Lucas, *The Low Countries*, p. 42; Lot, *L'art militaire*, I:268; and Hans Delbrück, *History of the Art of War Within the Framework of Political History*, trans. W.J. Renfroe, Jr. (Westport, Conn., 1984), III:540. While these authors never indicate the problems presented by the *Annales Gandenses* in studying what occurred at Mons-en-Pévèle, all use this source in their narrative of the battle. Other historians, namely Verbruggen (*Krijgkunst*, pp. 323–35), Funck-Brentano (*Philippe le Bel*, pp. 474–75), and Henri Nowé (p. 91), all have no difficulty in recognizing that this was a French victory; each also uses the *Annales Gandenses* as a source.
10 See *Chronographia regum Francorum*, I:154; *Chronicon comitum Francorum*, p. 173; Gilles li Muisit, p. 201; *Chronique de Flandre*, I:495; *Continuatio chronici* of Guillaume de Nangis, I:343; and Jean de Paris, p. 643.
11 *Annales Gandenses*, p.57.
12 For the estimate of 100,000 men see *Chronique Normande*, p. 25; *Rijmkroniek van Vlaenderen*, p. 809; and Jean Desnouelles, p. 194. For other comments on the size of the French force see *Chronicon comitum Flandriae*, p. 173; Giovanni Villani (ed. Muratori), col. 413; Ottokar von Stiermarken, p. 1001; *Grandes chroniques*, VIII:239; Ives, p. 204; Jean de Paris, p. 643; and *Continuatio chronici* of Girard de Franchet, p. 24.
13 See Verbruggen, *Krijgkunst*, p. 324.
14 Guillaume Guiart, pp. 290–91.

only three 'perdriaus' and two 'espringales.' These sources agree, however, that despite some initial damage caused by these weapons, in the long run they proved to be an inconclusive factor in the battle, the Flemings having destroyed them long before the actual fighting began.[15]

The French army was led by Philip himself who handled his military leadership as if he were leading a Crusade. He had prepared for the campaign by offering prayers for victory in the most sacred of French churches, the church at Saint-Denis, where he had also obtained the *oriflamme*, a banner of almost relic reputation which was only to be used in fighting against heretics or heathens.[16] Assisting Philip in his command were his constable and two marshals, the most important military leaders in the kingdom. Philip had also requested the aid and leadership of William of Hainault and Holland, but the count had declined because of ill health.[17]

The Flemish army arrived at Mons-en-Pévèle later than the French and set up their camp opposite to them, but within their sight.[18] Their numbers are reported to be larger than the French, with calculations ranging as high as 200,000;[19] modern historians claim a smaller, although equally impressive, 12,500 to 15,000 tally.[20] All the Flemish soldiers were on foot, armed with godedags and lances.[21]

The morale of the Flemings was high. They desired to fight the French king, and they believed that they could defeat him. They were, according to the bourgeois of Valenciennes, inspired by their need to 'defend themselves and their heritage.'[22] Moreover, the *Annales Gandenses* reports that when they heard of the defeat of their companions at Zierkzee they were 'for the most part . . . stimulated rather than dejected' by the news, 'since they believed they would get their own back for Guy [of Namur]'s loss from the king and his army.'[23]

The Flemings set up their line opposite the French. This made the opposing lines, again according to the *Annales Gandenses*, 'so close that the crossbowmen of one could have shot at the other.'[24] The Flemings were ordered in a defensive formation

---

[15] *Chronique Artésienne*, pp. 85–86 and Guillaume Guiart, pp. 288, 291–93. See also *Chronicon comitum Flandriae*, pp. 173–74.

[16] See *Chronographia regum Francorum*, I:150 and *Chronique de Flandre*, I:493. On the *oriflamme* see Philippe Contamine, *L'oriflamme de Saint-Denis aux XIVe et XVe siècles* (Nancy, 1975).

[17] The constable and marshals are only mentioned before the battle (see *Chronographia regum Francorum*, I:152–53); they are not mentioned at Mons-en-Pévèle although they surely would have been there. On the request for aid from William of Hainault and Holland and his illness keeping him away from the battle see *Chronographia regum Francorum*, I:151–52.

[18] On the Flemish arrival at Mons-en-Pévèle see *Chronographia regum Francorum*, I:154; *Chronique Artésienne*, p. 84; *Récits d'un bourgeois de Valenciennes*, p. 120; and *Chronique de Flandre*, I:495.

[19] On the estimate of 200,000 see Jean Desnouelles, p. 194 and *Chronique Normande*, p. 25. *Rijmkroniek van Vlaenderen* estimates a smaller, although still outrageous, 160,000 size force.

[20] See Verbruggen, *Krijgkunst*, p. 324.

[21] See Guillaume Guiart, pp. 291–92.

[22] *Récits d'un bourgeois de Valenciennes*, p. 121. See also *Chronographia regum Francorum*, I:154; *Chronique de Flandre*, I:276; and *Ancienne chronique de Flandre*, p. 394.

[23] *Annales Gandenses*, p. 65: 'Sed Flandrenses, rumore predicto non concussi pro majori parte, sed magis exacerbati, credentes se damnum Guidonis et sperantes a rege et suo exercitu recuperaturos.'

[24] *Annales Gandenses*, pp. 63–64: 'Cumque duo hostiles exercitus sic ordinati in tantum essent propinqui, quod balistarii unius exercitus in oppositum sua spicula poterant jaculari . . .'

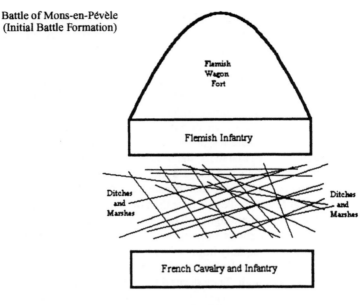

Battle of Mons-en-Pévèle
(Initial Battle Formation)

Flemish
Wagon
Fort

Flemish Infantry

Ditches
and
Marshes

Ditches
and
Marshes

French Cavalry and Infantry

French Camp

similar to that which had been successful at Courtrai, but with the addition of a quasi-fortification made with their wagons and carts at their rear and on their flanks. The *Annales Gandenses* describes this fortification:

> ... some Flemings detailed for the purpose sent away all the drivers with the horses and mares drawing the wagons, and made a sort of fortification out of the wagons in their rear of their own line, connecting one with another, but taking off one wheel from each, so that the French, if they wished to encircle them, should not be able to attack them from the rear.[25]

Jean de Paris provides a more 'wild west' description of this defensive formation describing a 'fortress' of carts and wagons which were circled 'so that they [the Flemings], in necessity, might be able to make a stand and fight inside such a circle.'[26]

There also seems to have been some marshes and ditches separating the two lines. These may have been simply natural hindrances as there is no mention of their construction for the battle. However, that the Flemings knew of their existence and planned their formation accordingly is attested to by Guillaume Guiart who reports

[25] *Annales Gandenses*, p. 66: par '. . . aliqui Flandrenses ad hoc ordinati, dimissis omnibus aurigis cum equis et equabus trahentibus currus, de ipsis curribus a tergo aciei sue quasi quamdam munitionem unum alteri connectendo composuerunt, a quolibet una rota ablata, ne Franci, si eos voluissent circumequitare, ipsos possent a tergo invadere.'
[26] Jean de Paris, p. 643: 'Flandrenses autem astute fecerant quasi munitionem de suis curribus et quadrigis, magnum terrae spatium hujus modi vehiculis circumdantes, ut infra talem circuitum possent in necessitate consistere et pugnare.' See also *Chronographia regum Francorum*, I:155–56 and *Chronique Artésienne*, p. 84.

that the Flemish leaders told their soldiers that the ditches would save them as they had at Courtrai. In fact, the marshes and ditches had little effect on the outcome of the battle.[27]

On August 13, with a flurry of crossbow fire, the Flemish troops tried to provoke the French to do battle.[28] The French armed themselves and assembled for a charge on the Flemish line.[29] Whether a charge actually occurred at this time however is questionable, as only the *Annales Gandenses* claims that it took place. Even then, the anonymous author of this chronicle contends that it was stopped before actually encountering the Flemish infantry.[30] Other writers report only skirmishing – crossbow fire, artillery fire and small raids – between the two sides at this time. According to the *Chronicon comitum Flandriae*, the French hoped that this skirmishing would fatigue the Flemings and cause them to withdraw from the field.[31]

This was not to be the result; nor did battle ensue at this time. Instead, fighting was halted so that a peace parliament could be called to discuss the rebellion without further bloodshed. This is a difficult scenario to investigate because there are several differing stories about this peace council. It does seem certain that such a parliament took place on the battlefield and that the battle was stopped until the question of peace was resolved as so many sources report it, but these sources differ on who asked for peace and on whom the blame should rest for peace not being declared.

On the one hand, there is a tradition among contemporary writers that it was the Flemings who desired peace at Mons-en-Pévèle. Both the author of the *Chronique Normande* and Jean Desnouelles relate a story that has the Flemings beginning to lose the battle and asking the count of Savoy, whose friendship they had recognized in the past, for assistance in obtaining a peace accord to stop further fighting. This is a request which the count was more than willing to grant if the Flemings promised 'to give and ordain one hundred chapels where masses might be directed for the French who were slain at Bruges and elsewhere.'[32] The Flemings readily agreed to this offer, but peace was thwarted when Philip refused to accept these conditions and chose instead to pursue the engagement.

Other sources claim that it was the French who desired peace on this day and that this was denied them by the Flemings. Guillaume Guiart, for example, claims that the hunger, thirst and filth of the battlefield began to demoralize the French troops who thus were encouraged by the talk of peace.[33] Some authors also comment on the intense heat of the noonday sun which fatigued the French soldiers causing them to disarm and disorganize. Indeed, Jean de Paris claims that the heat and thirst endured

---

[27] Guillaume Guiart, p. 291. See also *Annales Gandenses*, p. 70.
[28] See *Annales Gandenses*, pp. 63–64.
[29] See *Ancienne chronique de Flandre*, p. 394.
[30] *Annales Gandenses*, pp. 66–67.
[31] *Chronicon comitum Flandriae*, pp. 173–74. See also Guillaume Guiart, p. 286 and *Chronique Artésienne*, pp. 85–86.
[32] *Chronique Normande*, p. 25: '. . . il leur voulsist pardonner leur meffait pour donner et ordonner cent chappelles, ou on diroit messes pour les Francois, qui avoient este occis a Bruges et allieurs.' See Jean Desnouelles, p. 194 and *Chronographia regum Francorum*, I:155.
[33] Guillaume Guiart, p. 294.

by the French was so bad that 'many died in camp from their great thirst, including the count of Auxerre and others.'[34] All of these authors generally blame the Flemings for refusing to grant peace to the French at Mons-en-Pévèle, claiming instead that the rebels used this opportunity to treacherously attack the demoralized enemy.[35]

A final variant on this story is found in the *Annales Gandenses*. Here it is reported that it was the French king who pushed for peace, but that the Flemings 'who were always desirous of peace' also welcomed a conference which might end the battle. However, the call to peace was merely a ruse used by Philip IV to reform his army. The Ghentenaar annalist writes:

> But while negotiations as to peace were going on between the parties, and orders had been given in both hosts that all should remain inactive and do each other no injury, the king, who had large numbers of horse, sent one company of horse, with many foot, against the left flank of the Flemish army, and another against the right, as though to attack the Flemings from the rear.

The Flemings, 'perceiving the deception,' thus withdrew from the peace negotiations and returned to their line. In the process, a knight, whom the *Annales Gandenses* reports bore the 'cognizances' of the count of Savoy, was calling for a truce; but, he was killed by the Flemings, 'not wanting to hear any more about peace.'[36]

On August 18, after the failure of the peace parliament, the battle resumed. Unlike the skirmishing five days earlier, contemporary writers do not report who initiated this new phase of fighting. It may have been a French initiative, however, as they opened the battle by charging into the Flemish line in a fierce cavalry charge imitative of that attempted at Courtrai. Fighting became so vicious during this phase of the battle that Guillaume Guiart, who may have participated during these French attacks of the Flemish line, sums it up simply: 'death and blood dwelt there.'[37]

The 'horrible and cruel' battle continued into the midday.[38] The French fought well, but the Flemings held their position; both sides took heavy casualties. Soon it became apparent that the Flemings were beginning to win. Panic ran through the

---

[34] Jean de Paris, p. 643: 'Franci namque ex calore et siti plurimum fuerunt tunc gravati, ita quod plures ex maxima siti in campo obierunt, ut comes Antissidorensis aliique plures.' See also Jean Desnouelles, p. 194.

[35] See Ives, p. 204; *Continuatio chronici* of Guillaume de Nangis, I:343; and Jean de Hocsem, p. 121.

[36] *Annales Gandenses*, pp. 67–68: '... ex parte regis petitum est cum maximo dolo, ut pace tractatus haberetur. Flandrenses igitur, qui semper pacem desiderabant, in tractatum consenserunt. Sed dum de pace inter partes tractaretur, et in utraque acie esset proclamatum, quod omnes starent in quiete, et unus alteri non noceret, rex, qui in equitibus abundabat, unam aciem equitum cum multis peditibus misit versus sinistrum latus exercitus Flandrensis et aliam versus dextram, quasi per eos Flandrensibus a tergo noceret. Qui dolum cognoscentes, ulterius in quiete stare nolentes, sicut prius pugnare ceperunt. Venit autem quidam eques de exercitu regis cum fortissimo equo et optime armatus, signis bellicis comitis ornatus Sabaudie, clamans dolose, "Pax! Pax!" quem Flandrenses, dictum comitem esse credentes, occiderunt, nihil audire volentes ulterius de pace.'

[37] Guillaume Guiart, p. 293: 'Mort et sanglent ileuc demeure.' (Guiart's entire description of this phase of the battle appears on pp. 291–93.) See also *Chronographia regum Francorum*, I:156 and Ives, p. 204.

[38] See *Ancienne chronique de Flandre*, p. 394.

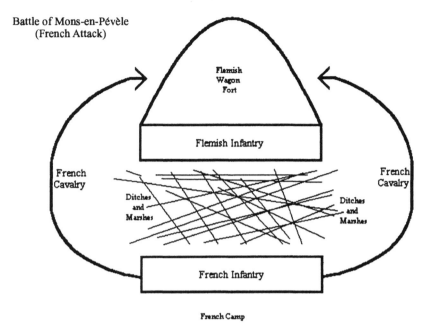

Battle of Mons-en-Pévèle
(French Attack)

French army, and several began to flee from the battlefield. The *Chronographia regum Francorum* describes the scene:

> A marvelous battle was fought on both sides. And when they had fought most fervently for a long time, the Flemings prevailed so strongly and enthusiastically that the French retreated and left the field, as if they were semi-conquered.[39]

Something had to be done to prevent a Flemish victory. The French leadership chose to attack the flanks of the Flemish line, hoping that such a maneuver might divert attention from the frontal assaults and perhaps break the Flemish defensive formation. As such, the attack on the flanks proved somewhat successful reaching the Flemish wagon fortification and sacking their camp. An attempt was also made to disassemble the wagons to allow for a rear assault on the Flemish line. But, the Flemings countered this by sending some troops against the French ultimately chasing them from the camp and preventing further damage to their fortification.[40] The infantry line continued to hold its position.

The length of the battle and the August heat began to take its toll on both armies.

---

[39] *Chronographia regum Francorum*, I:157: 'Factaque est pugna mirabilis ab utraque parte; que cum ferventissima jamdiu durasset, prevaluerunt Flamingi ita fortiter et animose quod Gallici jam se retrahebant et per campos dividebantur, quasi semivicti.' See also *Annales Gandenses*, p. 67; Ottokar von Stiermarken, p. 1001; Gilles li Muisit, p. 201; *Chronique de Flandre*, I:495–96; and *Chronique anonymé Française*, p. 136. Jean de Paris (p. 643) does not agree with these other accounts, claiming instead that the Flemings lost this phase of the battle.
[40] *Annales Gandenses*, pp. 68–69 and Ottokar von Stiermarken, p. 1002. The *Annales Gandenses* contends that this attack was by both French cavalry and infantry.

Fatigue and thirst plagued all involved in the fighting, but the French seem to have been especially affected by it. They wore heavier armor than did their opponents, and they had been faced with the demoralization of constant defeat. Jean Desnouelles reports that this led to disorder among the French army, many of whom were trying to remove their armor to prevent heat prostration.[41] This did not work, however, as the _Annales Gandenses_ notes that many died without being wounded, suffocating 'through the weight of their armor and the summer heat.'[42]

As the battle had turned to their side, some of the Flemish leaders, including John and Henry of Namur, retreated to Lille with their tired troops, leaving William of Jülich, Robert of Namur and Philip of Chieti to continue to fight the French.[43] The remaining Flemish leaders then met in council to plan how to end the battle; they decided to make a conclusive attack with their infantry line on the French camp hoping to drive their enemy from the field.[44]

The Flemish attack was brutal and initially successful. The discouraged French troops still facing the infantry line were taken by surprise and fled to the rear. Soon the Flemings were among the French camp, and they began to threaten Philip the Fair. More contemporary chronicles comment on this attack, and the subsequent French recovery, than any other part of the battle at Mons-en-Pévèle. It seems to both the French and Flemish authors that this was the deciding point of the battle, a point when the success of the French army against the Flemings was determined.[45] The Flemings must have felt the same, for the sole purpose of this battlefield venture, according to the _Chronique Artésienne_, was to try and reach the French king and possibly to kill him, thereby gaining victory.[46]

The contemporary chronicles contend that the Flemish attack on the French camp nearly succeeded in its goal of killing Philip. Ives reports that the Flemings slew all of the king's bodyguard save two,[47] and the _Chronicon anonyme regum Franciae_ claims that only one man separated Philip from the Flemings and that this knight was decapitated assisting the king onto his horse.[48] Several chroniclers also mention the destruction of the _oriflamme_ in this attack.[49]

Most descriptive in its narrative of this scene is the _Annales Gandenses_ which

---

41 Jean Desnouelles, p. 194. See also Guillaume Guiart, p. 294 and Jean de Paris, p. 643.

42 _Annales Gandenses_, pp. 69–70.

43 See _Annales Gandenses_, p. 70.

44 See _Annales Gandenses_, p. 70 and _Chronique Artésienne_, p. 86.

45 See Guillaume Guiart, p. 296; _Annales Gandenses_, pp. 71–72; _Chronographia regum Francorum_, I:157–58; _Chronique Artésienne_, pp. 86–87; _Chronicon comitum Flandriae_, p. 174; Jean de Paris, p. 643; Jean Desnouelles, p. 194; _Récits d'un bourgeois de Valenciennes_, p. 121; Ives, pp. 204–05; Gilles li Muisit, p. 201; _Ancienne chronique de Flandre_, p. 394; _Chronique anonymé Française_, p. 136; _Continuatio chronici_ of Guillaume de Nangis, I:344; _Chronique Normande_, p. 26; _Grandes Chroniques_, VIII:241; _Chronique de Saint-Denis_, p. 678; Geoffroi de Paris, p. 117; _Rijmkroniek van Vlaenderen_, p. 809; Giovanni Villani (ed. Muratori), col. 415; Ottokar von Stiermarken, pp. 1001–03; Jean de Winterthur, p. 32; and _Chronicon anonyme regum Franciae_, p. 18.

46 _Chronique Artésienne_, p. 86.

47 Ives, p. 204.

48 _Chronicon anonyme regum Franciae_, p. 18.

49 _Chronographia regum Francorum_, I:161; _Ancienne chronique de Flandre_, p. 395; and _Chronique anonymé Française_, p. 136.

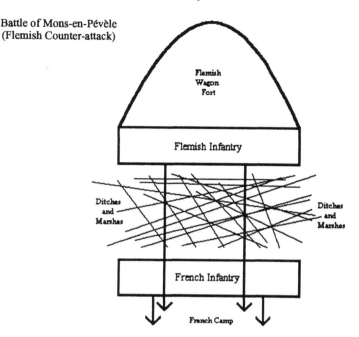

Battle of Mons-en-Pévèle
(Flemish Counter-attack)

Flemish Wagon Fort

Flemish Infantry

Ditches and Marshes

Ditches and Marshes

French Infantry

French Camp

asserts that Philip was fiercely attacked, but defended himself nobly and bravely until his horse was killed under him. However, the Flemings were unable to recognize the fallen king and thus his life was spared. The anonymous Ghentenaar annalist writes:

> [The Flemings] did not know how to distinguish him from the others lying on the ground, for his bodyguard, as a precaution in the peril of the conflict, had removed his surcoat, adorned with the sign of the lilies, so that he should not be recognized by the enemy, who would have more gladly killed him than anyone else.[50]

The *Annales Gandenses* continues the story by maintaining that finally a group of Philip's fleeing knights came upon him lying stunned on the ground and helped him to mount a horse. But Philip had difficulty guiding his steed which was attacked and wounded by a Flemish soldier. Fortunately, the horse led the stunned king back towards his own troops and he was saved.[51]

Philip the Fair soon recovered, and provoked by the attack which had come close to killing him, he rallied his army and led a counterattack against the Flemings. The *Chronographia regum Francorum* has left a compelling description of Philip at this time:

[50] *Annales Gandenses*, p. 71: 'Nesciens ipsum inter alios prostratos discernere, eo quod custodes predicti in periculo conflictus pre timore supertunicale suum bellicum, suo signo, scilicet liliorum, decoratum, ne ab hostibus, qui libentius ipsum quam aliquem alium occidissent, agnosceretur, abruperant.'

[51] *Annales Gandenses*, p. 71.

The king was nobly armed with his regal arms, and he sat upon his war horse holding a metal mace in his hands . . . and finally that most ferocious lion entered into the middle of the battle killing here and there and slaying all whom he touched with his mace. For he held himself so powerfully then that by his own bodily strength and no other were the Flemings suppressed.[52]

The *Chronique de St. Denis* adds that by doing this he was able to demonstrate how 'very confident and brave' he was to his enemies, striking fear among them and causing them to flee.[53]

It was Philip's ability to rally his fleeing army against the Flemish attackers which led to the French victory. Jean de Paris writes:

And when most of the king's army had fled terrified from the sudden invasion and confusion of the Flemish army, the king whom we ought to praise very highly in this, taking on an air of constancy and bravery, remained with few men, and he gave heart and courage to those fleeing and trembling with fear, that returning they obtained a pleasant victory from the Flemings that very evening and night.[54]

This counterattack fought by both French knights and infantry caught a disordered Flemish army unprepared for such an assault. After only a small amount of defense they turned and fled in rout;[55] the French troops pursued the fleeing Flemings well into the night.[56]

It is this last part of the battle with which the *Annales Gandenses* differs in its story. It contends that rather than returning to the battle and rallying his troops to victory, Philip was 'forced and compelled' by his soldiers to take flight, despite not wishing to leave the battlefield. His army fled with him. The Flemings then plundered the French camp before returning to the battlefield to celebrate their victory. Finally, these Flemings joined their comrades at Lille. But, this was not because they had lost the battle, simply because they had run out of food. The annalist writes:

From a high and elevated position, where they [the Flemings] united to rest for a short time, they watched with joy the French returning with their troops and companies, their torches and great wax tapers lighted, seeking in great sorrow their noble dead, slain, crushed, or choked in the pits and ditches, and showing no

---

[52] *Chronographia regum Francorum*, I:157–58: 'Rex vero nobiliter indutus suis armis regalibus et sedens super dextrarium suum tenesque machiam ferream in manibus suis . . . et tanquam leo ferocissimus intravit medium belli, percutiens hinc et inde et prosterens quoscumque attingebat de machia. Nam ita valide tunc se habuit, quod propria strenuitate corporis sui et non alterius, Flamingi refutati sunt.'

[53] *Chronique de Saint-Denis*, p. 678.

[54] Jean de Paris, p. 643: 'Cumque plurimi de regis exercitu ex invasione subita et tumultu Flandrensis exercitus perterriti fugerunt, rex, in hoc laudandus quamplurimum, constantiam et audiciam assumens, remansit cum paucis, deditque cor et audiciam tantam fugientibus ac trepidantibus prae timore, quod revertentes satis pulchram victoriam eadem vespere et nocte de Flandrensibus habuerunt.'

[55] See *Chronographia regum Francorum*, I:158.

[56] On the pursuit of the Flemings see *Chronographia regum Francorum*, I:159–60; *Chronique Artésienne*, p. 87; *Ancienne chronique de Flandre*, p. 395; *Chronique de Flandre*, I:496; and Ottokar von Stiermarken, p. 1003.

desire for further battle, although the moon rose in clear splendor. On the said hill, however, they could not find victuals sufficient for their number, or coverings, or tents to shelter them. So after consultation they went away towards Lille, not as vanquished or in flight, for there was none to pursue them, but driven by hunger and necessity.[57]

But the *Annales Gandenses* is alone in its assertion of Flemish victory; all other contemporary sources report a French victory.

Philip the Fair greeted the victory with much thanksgiving. He had subdued the Flemings, restoring peace to his torn kingdom, and he responded, according to the *Chronicon anonyme regum Franciae*, by giving a gift of one hundred *l.p.* to those knights who stayed with him when it seemed that the Flemings would defeat them; to the son of the knight who was slain helping him mount his horse, the king gave five hundred *l.p.*[58] Philip also celebrated the victory by giving gifts to several important churches in his kingdom.[59]

But Philip also grieved over those men lost on the battlefield. Both sides had suffered heavy losses at the battle of Mons-en-Pévèle. Estimates of Flemish dead range from a low of 4,000 noted in the *Annales Gandenses* to a high of 70,000 found in the *Chronicon anonyme regum Franciae*. The French may have lost as many or perhaps more, although the only tally given by contemporary sources is that of 9,000 found in the *Annales Gandenses*.[60]

Some of the most interesting anecdotes of the battle concern the deaths of two of the prominent Flemish leaders: Pieter de Coninck, the man responsible for the Bruges Matins massacre which had prompted the rebellion in 1302, and William of Jülich, the leader of the Flemish army and the man chiefly credited with the strategy which

---

[57] *Annales Gandenses*, p. 73: 'Ex quo loco, cum in eo aliquantulum more quiescentes contraherent, alto et eminenti viderunt cum gaudio Francos cum turmis et cuneis reversos, accensis faculis et cereis suis magnis torcis, cum maxima mestitudine mortuos suos nobiles occisos vel oppressos, suffocatos per puteos et fossata requirere, nec eos, quamvis luna ascenderet splendendo clare, amplius velle de bello curare. In dicto itaque monte, quasi nihil victualium quod multitudini eorum sufficeret, nec cooperimenta, nec tentoria aliqua, quibus tegerentur, invenientes, non ut victi vel fugati, quia nullus eos insequebatur, versus Insulam inito consilio abierunt, sed inedia et necessitate coacti.'

[58] *Chronicon anonyme regum Franciae*, p. 18.

[59] While besieging Lille, a few days after his victory at Mons-en-Pévèle, Philip gave an annuity of one hundred *l.p.* to the church of St. Denis in commemoration of the victory in Flanders; he also promised an equestrian statue of himself for the Notre Dame Cathedral in Paris. These gifts are enumerated and pledged by Philip in a letter written at the siege of Lille in September 1304. Copies of this letter can be found in *Gallia christiana* (Paris, 1744), VIII:374–75; Michel Felbien, *Histoire de l'abbaye royale de Saint-Denis en France* (1707; rpt. Paris, 1973), p. cxxx; and Caesar Egassio Du Boulay, *Historia universitatis Parisiensis*, (1668; rpt. Frankfurt, 1966), IV:71. Philip made similar offerings in commemoration of the victory to two churches, Mont-Saint-Michel and the Notre Dame de Boulogne, which he visited on his return trip home to Paris. See *Chronique anonymé Française*, p. 136.

[60] *Annales Gandenses*, p. 75; and *Chronicon anonyme regum Franciae*, p. 18. See also *Chronique Artésienne*, p. 87; Jean de Paris, p. 643; *Chronicon comitum Flandriae*, p. 174; *Ancienne chronique de Flandre*, p. 394; *Récits d'un bourgeois de Valenciennes*, p. 122; Jean Desnouelles, p. 195; *Continuatio chronici* of Guillaume de Nangis, I:344–45; *Chronique de Saint-Denis*, pp. 678–79; *Chronique anonymé Française*, p. 136; *Rijmkroniek van Vlaenderen*, p. 810; and *Chronique Tournaisienne*, in *Chronique Artésienne et Tournaisienne*, ed. F. Funck-Brentano (Paris, 1898), p. 87 n1.

resulted in the Flemish victory at Courtrai. Concerning the death of Pieter de
Coninck, the *Chronographia regum Francorum* records that, after the battle was won
and the Flemings had left the field, a riderless Flemish horse was found 'adorned by
the wooden image of St. George.' Said to be the horse of Pieter de Coninck, it was
concluded that he had made this image in an effort to gain the intercession of God.
That this horse was without its rider, who was presumed to be slain, was a message
to the French that God had been with them and not with the Flemings.[61]

More colorful stories accompany the death of William of Jülich. Almost all
contemporary sources report that William was killed during the last stages of this
battle, trying to rally his fleeing troops, and that it was important ultimately in the
defeat of the Flemings; but by whom or how William was killed is contested by the
contemporary authors. The *Récits d'un bourgeois de Valenciennes* claims that the
credit for William's death ought to be given to Charles of Valois, the king's brother,[62]
while three other chronicles, Jean Desnouelles' *Chronicon*, the *Chronique Normande*, and the *Chronique Tournaisienne*, claim that William was killed by Renaud
of Dammartin, the count of Boulogne, out of vengeance for the death of his father
at Courtrai.[63] The *Chronographia regum Francorum* agrees with these latter conclusions on who was responsible for the death of the Flemish leader, but its account is
very different from the other sources:

> Meanwhile, William of Jülich . . . seeing that he was unable to flee, constricted
> not a little by the heat and thirst, unshod his feet, and also those with him taking
> up their sword points placed the pommels into their mouths so that they might
> extinguish their thirst, thus awaiting death. Immediately the count of Boulogne
> . . . attacked them and cut off the head of the aforementioned William, count of
> Jülich, and the others perished by the sword.[64]

As well, three sources, the *Chronographia regum Francorum*, the *Récits d'un
bourgeois de Valenciennes* and the *Ancienne chronique de Flandre*, note that after
the battle a man, described as a 'client' by the *Chronographia*, delivered the head of
William of Jülich to Philip's tent, but that the French king 'did not care to receive'
this prize.[65]

Again it is the *Annales Gandenses* which differs from the other contemporary
sources on this story. For one thing, the annalist is certain that William's death came
honorably on the battlefield: 'when pursuing the enemy [William of Jülich] either
perished by suffocation being crushed after falling (for he was of slender build,

---

[61] *Chronographia regum Francorum*, I:161.

[62] *Récits d'un bourgeois de Valenciennes*, p. 122.

[63] Jean Desnouelles, p. 194; *Chronique Normande*, p. 26; and *Chronique Tournaisienne*, p. 87n1.

[64] *Chronographia regum Francorum*, I:158–59: 'Interea Guillelmus . . . videns quod evadere non
valebat, nimium constrictus calore et siti, discaltiavit pedes suos; qui quidem et qui cum eo erant,
sumptis mucronibus suis, ponebant pomalia in oribus suis ad extinguendam sitim, sic mortem
expectantes. Porro comes Bolonie, qui prius perceperat quod evadere vellent et ob hoc viam, qua
possent fugere, clauserat, percipiens eorum dolorem, aggressus est eos abscinditque caput prefati
Guillelmi, comitis Juliocensis: ceteri vero gladiis interierunt.'

[65] *Chronographia regum Francorum*, I:161; *Récits d'un bourgeois de Valenciennes*, p. 122; and
Ancienne chronique de Flandre, p. 395.

courageous though he was), or, as the French assert, when in pursuit of them with a company of about eighty men.'[66] At the same time, he dispels some of the folklore which had arisen around the death of this Flemish leader:

And because afterwards no certain trace of his body or his arms could be found, either by the French or the Flemings, the common Flemish folk for a long time afterwards said that he had been spirited away by the magic to which he was devoted, and later, at a fitting time, when they were in great military peril, would return. But these are frivolous and fabulous tales. For it is certain that he perished that day, even though no trace of his body or his arms could be found among the slain or smothered. The same happened with regard to many nobles at Courtrai. It is said that a certain most wicked enchanter of his household, who was with him, promising a certain magic incantation which he had learned for himself that he could become invisible to the enemy and others whenever he wished or found it necessary. But the said incantation availed him nothing, so far as saving his life went. I do not know if it was of use in concealing his body; for it is easy for demons to hide some dead body.[67]

The *Annales Gandenses* also dispels the notion that William's head had been delivered to the French king after the battle, contending instead that the head was that of 'a certain chaplain of Ghent, rather like him.'[68]

As can be seen from a narrative of the battle of Mons-en-Pévèle, this was not, as Charles Oman insists, the vindication of fourteenth-century French cavalry warfare.[69] Indeed, it was not until the end of the battle, after the failure of the Flemish attack on the French camp, that the French knights played any role in realizing the victory. Even then, at least according to the author of the *Chronique de Saint-Denis*, it was not the cavalry alone which defeated the Flemings, but a combination of cavalry and infantry, fighting together, which crushed the attack on the camp.[70]

All else points to a distinct infantry superiority on the battlefield of Mons-en-Pévèle. Despite not arriving first on the field, the Flemings ordered themselves precisely as they had at Courtrai: in a single line of infantry formed as a defensive unit prepared to meet the onslaught of French knights. And while they were unable

[66] *Annales Gandenses*, pp. 73–74: 'Inter quos fuit precipuus Wilhelmus Juliacensis, qui insequens hostes vel oppressionis et casus suffocatione interiit (erat enim tenuis complexionis, licet esset animosus), vel, ut Franci asserunt, eos insequens, cum parvo cuneo circiter lxxx virorum.'

[67] *Annales Gandenses*, p. 74: 'Et quia postea nullum indicium certum corporis ejus vel armorum a Francis nec a Flandrensibus poterat inveniri, vulgares Flamingi longo postea tempore arte magica, cui inserviebat, ipsum affirmabant ablatum, et in posterum, tempore suo competenti, quando ipsi in majori essent belli periculo, rediturum. Sed hec frivola eunt et fabulosa. Certum est enim quod isto die periit, quamvis indicia corporis vel armorum ejus inter multos occisos vel oppressos non poterant inveniri; hoc enim de multis nobilibus accidit in Curtraco. Dicitur quidam pessimus incantator de familia sua mala (et tunc cum eo erat) ipsum decepisse, quia promiserat sibi, quod quadam magica incantatione, quam sibi didicerat, quandoque vellet et indigeret, hostibus et quibuscunque aliis invisibilis fieret. Sed dicta incantatio nihil sibi hic profuit, quantum ad vite conservationem; facile enim est demonibus corpus aliquod admortuum occultare.'

[68] *Annales Gandenses*, pp. 74–75: '. . . numquam fuisse Wilhelmi, sed cujusdam capellani de Gandavo sibi aliquantulum similis, qui in bello corruit et quem ego bene novi.'

[69] Sir Charles Oman (1905), II:118.

[70] *Chronique de Saint-Denis*, p. 678.

to prepare the battlefield by digging ditches as they had done at Courtrai, they were well aware of the natural hindrances which lay between themselves and the French – marshes and perhaps irrigation ditches – and, according to Guillaume Guiart, they planned their formation in order to take advantage of them. Furthermore, with the frequently mentioned construction of the wagon-fortress, they prepared the field behind and to the sides of their line in order to protect themselves from attacks in their rear and on their flanks. This fortification also prevented easy flight if the Flemings began to lose.

The French, too, may have been aware of the vulnerability of their knights in a charge against this well prepared Flemish infantry line. Perhaps this is why the *Chronicon comitum Flandriae* contends that the French initially only skirmished, hoping that by this the Flemings would grow fatigued and give up the field without necessitating a charge by the French knights. This also could be the reason behind Philip's use of artillery on the battlefield, as this was uncommon in the early fourteenth century. If he could have broken the Flemish line with the fire from these weapons, he could then have countered with an effective cavalry charge. But, the life of the artillery at the battle was short-lived, for little is mentioned further about it except that it was easily destroyed by the Flemings in the skirmishes which preceeded the August 18 fighting. Finally, if the *Annales Gandenses* is to be believed, the French did try a 'feigned' cavalry charge in the first phase of the battle which stopped short of hitting the Flemish line. Perhaps this was also an attempt by Philip to see if the infantry formation would break; however, when it did not, another tactic was tried – a peace parliament.

If this was the case, it gives credence to the story told by several of the contemporary writers, including the eyewitness Guiart, that the peace parliament was summoned by the French. Perhaps it also gives credence to the rather cynical statement of the anonymous author of the *Annales Gandenses* that the peace conference was only a 'crafty' artifice used by the French king to hide the reformation of his army.

If it occurred, the reformation must not have worked, for when battle began again, after the failure of the peace parliament, the French returned to the strategy which had met with failure at both Courtrai and Arques: they charged on horseback into the solidly formed Flemish infantry line. And, as at both of those battles, the charge was entirely ineffective. The infantry line held, the horses stopped, and the cavalry began to lose. The French attempted cavalry charge after cavalry charge, but they neither broke the Flemish line nor disrupted it sufficiently to gain even the slightest victory. Thus, the French were forced to alter their battle plans. A contingent of horse and foot was even sent against the flanks of the Flemings which pierced their wagon fortification. But, they too were incapable of disrupting the Flemish line and were easily put to flight by a counterattack.

Furthermore, although there were heavy casualties on both sides, it was not the Flemings who tired first. The French knights, dressed in heavy armor and having to wage a constant offensive battle, were the ones who became more quickly fatigued and thirsty, and several of them deserted the battlefield.

Thus, all hinged on the success of the Flemish attack on the French. While the

Flemings had not been defeated by endless French cavalry charges, they had also not gained victory over their opponents. The French kept charging, despite their frequent setbacks, and they showed no signs of surrender. Moreover, unlike at Courtrai, the French leader himself, in this case the king, did not take part in the cavalry charges, and therefore was still alive. As well, fatigue began to affect the Flemish army, and some had already retired from the battlefield. Consequently, the Flemish leaders recognized the need to attack the French and drive them from the field.

The charge began in an ordered fashion; without breaking ranks, the Flemish line advanced against the French who were immediately facing them. This brought instant success, with the French troops fleeing to the rear. But, the French camp did not join in the rout, and the Flemish line found itself among the tents of the French battling all the way to the king.

At this point it becomes interesting to ponder what might have occurred had the Flemings succeeded in killing or capturing the king. The battle undoubtedly would have had a different result. But, saved by his bodyguard's dramatic defense, Philip IV was not killed, and ultimately he was able to rally his troops and counter the Flemish attack. Finally, the Flemish line had broken, although not by any action of the French. The tents and other camp equipment had so disrupted the line that their defensive formation was impossible to hold. This then allowed the French to charge easily through the Flemings, killing many and sending the others fleeing from the field. A few Flemish soldiers, led by William of Jülich, did try to regroup, but their numbers were too few to withstand a French assault, and, as asserted in the *Chronographia regum Francorum*, they were also very fatigued and dehydrated so that their defense was very weak, and all were killed. In the end then, it was the early success of the Flemish charge which eventually led to their defeat. They had disordered themselves with their attack on the French camp, and this, coupled with the very quick French recovery inspired by the king himself, led to the defeat of the Flemish infantry at Mons-en-Pévèle.

The impact of the French victory at Mons-en-Pévèle may never be entirely understood. While it seems that some lessons learned at Courtrai and Arques about sending knights against a solid infantry line altered the maneuvers of the French army at Mons-en-Pévèle, on the whole it appears that the French were unwilling to change their battlefield tactics. They were destined later, at Crécy and elsewhere, to repeat the same tactical mistakes – continually charging their knights into infantry – and this brought frequent defeats.

Therefore, the impact of Mons-en-Pévèle may have been to hide the problems knights faced when encountering defensive infantry formations. The defeat at Courtrai could be blamed on the ditches and other battlefield hindrances prepared by the Flemings, on the poor leadership of French generals, on the pride of their soldiers, or simply on the swing of the wheel of fortune. As well, the result of these battles could also be laid at the feet of the Flemish rebel leaders, especially William of Jülich and Pieter de Coninck, and perhaps this is the purpose behind the rather lengthy and anecdotal stories of their deaths. The death of a losing military leader is always of interest to contemporary chroniclers, but in the case of the battle of Mons-en-Pévèle the extent to which most of the major accounts go to explain how

William of Jülich died, and what happened to his body, must have other underlying significance. Perhaps it was because of the success William had at Courtrai and Arques, not only as a rebel leader, but also as a leader of non-chivalric infantry forces that necessitated a description of his death. This in turn would assure the French and Flemings that he was dead and incapable of rising again, while at the same time it would show that the infantry victories at Courtrai and Arques were accidents, led by a general who eventually met his fate at the hand of a knight, either the king's brother, Charles of Valois, or the vengeful Renaud of Dammartin, the count of Boulogne.

IV

THE BATTLE OF LOUDON HILL, 1307

ON MARCH 25, 1306, ROBERT BRUCE crowned himself king of Scotland at the castle of Scone, the traditional site of Scottish royal coronations. In doing so he confirmed his intention to open a second phase of the Scottish rebellion against the English king, Edward I.

Robert Bruce was an unusual candidate to lead this phase of the rebellion. Prior to 1297, the Bruce family was loyal to Edward. Hoping eventually to gain the Scottish throne left vacant by the deaths of Alexander III (1286) and his granddaughter, Margaret, (1290), both Robert and his father, also named Robert, had done fealty and homage to Edward as late as 1296. Still hoping for coronation, the Bruces neither participated in nor condoned the rebellions of other Scottish nobles against England in the previous decade.[1] However, by May 1297 when the Scottish rebellion began again, Robert Bruce had become impatient with Edward's reluctance to fill the vacant northern throne. As earl of Carrick he joined the other nobles in a rebellion led by William Wallace.[2]

William Wallace proved to be a disappointing military leader. Despite having a rather large and enthusiastic Scottish army, as well as the blessings of both King Philip IV of France and Pope Boniface VIII, and despite initially defeating the English army at the battle of Stirling Bridge, fought on September 11, 1297, Wallace suffered a critical loss to the English knights at the battle of Falkirk, fought on July 22, 1298.[3] The Scottish rebellion seemed at an end. Robert Bruce was not involved in the defeat at Falkirk, but was named as one of the rebel leaders, and as such was

---

[1] The best modern history of Robert Bruce is undoubtedly G.W.S. Barrow's *Robert Bruce and the Community of the Realm of Scotland*, 3rd ed. (Edinburgh, 1988). A less satisfactory, but also recent biography of Bruce is Ronald McNair Scott, *Robert the Bruce: King of Scots* (New York, 1982). For Robert Bruce's early life see Barrow, pp. 20–38 and Scott, pp. 3–37. For his and his father's allegiance to Edward I before 1297 see Barrow, pp. 39–68. On the latter point see also Ranald Nicholson, *Scotland: The Later Middle Ages* (Edinburgh, 1974), p. 51; F.M. Powicke, *The Thirteenth Century, 1216–1307* (Oxford, 1953), pp. 606–14; Michael Prestwich, *Edward I* (London, 1988), pp. 366–69; and *The Three Edwards: War and State in England, 1272–1377* (London, 1980), pp. 42–47.

[2] On the origins of the 1297 rebellion see Barrow, pp. 79–83; Scott, pp. 38–42; and Prestwich, *Edward I*, pp. 476–79. The standard work on the Scottish rebellion is Evan M. Barron, *The Scottish War of Independence: A Critical Study*, 2nd ed. (Inverness, 1934), but it is dated and has been revised almost completely by Barrow. For Barron's discussion of the 1297 rebellion see pp. 18–67. On the relationship between Bruce and Wallace see Andrew Fisher, 'Wallace and Bruce: Scotland's Uneasy Heroes,' *History Today* 39 (February 1989), 18–23.

[3] The standard description of the battles of Stirling Bridge and Falkirk is found in Oman (1905), II:75–81. Ferdinand Lot also discusses Falkirk (I:323–24). See also Barron, pp. 68–78; John E. Morris,

pursued by Edward I after the battle. He was forced to go into hiding along with many of the rebellious Scottish nobles.[4]

Robert Bruce reappeared in February 1304 as he and most other Scottish nobles surrendered to the English and renewed their oaths of fealty and homage. The nobles lost no land or titles, and there was no exchange of hostages or judicial action taken against them. Moreover, a new government was established in Scotland which, although being led by English nobles in the dominant positions of lieutenant and treasurer, did contain some Scottish representation on the advising council. Among this leadership was John Comyn, who was chiefly responsible for the reconciliation of the Scots and the English, and Robert Bruce.[5]

But peace was short-lived. Two years after renewing his oaths of fealty and homage to Edward, Robert Bruce rebelled against the English king, murdered John Comyn, and crowned himself king of Scotland.[6] Although some historians contend that this was a rash act precipitated by an argument with Comyn, it seems more likely that Bruce had carefully planned his *coup-d'état*. Bruce knew that Edward I was ill, and that he was unlikely to lead an invading army into Scotland. Furthermore, Comyn was a symbol of Scottish submission to England. His death would be a symbolic gesture which would unite the Scottish people in a rebellious fervor.[7] At the same time, Robert Bruce's coronation as king returned the rule of Scotland to its rightful lords, the Bruce family able to trace its claim to the throne through Alexander II.[8]

News of Robert Bruce's rebellion reached Edward at the end of February. On May 22, 1306, in a colorful oration delivered after the knighting of his son, the future Edward II, at an Arthurian feast now known as the Feast of Swans, Edward I insisted that he would avenge the death of Comyn. Swearing on the roast swans which made up the chivalric centerpiece on the banquet table, he promised that he would not sleep more than one night in the same place until he reached Scotland with an army to put down Bruce's rebellion. This campaign, the king promised, would be the catalyst behind his greatest military adventure, one which would conclude in the Holy Land.[9]

Edward summoned his army to meet him at Carlisle in July 1307. In the meantime, however, he appointed Aymer of Valence, his half-cousin and brother-in-law to Comyn, to be his special military lieutenant in Scotland. The king commissioned

The Welsh Wars of Edward I (Oxford, 1901), pp. 282–94; Barrow, pp. 83–104; Scott, pp. 42–52; and Prestwich, *Edward I*, pp. 478–83.

4   See Barrow, pp. 104–31; Scott, pp. 53–64; F.M. Powicke, pp. 692–94; and M. Keen, *England in the Later Middle Ages: A Political History* (London, 1973), pp. 35–37.

5   See Barrow, pp. 132–44; Scott, pp. 64–73; F.M. Powicke, p. 713; and Keen, p. 37.

6   See Barrow, pp. 145–64; Scott, pp. 73–76; Nicholson, *Scotland*, p. 71; F.M. Powicke, pp. 713–14; Prestwich, *Edward I*, pp. 505; and T.M. Smallwood, 'An Unpublished Early Account of Bruce's Murder of Comyn,' *Scottish Historical Review* 54 (1975), 1–10. For this murder Bruce was excommunicated.

7   For a discussion on the different historical interpretations of this *coup d'état* see Barrow, pp. 145–53 and F.M. Powicke, pp. 713–14.

8   On Bruce's royal lineage see F.M. Powicke, p. 611 n.1 and Barrow, pp. 39–40.

9   Several sources mention the Feast of the Swans. The most colorful narrative is that of Prestwich, *The Three Edwards*, pp. 34–35. See also F.M. Powicke, p. 515; Barrow, pp. 153–54; and Scott, pp. 79–80.

Valence to harass Bruce and to try to demoralize the Scots so that the rebellion might be contained until the larger army arrived the following summer. Edward also sent his son to aid Valence in this task.

Initially, Valence was very successful against the Scottish leader. By the end of summer, Bruce's rebellion had nearly collapsed. Valence had met and defeated Bruce's army at Methven on June 20, and this was followed by a second defeat at Dalry fought two months later.[10] Meanwhile, Edward, the prince of Wales, had also captured Bruce's castle at Lochmaben. Many rebels had been captured and executed, including a number of Bruce's own family members. But Robert Bruce himself had escaped capture, and by the end of the campaigning season he, and with him the rebellion, remained alive.[11]

After this successful beginning, however, nothing went right for the English cause. Edward I became increasingly ill on his journey north and was unable to proceed further than Carlisle. His efforts to arrange a parliament in January to discuss the Scottish situation also were unsuccessful. Furthermore, in February, Bruce once again eluded capture, despite being encircled by Aymer of Valence's army in the neighborhood of Glen Trool.[12] Bruce went north followed by Valence, and finally the two armies met on May 10 at the battle of Loudon Hill. This time the outcome did not favor the English. Robert Bruce won a certain victory, handily defeating the English cavalry.

The victory was a stunning upset of the English strategic plans. Aymer and his army fled to Carlisle where he met the ill Edward and resigned his commission in disgrace. The remaining English armies too were recalled, so that a new offensive could be undertaken. However, before that happened Edward I died (on July 7), turning the responsibilities of English rule, including the handling of the newly motivated Scottish rebellion, over to his son who became Edward II.[13]

Burdened by his new responsibilities, Edward was unable to respond promptly to Robert Bruce's victory. The rebellion grew in numbers and morale. A now famous letter, dated May 15, 1307 and attributed to Alexander Abernethy, recounts the spirit of the Scottish people following Bruce's victory at Loudon Hill:

> I hear that Bruce never had the good will of his followers or of the people generally so much with him as now. It appears that God is with him, for he has destroyed

---

[10] The tactical action of both of these battles is difficult to determine from the original sources; as such, I am unable to write more at length on them in this work.

[11] For a description of the events of 1306 see Barrow, pp. 154–61; Scott, pp. 80–100; Nicholson, *Scotland*, pp. 72–75; F.M. Powicke, pp. 715–17; Barron, pp. 236–59; Prestwich, *Edward I*, pp. 507–09; and Keen, p. 38. Among the relatives of Robert Bruce captured during this year were his second wife, Elizabeth de Burgh, his daughter, Marjorie, three sisters, Elizabeth Siward, Christina Seton, and Mary Bruce, and three brothers, Neil, Thomas and Alexander. Only the three brothers were executed although Mary was confined in a wooden cage at Berwick.

[12] On Edward's attempt to call a parliament in January 1307 see Barrow, pp. 161–64 and Keen, p. 38. On Bruce's escape at Glen Trool see Barrow, p. 172 and Scott, pp. 100–02.

[13] On the transformation of English power after the death of Edward I see Prestwich, *Edward I*, pp. 556–58. On the impact of the victory on Scotland see Barrow, pp. 172–74 and Scott, pp. 104–06.

King Edward's power both among the English and Scots. The people believe that Bruce will carry all before him . . .[14]

It would not be until 1310 that Edward II again would return to Scotland to fight Robert Bruce, the Scottish king.

Unlike most of the battles fought in the early fourteenth century, the battle of Loudon Hill is recorded in only one source, John Barbour's historical poem *The Bruce*.[15] Despite its historical significance, only one English chronicler, Thomas Gray, mentions the battle, and his chronicle contains no details beyond simply recording it as a Scottish victory. No other English source chronicling the Scottish rebellion even mentions this battle, and this reticence is echoed by the Scottish chronicles which discuss the life of Robert Bruce.[16] This silence in itself seems odd, especially when compared to the large number of contemporary records on the battle of Bannockburn fought seven years later. Coupled with the fact that John Barbour's poem was not written until 1376, the absence of a large number of sources has led most medieval military historians to neglect or to downplay the battle's significance.[17] Still, Barbour's poem, composed in Middle English, is considered by most scholars to be of great historical accuracy.[18] Moreover, its narration of the battle of Loudon Hill shows Bruce's successful use of infantry against cavalry, a feat which he would duplicate later at the battle of Bannockburn.

Barbour begins book VIII of his poem after Robert Bruce's escape from Valence at Glen Trool. Bruce traveled north followed by an angered Valence who was harassed in his pursuit by Bruce's lieutenant, James, lord of Douglas.[19] Finally, Bruce's army, all infantry, arrived at Loudon Hill where he was sent a message from Valence challenging him to battle on the plains near the hill. Bruce received Valence's challenge, and, recognizing the need to eventually fight the English army despite having a much smaller army than his English counterpart, he accepted the

---

[14] This letter is found in *Calendar of Documents Relating to Scotland*, ed. J. Bain (Edinburgh, 1883), II:#1926. The translation I have used is found in Barrow, pp. 172–73.

[15] While there are several editions of Barbour's *Bruce*, the most accessible and widely used is that edited by Walter W. Skeat (*The Bruce, or the Book of Robert de Broyss, King of Scots (1286–1332)*, Early English Text Series, 2 vols. (1870–77; rpt. Oxford, 1968)). Barbour's description of the battle of Loudon Hill is found on I:177–92.

[16] Thomas Gray, pp. 34–35. Later Scottish chronicles mention the battles of Methven and Dalry but omit mention of Loudon Hill. See John of Fordun, *Chronica gentis Scotorum*, ed. W.F. Skene (Edinburgh, 1871), I:340–42 and the *Liber Pluscardensis*, ed. F.J.H. Skene (Edinburgh, 1877), I:231–33.

[17] The only military historian who discusses the battle is Oman (1905), II:83–84, but his narrative is quite short. Barron's description of the battle is also quite short (pp. 262–63). Even Aymer of Valence's biographer, J.R.S. Phillips, does not discuss the battle at any length, despite Valence's defeat there being the reason for his retirement from military leadership. See *Aymer de Valence, Earl of Pembroke, 1307–1324: Baronial Politics in the Reign of Edward II* (Oxford, 1972).

[18] On the historical veracity of John Barbour's poem see George Neilson, *John Barbour, Poet and Translator* (London, 1900) and Barrow, pp. 312–13.

[19] Barbour, I:177–81.

challenge.[20] Valence was pleased with Bruce's desire to fight him for he felt that the English cavalry would easily triumph over the Scottish infantry:

> For he thought, through his great might,
> If the king appeared to fight,
> That, through the great chivalry
> That was in his company,
> He would so overwhelm the king,
> That there would be no recovery.[21]

But, the Scottish army was already at Loudon Hill, while the English force had not yet arrived. So, Bruce was able to reconnoiter the battlefield, establish his position, and prepare the field to disrupt the charges of the English cavalry. He discovered that while the plain itself was flat and dry, on one side there was a morass, 'deep and wide,' which could be used as a border for fighting.[22] However, the field was still too wide for an infantry army to fight cavalry, and thus Bruce decided that alterations were needed to aid him in fighting the English. He therefore cut three large and deep trenches across the field, leaving small gaps in them which would decrease the number of cavalry who could charge the infantry line. Robert Bruce also hoped that these trenches would slow down the progress of the English cavalry charges so that their shock might be lessened.[23] Bruce then gathered his army, numbering only 600 and camped beyond the trenches.[24]

On the day of battle, Aymer of Valence assembled his army, numbering 3,000, and marched to Loudon Hill. The sun was shining and the cavalry, ordered in two lines, were impressive to their Scottish opponents. Barbour describes the chivalric array:

> The sun rose, shining and bright,
> So that it glimmered on the large shields.
> . . .
> Their helmets were brightly polished,
> Again, on them the sun glistened;
> Their spears, their pennons, and their shields
> Illuminated the entire field with bright light.
> Their best, brightly colored armor,
> And horse the shade of such color,

---

[20] Barbour, I:181–82.

[21] Barbour, I:182–83:

> For he thoucht, throu his mekill mycht,
> Gif the king durst apeir to ficht,
> That, throu the gret chevelry
> That suld be in his cumpany,
> He suld swa ourcum the king,
> That thar suld be na recouering.

[22] Barbour, I:183.

[23] Barbour, I:183–84. Barbour claims that these gaps were so narrow that they would only allow the passage of 500 knights charging side by side. This still seems to be rather high number and may indeed be an exaggeration.

[24] Barbour, I:184.

Battle of Loudon Hill

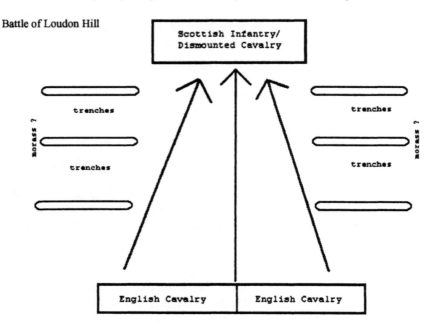

And coat-of-arms of such color,
And hauberks, that were as white as flour,
Made them glow, so that they appeared
to be angels of a heavenly kingdom.[25]

To offset this impressive and imposing display, Bruce addressed his soldiers, reminding them that they would be killed for rebelling against the English king if they failed to win the battle. They should therefore fight 'hardely,' meeting the first line's charge bravely and solidly, so that the second line would be terrified of repeating the same unsuccessful result. Bruce also promised his troops that victory would bring happiness and valor. The Scots responded: 'Sir, if God wishes, we will do it / so that no disgrace shall be placed on this deed.'[26] Bruce then led his men in

[25] Barbour, I:184–85:

> The sone wes rysyn schynand bricht,
> That blenknyt on the scheldis braid.
> . . .
> Thair basnetis burnyst var brycht,
> Agane the sone [glemand] of licht;
> Thair speris, thair pennownys, & thar scheldis
> Of licht Illumynit all the feldis.
> Thair best [&] browdyn bricht abneris,
> And hors hewit on seir colour,
> And cot-armouris off seir colour,
> And hawbrekis, that war quhit as flour,
> Maid thame glitterand, as thai war lik
> Till angellis he, of [hewinis] rik!

[26] Barbour, I:186: 'Schir, gif god will, we sall sa do / That no repruf sall ly thar-to.'

a battlefield prayer, and they prepared for the English attack by moving to the first trench and ordering their defensive line formation.[27]

Aymer of Valence saw the formation of the Scots among the trenches, but he still did not feel that there would be any difficulty in achieving a quick victory given his larger numbers and the fact that his cavalry faced only infantry. He too addressed his troops, promising them that they would gain rewards and renown by defeating the rebels.[28] The trumpets then announced the beginning of battle, and the English cavalry charged into the Scots. The Scottish infantry in turn met the charge '. . . with such vigor / that the best and the most valorous / were dragged to the ground at the meeting.'[29] Before long the tide of battle began to favor the Scots. The English cavalry charge was powerful and impressive, but by the time it hit the line of Scottish infantry its impact had deteriorated, disrupted by the trenches placed on the battlefield. Their Scottish opponents, on the other hand, held their position, using their line first to stop the charge and then to push the cavalry back. Scottish spears killed both men and horses, while other cavalry, trying to escape the infantry, were thrown from their mounts into the trenches and morass:

> The king's men, who were worthy,
> With their spears so sharp,
> Stabbed both men and horses,
> Until red blood flowed freely from the wounds.
> The wounded horses tried to flee,
> And charged their own men in their flight,
> So that those who were in the vanguard,
> Were thrown here and there into the trenches.[30]

Among the Scots fought Robert Bruce himself, and his military exploits boosted morale within his own force while inspiring fear among the English.[31]

Soon the battle was over. The field was covered with dead and dying English cavalry and their horses. The Scots too had suffered losses, but they were small in comparison to their chivalric opponents'.[32] Still in line, and still led by Robert Bruce,

---

[27] Barbour, I:186–87.

[28] Barbour, I:187.

[29] Barbour, I:188: '. . . vith sa gret vigour / That the best and of mast valour / Var laid at erd at thair metyng.'

[30] Barbour, I:188–89:
> The kingis men, that worthy war,
> With thair speris that scharply schar,
> Stekit men and stedis bath,
> Till red blude ran of voundis rath.
> The hors that [woundyt] war can fling,
> And ruschit the folk in thair flynging,
> Swa that thai that than formast war
> War stekit in soppis heir and thar.

[31] Barbour, I:188. Also singled out for their bravery in battle were James of Douglas and Edward Bruce, Robert's brother.

[32] Barbour, I:189. No estimates of casualties on either side are given by Barbour although he does indicate that when Bruce advanced after the fleeing English troops only 500 soldiers went with him

the Scottish infantry began to advance across the field in pursuit of the fleeing soldiers. Seeing this rout, the English rearguard, which had yet to enter the fray, turned and fled as well. Aymer of Valence tried to rally his troops, but finally he too was forced to flee from the field; the English had lost the battle of Loudon Hill.[33]

The Scots left the battlefield with their prisoners. They were obviously elated with the victory, and they praised Bruce for leading them against the English. Barbour ends his narration of the battle by writing:

> They were without a doubt happy;
> Because they knew that they had won,
> As the king had helped them so.
> From that they gave him more homage.
> Then his power grew more and more.[34]

There are several similarities between this battle and that of Courtrai fought five years previously. Despite being challenged to battle by the English, a challenge which included the site of the battlefield, Robert Bruce was given the opportunity to choose on what part of the field the fighting was to take place. Arriving at the site first, he was able to survey the area, noting its natural hindrances to fighting, and to prepare it to serve his advantage in battle. He knew that he was fighting with a small infantry army against a larger cavalry force, and he used this to formulate his battle plan. Although he found a morass bordering the battlefield, he judged the plains to be too large to serve his purposes. Therefore, he directed that the field be narrowed by digging three large trenches across it. He then ordered his troops in a defensive line with the intention of standing against the charge of English cavalry.

On the English side, as with the French at Courtrai, there was no concern for the pre-battle activities of the Scots. Despite seeing the trenches, and perhaps knowing that they would decrease the number of cavalry who could charge at one time, the English army proudly formed their mounted shock formation and surged forward. Their display was impressive and their charge seemed powerful, and yet they lost. The Scottish infantry simply held their line, and their opponents on horseback could not pierce their formation. Again as at Courtrai, the warhorses must have stopped, and this allowed the infantry to use their weapons advantageously against the heavily armored cavalry. Horses became a target, as did the fallen cavalry with the weak joints of their armor exposed.

---

indicating a possible loss of one hundred men. Oman (1905, II:85) reports that one hundred English knights were killed there, but he gives no source for his tally, and I have yet to find any mention of this elsewhere.

[33] Barbour, I:189–90. The English rearguard probably contained infantry, but Barbour does not report who was in that formation, only that they fled with the routed cavalry.

[34] Barbour, I:191:

> So war thai blith forouten dout;
> For feill that wonnyt thaim about,
> [Fra] thai the king saw help him swa,
> Till him thar homage can thai ma.
> Than vox his power mair and mair.

Robert Bruce rejoiced in the defeat of the English. Although we are not told what he thought about the battle, or whether he believed that it was his tactics which achieved victory, the next time a serious threat was made against his claim to the throne, at Bannockburn in 1314, he repeated many of his Loudon Hill tactics and again achieved victory. At Bannockburn, however, Bruce did not face and defeat a lieutenant of the king but the king himself, Edward II.

V

THE BATTLE OF KEPHISSOS, 1311[1]

THERE ARE PERHAPS few more interesting medieval military organizations than the Catalan Grand Company. A band of mercenaries by definition, they are more appropriately described as a loose-knit group of late medieval warriors, largely infantry troops, who travelled widely throughout the eastern Mediterranean region. Effectively leaderless for most of their early history, during that period the Catalan Company still faced and defeated armies made up of Turkish, Caucasian, Genoese, Thracian, Macedonian, Athenian, Byzantine, Burgundian, and French soldiers. In doing so they captured large amounts of land, dominating and ruling most of Greece throughout much of the fourteenth century – Kenneth M. Setton's dates are 1311–1388.[2]

The Catalan Company was organized late in 1302 by Roger de Flor of Brindisi. Once a Knight Templar and very much an experienced warrior, both on land and sea, Roger de Flor gathered together a group of experienced Spanish soldiers who had taken the side of Frederick II against the Napolese Angevins in the War of the Sicilian Vespers which had lasted for more than twenty years. Having fought for so long, most of those who joined his company had little else they could do for employment.[3] The Company was not small; most historians estimate a number of 6,500, 4,000 of whom were 'the famed and formidable almugávares', infantry troops of outstanding

---

[1] There are several spellings of this battle, which was named after the river near where it was fought. I have chosen to use the Greek. Other spellings include Cephissus and Céfu. Jep Pascot, *Les almugavares: Mercenaires catalans du moyen âge (1302–1388)* (Brussels, 1971), pp. 149–55 calls the battle Copaïs after a nearby lake.

[2] Kenneth M. Setton, *Catalan Domination of Athens, 1311–1388* (Cambridge, 1948) is the seminal work on the Catalan Company. Other works of importance include: Pascot; Kenneth M. Setton, 'The Catalans in Greece, 1311–1380,' in *A History of The Crusades*, ed. K.M. Setton, vol. III: *The Fourteenth and Fifteenth Centuries*, ed. H.W. Hazard (Madison, 1975), pp. 167–224; R. Ignatius Burns, 'The Catalan Company and the European Powers, 1305–1311,' *Speculum* 29 (1954), 751–71; David Jacoby, 'La "compagnie catalane" et l'état catalan de Grèce. Quelques aspects de leur histoire,' *Journal des savants* (1966), 78–103; Nicolas Cheetham, *Mediaeval Greece* (New Haven, 1981), pp. 130–51; and J. Longnon, 'The Frankish States in Greece, 1204–1311,' in *A History of The Crusades*, ed. K.M. Setton, vol. II: *The Later Crusades*, ed. R. L. Wolff and H.W. Hazard (Madison, 1969), pp. 270–74.

[3] Setton, *Catalan Domination*, pp. 2–3; Pascot, pp. 32–44; Setton, 'Catalans,' pp. 168–69; Burns, p. 752; Jacoby, pp. 79–81; Cheetham, pp. 134–35; Longnon, p. 270; and Norman Housley, *The Later Crusades, 1274–1580: From Lyons to Alcazar* (Oxford, 1992), p. 161. The Catalan Company initially was made up of Catalan, Aragonese, Majorcan, and Navarrese soldiers. Later, Turks, Byzantines, Thracians, and Macedonians joined the mercenary group.

skill and ability.[4] The Byzantine Emperor, Andronicus II Palaeologus, was looking for experienced soldiers, hoping to import an army to face the growing power of the Ottoman Turks in the eastern Mediterranean. He could pay well, and the Catalan Company jumped at the opportunity to put their skills to use again.[5]

By August 1303, the Company had their first success, by sacking the island of Ceos. The following month they arrived in Constantinople. Quickly they were put up against the Ottomans in Asia Minor, and just as quickly they began to push them back from the Byzantine capital. Soon they had won so much favor and were so feared in Byzantium that Roger de Flor, now with the title 'Caesar,' had even married into the Palaeologi family. But this turned out to be a bad decision, for he was murdered by the same family in April 1305.[6]

Devoid of their founder and leader, but respected and feared by all in the east, the Catalan Company withdrew from Constantinople but refused to return to the western Mediterranean. They went instead to the Gallipoli peninsula where they established their first state.[7] This state did not last long. In June 1307, the Company left Asia Minor and moved into the west. They traveled swiftly. With little opposition, the Company, now bolstered by Turkish and Greek recruits, quickly conquered Thrace and Macedonia, and by spring 1309 they entered Thessaly, threatening Athens, Thebes, and the lower Greek peninsula.[8] Walter (Gautier) I of Brienne, the Frankish duke of Athens, did what little he could to stop their advancement: rather than fighting against them, he hired them to fight for him. For six months, until the end of 1310, they waged war for their new employer, taking more than thirty villages, towns, and strongholds, conquering other rulers of Greece, in Thessaly and Epirus, and even attacking Byzantine forces in the southern peninsula.[9]

But the wisdom Walter had shown in hiring instead of firing the Catalan Company, now disappeared. After so many victories he sought to dismiss them still owing four months wages. Instead, he selected 500 of the mercenaries – 200 knights and 300 almugávares – paid them their wages, gave them lands and titles, and then requested that they keep their comrades out of Athenian territories. The rest of the Catalan Company moved into fortifications in southern Thessaly, but they refused to be so easily dismissed, and during the end of 1310 and the beginning of 1311 both they and the duke of Athens prepared for battle. A blow to the Athenian military strength came with the defection of the 500 Company soldiers whom the duke of Athens had

---

[4] Setton, *Catalan Domination*, p. 3; Pascot, p. 44; and Burns, p. 752.
[5] Setton, *Catalan Domination*, p. 2; Burns, p. 752; and Jacoby, p. 79.
[6] Setton, *Catalan Domination*, pp. 3–4; Pascot, pp. 47–85; Setton, 'Catalans,' p. 169; Burns, p. 752; Jacoby, pp. 80–81; Cheetham, pp. 134–37; and Housley, p. 161.
[7] Setton, *Catalan Domination*, p. 4; Pascot, pp. 87–123; Setton, 'Catalans,' p. 169; Jacoby, pp. 81–86; and Longnon, p. 270. At Gallipoli, the Catalan Company was forced to defend themselves not only against the Byzantines, but also against the Genoese and Caucasians.
[8] Setton, *Catalan Domination*, pp. 4–5 and Pascot, pp. 125–40. Pascot claims that the Catalan Company vacated Gallipoli because of discord among the Company. Setton believes that it was because the Catalans had devastated the peninsula and were unable to continue to feed themselves.
[9] Setton, *Catalan Domination*, pp. 7–8; Pascot, pp. 140–49; Setton, 'Catalans,' pp. 169–70; Cheetham, pp. 132, 137–40; Longnon, pp. 270–71; and Housley, pp. 161–62.

separated from the rest of the mercenary band; they rejoined their comrades.[10] A more major blow came on March 15, 1311, when the still outnumbered Catalan Company met and defeated the duke of Athens and his Frankish knights at the battle of Kephissos. Athenian losses were numerous; Walter of Brienne was among the dead on the field. Greece was now the land of the Catalan Company.[11]

There are only three sources for the battle of Kephissos and all are written from the Catalan perspective. The longest and most detailed is Ramón Muntaner's *Crònica*, written sometime before his death in 1336. The second is the Aragonese version of the *Chronique de Morée* known as the *Libro de los fechos et conquistas del principado de la Morea* which was compiled during the first half of the fourteenth century under the direction of the Don Fray Johan Ferrandez de Heredia, Master of the Hospital of St. John of Jerusalem.[12] And the third is found in Nikephoros Gregoras's *Byzantina historia* written in Constantinople c.1359. Although composed a great distance from and much later than the battle of Kephissos, Gregoras' narrative seems to have been taken from Catalan or Turkish participants.[13] There is no source on Kephissos written from the Athenian position.

Probably because there are no original sources written on the battle of Kephissos from the Athenian perspective, there is little disagreement in the story given by Ramón Muntaner, the Aragonese version of the *Chronique de Morée*, and Nikephoros Gregoras.

In 1311 there was undoubtedly no military force more experienced in warfare than the Catalan Company. Although there is little record of them fighting full-scale battles before Kephissos, they were involved in the raids, chevauchées, and sieges, both against armed forces and unarmed civilians, that generally characterized late medieval warfare. They had also fought several small engagements at which their battle tactics would have been strengthened. As well, their military training had been developed by fighting several different foes, from the peasant factions quickly put together to defend the lands of Thrace and Macedonia to well-organized and armed professional Byzantine Imperial contingents.

The Catalan Company was also quite numerous for a mercenary band. The Aragonese *Chronique de Morée* indicates that at the time of the battle of Kephissos the Company numbered 6,000, 2,000 of whom were cavalry and 4,000 infantry.[14] This number was not much smaller than the initial recruitment count given by Ramón

---

[10] Setton, *Catalan Domination*, pp. 8–9; Setton, 'Catalans,' p. 170; Cheetham, p. 140; Longnon, p. 271; and Housley, p. 162.

[11] Setton, *Catalan Domination*, pp. 9–13; Pascot, pp. 149–54; Setton, 'Catalans,' pp. 167, 170–71; Jacoby, p. 87; Cheetham, pp. 140–42; Longnon, pp. 271–72; Housley, p. 162.

[12] Ramón Muntaner, *Crònica*, trans. H.M. Goodenough (London, 1921), II:575–78 and *Libro de los fechos et conquistas del principado de la Morea compilado por comandamiento de Don Johan Ferrandez de Heredia*, ed. A. Morel-Fatio (Geneva, 1885), pp. 119–21.

[13] Nikephoros Gregoras, *Byzantina historia*, ed. J.-P. Migne, *Patrologia Graeca*, 148 (Paris, 1865), 411–22.

[14] *Libro de los fechos*, p. 120.

Muntaner,[15] although Nikephoros Gregoras indicates that more than 1,100 Turks had been added to the Company total before their invasion of Thessaly.[16]

The Athenian army was much larger, with Nikephoros Gregoras counting 6,400 knights and 8,000 foot, and Ramón Muntaner enlarging the latter figure to 24,000.[17] These numbers are probably exaggerations, at least that is the conclusion of most modern historians, yet there is little doubt that the Athenians outnumbered the Catalan Company. Indeed, the Aragonese version of the *Chronique de Morée* reports that when the Company saw the number of their enemy at Kephissos, 'that great multitude of men,' they tried to make peace.[18] Many of these troops were also mercenaries themselves, with Muntaner estimating 700 'Frankish' knights fighting for the duke of Athens.[19]

But while outnumbering the Catalan Company, the Athenians certainly did not have the same level of military experience as did their counterparts. After all, it was because of their experience that the Catalans had been hired as warriors by Walter of Brienne in 1309. This relative lack of experience may have been a significant factor in the Athenian loss at Kephissos.

The story of the battle of Kephissos opens with the hiring and then firing six months later of the Catalan Company by the duke of Athens, Walter of Brienne. This was an odd occurrence, claims Ramón Muntaner, as Walter had 'made himself beloved by the Catalans and spoke Catalan.' In turn, the Company had responded by fighting valiantly for the duke, recovering much territory which had been taken from him by the Byzantines and others.[20]

Still, there was the question of money. The Catalan Company had been in the employ of Athens for six months, but had only been paid for two. This is when Muntaner claims that Walter of Brienne decided, 'when he saw that he was at peace with all his neighbours,' on 'a very wicked plan': he would choose 500 of the Catalans and bribe them to stay with him, paying them for their past service and giving them land in the duchy. The others he commanded to be driven from his duchy without paying what was owed to them. In devising this plan, Walter was certain that the mercenaries who remained would defend him against those whom he had driven away.[21]

There were two grave miscalculations made by the duke in this plan. First, instead of leaving Greece as ordered, the Catalan Company retreated into some of the strongholds which they had recently won. While the Aragonese *Chronique de Morée* insists that the Company only wanted to remain in peace there, these were technically the duke's holdings, and thus it appears that the Catalans were staying close enough to Athens to monitor the situation and to wait for an opportunity to gain vengeance

[15] Ramón Muntaner, pp. 485–86.
[16] Nikephoros Gregoras, pp. 414–15.
[17] Nikephoros Gregoras, pp. 423–24 and Ramón Muntaner, p. 576.
[18] *Libro de los fechos*, p. 120. See also Setton, *Catalan Domination*, p. 9; Pascot, pp. 151–52; and Cheetham, p. 140.
[19] Ramón Muntaner, p. 576.
[20] Ramón Muntaner, pp. 575–76 and *Libro de los fechos*, p. 119.
[21] Ramón Muntaner, p. 576. See also *Libro de los fechos*, pp. 118–19.

for their mistreatment by the duke.[22] Second, although mercenaries by occupation, money and lands alone could not force the 500 Catalans who had been paid to stay behind to fight against their comrades. When placed in a battle situation at Kephissos, they refused to contend against the Company and instead joined with them in fighting the Athenians. However, at the time the duke did not worry about this defection, as, perhaps anticipating its occurrence, he had gathered a large army of other soldiers to fight his war.[23]

Walter of Brienne was to fight this war on a field chosen by the Catalans. According to Ramón Muntaner, the Catalan Company knew when the Athenian army marched against them, and that in response, together 'with their wives and their children,' they traveled to a 'beautiful plain near Thebes'. It was an easily defensible position, Muntaner reports: 'in that place there was a marsh, and of that marsh the Company made a shield for themselves.'[24] Nikephoros Gregoras adds that the Catalan Company further prepared the field by 'irrigating' it with more water brought in from the nearby river. But the Company themselves were not to be bogged down by this water as Gregoras also reports that the Company were able to form their line on 'a flat land, green with grass.'[25] To reach the Catalans, standing on this dry ground, the Athenians would have to charge across a marsh, certainly an insurmountable obstacle.

So why did the Athenians choose to attack the Catalans at Kephissos? The answer is not clear in the sources, except that the Aragonese *Chronique de Morée* seems to indicate that the large size of the Athenian contingent gave the duke much confidence in facing the Catalan Company, no matter what battlefield obstacles lay in his way. This is also indicated in the speech given by Walter to the 500 Catalans who wished to join their former compatriots: 'And the [duke] told them to go, and bad luck go with them, that it was well that they should die with the others.'[26] Furthermore, the Company themselves may have encouraged this confidence first by the decision of the Turks within the Company to refuse to fight, as Ramón Muntaner records, 'thinking it [the battle] was done by an agreement between the two sides, in order to destroy them,' and second by trying to make peace with the Athenians at the onset of the battle. By refusing to make this peace, however, the duke forced the Catalans to decide, in the words of the anonymous author of the Aragonese *Chronique de Morée*, that it was 'better to die in battle than to surrender to his mercy.'[27]

Choosing the field was only part of the Catalan tactics at Kephissos. They also ordered themselves in a defensive formation, as a solid line beyond the marsh. Whether this line included both cavalry and infantry or infantry with dismounted cavalry as in other early fourteenth-century battles cannot be known from the original

---

[22] *Libro de los fechos*, pp. 119–20 and Ramón Muntaner, p. 576.
[23] Ramón Muntaner, pp. 576–77.
[24] Ramón Muntaner, p. 576.
[25] Nikephoros Gregoras, pp. 419–22.
[26] *Libro de los fechos*, p. 120 and Ramón Muntaner, pp. 576–77. The speech of the duke is reported only in Muntaner.
[27] Ramón Muntaner, p. 577 and *Libro de los fechos*, p. 120: '& ellos, viendo que non los queria recebir finon á mercer.'

Battle of Kephissos

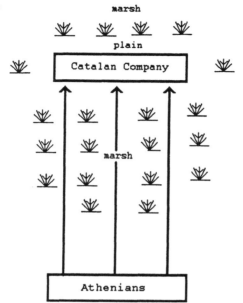

sources. However, all three sources are interested in and do describe the Athenian offensive formation which charged at this line. This is reported to be a cavalry line made up of knights – 200 French knights 'all with gold spurs' according to Muntaner – with a few infantry following led by Walter of Brienne himself.

This charge failed miserably, although what caused its failure is in dispute. Ramón Muntaner, for example, describes what happened simply and without many details:

> What shall I tell you? The horses of the count, at the noise the almugavars made, turned towards the marsh, and there the count and the banner fell, and all those who were in the van.[28]

But Nikephoros Gregoras has a more spectacular determination for why the charge ended in defeat. After discussing the water-filled state of the battlefield, the Byzantine chronicler writes: 'so that it slowed and stopped the unstable charge of the horses whose hooves, mired in the mud, were able to be moved only with difficulty.'[29]

Despite the author's distance geographically and chronologically from the battle, it is Gregoras' description of the charge's failure which has been accepted by most modern historians; although, to be accurate, they get this depiction of events not from Nikephoros Gregoras, but from the seventeenth-century *Catalan Chronicle* of Francisco de Moncado. Attributing his narrative to Gregoras, Moncado expands the original author's report of the Athenian charge:

[28] Ramón Muntaner, p. 577.
[29] Nikephoros Gregoras, pp. 421–22.

The Duke with the first troop of the vanguard rushed to close with a squadron of infantry that was on the other side of the submerged fields, the cavalry furiously pushed forward without noticing that it was in the midst of the marsh. At the same time the Almugavars, swift moving and unencumbered, with darts and swords fell upon those who, weighted down with iron, were wallowing with their horses in the mud and slime. The rest of the troops came up to help the Duke and fell into the same danger.[30]

Surely this could have occurred, but as it is not so mentioned in Muntaner's chronicle or in the Aragonese *Chronique de Morée*, although such a colorful episode should have elicited comment, there may be some doubt as to its accuracy. It could also be that the marsh did not bog down and stop the charge but merely hindered it from reaching the Catalan line with full force. In fact, this interpretation more easily allows for the statements made by both Muntaner and the Aragonese *Chronique* after their mention of the charge that the Company fought very well against the attacking force. The Aragonese chronicler claims that the Catalans fought 'como hombres desesperados,' while Ramón Muntaner writes that 'the battle was very hard; but God, Who always helps the right, helped the Company.'[31] These are hardly descriptions of combat against an entrapped enemy. As well, at this point in the battle, seeing that it was not simply a plan to destroy them, the Turks rejoined the Catalan Company, and added their attacks against the Athenians.[32] This too might not have happened if the Athenian charge had been stopped in the mud.

In the initial charge, Walter of Brienne lost his life. Nikephoros Gregoras blames him directly for the defeat:

Truly the opinion and arrogance of the prince differed much from correct reason. For he hoped not only to defeat the Catalans, but also to take all of their lands and towns all the way to Byzantium. But a while later the opposite occurred.[33]

Many others also fell at Kephissos. Ramón Muntaner numbers the dead infantry at 20,000, while Gregoras reports a loss of 6,400 cavalry and 8,000 foot, equalling the total number which he says fought in the battle. Muntaner also claims that of the 700 French knights who fought with the Athenians, only two survived. Undoubtedly these are all exaggerations, although the large numbers may simply demonstrate the overwhelming defeat had by the Athenians that day.[34]

The defeat was significant and perhaps even could be defined as decisive. Ramón Muntaner's concluding words are simple and direct, but they reveal much: 'And so

---

[30] Francisco de Moncado, *Expedición de los Catalanes y Aragoneses contra Turcos y Griegos* (Madrid, 1941), p. 230. This has been translated in *The Catalan Chronicle of Francisco de Moncado*, trans. F. Hernández, ed. J.M. Sharp (El Paso, 1975), pp. 217–18. Moncado's explanation of battlefield events has been accepted by Setton, *Catalan Domination*, p. 11; Pascot, p. 153; Setton, 'Catalans,' p. 171; Cheetham, p. 141; and Longnon, p. 271.

[31] *Libro de los fechos*, p. 120 and Ramón Muntaner, p. 577.

[32] Ramón Muntaner, p. 577.

[33] Nikephoros Gregoras, pp. 421–22.

[34] Ramón Muntaner, p. 577 and Nikephoros Gregoras, pp. 421–22. See also *Libro de los fechos*, p. 120.

the Company . . . had won the battle and all the Duchy of Athens.'[35] They would hold the duchy for more than seventy years.

Despite the size and cavalry domination of the Athenian force, and despite the initial Turkish unwillingness to fight with the Catalan Company, which significantly decreased their numbers, the smaller army seems to have easily won the battle. Why? In assessing the battle of Kephissos, two important factors must be considered: First, the Catalan Company chose a battlefield with obvious natural defensive advantages. In particular, a marsh ran across the field. This allowed the Company to order their line in a defensive formation on flat land, with the Athenians forced, if they wanted to fight a battle against their mercenary foes, to cross the marsh to reach them. The Catalan Company may also have prepared this field further by adding even more water from the nearby river.

Second, while all signs indicated that the Athenians should not charge their cavalry into the Catalans across such a field, they did so anyway. The lure was not archery fire as in some other early fourteenth-century battles, but pride. Walter of Brienne simply could not understand how his large, noble, cavalry-based force could be defeated by a much smaller, largely infantry army. As Gregoras indicated, this may have been against 'correct reason,' but it did convince the duke that a charge could be successful. It was not. Walter's pride cost him his life and lands and the lives and lands of many of his retainers. For whether the charge became mired in the mud and stopped, thus allowing for a more mobile and lighter infantry counterattack to defeat them, or simply became disordered by the marshy conditions of the battlefield, thus allowing the defending line to stop the confused and disrupted charge and to defeat it within their defensive formation, the result was the same, victory for the Catalan Company.

[35] Ramón Muntaner, p. 577.

VI

THE BATTLE OF BANNOCKBURN, 1314

With his victory at Loudon Hill in May 1307 and the death of the English king, Edward I, in July 1307, Robert Bruce gained virtual control over all of Scotland. Loudon Hill had given Bruce strong credibility as a leader, and even those who opposed his right to the throne or doubted his ruling capabilities before his crowning now accepted their new king without much hesitation. Also adding to Robert Bruce's credibility was the fact that a strong English opponent in Edward I was replaced by a much less strong heir, Edward II; the new English king's military, political, and personal weaknesses were recognized long before his crowning. This, coupled with the prevailing story in Scotland that in a vision an English knight had seen Edward I residing and being tormented in hell, seemed to indicate that God was now favoring the Scots and had given His divine approval to the reign of their King Robert I.[1]

From 1307 to 1310 Robert Bruce ruled Scotland with few complications or hindrances from England. This gave the Scottish king time to solidify his kingdom and to unify his followers. Those who continued to oppose Robert were dealt with without mercy. For example, from the end of 1307 to the end of 1309 the Scottish king campaigned against the Comyn-Balliol adherents throughout his kingdom, causing them to surrender their castles and lands; some joined the side of Bruce, while others were forced to flee to the protection of English borders. Indeed, so fervent was Bruce's military enthusiasm during this campaign that when he fell ill in December 1307, he continued to lead his army from a litter. Each foe he faced quickly wrote an appeal for aid to Edward II, but on every occasion no relief came and defeat quickly followed. By Christmas 1309, two-thirds of Scotland was securely under the control of Robert Bruce, and almost all opposition to his rule was either neutralized or crushed. Only the little populated northern hinterlands and the castles of Stirling, Perth, and Dundee, able to be supported by the English navy, remained hostile to his authority.[2]

After 1309, Robert Bruce turned his efforts to more peaceful means of ruling. Parliaments began to be held, the treasury filled, and positions allotted. Profiting

[1] Nicholson, *Scotland*, p. 76.
[2] Barrow, pp. 173–83; Scott, pp. 104–15; Barron, pp. 273–375; John E. Morris, *Bannockburn* (Cambridge, 1914), p. 19; W.M. Mackenzie, *The Battle of Bannockburn: A Study in Mediaeval Warfare* (Glasgow, 1913), pp. 3–5; Nicholson, *Scotland*, pp. 77–81; Prestwich, *Three Edwards*, p. 53; May McKisack, *The Fourteenth Century* (Oxford, 1959), pp. 32–33; and A.A.M. Duncan, 'The War of the Scots, 1306–23,' *Transactions of the Royal Historical Society* 6th series, 2 (1992), 139–48.

from this especially were the large number of lesser nobles and small landowners who had supported the king since his ascension and now began to benefit from that support.[3] Diplomacy with France also began again, with new Franco-Scottish relations agreed to. A Norwegian-Scottish treaty was signed on October 29, 1312. And Robert Bruce also initiated diplomatic relations with Flanders and Germany, bringing increased economic prosperity and security to his kingdom.[4]

In late 1310, Edward II finally decided to invade Scotland. But this expedition was destined for failure as, despite a successful excursion into Scotland led by the king's favorite, Piers Gaveston, few of the English forces were able or willing to move from Berwick, remaining in garrison there until the summer of 1311.[5] Despite its impotence, Bruce seized upon the 'invasion' as an excuse to raid the marches of England, attacking frequently during the next three years, carrying off large amounts of booty, and forcing the inhabitants to agree to costly truces to protect their lands and agricultural livelihoods. During these years Robert Bruce also conquered Perth and Dundee.[6] Finally, in May 1313 Edward Bruce, while his brother invaded the Isle of Man, besieged Stirling Castle. By summer a truce had been agreed to: if an English army did not come within three miles of the castle by Midsummer's Day 1314, Stirling would peacefully capitulate. The next move was to be Edward's. He could undertake an invasion of the Scots, something that he had been unable to do in 1310, and perhaps win; or he could do nothing and not only lose Stirling Castle but also continue to lose credibility at home among those who were awaiting an opportunity to remove him from the English throne. The answer was simple: gather an army and march to the relief of Stirling.[7]

Edward II used this incident to counter his baronial opposition in England, impressing almost everyone of the necessity of participating in this military adventure. By March 1314 preparations began for the invasion, and by May, a large English army gathered at Berwick and began to march into Scotland. By June 23, one day before the truce was to expire, Edward's force came within three miles of Stirling Castle. However, between him and the castle stood Robert Bruce's army,

[3] Barrow, pp. 183–86; Scott, pp. 116–19; Barron, pp. 363–71; and Nicholson, *Scotland*, pp. 81–82.
[4] Barrow, pp. 183–84, 190, 198–200; Scott, pp. 120, 130 and Nicholson, *Scotland*, p. 82. However, a formal Franco-Scottish alliance would not be signed until April 1326.
[5] Scott, pp. 119–26; Barron, pp. 379–84; Morris, *Bannockburn*, pp. 19–20; Mackenzie, pp. 5–9; Nicholson, *Scotland*, pp. 82–83; McKisack, pp. 11–12; and M.R. Powicke, 'Edward II and Military Obligation,' *Speculum* 39 (1956), 97–98.
[6] Barrow, pp. 190–95; Scott, pp. 128–36; Barron, pp. 392–418; Morris, *Bannockburn*, pp. 20–21; Mackenzie, pp. 9–14; Nicholson, *Scotland*, pp. 83–84; Prestwich, *Three Edwards*, p. 53; McKisack, pp. 32–34; Duncan, pp. 146–49; Jean Scammell, 'Robert I and the North of England,' *English Historical Review* 73 (1958), 385–86; J.A. Tuck, 'War and Society in the Medieval North,' *Northern History* 21 (1985), 35–36; and Michael Prestwich, 'England and Scotland during the Wars of Independence,' in *England and Her Neighbours, 1066–1453: Essays in Honour of Pierre Chaplais*, ed. M. Jones and M. Vale (Woodbridge, 1989), p. 195.
[7] Barrow, pp. 195–202; Scott, pp. 136–42; Barron, pp. 418–28; Morris, *Bannockburn*, pp. 20–21; Mackenzie, pp. 14–18; Nicholson, *Scotland*, pp. 84–86; Prestwich, *Three Edwards*, p. 54; and McKisack, p. 34.

outnumbered, but prepared, if needed, to fight the English force.[8] A two day battle ensued, and at the end, the unexpected had occurred. Edward II was defeated, barely escaping his own capture, and the English soldiers, those who had not been killed or taken as prisoners, were rushing back to their own borders.[9] It would be the most significant victory in Scottish history, a result which all future rebels would try to imitate, but at which none would succeed.

Like Courtrai and completely unlike Loudon Hill, there is a large number and great variety of impressive accounts of the battle of Bannockburn written by contemporary or near contemporary authors from both sides. Obviously such a striking victory by a smaller and less experienced force over an army made up of the most noble English knights and led by their king fascinated and awed many. Scottish commentators tried diligently to explain why they had won, while their English counterparts tried equally as diligently to rationalize why they had lost.

Unfortunately, no contemporary Scottish account of the battle exists, the most detailed report coming from John Barbour's c.1375 narrative poem on Robert Bruce which was of such great importance in explaining the Scottish king's tactics at Loudon Hill. Other, much smaller accounts of the battle can be found in three Latin works, John Fordun's *Scotichronicon*, written c.1384, the *Liber Pluscardensis*, and Walter Bower's continuation of Fordun's *Scotichronicon* – which also contains much new material about Bannockburn – both written in the early to middle fifteenth century. Strangely, Andrew of Wyntoun's lengthy *Orygynale Cronykil of Scotland* contains nothing about the battle, although a short account can be found in his *Brevis cronica*, written in Middle English at the beginning of the fifteenth century.[10]

The English accounts of Bannockburn, although none as extensive as Barbour's narrative, are both more numerous and more contemporary. Lengthy discussions of the battle can be found in John of Trokelowe's *Annales*, written c.1330, Geoffrey le Baker's *Chronicon*, written starting in 1341, the anonymous *Chronicon de Lanercost*, c.1346, the *Vita Edwardi II*, written c.1348 by an anonymous clerk at St. Paul's in London, Thomas of Burton's *Chronica monasterii de Melsa*, written at the end of the fourteenth century, and Thomas Walsingham's *Historia Anglicana*, written in the early fifteenth century. Other, shorter descriptions are in Adam Murimuth's *Continuatio chronicorum*, written and updated between 1325 and 1347, Henry Knighton's *Chronicon*, c.1360, *The Anonimalle Chronicle*, written c.1381 in French at St. Mary's

---

[8] Barrow, pp. 203–10; Scott, pp. 143–46; Barron, pp. 429–49; Morris, *Bannockburn*, pp. 57–60; Mackenzie, pp. 19–41; Nicholson, *Scotland*, 86–87; McKisack, pp. 34–35; and Duncan, pp. 149–50.
[9] Morris, *Bannockburn*, pp. 60–93; Mackenzie, pp. 42–111; Barrow, pp. 211–32; Scott, pp. 146–65; Barron, pp. 450–77; Oman, (1905), II:84–100; Delbrück, III:438–42; Nicholson, *Scotland*, pp. 87–90; Prestwich, *Three Edwards*, pp. 54–55; and McKisack, pp. 35–39. Morris, MacKenzie, Barrow, Scott, Barron, Oman, and Delbrück have all written extensive accounts of the battle. I have chosen, however, to write my account of the battle solely from the original sources and have used these other accounts only sparingly, even when these authors agree with my interpretation of what occurred on the battlefield.
[10] John Barbour, II:257–330; John Fordun, *Chronica gentis Scotorum*, ed. W.F. Skene (Edinburgh, 1871), I:346–47; *Liber Pluscardensis*, ed. F.J.H. Skene (Edinburgh, 1877), I:237–39; Walter Bower, *Scotichronicon*, ed. D.E.R. Watt (Aberdeen, 1991), VI:349–77; and Andrew of Wyntoun, *Brevis cronica* (Edinburgh, 1879), III:336.

Abbey in York, the *Eulogium historiarum*, from the monastery at Malmesbury, which was begun in 1367 and continued until 1413, and *The Brut*, which was written and rewritten mostly in the fifteenth century.[11] There are also three contemporary poems on the battle of Bannockburn: one, composed in Middle English before 1352, by Laurence Minot is quite renowned, while two others, one anonymous and one by Robert Baston, both written in Latin, are less well known.[12] Perhaps the most interesting account of the battle is a long one written c.1355 by Thomas Gray in his *Scalachronica*. What makes this account so unusual is that Gray, a soldier who may have fought against the Scots at Neville's Cross in 1346, began his work, written in Old French, while in an Edinburgh prison. As well, his father, also named Thomas, was captured at Bannockburn. Consequently, he includes some information which appears nowhere else and which he may have learned from his captors.[13]

> O famous race unconquered through the ages, why do you, who used to conquer knights, flee from mere footmen? At Berwick, Dunbar, and Falkirk, you carried off the victory, and now you flee from the infantry of the Scots.[14]

With these words the anonymous author of the *Vita Edwardi II* asked the question that was on the lips of perhaps every Englishmen who learned of the defeat of their forces against the Scots. How could the English have lost? They were a large and quite experienced force, outfitted with the best arms and armor and led by the greatest military leaders of the land. Moreover, they were a cavalry-based force, whose horsed troops should have easily trampled down their rebellious and 'rustic' infantry opponents.

With the siege of Stirling progressing and the Scottish ultimatum delivered south to Edward II, the English king resolved to go north with a relief army. As Walter Bower reports:

> But the new King Edward, ablaze with strident anger on hearing of the illustrious deeds of King Robert, and weighing up the innumerable evils and infinite losses

---

[11] John of Trokelowe, *Annales*, ed. H.T. Riley (London, 1866), pp. 83–87; Geoffrey le Baker, *Chronicon*, ed. E.M. Thompson (Oxford, 1889, pp. 7–9; *Chronicon de Lanercost*, ed. J. Stevenson (Edinburgh, 1839), pp. 224–27; *Vita Edwardi II*, ed. and trans. N. Denholm-Young (London, 1957), pp. 49–57; Thomas of Burton, *Chronica monasterii de Melsa a fundatione usque ad annum 1396*, ed. E.A. Bonds (London, 1868), II:329–32; Thomas Walsingham, *Historia anglicana*, ed. H.T. Riley (London, 1863), I:139–41; Adam Murimuth, *Continuatio chronicorum*, ed. E.M. Thompson (London, 1889), pp. 20–21; Henry Knighton, *Chronicon*, ed. J.R. Lumby (London, 1889), I:409; *The Anonimalle Chronicle, 1307 to 1334*, ed. W.R. Childs and J. Taylor (Leeds, 1991), pp. 86–89; *Eulogium historiarum sive temporis*, ed. F.S. Haydon (London, 1863), III:194–95; and *The Brut, or the Chronicles of England*, ed. F.W.D. Brie (London, 1908), I:207–08.

[12] Laurence Minot, *Poems*, ed. J. Hall (Oxford, 1897), pp. 4–6; 'The Battle of Bannockburn,' in *Political Songs of England*, ed. T. Wright (London, 1839), pp. 261–67; and W.D. Macray, ed., 'Robert Baston's Poem on the Battle of Bannockburn,' *English Historical Review* 19 (1904), 507–08.

[13] Thomas Gray, *Scalachronica*, ed. J. Stevenson (Edinburgh, 1836), pp. 140–43.

[14] *Vita Edwardi II*, p. 54: 'O gens inclita multis retro temporibus inuicta, cur fugis pedites que uincere solebas equites? Apud Berewyke, Dounbar et Foukyrk, triumphum reportasti, nunc Scotis peditibus terga dedisti.'

brought upon him and his man by the same king, prepared new wars to punish the said acts.[15]

It was an impressive force, filled with 'a large number of worthy men,' according to John Barbour. And while the exact number can never be known – contemporary chronicles exaggerate the total, placing the it between 100,000 and 340,000[16] – it may have equalled the English army which invaded France in 1340 both in size and noble leadership. John of Trokelowe notes that 'all who owed him [Edward II] military service' were assembled at Berwick for the Scottish invasion by the king.[17] Indeed, of all the leading English barons and knights, only four earls were absent from the force: Lancaster, Warren, Arendale, and Warwick.[18]

Perhaps most significant for this study was the large number of cavalry troops included among the English army. Of the 100,000 troops which John Barbour counts, 40,000 are cavalry with 3,000 of those equipped with horses covered with armor; of the 340,000 Walter Bower tallies, 300,000 were cavalry.[19] These are definite exaggerations, but they do indicate the opinion of contemporaries that the English force was composed of many horsed warriors. Whatever conflict this army was to fight would undoubtedly be cavalry-based. John Barbour writes: 'There were so many knights, that they believed that if they were to do battle, there would be no strength which could withstand their might.'[20]

Justified or not by their large numbers, the English pride is remarked on by all sources, English and Scottish. An anonymous poet remarks simply: 'There were in the army many nobles, knights who were too showy and pompous.'[21] The author of the *Vita Edwardi II* is more eloquent:

> There were in that company quite sufficient to penetrate the whole of Scotland, and some thought if the whole strength of Scotland had been gathered together,

---

15 Walter Bower, VI:350–51: 'At Eadwardus novus rex acriori ira accensus audiens illustres actus regis Roberti, perpendensque innumera mala et infinita dampna sibi et suis per eundem regem illata, in vindictam premissorum nova bella parabat.' See also John Barbour, II:257–58; Thomas Gray, p. 140; 'The Battle of Bannockburn,' p. 262; John Fordun, I:346–47; and *Liber Pluscardensis*, I:237.

16 The tallies include: 100,000 (John Barbour, II:261); 300,000 (Andrew of Wyntoun, *Brevis cronica*, III:336; *Liber Pluscardensis*, I:183; and a poem appended to Walter Bower, VI:357); and 340,000 (Walter Bower, VI:361). The *Vita Edwardi II* (p. 50) is much more realistic in its tally, but only includes a count of cavalry, 2,000+, and records no figure of infantry or archers. Modern historians have considerably decreased the numbers of English soldiers. Morris, for example, sees only 17,500 troops with Edward II (*Bannockburn*, p. 41). Barron (pp. 430–31) tallies 17,000. And MacKenzie (pp. 22–30) counts 20,000. Barrow (pp. 205–06) agrees with Morris.

17 John of Trokelowe, p. 83. This statement was used also by Thomas Walsingham, I:139.

18 John Barbour, II:260–61; John of Trokelowe, p. 83; *Chronicon de Lanercost*, p. 224; *Vita Edwardi II*, pp. 49–50; Thomas Walsingham, I:139–40; and Robert Baston, p. 508.

19 John Barbour, II:262–64 and Walter Bower, VI:361. Modern historians have also decreased this number. Barrow, for example, sees no more than 7,000 to 10,000 soldiers in the Scottish army (pp. 208–09). Barron (pp. 432–33) and Mackenzie (pp. 31–32) give a smaller number of 7,000.

20 John Barbour, II:264: 'Thai war so cheuelrus, that thai / Trowit, gif thai com to the ficht, / Thair suld no strynth with-stand thar mycht.'

21 'The Battle of Bannockburn,' p. 263: 'Erant in excercitu plures generosi, / Milites in exitu nimis et pomposi.'

they would not have stayed to face the king's army. Indeed all who were present agreed that never in our time has such an army gone forth from England.[22]

Although they perhaps could not anticipate the extremely large outpouring of English support for the relief of Stirling Castle, the Scots had had a long time to prepare for this invasion. Like Edward II, Robert Bruce also made a recruitment call to his countrymen, encouraging them to fight 'manfully' for the 'fredome of this cuntre.'[23] 'The trumpet was sounded,' writes Robert Baston, and troops came to the sound.[24] Weapons and armor were also gathered and manufactured.[25]

But the Scottish numbers would not, and perhaps in agreement with the author of the *Vita Edwardi II*, could not equal those of the English force. Only the Scottish chroniclers seem concerned with the strength of the Scottish army, with John Barbour and Andrew of Wyntoun alone assigning them a number, 30,000, far smaller than their numbers for the English army – 100,000 and 300,000 respectively.[26] John Fordun and Walter Bower are content simply to describe them as 'few men,' while the *Liber Pluscardensis* uses a comparative tone: 'King Robert [had] an army small in comparison to the multitude of the said king of England.'[27]

But the defending troops were very spirited, ardently willing to fight an invading army in defense of their own lands. John Barbour describes at great length the religious devotion of the Scots, an assertion echoed by the English Thomas of Burton. Burton, a monastic chronicler who was not a supporter of Edward II, writes that while the English were proud, 'confident in their strength and numbers,' the Scots were 'humble, confessing, armed with the Eucharist, and placing their trust in God alone.'[28]

They also had good leaders, far more experienced in warfare through their years of conflict in Scotland and on the English marches than their counterparts.[29] Particularly imposing in his military leadership abilities was Robert Bruce. By 1314 he was a hero to his troops and a legend to his enemies. His presence alone could

---

[22] *Vita Edwardi II*, p. 50: 'Fuerunt in societate illa satis sufficientes ad penetrandum totam Scotiam, et iudicio aliquorum, si tota Scotia collecta fuisset in unum, non exspectaret regis exercitum. Revera hoc fatebatur tota comitiua, quod tempore nostro talis exercitus non exiuit ab Angliam.' See also Geoffrey le Baker, p. 7 and Walter Bower, VI:351–52.

[23] John Barbour, II:259 and Thomas Gray, p. 140.

[24] Robert Baston, p. 508.

[25] John Barbour, II:260.

[26] John Barbour, II:266–67 and Andrew of Wyntoun, *Brevis cronica*, III:336.

[27] John Fordun, I:347; Walter Bower, VI:353; and *Liber Pluscardensis*, I:237. The only English chronicler reporting a description of the Scottish army is the *Anonimalle Chronicle* which refers to them as a 'grant poer' (pp. 88–89). However, it is difficult to understand how the chronicler uses the adjective 'grant' in describing the Scots as he follows this statement with a note that they 'strongly' fought the English in the battle.

[28] John Barbour, II:271–73, 276 and Thomas of Burton, II:331: 'Angli vero summe elati, in viribus et multitudine confidentes, Scotti vero contriti, confessi, viaticoque muniti, solum Deum protectorem acclamantes.'

[29] On the Scottish leaders see John Barbour, II:265–66.

make up for some of the numerical advantage of the English, especially as they were led by the 'inept' Edward II, to use Thomas of Burton's term.[30]

As there was to be no surprise to Edward's invasion, the English army moved with much ostentation and violence through Scotland to Stirling Castle.[31] With it was a large logistical train, containing many wagons filled with armor, tents, furniture, wine, wax, and food.[32] But this did not slow it down much, as the army made rapid progress, so rapid, insists the author of the *Vita Edwardi II*, that it was quite fatigued by the time it arrived at Bannockburn; thus the Scots were at an advantage in the battle:

> Brief were the halts for sleep, briefer still for food; hence horses, horsemen and infantry were worn out with toil and hunger, and if they did not bear themselves well it was hardly their fault.[33]

While the English had to travel a large distance to arrive at the battlefield, Robert Bruce's army was much closer. This enabled Bruce to locate a good battlefield site and, as he had done at Loudon Hill, to prepare it to his army's advantage. Bruce's site was known as New Park, a flat field bordered by trees and marshes through which the English had to march on their way to Stirling Castle.[34] According to John Barbour, Robert Bruce needed the flat field for his defensive infantry formation – if the Scots fought on horseback, Bruce knew that the English would defeat them. However, the Scottish leader also knew that Edward II would try to break his infantry line with cavalry charges, and that a flat field would facilitate those charges unless some modifications could be made to it.[35] Ditches to narrow a cavalry charge, like those that the Scots had dug at Loudon Hill, were not needed at Bannockburn, as the bordering trees and marshes served that function. Yet, smaller ditches and pits dug in the battlefield proper would serve to disrupt the cavalry charges, disordering them and resulting in a loss of impact when the horses reached the infantry line. So they were dug. Geoffrey le Baker describes these battlefield hindrances:

> . . . the Scots selecting the battlefield for the greatest possibility of victory, dug extended ditches three feet deep and three feet wide from the right to the left flanks of the army, filling them with a brittle plait of twigs, reeds, and sticks, that is a 'trellis,' and covering them with grass and weeds. Infantry might be aware of a safe passage through these, but heavy cavalry would not be able to pass over them.[36]

---

[30] Thomas of Burton, II:329–30. See also John Barbour, II:270–71; Walter Bower, VI:357; and Henry Knighton, I:409

[31] *Chronicon de Lanercost*, p. 225; John Barbour, II:261–64; and Walter Bower, VI:352–53.

[32] John Barbour, II:261–62 and *Vita Edwardi II*, p. 50.

[33] *Vita Edwardi II*, p. 51: 'Breuis erat mora capiendi sompnum, sed brevior erat mora sumendi cibum; unde equi, equites et pedites, labore et fame fatigati, si minus bene rem gererent non erant culpandi.'

[34] John Barbour, II:268. There is some dispute on the site of this battle. For descriptions see Morris, *Bannockburn*, pp. 60–66; Barrow, pp. 211–25; and Oman, II:85–86.

[35] John Barbour, II:268.

[36] Geoffrey le Baker, pp. 7–8: '. . . Scoti, campi locum nacti victoribus maxime oportunum, subfodiebant ad mensuram trium pedum in profundum et ad eiusdem mensure latitudinem fossas protensas in longum a dextro in sinistrum cornu exercitus, operientes illas cum plexis fragilibus ex virgulis et

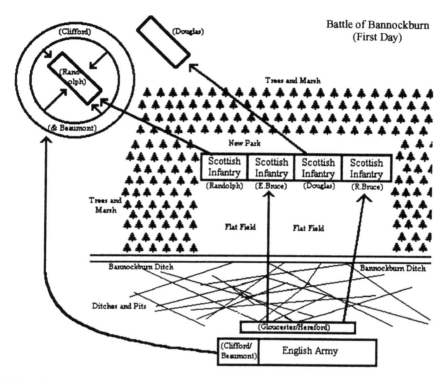

Walter Bower gives it a class interpretation; lesser individuals were able to defeat their betters by using a simple 'machina plena malis':

> A contrivance full of evils is fashioned for the feet of horses. / trenches set with stakes, so that they cannot pass without tumbles. / The ordinary folk have dug the pits so that the cavalry may stumble over them.[37]

With the ditches and pits dug, and hearing the approach of the English army, Robert Bruce, who had previously split his troops into four divisions, under the command of Thomas Randolph (Earl of Moray), Edward Bruce, Walter Stewart/ James Douglas, and Bruce himself respectively, ordered them in their planned infantry formation. It was a solid formation which stood ready for battle, waiting for someone to attack them, states John Barbour.[38]

However, there was a delay in the English advance. Although their approach had been apparent to the Scots since they had entered Scotland, as they neared the

---

viminibus sive cratibus, id est "herdeles", cespite et herbis superstratis, peditibus quidem perviis saltim consciis cautele, set equitum pondera non valentibus sufferre.' See also John Barbour, II:271–72. A discussion of the nineteenth-century excavation of some of the Bannockburn pits and ditches can be found in Morris, *Bannockburn*, pp. 62–63.

[37] Walter Bower, VI:370–73: 'Machina plena malis pedibus formatur equinis, / concava cum palis, ne pergant absque ruinis. / Plebs foveas fodit ut per eas labantur equestres.'

[38] On Bruce's troop division see John Barbour, II:269–70. (Douglas and Stewart combined leadership of the third division.) On the Scots order before battle see Barbour, II:273–74.

battlefield they stopped. Why this occurred has always been somewhat of a mystery. No original source discusses the reasons for the English delay, although Barbour gives the impression that Robert Bruce was surprised by the lack of an attack, sending two of his leaders, James Douglas and Robert Keith, to reconnoitre the enemy force. They reported only their amazement at the size and splendor of their foe. (Bruce had them lie to his troops for fear that they might flee when told what they had to face.[39])

It was late in the day, June 23, perhaps too late for the English troops to advance on the Scottish position. But if this was the reason for the lack of a prompt English attack, Edward II blundered by sending a small number of troops (800) under the leadership of Lord Robert of Clifford and Henry of Beaumont, a 'company,' to use Barbour's term, to relieve the siege of Stirling Castle.[40] Why he did this is yet another mystery. Perhaps Edward believed that this small force could slip past the Scots, 'for they knew well where the King [Robert Bruce] was,' and give relief to the castle. If this was what he thought, however, the English king was gravely mistaken. For as the company proceeded towards the castle, Thomas Randolph's division rushed from the woods (his position in the main Scottish line was bordering the woods) and attacked them.[41] Randolph had only 500 men, but he was prepared to fight the larger force. Still, the size differential was significant, and the Scots immediately ordered themselves in a defensive formation, setting up 'back to back with their spear points outward,' as the English troops moved in to surround them. Although outnumbered, the formation was solid and strong. The English quickly began to take casualties, including Sir William Dancourt, one of the noble leaders, as the Scots speared both men and horses.[42] Thus the English were forced to hold back from their accustomed hand-to-hand combat and to throw 'spears, darts, and knives' into the Scottish line; when these were gone, they even threw their maces and swords, all in an effort to try and disrupt or break the Scottish formation. This stalemate continued for a long time, the English surrounding an unwavering Scottish line. Finally, John Barbour reports that both sides began to suffer from the heat of the day: 'On both sides they became so fatigued / from the fighting and the sun's heat, / that their flesh became wet with sweat.'[43] The dust and smell also rose and blinded all in combat. But neither side withdrew.

Seeing Randolph's troops surrounded and fatigued, James Douglas approached

---

[39] John Barbour, II:274–76.

[40] John Barbour (II:277–82), Thomas Gray (pp. 141–42), and *Chronicon de Lanercost* (pp. 225–26) are the only original sources which discuss this initial phase of battle. (Other sources pick up the story when the two main armies enter the fray.) Gray differs from Barbour in that he records the movement of the English vanguard against the main Scottish force before the encounter between Randolph and the English. The *Chronicon de Lanercost* gives no chronology. Despite Gray's father, also named Thomas, being captured in this battle, I have accepted Barbour's chronology because of the greater intricacy of his account.

[41] The *Chronicon de Lanercost* (pp. 225–26) contends that Edward II knew that the Scots were in the woods and that Clifford's expedition was in part trying to draw them out.

[42] Thomas Gray (p. 142) reports that his father was captured at Bannockburn when his horse was speared and he was brought down.

[43] John Barbour, II:280: 'On athir half thai war so stad, / For the [rycht] gret heit that thei had, / Of fechting and of sonnys het, / That all [thair] flesche of swat wes wete.'

Robert Bruce and asked permission to enter the battle, hoping that such an action might relieve the beleaguered Scottish line. Initially, Bruce refused Douglas' request, fearing that a weakened main force might provoke the attack of Edward II, but when Douglas repeated his request, the Scottish king gave in.[44] Douglas' entry into the battle moved it into a second, more violent phase.

Douglas' movement was noticed by the English troops, and it excited them. Barbour insists that Edward II did not favor a fight that late in the day, early evening. But the vanguard, under the leadership of Gilbert of Clare, the earl of Gloucester, and Humphrey of Bohun, earl of Hereford, refused, or at least may have been too far separated from the main body of English troops, to heed the king's words, for it rushed after Douglas' soldiers.[45] Perhaps, the *Vita Edwardi II* insists, the English vanguard misinterpreted Douglas' advance in relief of Randolph's force as a flight from the battlefield, and wishing to take advantage of the situation charged in pursuit; the Scots being on foot and the English on horse made this a viable option.[46] Thomas Gray, however, maintains that the English vanguard was merely advancing onto the battlefield without attempting anything against Douglas' force.[47]

Whatever the reason for their action, what the English troops found, to what most chroniclers claim was their surprise, was the main Scottish body ready to fight against them. Led by Robert Bruce himself, 'with his own axe in hand,' the remaining two divisions of Scottish troops immediately broke from their formation and attacked the surprised and somewhat trapped English vanguard.[48] Seeing Robert Bruce on the battlefield – he wore a distinguishable crown on his bascinet – gave at least one English knight, Sir Henry of Bohun, the opportunity for heroism, as he rushed to strike the Scottish leader. The two met: Bohun slashed with his weapon and missed; Bruce buried his axe in Bohun's helmet, killing his foe with a blow so powerful that it broke the handle of the axe. This display, Barbour reports, which was seen by almost all of the troops on both sides, caused the Scots to fight with more enthusiasm and the English to retreat from the field. The Scots pursued their foes, but most of the English were able to escape.[49]

While this was going on, Randolph's force was still engaged with Clifford's. Douglas' men approached the conflict to relieve it, but their presence alone seemed to turn the tide of the battle in favor of the Scots. Indeed, John Barbour asserts that Douglas' troops never even entered the combat, for once the English saw their approach, they wavered and made an opening in their encirclement of Randolph's division. This gave Randolph the advantage, and with Douglas halting his troops so that he might not distract from the honor of victory Randolph deserved – 'it would be a sin for him to lose his well-earned honor' – the Scots increased their fighting

---

[44] John Barbour, II:281–82.
[45] John Barbour, II:283.
[46] *Vita Edwardi II*, p. 51.
[47] Thomas Gray, p. 141.
[48] John Barbour, II:283–84.
[49] John Barbour, II:284–86; Thomas Gray, p. 141; *Vita Edwardi II*, p. 51; and John Trokelowe, p. 84.

intensity and broke through the surrounding English army, sending it in rout. Many on both sides had been slain, but the English losses numbered many more.[50]

The Scots rejoiced in their victory. Although the main English body as yet had not been encountered, the Scots had been victorious in both of the small conflicts of the day. Thomas Randolph's troops had seen the most brutal of the fighting, and they were justly praised for their victorious deeds. As well, Robert Bruce had himself been embroiled in the combat, and he had proven his fighting capabilities against a renowned English knight. He was rebuked by his nobles, who felt that he had needlessly put himself in danger; from his troops he received only increased affection and loyalty.[51] As the Scots encamped for the night, they no longer feared the upcoming day and its inevitable fight with the main body of English troops. They had the assurance that God was on their side, and when Robert Bruce spoke to them, warning them to be cautious against pride and asking them to be prepared for what they would encounter the next day, he repeated the advantages that the Scots had over the English: they had right on their side; they would gain much from the capture of English riches; and they were fighting for their wives, children, and freedom. But they would need discipline in order to win. Bruce believed that the English would try cavalry charges against the Scottish infantry line, and this meant that the Scots must defend themselves strongly and boldly with their spears. They must also not break for looting until the battle was over. Finally, he assured those fighting that if they were to die in the battle, their heirs would have immediate possession of their property without fines, for honor required this. He concluded his speech by asking his soldiers to remain prepared for battle throughout the night; they slept armed and in order.[52]

There was no joy in the English camp. Most had seen Gloucester and Hereford's defeat, and when Clifford's return brought news of his lack of success, the English troops became extremely downcast and disheartened.[53] Some even expected the Scots to attack during the night.[54] Their feelings seem to have been expressed in Walter Bower's recorded words of an English poet captured at the battle:

Ill-omened Sunday opens the preliminaries of the disaster / befalling the sons of England; hence issues discord from its very mouth. / The dry ground of Stirling sustains the first conflicts. /Splendid is the attacking host, but soon it takes a downward turn. / Great is the grief, grief enhancing grief; / fierce is the frenzy, frenzy inflaming frenzy; / louder grows the clamour, vanguard assailing vanguard; / feeble the valour, valour foiling valour; / fierier the ardour, ardour firing ardour; / more hesitant the fighters, waverer reproaching waverer; / bewilderment is audible, bewilderment redoubling bewilderment; / resistance is worn down, order

---

50 John Barbour, II:286–88.
51 John Barbour, II:288–89.
52 Robert Bruce's speech to his troops is recorded in John Barbour, II:289–95.
53 John Barbour, II:295–96.
54 *Vita Edward II*, p. 51.

losing order; / uproar uprises, blood shedding blood; / now fear is recognizable, fear afraid of fear.[55]

The English nobles tried to boost the morale of their troops by declaring that the battle on the next day, the one in which the main English body would take part, would have a different result. But their words brought little comfort, as the English army spent a miserable, sleepless night, made even more uncomfortable by their camp, on what Thomas Gray describes as an 'evil, deep wet marsh.'[56]

The Scots began the next day by gaining the defection of Alexander Seton, a Scotsman who had been before this time in the service of Edward II. According to Thomas Gray, the only chronicler who reports his defection, Seton left the English when he had witnessed their discouragement in losing to the Scots on the previous day. This discouragement he reported to Robert Bruce; he also reported that the English were planning a 'sudden, open attack.'[57]

No doubt Seton's news further excited the Scottish troops, and, although it probably did not set the tactics which Robert Bruce had planned in fighting the English that day, it certainly confirmed his plan. He would order his troops in an infantry formation and prepare for English cavalry charges. The *Chronicon de Lanercost* describes the Scottish formation as one of two lines and a rearguard; all other sources simply report three lines. All commentators maintain that only infantry formed these lines. John of Trokelowe and Thomas Walsingham claim that Bruce used only infantry because he feared that if he were to use cavalry as the Scots had at Falkirk, the same result, defeat, would occur. But Trokelowe also adds that the Scottish king himself was dismounted, with his other leaders, 'so that danger having been equalized between the nobility and the commoners no one thought about flight.'[58] For whatever reason, the Scots looked impressive in their infantry formation. They were well armed, notes the *Vita Edwardi II*: 'each was furnished with light armor, not easily penetrable by a sword. They had axes at their sides and carried

---

[55] Walter Bower, VI:372–73: 'Dira dies solis pandit premordia molis / Angligene prolis; hinc exit ab ore suo lis. / Arida terra gerit Strivelini prelia prima; / Splendida turba ferit, sed tandem tendit ad ima. / Est dolor immensus, augente dolore dolorem; / est furor accensus, stimulante furore furorem; / est clamor crescens, feriente priore priorem; / est valor arescens, frustrante valore valorem; / est calor ardescens, urente calore calorem; / est gens demescens, reprobante minore minorem; / est stupor auditus, geminante stupore stuporem; / est populus tritus, perdente tenore tenorem; / surgit rugitus, fundente cruore cruorem; / nunc timor est scitus, metuente timore timorem.' According to Bower, this English poet, 'the most famous poet in the whole kingdom of England,' a Carmelite friar, had been taken by Edward II to Bannockburn because he was certain of victory there. He had been captured after the battle and forced to compose a poem on the battle in order to gain his release (VI:367).

[56] Thomas Gray, p. 142. See also John Barbour, II:296–98 and *Vita Edwardi II*, p. 51.

[57] Thomas Gray, p. 142.

[58] John of Trokelowe, p. 84: 'Robertus vero le Brois, qui se Regem Scotiae clamitabat, pedes, cum suis consortibus, totum exercitum suum praecedebant, ut sic, periculo inter majores et minores coaequato, nemo de fuga cogitaret,' and Thomas Walsingham, I:140. On the Scottish formation see also *Chronicon de Lanercost*, p. 225; *Vita Edwardi II*, p. 52; Geoffrey le Baker, p. 8; and Thomas Gray, p. 142. Thomas Gray (p. 140) uses the word 'schiltrom' to describe the Scottish formation. However, John Barbour (pp. 299–300, 312) uses the same term to describe the English formation.

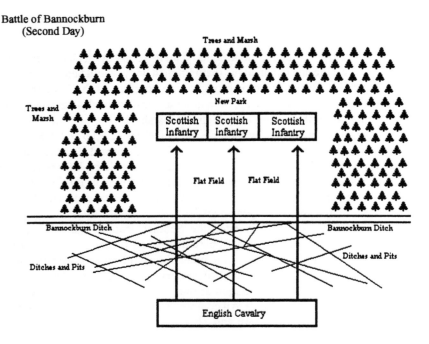

Battle of Bannockburn
(Second Day)

lances in their hands.'[59] John of Trokelowe insists that the formation would be difficult to defeat: 'These elect men, certainly spirited, set up an impenetrable line armed with sharpened axes and other arms of war and with shields placed thickly among them.'[60] Before this formation, Robert Bruce unfurled his banners and set them among the troops. He also knighted two men who had displayed valor on the day before, Walter Stewart and James Douglas. Finally, he led his men in prayer.[61]

At the same time, the English also prepared for battle. However, their array seems to have been more sloppy than the Scottish one. Using the term 'schiltrom,' John Barbour records that the English were crowded together in a group, although whether this was because of the terrain on which they were ordered or out of fear, the Scottish writer does not know. Barbour does report that the English vanguard was well ordered and anxious for conflict. Still, even without the harmony of the Scots, the English army was imposing, their armor shining 'like angels,' and they were numerous, covering a large amount of ground.[62]

There were two distinct groups of English soldiers. One consisted of infantry and archers, with the other of cavalry. Not yet mounted, all sources agree that the cavalry

[59] *Vita Edwardi II*, p. 52: 'sed erat unusquisque eorum leui armatura munitus, quam non faciliter penetraret gladius. Securim habebant ad latus et lanceas ferebant in manibus.'
[60] John of Trokelowe, p. 84: 'viri quidem electi, animosi valde, securibus praeacutis caeterisque armis bellicis decenter communiti, conserta ante se scutorum spissitudine, cuneum impenetrabilem statuerunt.'
[61] John Barbour, II:298–301 and *Chronicon de Lanercost*, p. 225.
[62] John Barbour, II:299–300 and Geoffrey le Baker, p. 8.

was to be the primary attackers in the battle, for, in the words of Thomas Gray, 'they were not accustomed to fight on foot.'[63] The English too were well armed and anxious for the battle to begin.[64]

However, before the English could attack, Edward II called an impromptu council of war. The reason, Barbour decides, was because the king was surprised at the Scottish infantry formation, expecting it seems a cavalry array. 'How will we fight the Scots?' he is reported to have said. One English knight, Sir Ingraham Umphraville, proposed that the army retreat behind their camp, as if in flight, causing the Scots to break ranks to loot the English tents. Then the more numerous English troops could sweep in and easily defeat their opponents. Edward II dismissed this plan, as he refused to retreat. Moreover, he had just noticed the Scots kneeling in prayer and believed that they were kneeling for mercy. Thus he proposed an immediate cavalry charge, a tactic objected to by both Umphraville and Gloucester. Ignoring their protestations, Edward mounted his own horse and joined his cavalry line.[65]

Both sides now awaited the first attack. John of Trokelowe describes the action:

> Both armies prepared for battle and at about the third hour of the day the lines of both parties, approaching each other, showed a formidable sight to those who saw them. For the din of the trumpets and clarions, the neighing of the horses, the motion of the standards, the calls of the leaders which sounded in their midst, could frighten the hearts of even the bravest men.[66]

There may also have been an exchange of archery fire, short in duration and English dominated, but only the *Chronicon de Lanercost* reports it.[67]

Who initiated the attack between the two main armies on June 24 is in dispute among the original sources. John Barbour, John of Trokelowe, Walter Bower, and the *Chronicon de Lanercost* all contend that it was the English cavalry who first charged into the Scottish formation,[68] while the *Vita Edwardi II* indicates a Scottish charge:

> They advanced like a thick-set hedge, and such a line could not easily be broken. When the situation was such that the two sides must meet, James Douglas, who commanded the first line of the Scots, vigorously attacked the Earl of Gloucester's line.[69]

---

[63] Thomas Gray, p. 142: 'qi nestoint my acoustomez pur descendre a coumbatre a pee.' See also John Barbour, II:299–300; Geoffrey le Baker, p. 8; Thomas Walsingham, I:140; and Walter Bower, VI:369. Walsingham orders the infantry in front of the cavalry, while Baker has the horse before the infantry.
[64] Walter Bower, VI:369.
[65] Only John Barbour reports this council (II:300–02), with the *Vita Edwardi II* (p. 52) the only chronicle noting the disagreement of Gloucester.
[66] John of Trokelowe, p. 84: 'Uterque exercitus ad pugnam se parabat, et circa horam diei tertiam acies utriusque partis, sibi invicem appropinquantes, formidabile spectaculum intuentibus ostendebant. Clangor enim tubarum et lituorum, hinnitus equorum, motio vexillorum, clamor exhortantium, qui in eorum congressu resonabant, corda poterant terruisse magnanimorum.'
[67] *Chronicon de Lanercost*, p. 225.
[68] John Barbour, II:302; John of Trokelowe, p. 84; Walter Bower, VI:373; and *Chronicon de Lanercost*, p. 225.
[69] *Vita Edward II*, p. 52: 'Ibant etiam quasi sepes densa conserti, nec leuiter potuit talis turma

Why one of the most contemporary chronicles would disagree both with these other accounts and with Robert Bruce's standard infantry tactic, as shown both the day previously in Randolph's stand and at Loudon Hill, is uncertain. However, the anonymous author of this chronicle could be simply in error, especially as he will later compare the battle to that fought by the Flemings at Courtrai.[70]

The first English attack struck the Scottish line with great impact but with no penetration. The battle continued for a very long time. John of Trokelowe recounts the scene:

> On one side stood the magnates of England advancing with their troops strongly against the Scots. On the other side, the leaders of the Scots stood defending themselves strongly. And the troops clashing against each other fought a most bloody battle. The crash of the lances, the ringing of the swords, the noise of hasty blows, the groan of the dying, the lamentation of the wounded, being heard in this conflict seemed to split the air. For a long time it was fought at the front of the lines with the ringing of many swords and both armies fighting strongly against each other.[71]

Many English charges were made, and at times it seemed that the Scottish line would break under the fierce attacks of the cavalry. Still, there was no penetration of the solid infantry formation.[72] The Scots fought 'with all their might and all their means; they attacked like madmen,' writes John Barbour.[73] Even the Scottish camp followers

---

penetrari. Cum autem ad hoc uentum esset ut congredi simul oporteret, Jacobus Douglas, qui prime turme Scotorum preerat, aciem comitis Gloucestrie acriter in uasit.' N. Denholm-Young's translation of 'turma' as phalanx makes little sense in a medieval military context. I have chosen to use the more generic 'line' in my translation.

[70] *Vita Edwardi II*, p. 56. There may be more to this account when we look also at Thomas Gray's narrative of the battle. Gray's description of the charge in its original Old French language reads:

> Lez auaunt ditz Escotez uindrent de tot aleyn en schiltrome, assenblerent sur lez bataillis dez Engles, qi entassez estoint, qi rien remuerent deuers eaux tanque lours cheueaux estoient enbuaillez dez launcez lez gentz dereir dez Engles (p. 142).

This has been translated by Herbert Maxwell as,

> The aforesaid Scots came in line of 'schiltroms,' and attacked the English columns, which were jammed together and could not operate against them [the Scots], so direfully were their horses impaled on the pikes (Glasgow, 1907, pp. 55–56),

and thus seems to agree with the *Vita Edwardi II*. But I think that Maxwell has mistranslated this, that it is not the English which are jammed together, but the Scots.

[71] John of Trokelowe, pp. 84–85: 'Stant hinc magnates Angliae, cum suis turmis Scotos fortiter insilientes. Stant inde duces Scotorum, sese viriliter defendentes. Et collidentibus ad invicem catervis, bellum cruentissimum commiserunt. Fragor lancearum, tinnitus gladiorum, ictuum strepitus repentinorum, gemitus morientium, vulneratorum lamentatio, in ipso conflictu audita, aera perturbare videbantur. Multo tempore nimis gladiis circa capita tinnientibus altercatum est, et decertantibus utrinque viriliter partibus ex adverso.' See also John Barbour, II:302, 312; *Chronicon de Lanercost*, p. 225; and Thomas Walsingham, I:140.

[72] See, for example, John Barbour, II:303–05.

[73] John Barbour, II:311: 'With all thar mycht and all thar mayne / Thai layd on, as men out of wit.' On the battle in more detail see Barbour, II:302–14.

chose a captain and joined in the attack.[74] Walter Bower's English poet puts his report in verse:

> Scots no longer remote but close at hand. / The ordinary folk bang and clang; but, when the impact touches them, / they beat their breasts. Battered by blows, their morale breaks. / The overweening enemies of the Scots are shrunken.[75]

English and Scottish archers also engaged in the battle. But they had very little effect, at least according to John Barbour, who is the only source which mentions their participation in detail: the Scottish archers only annoyed the English cavalry, while the English archers might have been more effective had not Robert Bruce sent a contingent of horsed warriors under the command of his marshal, Robert Keith, to successfully disperse them.[76]

As the battle raged on, the ditches and pits dug by the Scots prior to the fighting became a factor. The English cavalry initially seems to have passed over these impediments without any difficulty. But, as they had been unable to penetrate the Scottish line and began to be pushed back, they also began to fall into the pits and ditches, 'tumbling one over the other,' notes Thomas Gray.[77] One ditch in particular, after which the battlefield 'Bannockburn' was named, created special problems according to the *Chronicon de Lanercost*:

> Another misfortune which happened to the English was that, although they at first had crossed a great ditch called Bannockburn, into which the tide flows, and now in confusion wanted to recross it, in the press many nobles and others fell into it with their horses. And while some escaped from it with much difficulty, many were never able to remove themselves from the ditch. Thus Bannockburn was in the speech of Englishmen for many years after.[78]

Yet, perhaps the biggest blow to the English attacks came with the death of Gilbert of Clare, earl of Gloucester. He was young, but his noble rank had given him command over the vanguard on the day previously, and, although his fighting then had been unsuccessful, it seems he had retained some leadership responsibilities on the second day of battle. By losing on the first day, Gloucester had to prove his valor and military capability, and so he pressed with as much courage and strength as he could muster. It may have cost him his life. John of Trokelowe writes:

---

[74] John Barbour, II:308–09.

[75] Walter Bower, VI:372–73: 'admotos Scotos ab eis non longe remotos. / Plebs plangit clangit; sed quam congressio tangit, / nunc pangit. Frangit vires quas ictibus angit. / Magnifici modici Scotorum sunt inimici.'

[76] John Barbour, II:307–09. See also Geoffrey le Baker, pp. 8–9. The existence of Scottish cavalry obviously goes against the contention of most sources that all of the Scots were dismounted.

[77] Thomas Gray, p. 142.

[78] *Chronicon de Lanercost*, p. 226: 'Aliud etiam infortunium accidit Anglicis, quia, cum paulo ant transissent unam foveam magnam, in quam intrat fluxus maris, nomine Bannokeburne, et jam confusi vellent redire, multi nobiles et alii prae pressura cum equis in illam ceciderunt, et aliqui cum difficultate magna evaserunt, et multi nunquam se explicare de fovea potuerunt; et ideo Bannokeburne in ore Anglicorum erat per multos annos sequentes.'

Many fell having been fatally wounded. When Gilbert, count of Gloucester, saw this he was very angry on account of the enemy's fierceness; he urged his comrades to rush in on the effeminate Scots unaccustomed to fighting the gathered English; and wishing to win a name for himself, he presented an example to them as a bellicose boar. In the heat of anger he attacked the troops of the enemy with their blood inebriating his sword. For whomever he struck with his sharp blade, he cut off a head or some other limb. Finally, thirsting so for their deaths, the equilibrium of the entire battle was turned around to such a degree that the points of the lances being applied to each part of his body, stabbing several places, he was knocked to the ground, and his head was struck on all sides by the clubs of the enemy, until he breathed out his soul under the horse's feet.

Seeing the death of one of their important leaders, English morale was broken and several soldiers took flight. John of Trokelowe concludes: 'Seeing him thus to be killed, all of the rest of his army, gripped with fear, fled, alas, leaving their lord slaughtered on the battlefield.'[79]

Soon all of the English troops were fleeing from the Scots, leaving only a few valiant soldiers to fight on in vain.[80] Ultimately, even the king, Edward II, fled, having shown his own expertise on the field. The Scots pursued him and all others who had not been captured or killed; although the king escaped with difficulty, many others could not and added their numbers to the Scottish prisoners.[81] A large number of English lay dead and dying on the battlefield. Only John Barbour reports a total number killed, 30,000,[82] with most other sources which tally the deaths concerned only with the number of nobles killed, a number which ranges from 154 to 700.[83]

---

[79] John of Trokelowe, p. 85: 'Quod cum videret G[ilbertus] Comes Gloverniae, indignatus est valde super eorum feritate; suos commilitones exhortatur, ut in Scotos effoeminatos, congressiones Anglicanas expectare non solentes, irruant truculenter; et, nomen militiae sibi volens acquirere, exemplum suis in seipso praetendens, ut aper bellicosus, in incendio irae suae turmas hostium invasit, gladium suum cruori eorum inebriando. Que[m]cunque enim mucrone suo attingebat, caput ei, aut membrum aliquod, amputabat. In ipsum tandem, eorum necem ita sitientem, pondus totius proelii conversum est; adeo ut lancearum cuspidibus ex omni parte sui corporis applicatis, impingentibus hinc inde diversis, ad terram prosternitur, et caput ejus clavis hostium undique malleatur, donec animam, cum sanguine, sub pedibus equinis exhalaret. Reliqui vero omnes de exercitu suo, videntes eum sic occubuisse, timore perterriti, fugam inierunt, dominum suum, in campo trucidatum, proh O dolor! relinquentes.' On Gloucester's death see also Geoffrey le Baker, p. 8; *Vita Edwardi II*, pp. 52–54; Adam Murimuth, p. 21; Thomas Walsingham, I:140–41; John Fordun, I:339; *Liber Pluscardensis*, I:183; and Walter Bower, VI:375. On his death causing the English flight see *Vita Edwardi II*, p. 54. There is absolutely no corroboration for the story recorded in the anonymous poem, 'The Battle of Bannockburn,' that Gloucester was betrayed by one of his retainers, Bartholomew.

[80] John Barbour, II:316.

[81] John Barbour, II:316–22, 326–29; Thomas Gray, pp. 142–43; John of Trokelowe, p. 85; Geoffrey le Baker, p. 9; *Vita Edwardi II*, pp. 54–55; *Anonimalle Chronicle*, p. 89; Adam Murimuth, p. 21; Thomas of Burton, II:331; Thomas Walsingham, I:141; *The Brut*, I:208; John Fordun, I:347; and Andrew of Wyntoun, *Brevis cronica*, p. 336. The ransoms paid to the Scots for their noble prisoners are mentioned by several authors: *Vita Edwardi II*, p. 55; *Anonimalle Chronicle*, p. 89; Adam Murimuth, p. 21; Thomas Walsingham, I:141; *Eulogium historiarum*, III:195; John Fordun, I:347; *Liber Pluscardensis*, I:238; and Walter Bower, VI:353.

[82] John Barbour, II:321.

[83] These numbers include: 154 (Thomas Walsingham, I:141); 300 (*Eulogium historiarum*, III:195); and 700 (John Barbour, II:323). Other chronicles which mention the large numbers of English dead

The Scots' death toll was far less, with John Barbour – the only original source even mentioning Scottish dead – reporting only two slain knights.[84]

For the Scots the battle of Bannockburn was a sign from God that He was with them in their search for independence from the English, and that Robert Bruce was His 'divine right' ruler of their blessed land.[85] The English chroniclers have more difficulty in judging why their forces lost. For the *Chronicon de Lanercost*, it was Edward II's sinfulness which led to defeat for he 'did and said things to prejudice and injure the saints.'[86] For the *Vita Edwardi II*, it was the 'proud arrogance of our men [which] made the Scots rejoice in victory.'[87] Only John of Trokelowe looks to what occurred on the field:

> I do not know to which misfortune I should assign the cause of this defeat; unless perhaps because the English advanced impetuously and more inordinately than was befitting. For their men and beasts were exhausted on account of their great haste, and they were weak, indeed made weak from hunger and lacking the revitalization of sleep. For the Scots, awaiting the attack on their own ground, most speedily hastened to a place of battle known to them and unknown to the English, revived to a fullness with food as well as sleep, organized for battle in thick lines and troops.[88]

Trokelowe is mostly correct in his determination of what caused the Scottish victory at Bannockburn. It is true that the English advance was impetuous, and that it became quickly disordered and confused when it was unable to penetrate the Scottish line. It is also true that the English troops were fatigued and hungry, both on their arrival at Bannockburn and on the morning of the second day of the battle after spending a sleepless, uncomfortable night encamped in the marshlands on the edge of the battlefield.

It is also true that the Scots chose the battlefield and reached it first, were less fatigued and hungry, and had ordered in thick lines of troops. But here Trokelowe does not wholly understand how these factors enabled a Scottish victory. His assertions are simply incomplete. Not only was it important that the Scots selected Bannockburn as the field of battle because they knew the site and the English did not, but because they selected a battlefield site which enabled their formation, on flat land, and hindered their opponent's attacks, with trees and marshes narrowing

---

but do not give a count are: John of Trokelowe, p. 87; Geoffrey le Baker, p. 8; *Vita Edwardi II*, p. 55; *Anonimalle Chronicle*, p. 89; Henry Knighton, I:409; *The Brut*, I:208; *Liber Pluscardensis*, I:238; and Walter Bower, VI:353, 375.

[84] John Barbour, II:323–24.

[85] See, for example, *Liber Pluscardensis*, I:238–39 and Walter Bower, VI:355, 357, 359–63.

[86] *Chronicon de Lanercost*, pp. 224–25.

[87] *Vita Edwardi II*, p. 56: 'Certe superba nostrorum presumptio Scotos fecit gaudere triumpho.'

[88] John of Trokelowe, p. 87: 'Causam qutem hujus ruinae, cui infortunio imputare valeam, ignoro; nisi forte, quod Anglici impetuose, nimisque inordinate, quam deceret advenerunt. Homines enim eorum, et bestiae, prae nimia festinatione lassi erant imbecilles, fame quidem tabefacti, et somni recreatione carentes. Scoti quidem, adventum eorum in terra propria expectantes, ad locum belli sibi notum, Anglicisque ignotum, tam cibo quam somno ad plenum refocillati, densis agminibus catervisque ad proeliandum despositis, maturius accesserunt.'

cavalry charges. This was further improved from the Scottish standpoint by the digging of pits and ditches which may not have hindered the initial attacks of the English, but did create hazards for the knights and horsemen once they were unable to penetrate the Scottish lines and began to be pushed back into them. Judging from most of the sources on the battle of Bannockburn, the ditches and pits caused many of the English deaths.

Yet, the fact that the Scots were more rested and less hungry than their English counterparts is only part of the reason for their spirited combat. The original sources, especially the Scottish authors, all remark on the impressive numbers and nobility of the English army and that this greatly frightened the Scottish warriors. But the Scots did not give in to their fears and flee from their foes. Instead, they fought 'like madmen,' says John Barbour, showing no fear and great morale. For this we must recognize the leadership ability of Robert Bruce. His participation in the first day of battle, even facing and killing an English knight, although reproved by his nobles and other leaders, brought him favor among his troops. So too did his order for the knights in his army to dismount and fight with the more common people on foot. And, while there is some dispute among the sources as to where he placed himself on the second day of battle – Thomas Walsingham puts Bruce in the front of the Scottish formation while the *Chronicon de Lanercost* places him in the rear[89] – there is no dispute about his active leadership in the fight on that day.[90] Moreover, Bruce's speeches to his troops, primarily the one given by him at the end of the first day of battle with its praises, cautions, and promises, was a great encouragement in building his soldiers' morale.

Finally, the thick lines of Scottish troops were perhaps the greatest factor in their victory. But again Trokelowe leaves out an essential part of the equation in not including the fact that these were infantry lines standing in defensive formation. This solid infantry formation, used both by Randolph's force on the first day and by the main army on the second, was unable to be penetrated and thus presented an impediment to victory that the English cavalry, no matter how well-armed, how noble, or how large, was able to overcome. Their attacks proved impotent, and eventually they were forced to try to save their lives by fleeing from the battlefield. It is no wonder that both Thomas Gray and the *Vita Edwardi II* can see the comparison between this battle and that at Courtrai, for as in the Flemings' victory there, at Bannockburn the Scottish infantry defeated a more numerous and more noble cavalry force. As the author of the *Vita Edwardi II* writes: 'Indeed I think it is unheard of in our time for such an army to be scattered so suddenly by infantry, unless when the flower of France fell before the Flemings at Courtrai.'[91]

Without a doubt Bannockburn was a great blow to the English. The defeat remained in the thoughts of many English writers for many years, but before too long

---

[89] Thomas Walsingham, I:140 and *Chronicon de Lanercost*, p. 225.
[90] See, for example, John Barbour, II:302–14.
[91] Thomas Gray, p. 142 and *Vita Edwardi II*, pp. 55–56: 'Siquidem a seculo recordor inauditum talem exercitum coram peditibus tam subito dispersum, nisi cum flos Francie coram Flandrensibus apud Coutray cecidit.'

even this loss was forgotten. The English army would learn valuable lessons from their defeat at Bannockburn, and the next time an English army faced the Scots, at Dupplin Moor in 1332, they would not repeat the mistakes of their battle of 1314. Nor would they repeat them at Halidon Hill in 1333 or at Neville's Cross in 1346 or in any other battle between the two lands during the remaining centuries of the Middle Ages. Indeed, John of Trokelowe may have been more of a prophet than he realized when he concluded his account on the battle of Bannockburn with these words: 'But let this outcome break no one, for the fates of battles are unknown. For the sword consumes now these and now those, and thus with fortune turning its wheel, the victory remained in this one turn to the Scots.'[92]

---

[92] John of Trokelowe, p. 87: 'Sed neminem frangat ista res; varii enim sunt oventus proeliorum, et fata eorum ambigua. Nunc enim hos consumit gladius, et nunc illos; et sic, fortuna rotam suam volvente, victoria Scotis illa sola vice remansit.' See also John Barbour, II:329–31.

VII

THE BATTLE OF BOROUGHBRIDGE, 1322

TWO GENERALIZATIONS might be made about medieval rulership: first, strong and weak rulers are almost always so because of their relative strong and weak military leadership, and second, weak rulership brought not only attacks from outside, but also, and sometimes more importantly, attacks from inside – civil war. These may be too simplistic, but if they are accepted, then there is no better archetype for the weak ruler than King Edward II of England.

No English king was less able to contend with the problems of his realm than was Edward II. Already witnessed within these pages was Edward's inability to solve Robert Bruce's 'outside' warfare, with English armies losing both at Loudon Hill in 1307 and at Bannockburn in 1314. But Edward also had to contend with attacks from inside his realm, and no better example of this can be found than in the case of the rebellion of Edward's cousin, the powerful lord and chief counsellor, Thomas, duke of Lancaster; but in this instance, it was a rebellion which ended in victory for the king at the battle of Boroughbridge fought on March 16, 1322.

It is unnecessary here to detail the conflict between Edward II and Thomas of Lancaster, which at times appears to be a roller coaster of favor and disfavor. But a few introductory comments must be mentioned to put the battle of Boroughbridge in context. First, it must be noted that this was not the only nor even the first conflict Edward II had with his nobles. Indeed, the baronial difficulties Edward had to a large part were inherited from his father, Edward I, and perhaps even from his grandfather, Henry III, and great-grandfather, John. But none of the difficulties Edward II faced, at least until he met his end at the hand of his son, Edward III, can compare with the 1322 rebellion led by Thomas of Lancaster.

The Edward/Lancaster conflict dates from the hatred held by Lancaster and most of the other barons of England towards the king's favorite, the handsome Gascon noble, Piers Gaveston. Edward's affection towards Gaveston is legendary and needs not be dealt with here. Suffice it to say, that when Gaveston was finally brought down, in 1312, it was Thomas of Lancaster, together with Guy Beauchamp, earl of Warwick, who abducted him from his captors, Aylmer of Valence, earl of Pembroke, and John, earl of Warenne; and it was Lancaster and Beauchamp who killed the king's favorite, despite an earlier promise of safe-passage to Gascony given him by Pembroke and Warenne.[1]

---

[1] J.R. Maddicott, *Thomas of Lancaster, 1307–1322: A Study in the Reign of Edward II* (Oxford, 1970), pp. 121–30; J.S. Hamilton, *Piers Gaveston, Earl of Cornwall, 1307–1312: Politics and*

Despite later pardoning them, Edward II never forgave his two barons, but there was little he could do about the situation. Thomas of Lancaster was perhaps the most wealthy and powerful of all the barons. Already holding vast lands of his own, in 1311 he had inherited even more when his father-in-law, Henry de Lacy, earl of Lincoln, died. At the time of Gaveston's murder, Lancaster held no fewer than five earldoms: Lancaster, Leicester, Lincoln, Derby, and Salisbury.[2]

Nor does it seem that many other nobles in the kingdom approved of Lancaster and Warwick's actions in the Gaveston affair. Especially Aylmer of Valence and John of Warenne, whose promise of safe-passage to Gaveston had been violated by his abduction and murder, seemed to believe that Lancaster and Warwick had chosen a more harsh solution to the problem than was necessary.[3]

Relations further soured in 1314 when Lancaster, again with Warwick in tow, refused the summons to join the king's army against the Scots; their absence in the campaign to some, including many of the other barons as well as the king, carried part of the blame for the English loss to Robert Bruce at Bannockburn. Yet, at the same time, the defeat at Bannockburn meant that there was a need for reconciliation between Lancaster and the king. To preserve the peace and security of his kingdom, Edward reluctantly decided to accept his wealthy baron's advice and to name him as his chief counsellor.[4]

Lancaster's rise to chief counsellor did not, however, bring an end to his conflict with Edward II or the other English barons. From 1316 to 1320 Lancaster wielded almost monopolistic control over the English government. But he was not a good leader, and his decisions, too often self-serving, continued to alienate the king and almost all of the other English prelates. Sometimes this governmental turmoil even erupted into open warfare, and on one occasion, in 1318, a major baronial civil war was averted only by the intercession of Pope John XXII's papal mediators.[5]

In 1320 a new baronial contingent arose to oppose Lancaster. It was led by the Despensers, Hugh the Elder and Hugh the Younger, father and son. Taking a cue from

---

Patronage in the Reign of Edward II (Detroit, 1988), pp. 93–99; T.F. Tout, *The Place of the Reign of Edward II in English History*, 2nd ed. (Manchester, 1936), pp. 87–90; Prestwich, *The Three Edwards*, pp. 84–85; McKisack, pp. 24–28; Keen, p. 54; Fryde, p. 22; and Phillips, pp. 31–37. On surrender terms between Pembroke and Gaveston see Phillips, pp. 33–34. The only modern biography on Piers Gaveston used to be Hamilton, but recently a new biography, Pierre Chaplais' *Piers Gaveston: Edward II's Adoptive Brother* (Oxford, 1994), has appeared which argues against many of Hamilton's theses, but none which affect this chapter.

[2] On Lancaster's estates, finances and retinue see Maddicott, pp. 8–66. See also James Conway Davies, *The Baronial Opposition to Edward II: Its Character and Policy* (London, 1918), pp. 107–10; Prestwich, *The Three Edwards*, pp. 85, 91; and Keen, pp. 54–55. On contemporary views of Lancaster see Fryde, pp. 19–20.

[3] Maddicott, pp. 130–31, 149–50, 154–59; Phillips, pp. 38–72; Hamilton, pp. 103–07; Prestwich, *The Three Edwards*, p. 85; McKisack, pp. 28–31; and Keen, p. 55.

[4] Maddicott, pp. 158–61; Tout, *Edward II in English History*, pp. 90–94; Fryde, p. 24; Davies, pp. 412–19; Phillips, pp. 72–82; Prestwich, *The Three Edwards*, p. 86; McKisack, pp. 39, 45–47; and Keen, p. 55.

[5] Maddicott, pp. 190–208, 213–39; Tout, *Edward II in English History*, pp. 110–22; Fryde, pp. 20, 25–26; Davies, pp. 502–03; Prestwich, *The Three Edwards*, pp. 87–89; McKisack, pp. 51–56; Keen, pp. 62–64; and Phillips, pp. 119–20, 154–77.

Piers Gaveston before them (and perhaps from Lancaster as well), the Despensers began to court the favor of the almost powerless king, who was unable to turn away from their attendance, especially that of the young and fair Hugh Jr. Edward II began to favor the Despensers as he had done Gaveston before them, especially when it came to granting them lands. This, of course, brought immediate enmity from the other barons of the realm, who conveniently forgot about their dislike of Lancaster and turned instead to anger against the Despensers. Civil war broke out in April 1321.[6]

Initially at least, Lancaster remained outside of the anti-Despenser coalition, not because he favored the Despensers, but because all of his enemies hated them. However, no major step against them could be made without Lancaster's assistance and, finally in May, he entered the conflict, calling together the anti-Despenser coalition who, in their words, 'bound themselves together to preserve peace and to defend the realm.' Action was taken. On July 15, 1321 they decided to march to London to remove the Despensers, who fled from the city; on August 19, Parliament sentenced them in absentia to a forfeiture of lands and banishment as 'evil and false counsellors, seducers and conspirators, and disinheritors of the crown, and enemies to the king and kingdom.'[7]

With the Despensers gone, the wrath of the barons (and also of the king) once again was directed towards Thomas of Lancaster. Edward was especially incensed, for he realized that this was the second of his favorites removed from him by Lancaster, and he began to speak out against his chief counsellor. Finally showing some strength, baronial adherents began to flock to the king, and Lancaster quickly found that only a few nobles remained by his side. Now the anti-Lancaster coalition, led by the king himself, began to march against Lancaster's lands and castles. Leeds, Chirk and Wigmore fell. The hated duke could only flee to the north, in an attempt to seek protection from the up-to-now neutral northern nobles or from the Scots (contemporary historians seem uncertain about this). But instead of gaining refuge, on March 16, 1322, Lancaster and his band were caught and defeated at Borough-bridge by Andrew Harclay, the sheriff of Cumberland.[8] All noble adherents to the rebellious duke who survived the battle, including Lancaster himself, were taken to York and tried for treason by the king. All were found guilty and were sentenced to

---

6 Maddicott, pp. 259–67; Tout, *Edward II in English History*, pp. 122–29; Fryde, pp. 37–45; Davies, pp. 469–72; Phillips, pp. 177–201; Prestwich, *The Three Edwards*, pp. 89–90; McKisack, pp. 58–61; and Keen, pp. 66–67. On the rise of the Despensers before 1320 see Fryde, pp. 27–36.

7 Maddicott, pp. 267–80; Tout, *Edward II in English History*, pp. 129–30; Fryde, pp. 45–50; Davies, pp. 472–84; Phillips, pp. 201–11; McKisack, pp. 61–64; and Keen, pp. 67–69. See also S.L. Waugh, 'For King, Country and Patron: The Despensers and Local Administration,' *Journal of British Studies* 22 (1983), 23–45.

8 Maddicott, pp. 292–311; Tout, *Edward II in English History*, pp. 131–34, 205; Fryde, pp. 50–57; Davies, pp. 503–04; Phillips, pp. 214–24; Prestwich, *The Three Edwards*, pp. 90–91; McKisack, pp. 64–67; and Keen, pp. 69–70. There is some dispute on the spelling of Harclay's name, with Phillips for one wanting it to be spelled 'Harcla;' all other secondary authors use the spelling 'Harclay,' and thus so have I.

death and the forfeiture of lands. Lancaster was beheaded on March 22. Others met similar fates.[9]

The victory would be almost as short-lived for Andrew Harclay as the loss was for Lancaster and his followers. For although being granted the earldom of Carlisle by the king as a reward for his service at Boroughbridge, by an irony of historical circumstance, within a year Harclay was arrested and executed for treason against Edward II. His crimes were surprisingly familiar: he was accused of harboring hostility against the Despensers and for allying with Robert Bruce.[10]

While the battle of Boroughbridge has engendered little interest among modern writers,[11] a similar lack of interest in what happened on the battlefield is not shared by contemporary authors. Among English chroniclers reporting the reign of Edward II, including all those who discussed the battle of Bannockburn, the battle at Boroughbridge plays an important role in their narrative of the Edward/Lancaster conflict. This is especially the case in the long accounts found in the *Chronicon de Lanercost* and the *Vita Edwardi II*, both of which favor Edward II, and *The Brut*, which favors Lancaster. Perhaps this is because Thomas of Lancaster's position of importance in the English court as well as his relationship to the king made his rebellion significant, or perhaps it is because the fight at Boroughbridge was one of the few 'victories' had by the king; for whatever reason, the details of the battle and the short campaign leading up to it can be fairly easily sketched out.

While all contemporary writers discuss other aspects of the Lancastrian conflict with Edward, the campaign which would lead to Boroughbridge begins only after the exile of the Despensers, when the king and his loyal earls set out to attack Lancaster and his adherents. Lancaster discovered the king's intentions while he and his closest ally, Humphrey of Bohun, earl of Hereford, were meeting at Lancaster's castle at Pontefract in south Yorkshire. The *Anonimalle Chronicle* claims that Hereford had fled to Pontefract with the news of Edward's approach because 'he thought that [Edward] would destroy them as he had done others.'[12] Thomas of Lancaster's

---

[9] Maddicott, pp. 311–23; Fryde, pp. 58–68; Phillips, pp. 224–25; Prestwich, *The Three Edwards*, p. 91; McKisack, p. 67; and Keen, p. 70. See also S.L. Waugh, 'The Profits of Violence: The Minor Gentry in the Rebellion of 1321–22 in Gloucestershire and Herefordshire,' *Speculum* 52 (1977), 843–69. On these trials see Fryde, pp. 58–59; J.G. Bellamy, *The Law of Treason in England in the Late Middle Ages* (Cambridge, 1970), pp. 49–51; George Sayles, 'The Formal Judgments on the Traitors of 1322,' *Speculum* 16 (1941), 57–63; and George L. Haskins, 'Judicial Proceedings Against a Traitor after Boroughbridge, 1322,' *Speculum* 12 (1937), 509–11. On the punishments of Lancaster's adherents see Fryde, pp. 59–86. For many years after the decapitation of Roger of Clifford, Lancaster's co-conspirator and son-in-law, his body was hung in a gibbet from the wall of the castle of York, subsequently giving the castle its more common name, Clifford's Tower.

[10] Fryde, pp. 156–58. Thomas of Burton (II:347) cites Harclay's hatred of the Despensers as the cause of his treason, while the *Chronicon de Lanercost* (p. 235) sees it as a result of his desire to marry Robert Bruce's daughter.

[11] Only T.F. Tout, 'The Tactics of the Battles of Boroughbridge and Morlaix,' *English Historical Review* 19 (1904), 711–13 and J.E. Morris, 'Mounted Infantry in Mediaeval Warfare,' *Transactions of the Royal Historical Society* 3rd ser. 8 (1914), 86–91 mention much about the battle.

[12] *The Anonimalle Chronicle, 1307 to 1334*, ed. W.R. Childs and J. Taylor (Leeds, 1991), p. 104–05: '. . . et penserent bien qil les voleit destruire si come il avoit fait autres . . .'

immediate response to the threat of Edward's attack is somewhat of a mystery. At least one chronicler, the anonymous author of the *Chronicon de Lanercost*, contends that Lancaster initially wanted to stay and fight the king's troops, 'yet on the advice of his people he retired with his army into the northern regions.'[13] But this chronicle is alone in that assertion, with all others reporting only that Lancaster and his force fled immediately to the north. The *Vita Edwardi II* even asks the question: 'But why does the Earl of Lancaster, so often accustomed to resist the king, now take to flight, particularly as he had with him the Earl of Hereford and the flower of English chivalry?'[14]

Beyond the *Chronicon de Lanercost*'s response, there are five possible answers to the *Vita Edwardi*'s question. First, three chronicles mention the failure of Lancaster's ally, Robert Holland (of Holland in Lancashire), to bring him reinforcements. It was Holland who, according to the *Vita Edwardi II*, had been put in charge of Lancaster's treasury and whose responsibility it was to hire an army 'of his best men.'[15] But it was a responsibility which Holland had failed to carry out. This brings an accusation of treason by the pro-Lancastrian *The Brut*,[16] while the *Vita Edwardi II* declares Robert Holland to have been 'an apostate in his lord's cause [who] deserted to the lord king,' a treacherous act even for the author of this pro-Edward treatise.[17] In any case, the lack of reinforcements must have significantly decreased Lancaster's expected army strength and encouraged his flight.

A second possible reason for Lancaster's flight may have been the large size of Edward's attacking force. At least this is the conclusion drawn by Thomas of Burton: 'But when the two counts saw that the king's troops were both more numerous and stronger than theirs, they retreated.'[18] And while the numbers of Edward's army cannot be known for certain – both the *Chronicon de Lanercost*'s estimate of 60,000 and the *Vita Edwardi II*'s of 300,000 are undoubtedly much exaggerated[19] – it was probably far larger than that of Lancaster and Hereford, especially if Robert Holland had failed to come with reinforcements as had been anticipated.

Third, if it was not the size of the king's army which caused Lancaster to flee, perhaps it was the ease with which the king, before Lancaster's march north, defeated a Lancastrian force in a small battle near the Trent River at the town of Burton. All six of the chronicles which mention this engagement agree that it led directly to the flight of Lancaster's force. The *Vita Edwardi II*, which contains perhaps the most

---

13 *Chronicon de Lanercost*, p. 242: 'Licet autem comes regem vellet ibi exspectasse et pugnasse cum eo, de consilio tamen suorum divertit cum exercitu versus partes boriales.'
14 *Vita Edwardi II*, p. 122: 'Sed quare fugit comes Lancastrie qui totiens solebat regi resistere, precipue cum haberet secum comitem Herfordiae et clariorem militiam totius Anglie?' See also Henry Knighton, I:424; Adam Murimuth, p. 36; *Chronicon de Lanercost*, p. 242; Thomas of Burton, II:341; Geoffrey le Baker, p. 13; *Anonimalle Chronicle*, pp. 104–05; Bridlington, p. 75; and *Brut*, I:217.
15 *Vita Edwardi II*, p. 122. See also Henry Knighton, I:424 and *Brut*, I:217.
16 *Brut*, I:217
17 *Vita Edwardi II*, pp. 122–23: '. . . sed prefixo die Robertus non venit, immo prevaricator in causa domini sui reddidit se domino regi.'
18 Thomas of Burton, p. 341: 'At, cum ipsi 2 comites acies regales plures esse suis et fortiores conspexissent, terga verterunt . . .'
19 *Chronicon de Lanercost*, p. 242 and *Vita Edwardi II*, p. 122.

lengthy discussion of this battle, reports that the king in his march to the north came to the bridge crossing the Trent at Burton where he sent 'a strong phalanx of cavalry and infantry, wishing to know if there would be any opposition to his crossing [of it].' But the king's investigating force found that Lancaster was defending the opposite side of the river at this point; and so a small and inconclusive skirmish – the *Vita* calls it a 'conflictum' – was fought for three or more days until the king's army found a ford higher up the river and crossed there. The anonymous author concludes: 'When the barons heard, and now saw for themselves that the king had crossed the river, they left the bridge, took to horse, and fled.'[20] None of the other sources is as explicit in its details about this battle as is the *Vita Edwardi II*, and in fact none describes anything more than the king winning the battle by force of arms.[21] But undoubtedly this very easy victory, whether accomplished by stealth or by strength, influenced Lancaster's decision to flee to the north.

Fourth, both the *Vita Edwardi II* and the *Vita et mors Edwardi II* report that Edward offered amnesty to any of Lancaster's rebels who wanted to return to his allegiance. Although neither chronicle mentions how many of his adherents deserted from Lancaster, the *Vita et mors* reports at least two desertions of note, Maurice Berkeley and Hugh of Audeley.[22] Lancaster's dwindling numbers, in the face of Edward's larger force, as well as the possibility of further desertions must have encouraged his flight.

Finally, there is the question of Lancaster's ties to Scotland. Was he in fact fleeing to the north because he had been promised aid by Robert Bruce? While no documentary evidence has been discovered linking Edward's chief councillor with Robert Bruce, and such an indictment may be merely a propaganda ploy, at least four chronicles claim that Lancaster was indeed trying to flee to his allies across the border. As the Bridlington chronicler puts it: 'it was common opinion that they had arranged to go to Scotland;'[23] and the *Vita Edwardi II* reports: 'they hoped to find a refuge in Scotland, because Robert Bruce, as was said, had promised help against the king.'[24] It is only one later chronicle, *The Brut*, which claims that Lancaster was not trying to reach Scotland. The anonymous author of this work reports instead that

---

[20] *Vita Edwardi II*, p. 122: 'Exinde conduxit exercitum usque ad magnum fluuium qui dicitur Trente. Est autem ibidem pons magnus qui uiam prebet transeuntibus. Premisit quoque rex ad pontem cuneum fortem armatorum et peditum, scire volens an aliquis impediret transitum suum. Venerat autem comes Lancastrie cum omni sequela sua in uillam de Burhtone ex parte alia. Cumque iam fuisset compertum quod rex disposuit transire fluuium, misit comes viros fortes armatos et pedites qui pontem defenderet. Verum cum per tres pluresque dies inter se partes dimicassent, ac ad eundem conflictum in crastinum redissent, reperit rex uadum superius, ubi transiit ipse et reliqua pars exercitus. Audientes itaque barones et iam uidentes quod rex flumen transisset, pontem reliquerunt, equos ascenderunt et fugam inierunt.'

[21] Thomas of Burton, II:341; Geoffrey le Baker, p. 13; *Anonimalle Chronicle*, pp. 104–05; *Vita et mors Edwardi II*, p. 303; and 'A Chronicle of the Civil Wars of Edward II,' ed. G.L. Haskins, in *Speculum* 14 (1939), 78.

[22] *Vita et mors Edwardi II*, p. 303 and *Vita Edwardi II*, p. 121.

[23] Bridlington, p. 76: 'Opinio tamen communis vulgi fuit quod disponebant usque Scotiam properasse.'

[24] *Vita Edwardi II*, p. 123: 'In Scotiam sperabant habere confugium, quia Robertus de Brutz, ut dictum erat, contra regem promiserat auxilium.' See also *Chronicon de Lanercost*, p. 242 and *Annales Paulini*,

Lancaster stopped short of going across the border because he did not want to be perceived as a traitor. In a speech to his troops the earl presents his reasons for this decision:

> Lords . . . if we go towards the north, men will say that we have gone to join the Scots; and so we shall be seen as traitors, because of the differences between King Edward and Robert Bruce, who has taken the kingdom of Scotland. And therefore I say, for myself, that I will go not further into the north.[25]

Whether an alliance with the Scots was the reason for Lancaster's flight to the north or not cannot be ascertained from the narratives of the Boroughbridge campaign. However, one thing is certain: if he was trying to reach the Scots, Lancaster failed to make it to the border before meeting his demise.

The chronicles relate little about Lancaster's journey north until he reached the Boroughbridge region. Only the anonymous Bridlington chronicler says anything at all, and then it is to condemn the rebels, for they 'despoiled all the lands and did many other criminal acts [on their journey to the north].'[26]

If it was his intention to do so, Lancaster should have easily reached Scotland too, as he was some distance ahead of the king, but he and his troops stopped at Boroughbridge, reports the author of the *Vita Edwardi II*, so 'that they might rest for the night.'[27] Here they encountered the unexpected: a sheriff, Andrew Harclay, who with his northern levies, was loyal to the king. More importantly, and more disastrously for Lancaster, these troops were very experienced in warfare, having fought in a number of border skirmishes against the Scots; some probably also participated at the battle of Bannockburn, eight years earlier.

Harclay was a capable leader, 'warlike and strong,' describes the Bridlington chronicler, who also adds that 'he had been commissioned by the king because of his valor to resist and stop those rebelling against the king.'[28] He had been on his way south to join up with the king's army in pursuit of the rebels when, according to the *Chronicon de Lanercost*, while stopping at the town of Ripon, 'he learned from a spy that the earl and his army were going to arrive the next day at the town of Boroughbridge,' only a few miles from Ripon. This gave him the chance to surprise

in *Chronicles of the Reigns of Edward I and Edward II*, ed. W. Stubbs, vol 1, RS (London, 1883), p. 302.

25 *Brut*, I:217: 'Lordes . . . if we gone toward þe north, men wil seyn þat we gon toward þe Scottes; and so we shul be holde traitoures, for cause of distaunce þat is bituene Kyng Edward and Robert þe Brus, þat made him Kyng of Scotland. And þerfore y say, as tochyng myself, þat y wil go no ferþer into þe North.'

26 Bridlington, II:75: ' . . . patrias spoliantes et alia facinora facientes . . .'

27 *Vita Edwardi II*, p. 123: ' . . . ut ibidem saltem una nocte requiescerent.' See also 'Chronicle of the Civil Wars,' p. 78.

28 Bridlington, II:75: ' . . . Andreas de Harcla, bellicosus et strenuus, virtute commissionis regiae sibi factae ad resistendum et refraenandum regi rebellantes. . .' See also Thomas of Burton, II:342 and *Brut*, I:217–28. On the commission of Edward II to Andrew Harclay, which was principally to stop any Scottish foray into England, see *Vita Edwardi II*, pp. 120–21.

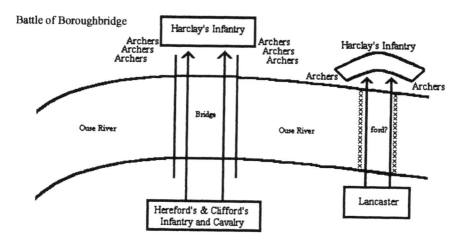

Lancaster's force, and thus 'pressing forward, at night, he arrived before the earl and occupied the bridge before him.'[29]

On the following day, March 16, Lancaster arrived at Boroughbridge, anticipating no opposition to his crossing of the Ouse River and continuing his journey north. But there stood Harclay's force, blocking Lancaster from further progress. The chronicles report very little about Harclay's army at Boroughbridge, and what is reported sometimes differs between these chronicles. For example, the Bridlington chronicler and the anonymous *Chronicle of the Civil Wars of Edward II* say that some of Harclay's force were knights – about fifty according to the *Chronicle* and about twenty according to Bridlington.[30] However, beyond Harclay, only Sir Symond Ward, the sheriff of York is mentioned by name, and then only in *The Brut.*[31] Furthermore, the *Chronicon de Lanercost* reports that most of these troops were from the counties of Cumberland and Westmoreland, 'all who were able to bear arms,' while the *Chronicle of the Civil Wars* records that they were almost all from the town of York.[32]

But the characteristic of Harclay's army which most impresses the contemporary historians, and which all agree upon, is that almost all of these troops were infantry soldiers armed with spears or pikes.[33] As well, Harclay in arriving at the place of battle ordered his men so that even the knights were forced to fight on foot. The *Chronicon de Lanercost* recounts:

> Sending his horse and those of his men to the rear, he ordered all his knights on foot and some pikemen at the northern end of the bridge, and opposite the ford or

---

[29] *Chronicon de Lanercost*, p. 243: 'de nocte igitur consurgens praevenit comitem, et praeoccupavit pontem de Burghbrigge.' See also *Vita Edwardi II*, p. 123 and *Brut*, I:218.
[30] 'Chronicle of the Civil Wars of Edward II,' p. 78 and Bridlington, p. 76. The *Vita Edwardi II* (p. 123) is the only chronicle which records the numerical strength of Harclay's force: 4000 soldiers. The *Anonimalle Chronicle* (pp. 106–07) notes only an army of 'grant poer.'
[31] *The Brut*, I:218.
[32] *Chronicon de Lanercost*, pp. 242–43 and 'Chronicle of the Civil Wars,' p. 78.
[33] See *Chronicon de Lanercost*, p. 243; Bridlington, p. 76; 'Chronicle of the Civil Wars,' p. 78; *Vita et mors Edwardi II*, p. 303; and Geoffrey le Baker, p. 14.

passage of water, he ordered other pikemen in a *schiltrom*, according to the manner of the Scots, to oppose the knights and the horses on which the enemy sat.[34]

Harclay's formation thus allowed him to take advantage of the fighting skill of his experienced infantry warriors. It should also be noted, as remarked on by the author of the *Chronicon de Lanercost*, that the formation around the ford was in the form of a *schiltrom*, 'according to the manner of the Scots,' thus revealing from where, at least in this author's opinion, this infantry formation had been learned.

Archers too are referred to among Harclay's soldiers, although how many there were is not mentioned, and only *The Brut* declares their placement on the sides of the infantry formation.[35] Yet, the accuracy of this declaration is doubtful. What would be the purpose of such a formation? Accurate archery fire into an opposing force across the Ouse River would be nearly impossible. And there was no need for archers to be placed on the flanks of the infantry to narrow the opposing cavalry charges as would become standard in later English formations – at Dupplin Moor, Halidon Hill, and Crécy – as the bridge and ford would serve to narrow sufficiently any cavalry charges made on these infantry positions.

Lancaster's army approached Harclay from the south side of the river, with the only access to the opposite shore being the bridge and a nearby ford, both guarded by his opponents. Lancaster's plan, according to the *Chronicon de Lanercost*, was to split his force in two: the earl of Hereford and Lancaster's son-in-law, Sir Roger of Clifford, would take their part of the army across the bridge to 'seize [it] from the pikemen standing there,' while Lancaster himself would take the second part of the army across the ford 'to seize the water and the ford from the pikemen' there. Both of these attacks were to be made on horseback.[36]

At this point in the narrative of the battle *The Brut* adds an interesting story not included in other contemporary writers' accounts. This chronicle reports that before the battle began, Lancaster, when he had seen the great 'power' which Harclay had brought with him and being 'very afraid,' called his opponent to him, hoping to persuade the sheriff to abandon the king and join the rebellion. Lancaster offered Harclay both land and leadership:

> and we will give to you the best part of five earldoms that we have and hold, and we will give you an oath that we will do nothing without your counsel and so that you would be well at ease with us.

But Harclay refused Lancaster's entreaty, causing the earl to threaten the sheriff:

---

[34] *Chronicon de Lanercost*, p. 243: 'et, dimissis retro equis suis et suorum, statuit in pedibus omnes milites et quosdam lancearios ad borialem partem pontis, et contra vadum sive transitum aquae posuit alios lancearios in scheltrum, secundum modum Scottorum, ad resistendum equitibus et equis in quibus adversarii considebant.'
[35] *Brut*, I:219. See also *Chronicon de Lanercost*, p. 243 and *Vita Edwardi II*, p. 124.
[36] *Chronicon de Lanercost*, p. 243.

At your word, Sir Andrew, I tell thee that before the year is done you shall be taken and held as a traitor, even more than you consider us now, and you shall die a worse death than any knight of England ever suffered.[37]

It is doubtful whether *The Brut*'s conversation with its prophecy of Harclay's eventual treasonous demise ever took place. But if it did, it was a last, desperate attempt by Lancaster to avoid battle, for it was necessary for him to fight the smaller force of Harclay at Boroughbridge quickly rather than linger or march elsewhere and risk running into Edward's larger force somewhere behind him.[38] So the battle was fought.

It is important at this point to note that neither Lancaster nor any of his lieutenants felt that they were in any danger of defeat. Certainly their cavalry, with so many knights among the force, should easily have defeated Harclay's infantry, despite, the fact that, as Geoffrey le Baker insists, they were unaccustomed to fight against infantry.[39] But, as the *Chronicon de Lanercost* puts it, 'another thing happened.'[40]

It is unclear from contemporary sources if both Hereford and Lancaster launched simultaneous attacks, or whether Hereford's force proceeded with the first assault. It does seem apparent, however, that whether Hereford's attack was launched first or not, it was the first to engage enemy troops, the bridge being easier to cross than the ford. Sir Humphrey of Bohun, earl of Hereford and Essex, was 'a bellicose man in all engagements, assuredly strong in body, most astute in mind and prudent enough in council,' wrote Geoffrey le Baker; he was 'a worthy knight, renown throughout all Christendom,' added *The Brut*.[41] He was also the brother-in-law to Edward II, whose friendship had wavered only in opposition to Piers Gaveston and the Despensers. Now he made the initial attack on a force commissioned by the king to put down his rebellion.

Hereford's attack was brief, and entirely unsuccessful; for not only was his charge stopped by the infantry formation on the other side of the bridge, but the earl himself was killed in the melee. Roger of Clifford, the second in command, was wounded, and he and the rest of the company were driven back to their side of the bridge, having

[37] *Brut*, I:218: 'Sire Andrew,' quod he, 'e mow wel vnderstonde how þat our Lord þe Kyng is ladde and misgouernede by miche false conseil, þrou Sir Hugh þe Spenser þe fader, & Sir Hugh þe sone, & Sir John Erl of Arundel, and þrou Maistre Robert Baldok, a false pilede clerc, þat is in þe Kyngus court duelling; wherfore y praye ow þat e wil come wiþ vs, wiþ al þe power þat e have ordeynede, and helpe to destroie þe venemye of Engeland, and þe traitoures þat bene þerin, and we wil if vnto ow þe best part of v Erldomes þar We haveþ & holdeþ; and We wil mak vnto ow an oth þat we wil neuer do þing wiþout our consel, and so e shul bene as wele at ese wiþ vs . . .' 'Sir Thomas! þat wolde nou t do, ne consent þerto, for no maner þing þat yhe might me eue, wiþouten þe wil and commaundement of our lord þe Kyng; for þan shulde y be holde a traitoure for evermore.' '. . . At on worde, Sir Andrew, y telle þe, þat or þis er be gon, þat e shal be take and holde for a traitoure, and more þan e holde vs nowe; and in worse deth e shul die, þan euer dede Knyght of Engeland.'
[38] No chronicle indicates how close Edward's army was to Lancaster on the day of Boroughbridge, but because the king was able to arrive so quickly at the trials of the rebels after their defeat, his army must have been fairly close.
[39] Geoffrey le Baker, p. 14.
[40] *Chronicon de Lanercost*, p. 243.

escaped 'with difficulty.' The *Chronicon de Lanercost* gives the best account of what happened:

> For when the earl of Hereford ... and Sir Roger of Clifford and some other knights, in the manner of lions, had bravely entered upon the bridge before the rest of the troops, and had charged fiercely upon the enemy, pikes were thrust at the earl from all sides. And he fell immediately and was killed on the bridge with his standard-bearer and [other] knights ... Sir Roger of Clifford, though grievously wounded with pikes and arrows, and driven back, escaped with difficulty along with the others.[42]

It seems clear in this chronicle that Hereford's charge was made on horseback. However, the *Vita Edwardi II* avers that Hereford's force was dismounted 'for the bridge was narrow, and offered no path for horsemen in battle array.'[43] While it may seem more logical to agree with the *Vita Edwardi II*, it is in fact the *Chronicon de Lanercost* which is the more detailed and accurate source for this battle and is the narrative accepted by most historians for what occurred.[44] The *Chronicon de Lanercost* mentions only a cavalry charge by Hereford.

Lancaster's charge across the ford also met with disaster, although in this attack it appears that archery played a more major role than against Hereford, as again stated in the *Chronicon de Lanercost*:

> The earl [of Lancaster's] cavalry, when they tried to cross the water, could not enter it because of the number and density of arrows which the archers discharged onto them and their horses.[45]

No one appears to have been killed by the archery assault, but progress was slowed and confused, and after hearing of Hereford's death on the bridge, according to the *Vita Edwardi II*, 'their zeal for battle cooled off, and they at once retreated.'[46]

Completely overwhelmed, Lancaster was forced to seek a truce until the following

---

41 Geoffrey le Baker, p. 13 and *Brut*, I:219. See also *Vita et mors Edwardi II*, p. 303.

42 *Chronicon de Lanercost*, p. 243: 'Cum enim comes Herfordiae ... et dominus Rogerus de Clifford cum quodam milite, more leonum, audacter ante alios pontem intrassent, et in adversarios fortiter irruissent, infixae sunt comite lanceae circumquaque, et cito prostratus est et interfectus supra pontem cum vexillario suo ... dominus autem Rogerus de Clifford, graviter vulneratus cum lanceis et sagittis et repulsus, cum aliis vix evasit.' On the death of Hereford see also *Vita Edwardi II*, p. 124; *Anonimalle Chronicle*, pp. 106–07; Bridlington, p. 76; 'Chronicle of the Civil Wars of Edward II,' p. 78; Henry Knighton, I:425; and *French Chronicle of London*, p. 45. Thomas of Burton (II:342), the *Vita et mors Edwardi II* (p. 303), and *Brut* (I:219) all claim that Hereford was killed by a spear thrust from below the bridge, although neither of the most detailed accounts of the battle, the *Vita Edwardi II* or the *Chronicon de Lanercost*, make such an assertion.

43 *Vita Edwardi II*, p. 124: 'Erat enim pons strictus, nec uiam equitibus ad bellum procedentibus prebere potuit.'

44 See, for example, Morris, 'Mounted Infantry' and Tout, 'Tactics.'

45 *Chronicon de Lanercost*, p. 243: 'Equites autem comitis, qui voluerunt aquam transivisse, non potuerunt eam intrare prae multitudine et spissitudine telorum quae a sagittariis mittebantur in eos et in equos eorum.' See also *Vita Edwardi II*, p. 124.

46 *Vita Edwardi II*, p. 124: 'Alii uero, dum uadum transire nituntur. ab ymbre saggitarum misere atteruntur; sed post mortem comitis Herfordie sua virtus tepuit militie, et statim reuertuntur.' See also *Chronicon de Lanercost*, pp. 242–43.

morning so that he could regroup his remaining troops and take care of the wounded.[47] He had every intention to continue the battle on the following day, it seems, but during the night a large number of his soldiers deserted their lords and fled from the battlefield.[48] Thus Lancaster awoke not to fight but to flee from the field, realizing what would happen to him if was captured. Yet, he had nowhere to run, and before the day was over he and sixteen other knights were apprehended and taken to York to await trial and punishment. As the *Vita Edwardi II* recounts:

> On that same night the sheriff of York came with a large force to attack the king's enemies; relying on his help Andrew Harclay entered the town [of Ripon] very early, and taking the Earl of Lancaster and almost all the other knights and esquires scatheless, led them off to York and imprisoned them. Some left their horses and putting off their armor looked round for ancient worn-out garments, and took to the road as beggars. But their caution was of no avail, for not a single well-known man among them escaped. O calamity! To see men lately dressed in purple and fine linen now attired in rags, bound and imprisoned in chains![49]

Almost all chronicles record the details and results of the trials of treason against Lancaster and his fellow rebels; he was beheaded, being spared from the traditional hanging, drawing and quartering, because of his kinship with the king.[50]

Thomas of Lancaster's rebellion had been short-lived, defeated as it was by a rather rude bevy of northern infantry musters using a 'Scottish' formation. The *Vita Edwardi II* lauds the victory:

> [It was] a marvelous thing and one indeed brought about by God's will and aid, that so scanty a company should in a moment overcome so many knights. For the Earl's side were more than seven times as numerous as their adversaries. There were captured with the Earl of Lancaster and the other barons more than a hundred valiant knights. The number of esquires no less valiant was, I believe, much greater. Why therefore should they not have stood and fought manfully for their safety? Indeed the criminal is always fearful and so less effective in action. They saw that the whole countryside was up-in-arms in front of them, and thus their advance was blocked. They knew that the king's army threatened them from the rear, and therefore their retreat was not secure. Thus as men having no plan nor even time to deliberate, they fell into the hands of their enemies, etc.[51]

---

[47] *Chronicon de Lanercost*, p. 244; *Vita Edwardi II*, p. 124; Bridlington, p. 76; and 'Chronicle of the Civil Wars,' p. 78.
[48] *Chronicon de Lanercost*, p. 243 and Thomas of Burton, II:3422.
[49] *Vita Edwardi II*: pp. 124–25: 'Ipsa uero nocte vicecomes Eboraci cum magna cohorte uenerat inimicos regis invadere; cuius auxilio fretus Andreas de Herkelee uillam intrauit summo mane, et cepit comitem Lancastrie et omnes pene reliquos milites et scutarios sine uulnere, et perducens Eboracum reclusit in carcerem. Quidam equos reliquerunt, et exeuntes arma sua ueteres attritas uestes quesierunt sibi, et more mendicantium uiam incesserunt. Sed cautela non profuit, nam nec unus quidem famosus ex omnibus euasit. O monstum! uidere uiros purpura et bisso nuper indutos nunc attritis uestibus incedere, et uinctos in compedibus recludi sub carcere!'
[50] See Thomas of Burton, II:342; *Anonimalle Chronicle*, pp. 106–11; Bridlington, p. 76; 'Chronicle of Civil Wars,' p. 78; Geoffrey le Baker, p. 14; Henry Knighton, I:425; and *Brut*, I:219–20.
[51] *Vita Edwardi II*, p. 125: 'Res miranda et certe nutu Dei et auxilio promota, quod tam rara manu subito superatur tanta militia. Pars enim comitis numero armatorum partem persequentium excessit

The Brut's epitaph is more succinct and more sorrowful, but the sentiment is nearly the same: 'Alas, the shame and dishonor that the gentle order of knighthood had there at that battle.'[52]

Both of these chroniclers misjudge the cause of Harclay's victory. The knights cannot be blamed for their defeat. This was not a battle where the cavalry lost because of a poorly executed charge, for neither Lancaster's nor Hereford's cavalry charges are noted by the contemporary sources to have been in themselves disordered or confused. Nor could the cavalry charges have been delayed, for Edward II's main force, much larger than that of the rebels, was feared to be close at hand.

This was a battle won by infantry. Harclay's infantry formation – in a solid line across the end of the bridge and in a *schiltrom*, or semi-circle, around the end of the ford – was the determining factor in his victory over the more 'knightly' cavalry force of the earls of Lancaster and Hereford. No tally for Harclay's army is given by the chroniclers, but he would not have needed many soldiers, even if facing a larger, more powerful troop. For the bridge and ford caused a natural narrowing of the cavalry charges made against Harclay, and this ensured that his formation was not flanked. And as his infantry remained in formation, combined with the archers present among his troops, the opposing cavalry was almost powerless to breach the 'Scottish' formation. Because Edward's army was probably nearby, Lancaster's dual force of cavalry was forced to charge, and these charges ended in failure, capped perhaps at their climax with the death of Hereford. It was a final blow to the morale of an already demoralized rebel army, for they must have felt that this would be an easy victory. Although no death calculations are made for Harclay's soldiers by contemporary chroniclers, he probably did not lose many. On the other hand, Boroughbridge cost Lancaster the rebellion.

Never again would an English army fight as it had at Bannockburn. From this time until the end of the Middle Ages the chief tactic of the English was to dismount most of the cavalry and to order them in a solid infantry formation – in a line or, if warranted by geography, as at the ford at Boroughbridge, in a *schiltrom*. This once powerful and proud cavalry-based army had become little more than, as John E. Morris termed it, 'mounted infantry.' Was this recognized first at Boroughbridge in

---

in septuplum. Capti sunt enim cum comite Lancastrie et ceteris baronibus milites ualentes centum et amplius. Sed et scutariorum non minus ualentium multo maiorem credo fuisse numerum. Quare igitur non restitissent et pro salute sua uiriliter dimicassent? Revera cor delinquentium semper est pauidum et ideo minus valens ad negotium. Videbant totam patriam a fronte excitatam, et per hoc uiam eorum impeditam. Sciebant a tergo imminere regis exercitum, et propter hoc cursum retrogradum non esse securum. Vnde quasi homines non habentes consilium nec etiam tempus ad deliberandum, inciderunt in manus inimicorum, etc.'

52 *Brut*, I:220: 'Allas þe shame & despite, þat þe gentil ordre of Knyghthode þere hade at þat bataile!' Other chronicles give different, less militarily oriented causes for defeat at Boroughbridge. Geoffrey le Baker (p. 13) believes that defeat came because both sides had not concentrated on defeating the Saracens in the Middle East, while the monk of Bridlington (p. 76) saw the defeat of Lancaster as the fulfillment of Biblical prophecy – the fulfillment of Revelation's prophecy of the red horse riding forth in the last days, whose rider had been given the duty of taking peace from the land (Revelations 6:4) – and as the fulfillment of the prophecy of Gregory the Great to Maximus of Salona – that those who are sinful will be punished by military conquest and unhappiness.

Harclay's brilliant victory over Lancaster? We probably cannot know for sure. But perhaps it is better to recognize the influence of this positive image of infantry warfare rather than the negative one received by the English at their defeat at Bannockburn, the latter being credited most by modern historians for the change in English tactics in the early fourteenth century.

VIII

THE BATTLE OF CASSEL, 1328

THE PEACE OF Athis-sur-Orge, described by fifteenth-century historian Adrien de Budt as a peace of 'little stability,' brought almost no calm to the county of Flanders.[1] Constant turmoil filled the region as the peace treaty with its heavy indemnities caused a hatred of the French overlords unseen since before the battle of Courtrai. Although Philip the Fair extended the treaty of Athis-sur-Orge and its indemnities in 1309 with an added threat of a papal interdict and excommunication if it was broken,[2] violence erupted often in Flanders in the two decades following the battle of Mons-en-Pévèle.[3]

Most hard hit by the heavy indemnities brought down with the treaty of Athis-sur-Orge were the peasants of the Flemish coastal regions. They resented having to ransom nobles captured during the 1302-05 war who cared little about them and their region. Robert of Bethune, who succeeded as count of Flanders in 1305, allowed the payment of indemnities to lapse in an endeavor to keep his county peaceful and at least a little loyal to him.[4] But when Robert died and was succeeded in September 1322 by his grandson, Louis of Nevers, the payment of war indemnities became a central issue which the new count wanted to enforce. Louis, who had married one of the daughters of the French king, Philip V, was extremely loyal to the French crown, and he immediately set out to make his county subservient to French royal wishes.[5]

---

[1] Adrien de Budt, *Chronicon Flandriae*, in *Corpus chronicorum Flandriae*, i, ed. J.J. de Smet (Brussels, 1837), p. 311.

[2] See the documents contained in the *Codex diplomaticus Flandriae*, ed. Thierry de Limburg-Stirum (Bruges, 1879), I:31–51, 65–69.

[3] In 1309–10, a small rebellion arose in the Waasland. In 1311, at Ghent, the weavers of the city arose against their local nobles. In 1319, they repeated this revolt and with other Ghentenaars succeeded in attacking Rijsel as well. Finally, in 1320, a Brugeois contingent, under the command of Nikolaas Zannekin, attacked Sluys. See Henri Pirenne, *Histoire de Belgique*, II:76–82; William H. TeBrake, *A Plague of Insurrection: Popular Politics and Peasant Revolt in Flanders, 1323–1328* (Philadelphia, 1993), pp. 34–37; Jacques Sabbe, *Vlaanderen in opstand, 1323–1328: Nikolaas Zannekin, Zeger Janszone en Willem de Deken* (Bruges, 1992), pp. 14–15; and David Nicholas, *Medieval Flanders* (London, 1992), pp. 195–96.

[4] See Henri Pirenne, ed., *Le soulèvement de la Flandre maritime de 1323–1328* (Brussels, 1900), pp. iii, iv, xi; Pirenne, *Histoire de Belgique*, II:71; David Nicholas, *Town and Countryside: Social, Economic and Political Tensions in Fourteenth-Century Flanders* (Bruges, 1971), pp. 162–63; F.W.N. Hugenholtz, *Drie boerenopstanden uit de veertiende eeuw* ('s Gravenhage, 1978), pp. 22–23; and Jacques Mertens, 'De boerenopstand onder Zannekin,' in *Nikolaas Zannekin en de slag bij Kassel 1328–1978* (Dixmude, 1978), p. 98.

[5] See Lucas, *The Low Countries*, p. 46; TeBrake, pp. 45–50; Sabbe, p. 20; Nicholas, *Medieval*

Besides seeking the payment of these indemnities, Louis enacted other changes which further alienated his subjects. Within a year of his ascension, Louis had supplanted the influence of Bruges with that of Ghent, he had returned the pro-French party to its political prominence, and he had nearly eliminated Robert of Bethune's policy of local independence. The most sweeping blow to the Flemings (especially to the Brugeois) came on July 13, 1323 when Louis granted a monopoly of the waterways to his great-uncle, John of Namur, an outspoken foe of Bruges. This edict was in direct violation of the privileges of the town of Bruges which had long controlled the waterways at Sluys.[6] Count Louis, perhaps misunderstanding the feelings of his subjects, had delivered this edict while in Bruges, and when the townspeople heard it they revolted, cast the count into prison, marched on Sluys, burned it, and captured John of Namur. Another rebellion had begun.

The rebellion was directed by the weavers of Bruges, but fueled by the peasants of maritime Flanders.[7] Governmental changes were instituted, comital bailiffs were replaced by revolutionary 'captains,' and Robert of Cassel, the uncle of the imprisoned Louis of Nevers, and 'secretly hostile' to him, was asked to lead the people against their French overlords.[8] Only the town of Ghent, still loyal to the count and the king, stood in the way of complete rebel control of Flanders.

Finally, in November 1325, the new French king, Charles IV – Philip V had died in 1322 – decided that the Flemish rebellion warranted some military action. He raised an army and prepared a punitive expedition against the rebels. At the same time, he wrote a letter to Robert of Cassel promising him forgiveness if he quit the rebellion; another letter promised Ghent that it would not fall to the rebels.[9] The threat of French military involvement and the subsequent desertion of the rebellion by Robert of Cassel was enough to force peace on the rebels. A treaty was formally signed at Arques on April 19, 1326. Louis of Nevers was freed and restored to his rule. The demolition of all fortresses constructed since 1323 was ordered. The indemnities agreed upon at Athis-sur-Orge in 1305 were to be paid with the addition of an extra 10,000 *livres* coming to the count for his suffering. Robert of Cassel was

Flanders, pp. 209–11; Jan van Rompaey, 'De opstand in het vlaamse kustland van 1323 tot 1328 en de figuur van Nikolaas Zannekin,' in *Nikolaas Zannekin en de slag bij Kassel 1328–1978* (Dixmude, 1978), p. 104; and John Bell Henneman, *Royal Taxation in Fourteenth Century France: The Development of War Financing, 1322–1356* (Princeton, 1971), p. 55.

[6] See Nicholas, *Town and Countryside*, p. 161; TeBrake, pp. 49–50; Pirenne, *Soulèvement*, p. xv; Sabbe, p. 20; Rompaey, p. 105; Nicholas, *Medieval Flanders*, 213; and Jules Viard, 'La guerre de Flandre (1328),' *Bibliothèque de l'école de chartes* 83 (1922), p. 362.

[7] See Henri Pirenne, *Early Democracies in the Low Countries: Urban Society and Political Conflict in the Middle Ages and the Renaissance*, trans. J.V. Saunders (New York, 1971), p. 153.

[8] See TeBrake, pp. 51–98; Sabbe, pp. 25–53; Pirenne, *Soulèvement*, pp. xvi–xvii; Hugenholtz, pp. 28–30; Nicholas, *Medieval Flanders*, p. 131; J. Bovesse, 'Le Comte de Namur Jean Ier et les événements du comté de Flandre en 1325–1326,' *Bulletin de la commission royale d'histoire* 131 (1965), 385–454; Henri Pirenne, 'Documents relatifs à l'histoire de la Flandre pendant la première moitié du XIVe siècle,' *Bulletin de la commission royale d'histoire* 7 (1897), 477–93; and Henri Pirenne, 'Un mémoire de Robert de Cassel sur sa participation à la révolte de la Flandre maritime en 1324–1325,' *Revue du nord* 1 (1910), 45–50.

[9] See Henneman, p. 55.

pardoned, and the revolutionary captains were removed with the comital bailiffs restored to their posts.[10]

But the treaty of Arques did not end the rebellion. The revolutionary captains refused to surrender their positions to the returning bailiffs, and with a new intensity the rebellion began again. Louis fled to Paris early in 1327 to ask Charles for more military assistance, but the weak king had died and was succeeded on May 29, 1327 by Philip VI of Valois, Charles' cousin. Philip recognized the county of Flanders as an area of rebellion in an otherwise supportive kingdom.[11] Thus, as Edouard Perroy writes, he 'zealously embraced the feudal cause' responding to Louis' appeal with a resolve to punish the rebels and to avenge his loyal count.[12] Leading a large French army himself, Philip entered Flanders and encountered the rebel force. The battle of Cassel was the result. It was fought on August 28, 1328.

At the end of this day, the French were victorious. Few rebels escaped the slaughter. Philippe Contamine has calculated the Flemish loss at fifty percent of their force,[13] while contemporary sources number the Flemish casualties as high as 20,000. The French lost considerably fewer men, with possibly as few as seventeen knights having died on the battlefield.

With the defeat at Cassel, the rebellion met its end. News of the French victory traveled quickly to the northern rebels who fled to safety inside their town walls. Ypres and Bruges rapidly submitted to Philip and Louis, and peace once again returned to the French countryside.[14] Philip was merciful. Perhaps he had seen too much bloodshed at Cassel, or perhaps he felt that if he punished the Brugeois harshly they might rebel further against him. In any case he refused to allow the destruction of the towns and lands held by the rebels.[15] Instead he launched a program of war indemnities and land confiscations against the Flemings. Most of the landholding rebels lost their property, but few lost their lives.[16] Only Willem de Deken, the mayor of Bruges, was taken to Paris to be tortured and executed.[17]

As with the battles of Courtrai and Mons-en-Pévèle, there are a number of contemporary chroniclers who comment on the battle of Cassel. The anonymous

---

[10] The text of the treaty of Arques can be found in *Codex diplomaticus*, II:385–403. See also TeBrake, pp. 98–99; Pirenne, *Soulèvement*, pp. xxv–xxvi; Sabbe, pp. 52–53; Nicholas, *Town and Countryside*, p. 161; Hugenholtz, p. 30; Rompaey, pp. 120–21; and Henneman, p. 56.

[11] See TeBrake, pp. 108–19; Sabbe, pp. 55–64; Hugenholtz, pp. 106–07; and Nicholas, *Medieval Flanders*, p. 215.

[12] Edouard Perroy, *The Hundred Years War*, trans. W.B. Wells (London, 1951), p. 81.

[13] Contamine, p. 258.

[14] See Viard, pp. 375–80.

[15] See Pirenne, *Histoire de Belgique*, II:90; Pirenne, *Soulèvement*, pp. xxx–xxxi; TeBrake, pp. 123–25; Sabbe, pp. 72–75; and Hugenholtz, pp. 32–34.

[16] A scholarly 'cottage-industry' of confiscation records research seems to have developed after Pirenne first published his records in 1900 (*La soulèvement de la Flandre maritime*). Two later additions have come from Jacques Mertens: 'La confiscations dans la Chatellenie du Franc de Bruges après la bataille de Cassel,' *Bulletin de la commission royale d'histoire de Belgique* 134 (1968), 239–84 and 'De economische en sociale toestand van de opstandelingen uit het Brugse Vrije, wier goederen na de slag bij Cassel (1328) verbeurd verklaard werden,' *Revue Belge de philologie et d'histoire* 47 (1969), 1131–53. See also TeBrake, Appendix A, pp. 139–44.

[17] See TeBrake, pp. 123–24 and Pirenne *Soulèvement*, p. xxxi.

French authors of the *Grandes chroniques de France* and the *Chronographia regum Francorum*, Gilles le Muisit, the bourgeois of Valenciennes, the second continuator of Guillaume de Nangis' *Chronicon*, Willem Procurator, Giovanni Villani, and the authors of the *Chronicon comitum Flandriae*, the *Chronique de Flandre*, and the *Rijmkroniek van Vlaenderen* all include narratives of the battle.[18] To these narratives must be added the accounts written by two of the premier historical writers of the fourteenth century, Jean le Bel and Jean Froissart.[19] Also recounting the battle is Richard Lescot, writing c.1344 at the monastery of Saint Denis, and an anonymous work composed at Paris and now known as the *Chronique Parisienne anonymé de 1316 à 1328*.[20] Another source for the battle of Cassel is a series of letters written between September 6 and October 4, 1328 by Pope John XXII to Philip VI. Although they do not give a narrative of the battle itself, these letters do report some details of the conflict which are not mentioned in the other sources. More importantly perhaps, they report what details were important enough to be recounted to the Pope in Avignon only a few days after the battle was fought.[21]

However, unlike the battle of Courtrai and Mons-en-Pévèle, few contemporary descriptions of the battle of Cassel favor the Flemings or mourn their defeat. Even those sources written in Flanders, like the *Chronicon comitum Flandriae*, the *Chronique de Flandre*, and the *Rijmkroniek van Vlaenderen*, are opposed to this rebellion despite being favorable to the one fought in 1302–05. Perhaps this is due to the fact that none of these chronicles were written in Bruges or in the maritime region of Flanders, the areas involved in the 1323–28 rebellion. But, more likely there is an absence of sympathetic records of the battle because of the social character of the rebellion; it included peasants as well as townspeople. Nevertheless, it is still possible to reconstruct what occurred at the battle of Cassel, and to understand why the Flemish infantry lost to the French cavalry there.

Almost all of the contemporary accounts of the battle begin with the visit of Louis of Nevers to Philip VI at the latter's coronation to plead for assistance against his rebellious subjects. Louis needed this assistance, the continuator of Guillaume de Nangis' chronicle insists, because 'he had not been of such power to be able to oppose their evils and to extirpate the cause of the rebellions.'[22] However, Philip did not

---

[18] *Grandes chroniques*, IX:79–95; *Chronographia regum Francorum*, II:2–10; Gilles le Muisit, pp. 211–12; *Récits d'un bourgeois de Valenciennes*, pp. 150–52; the *Continuatio chronici* of Guillaume de Nangis, II:90–102; Willem Procurator, pp. 218–25; Giovanni Villani (ed. Muratori), cols. 656–57; *Chronicon comitum Flandriae*, pp. 202–07; *Chronique de Flandre*, I:342–47, 534–37; and *Rijmkroniek van Vlaenderen*, pp. 822–23.

[19] Jean le Bel, *Chroniques de Jean le Bel*, ed. J. Viard and E. Duprez, Société de l'histoire de France (Paris, 1904), I:93–94 and Jean Froissart, *Chroniques*, in *Oeuvres de Froissart*, ed. Kervyn de Lettenhove (Brussels, 1867), II:216–26.

[20] Richard Lescot, *Chronique*, ed. J. Lemoine, Société de l'histoire de France (Paris, 1896), pp. 3–7 and *Chronique Parisienne anonymé de 1316 à 1339*, ed. A. Hellot, in *Mémoires de la société de l'histoire de Paris* xi (1895), pp. 116–22.

[21] These letters, nos. 2222, 2223, 2238, 2249 and 2258, are found in *Lettres de Jean XXII (1316–1334)*, ed. Fayen, in *Analecta Vaticano-Belgica*, vol. 2 (Rome, 1908).

[22] *Continuatio chronici* of Guillaume de Nangis, II:90–91: 'Circa istud tempus, comes Flandriae suo

respond swiftly to Louis' request, choosing instead to deliberate for fifteen days before deciding whether or not to involve himself in the count of Flanders' civil war.[23] In the end, with the advice of his council, Philip agreed to Louis' plea so that the rebellion, in the words of the *Chronicon comitum Flandriae*, 'would not attract to it other communities in Picardy and France.'[24] Only then, Jean Froissart records, did Philip promise Louis that he would 'never return to Paris until you have taken peaceful possession of the whole of Flanders.'[25]

Once the decision to march against the Flemish rebels had been made, Philip began to gather men and money to proceed with his war. On June 18 he announced an *arrière-ban* which asked that both noble and non-noble knights assemble at Arras on July 31 to fulfill their military duty; if they could not come to Arras they were permitted to send a monetary substitute so that others would be permitted to go in their place.[26] The response was enthusiastic. Not only was there a 'large army' gathered in Arras at the end of July, but it is also reported that more than 231,078 *livres* were collected.[27] In fact, the army was so large, the *Chronographia regum Francorum* reports, that Philip needed first to march to the towns of Lille, St. Omer, and Tournai in order to gather food to feed them all.[28] It is also reported that before entering Flanders Philip visited Notre Dame Cathedral, the monastery of Saint Denis and several charitable houses in order to gain the favor of God in his military venture; at Saint Denis he also obtained the *oriflamme* to take with him into battle.[29]

Hearing of the approach of this large army, the Flemings too prepared for battle. However, despite much anticipation, the advent of war was not met with much

---

domino regi Franciae, sicut debebat, fecit homagium. Quo facto, comes dicto regi plurium subditorum suorum, et maxime de Brugis, de Ypra et de Cassello, et de pluribus aliis locis intolerabiles rebelliones exposuit, et quod ipse tantae potestatis non esset quod solus posset eorum malitiis obviare, et rebellionis materiam exstirpare. Unde et sibi a dicto rege fieri auxilium humiliter supplicavit.' See also *Chronographia regum Francorum*, II:2–3; *Chronique Parisienne anonymé*, p. 117; Richard Lescot, pp. 3–4; *Chronique de Flandre*, I:357; Jean Froissart, II:217; *Chronicon comitum Flandriae*, pp. 202–03; and *Chronique Normande*, p. 36.

23 See *Chronicon comitum Flandriae*, p. 203.

24 *Chronicon comitum Flandriae*, p. 203: 'Consilium fuit omnium, quod rex illuc exercitum mitteret in adjutorium comitis Flandriae ad domandum rebelles, ne, si terminos suos exirent, attrahere sibi possent communitates alias Picardiae et Franciae, et sic magnam confusionem facere nobilibus atque et regno.'

25 See Jean Froissart, II:217: 'Dont parla li roys Phelippes, et dist: "Loeis, biaux cousins, nous vous tenons pour conte de Flandres, et par le digne unction et sacrement que nous recevons hui, jammais ne renterons en Paris se vous avons mis en possession paisieulle de le content de Flandres." '

26 For example, the town of Montpellier sent the king a subsidy of 2,000 *livres* as a substitute for sending soldiers (C. Devic and J. Vaissette, *Histoire générale de Languedoc* (Toulouse, 1872), I:676–80. See also the *Continuatio chronici* of Guillaume de Nangis, II:92 and Henneman, pp. 70–71.

27 On the amount of money collected see Viard, p. 365. A number of contemporary sources are impressed by the size of the French army. See the *Chronique Parisienne anonymé*, p. 117; Gilles le Muisit, p. 211; and the *Annales Tielenses*, in *MGH SS*, xvi, ed. G.H. Pertz (Hannover, 1879), p. 26. There was resistance among some French towns to Philip's order to collect an armed force at Arras. As seen in a document contained in C. Devic and J. Vaissette, I:671–676, the inhabitants of Lunel refused to send troops or money to the king for his military expedition.

28 See *Chronographia regum Francorum*, II:3.

29 See the *Continuatio chronici* of Guillaume de Nangis, II:92–93 and the *Grandes chroniques*, IX:80–81.

enthusiasm by the Flemings. Still, a large army, drawn from the towns of Bruges and Ypres as well as from many smaller villages, seems to have gathered to face Philip.[30] According to the author of the *Grandes chroniques*, the Flemings were frightened at the prospect of fighting the French king and 'they did not know where he would attack.' Therefore, they divided their force into three separate groups: the rebels from Bruges and the area around Bruges were marched towards Tournai, those from Ypres and Courtrai towards Lille, and those from the areas of Veurne, Dunkirk, Cassel, and Poperinge marched towards St. Omer.[31] It was this last group which first saw the French, and they moved swiftly to a defensive position, ordering their force on the hill outside of the village of Cassel.[32]

There is some disagreement among the sources as to who led this army of rebels. While most chronicles report that the Flemings at Cassel had no leader,[33] Jean Froissart names Nikolaas Zannekin, a long-time leader of the rebels. Not only does Froissart name him as leader, but he also describes Zannekin in fairly positive terms as a man 'marvelously arrogant, hardy and scurrilous' who promised those who followed him that they would kill the king of France. He reports further that it was Zannekin's purpose to keep Louis of Nevers out of Flanders, 'to confound all his enemies' and to kill all those loyal to the king of France.[34]

The French army arrived at Cassel shortly after the Flemings, setting up their own camp at the base of the hill. Philip, knowing that this was not the entire Flemish force, also divided his army into three parts, sending Robert of Cassel with a small contingent to St. Omer and Louis of Nevers with an equally small force to Lille. The bulk of the French army stayed with Philip at Cassel.[35]

But Philip chose not to attack the Flemish army at Cassel. The Flemings had wisely selected terrain which was easy to defend. A hillside, like ditches or a marsh, meant that a cavalry charge would be disorganized and fatiguing, allowing a solid Flemish infantry line to withstand easily the mounted shock combat of the knights. Thus, unlike some of his predecessors, Philip chose to wait for a better opportunity to fight against his opponents; he sat at the base of the hill, in effect besieging the Flemings camped on top of it.

---

[30] See the *Chronique de Flandre*, I:534. Jean Froissart claims that this force numbered 16,000 soldiers, but he is the only chronicler who provides a number for the Flemings.

[31] See the *Grandes chroniques*, IX:82: 'Quant les Flamens virent que le roy avoit fait si grant semonse, si s'assamblerent et virent qu'il n'avoient point de seigneur de qui il peussent faire chevetaine, car touz les gentilz hommes du pays leur estoient failliz, et ne savoient de quel part le roy les devoit assaillir, ne de quel part il devoit à eulz venir.'

[32] See the *Chronique de Flandre*, I:344, 534.

[33] See the *Chronique Parisienne anonymé*, p. 118; *Grandes chroniques*, IX:82; *Récits d'un bourgeois de Valenciennes*, p. 150; and Willem Procurator, p. 222.

[34] Jean Froissart, II:218: 'Quant le chapitainne de ces Flamens, qui se nommoit Clais Dennequins, entendi que li rois de France, en sa nouvelle régnation, avoit juré que jamais il n'entreroit en Paris, ne entenderoit à aultre cose si averoit remis en Flandres le conte Loïs et confondus tous ses ennemis et nuisans, si s'enfellona grandement, et dist que chils rois poroit bien fallir à ses pourpos, et toutes fois pour lui brisier, il s'en meteroit en painne.' See Jacques Mertens, 'Zannekin of de evolutie van het beeld van een volksheld,' *De Frans Nederlanden. Les Pays-Bas Français* (1978), 24–37.

[35] See *Grandes chroniques*, IX:83–85; *Chronographia regum Francorum*, II:4–5; and *Chronique de Flandre*, I:343.

For three days the situation continued with little activity between the two armies. There were a few skirmishes, but these were small and ineffectual. According to the *Chronicon comitum Flandriae*, Philip also had brought or made a few artillery pieces which were used to try to harass the Flemish army, but these too had little effect.[36] Philip's army also pillaged and burned the land around Cassel, including the monastery of Wastina (although the *Chronicon comitum Flandriae* insists that Philip did not know of its destruction), and these fires were seen by the Flemings on the hill. This was done, claims the *Chronique de Flandre*, that 'by this they wished to draw the Flemings from the mountain.'[37]

The Flemings also tried to provoke their enemy to do battle during these three days. Several chroniclers report the Flemings trying to taunt the French. For example, the continuator of Guillaume de Nangis' chronicle reports that the Flemings 'for the purpose of deriding and mocking the army of the king and of all France,' raised a large dead cock on a colored spear and shouted that 'when this cock crows, the king will take Cassel.' He also reports that the Flemings mocked Philip VI's assumption of the French throne calling him an 'invented king.' This too was without effect as the French king held his ground below the Flemings and refused to fight against their well protected defensive order.[38]

It was the Flemish army which first decided to break from their defensive formation. Impatient in having received no reinforcements, irritated by the burning of their lands and the harassment of the French army, the Flemish troops had grown discouraged by their inaction. They decided to charge down the hill and attack the French. It was hoped that by surprising the French and perhaps even killing or capturing the king, the Flemings might be able to defeat them, or at least to stop the devastation around Cassel. To this end Nikolaas Zannekin spoke to his troops, an oration which the *Chronicon comitum Flandriae* recounts:

> Are we not strong men who have subjugated all of Flanders, and are we accustomed to fear no one? We are accustomed to fight no one more than the king of France, so that we might be able to humble his pride. And behold this king is before us with but a few men; let us attack him in our strength . . .

He was answered: 'Let us attack the king immediately!'[39]

---

[36] On the skirmishes between the French and Flemish armies before August 28 see *Grandes chroniques*, IX:85–86; *Chronographia regum Francorum*, II:5–6; and Richard Lescot, p. 6. On Philip's use of catapults see the *Chronicon comitum Flandriae*, p. 205.

[37] *Chronique de Flandre*, I:344: '. . . et par ce cuidèrent traire les Flamens jus de mont.' See also *Chronicon comitum Flandriae*, pp. 204–05; *Grandes chroniques*, IX:85–86; *Chronographia regum Francorum*, II:5–6; and Richard Lescot, p. 6.

[38] *Continuatio chronici* of Guillaume de Nangis, II:94–95: 'In dicto vero castro, in regis et totius Francorum exercitus derisum et subsannationem, in quodam eminenti loco posuerant Flammingi quemdam gallum permaximum de tela tincta, dicentes: "Quando gallus uste cantabit, rex Casselum capiet vi armorum." . . . Unde et subsannantes regi, dicebant eum et vocabant *Regem inventum*.' See also Richard Lescot, p. 6.

[39] *Chronicon comitum Flandriae*, p. 205: ' "Numquid non sumus nos viri fortes, qui nobis subegimus totam Flandriam, et neminem timere consuevimus? nullum magis solebamus appetere quam regem Francorum, ut ipsius superbiam humiliare possemus. Et ecce hic rex ante nos cum paucis: adeamus eum in fortitudine nostra. . ." "Tunc omnes acclamaverunt:" "Regem protinus invadamus." '

Thus, at the hottest part of the day, after the French had retired to their tents to rest, to play games, and to hold a war council, the Flemings swept down onto them and onto their king who, the continuator of Guillaume de Nangis maintains, was taking his 'accustomed nap.'[40] With an apparent sarcasm Gilles li Muisit describes the attack: 'The infantry attacked without noise and almost in silence. All had the intention of approaching the tents of the king and taking and killing him. They passed through many tents, killing and striking no one, and they did go silently.'[41]

The charge was initially effective in its surprise. After the battles of Courtrai and Mons-en-Pévèle, the French forces were accustomed to having the Flemish infantry hold its defensive position without an offensive attack. As the intended target of this attack, no one was more surprised than the king. In this the attack almost succeeded, for the Flemings nearly reached Philip. As the *Chronique de Flandre* recounts, the attackers reached the king's tent but were beaten back by his soldiers. Still, Philip was so shaken by the attack that he had difficulty arming himself, and he had to be assisted by his aides.[42] (Even the Pope knew of the threat to Philip's life, telling Philip that God had preserved the king's life 'so that you might know most certainly that the future victory would proceed from Him and that He might obligate you to his devotion.'[43])

Ultimately, however, the Flemish surprise attack failed. Although some of the French did flee, the attack did not defeat them, and soon they were able to regroup and form a counter-attack. Initially this counter-attack was led by Robert of Cassel – who had joined the main French force a few days previously – together with the marshals of the French army, Gaucher de Châtillon and Robert Bertrand, with later assistance by William of Hainault.[44] But, as soon as he was able to recover from his attack, the king himself entered the fray, and ultimately it was his presence that

---

[40] *Continuatio chronici* of Guillaume de Nangis, II:96–97. See also *Grandes chroniques*, IX:86–87; *Chronographia regum Francorum*, II:6–7; Jean Froissart, II:220; and *Récits d'un bourgeois de Valenciennes*, p. 150.

[41] Gilles le Muisit, p. 211: 'Quasi circa horam nonae, sine strepitu et quasi sub silentio, pedites omnes cum intentione accedendi ad sarcinas regis et ipsum capiendi vel occidendi, transierunt plura tentoria, neminem occidentes au concutientes, sed tacite ibant.'

[42] *Chronique de Flandre*, I:345. See also *Continuatio chronici* of Guillaume de Nangis, II:98; *Grandes chroniques*, IX:97; and *Chronographia regum Francorum*, II:7–8.

[43] John XXII, letter 2222: 'Sane, fili dilectissime, cum horrore quodam percepimus quod hostes ipsi usque ad tua tentoria . . . sed forsan permisit Altissimus ut certius cognosceres ab ipso futuram victoriam processisse teque ad suam devotionem ejusque beneplacita exequenda et artius evitanda que prohibuit, obligaret.' See also letter 2223.

[44] There is some dispute among contemporary writers as to who led the counter-attacks which defeated the Flemish surprise attack. Dutch chroniclers credit their count, William of Hainault and Holland, with the leadership of the counter-attacking troops. (See Willem Procurator, p. 223 and Jan Beke, p. 291.) This assessment is agreed to by the Liègeois Jean de Hocsem, p. 197. On the other hand, several French and Flemish sources see the counter-attacks led by Robert of Cassel and the French marshals, with William of Hainault's counter-attack coming later. (See *Chronographia regum Francorum*, II:7; *Grandes chroniques*, IX:336; and *Chronique de Flandre*, I:345.) Finally, the *Chronicon comitum Flandriae* (p. 205) claims that both Robert of Cassel and William of Hainault led counter-attacks. An interesting aside to this incident is the Tournaissien Gilles le Muisit's claim that it was the troops from Tournai who first saw the Flemish surprise attack and sounded the alarm (p. 211).

ensured victory. As the continuator of Guillaume de Nangis's *Chronicon* writes: 'And behold when the king was led down through the battle with his few, the whole army of knights, many fleeing the [Flemish] infantry, seeing the regal banners, all gathered to him.'[45]

After the unsuccessful surprise attack, the remnants of the Flemish army fell back into a crown formation to make a final defensive stand. But, according to the *Chronicon comitum Flandriae*, this maneuver was futile; the battle was effectively lost:

> But although in this order they resisted strongly and held themselves vigorously, this resistance profited them nothing since the leonine descendants of the Franks stabbed at them with lances wet with blood . . . Nevertheless, the Flemings in this resistance made a great slaughter of horses, and they strongly resisted the French because another exit for flight was not open to them, for they were surrounded on every side by knights.[46]

At the end of the battle the chroniclers report that the field was heaped high with dead rebels. Contemporary estimates of Flemish dead range from a low of 9,000 given by the *Chronicon comitum Flandriae* to a high of 22,000 recorded by the author of the *Chronique Parisienne anonymé*. Among the Flemish dead was Nikolaas Zannekin. No French casualty figures are given.[47] Hearing of the massacre at Cassel, the other two rebel armies quickly disbanded and returned to their homes hoping thereby to escape punishment.

Philip had defeated the rebellion and returned Louis of Nevers to his comital throne. At the same time, according to Guillaume de Nangis' continuator, Philip chastised Louis for being unable to keep the county peaceful. In a rather lengthy castigation, Philip cautioned the Flemish count to be just and to keep his lands at

---

45 *Continuatio chronici* of Guillaume de Nangis, II:98: 'Et ecce interim cum rex per divium cum suis paucis deducitur, visis regalibus insigniis totus exercitus, multis peditum fugientibus, ad eum quasi unus homo congregatur.'

46 *Chronicon comitum Flandriae*, pp. 205–06: 'Sed licet sic ordinati fortiter resisterent et vigorose se haberent, nihil tamen eis profuit haec resistentia, dum Francorum leonina progenies ipsos adeo lanceis cruore madentibus confoderet, quod ipsos vivere in tali perplexitate taederet. Faciebant nihilominus Flamingi in resistentia illa magnam stragem in equis, et viriliter resistebant Gallicis, eo quod non patebat eis aliquis exitus ad fugam ineundam: erant enim undique ab equitantibus circumclusi.'

47 These are the Flemish death totals as tallied by contemporary sources (from highest to lowest): 22,000+ (*Chronique Parisienne anonymé*, p. 119); 19,800 (*Grandes chroniques*, IX:90; Richard Lescot, p. 6); 16,000 (Jean le Bel, I:94); 15,000 (*Récits d'un bourgeois de Valenciennes*, pp. 151–52; Jean Froissart, II:222–23); 14,000 (*Gesta abbatum St. Trudoniensum*, p. 420); 12,000 (Gilles le Muisit, p. 211; *Chronographia regum Francorum*, II:9); 11,547 (*Continuatio chronici* of Guillaume de Nangis, II:99); 11,000 (*Chronique de Flandre*, I:357; *Rijmkroniek van Vlaenderen*, p. 823; *Chronique Normande*, p. 36); 10,000 (Jean de Hocsem, p. 197); and 9,000 (*Chronicon comitum Flandriae*, p. 206). The only chronicle which mentions the French dead is the *Chronique de Flandre*, and this chronicle notes only the names of a few slain knights without reporting a total calculation (I:346). As well, only Jean Froissart (II:217) and the *Grandes chroniques* (IX:88–89) call attention to Zannekin's death.

peace so that the French troops would not need to return. For if he was forced to do so, Philip is reported to have said, 'I will return not for your but for my utility.'[48]

To many modern historians, the battle of Cassel is a vindication of cavalry warfare in the early fourteenth century. Sir Charles Oman, for one, believed that the victory at Cassel confirmed the strength of the cavalry-based army against its infantry enemy, reaffirming his opinion that the Flemish infantry victory over the French cavalry at Courtrai was but an 'accident.'[49] Edouard Perroy agreed, noting that the French victory at Cassel was 'a fitting sequel to that [battlefield] on which the 'golden spurs' had been defeated.'[50] At least one contemporary chronicler agrees with this modern opinion. The anonymous author of the *Chronique Parisienne anonymé*, referring to the earlier French victory over the Flemings at Bouvines (in 1214) writes:

> But our Lord Jesus Christ, merciful to and full of pity for the king of France and his troops, as he otherwise had been in the battle against Ferrand of Flanders and others, did not allow the Flemings to hold on longer to their iniquities.[51]

But can this battle be dismissed as a simple case of knight over foot, one which affirms the continued success of mounted shock combat? Certainly it appears that before the battle the Flemings had carried on their fourteenth-century military tradition. They chose a defensive position, and while they did nothing to prepare the ground for a cavalry assault as they had at Courtrai and Mons-en-Pévèle, the choice of a hilltop for their infantry line provided suitable terrain to defeat any charge by opposing knights. Furthermore, for three days they waited for this attack, continually taunting the French in the hopes of drawing the knights into one of their accustomed wild and disordered charges. This is all attested to by the author of the *Grandes chroniques* who insists that the Flemings had realized that an offensive attack against the French would be ineffective and thus had consequently chosen their defensive positions at Cassel.[52]

Moreover, the attitude of Philip VI in initially encountering the Flemish army was to respect their defensive positioning and not to make what would have been a suicidal charge. He had no intention of repeating the mistakes made by Robert of

---

[48] *Continuatio chronici* of Guillaume de Nangis, II:101–02: 'Tota vero Flandria jam quasi quietata et sub obedientia regis posita, rex in praesentia baronum convocari fecit coram se comitem Flandriae, cui fertur sic dixisse: "Comes, ad requestam vestram huc veni, et forte quia negligens fuistis de justitia facienda. Ut tamen vos scitis, venire non potui sine mei et meorum maximis expensis et laboribus. Ecce de liberalitate totam terram vestram quietam et pacificam vobis restituo, expensas condono; sed de caetero caveatis ne propter defectum justitiae oporteat me redire, scientes quod si ob defectum vestrum rediero, non ad vestram sed ad meam utilitatem redibo." '

[49] Oman, I:118. This same opinion was repeated as late as the 1989 Annual Meeting of the American Historical Association in a paper delivered by Franklin J. Pegues entitled 'Cavalry and the Feudal Aristocracy in Thirteenth- and Fourteenth-Century England and France.'

[50] Perroy, p.81.

[51] *Chronique Parisienne anonymé*, pp. 120–21: 'Maiz Nostre Seigneur Jhesuchrist, misericord et piteable au roy de France et ès siens, comme aultrefoiz à este au fait de Ferrant de Flandrez et allieurs, ne souffry pas les iniquitez dez Flamens plus à tenir.'

[52] *Grandes chroniques*, IX:82.

Artois at Courtrai, Jacques of Bayonne at Arques, Aymer de Valence at Loudon Hill, Walter of Brienne at Kephissos, Edward II at Bannockburn, and Thomas of Lancaster at Bouroughbridge. Instead of attacking the Flemish infantry with his knights, he chose essentially to besiege their camp, hoping to provoke them into breaking their defensive order. This he accomplished by continually harassing the Flemings with skirmishes and artillery combined with the burning and pillaging of the lands surrounding the hill. In this the Flemish defensive position worked to their disadvantage. Being the only high ground for miles around, the hill at Cassel gave the Flemings an unhindered view of this destruction, and many whose homes and families were nearby must have felt concern for them. Ultimately, this resulted in the surprise attack which led to the demise of the Flemish infantry.

When the Flemish attack finally came, it proved to be less of a surprise than intimated by contemporary chroniclers. Although the attack seemed to have caught some of the French by surprise, including Philip VI, the fact that a counter-attack followed so quickly with the participation of such high-ranking lieutenants as Robert of Cassel, William of Hainault, and the two French marshals, Gaucher de Châtillon and Robert Bertrand, seems to indicate that at least part of the army was on alert for just such an occurrence. Moreover, the Flemish attack was rash and disorganized. The *Chronique Parisienne anonymé* recalls the stupidity of the surprise attack: '. . . around 20,000 Flemings, all inflamed by battle, in their fool-hardiness . . . descended from the hill.'[53] What began then as a Flemish instigated surprise attack turned quickly into a French cavalry charge which easily defeated a disordered and poorly led infantry.

Once the infantry did recover, reforming their defensive 'crown' formation on the hill, although apparently not on the hilltop as before the attack, they had some success against the French knights. But their numbers had now been so diminished and they were so demoralized that the French eventually defeated even that formation.

Perhaps then it is inaccurate to credit the cavalry with this victory, as Oman and Perroy have done; it may be more precise instead to blame the infantry for their own defeat. Had they not broken from their defensive position into a confused and disordered attack, Philip VI probably would not have attacked them. As he showed later in attempting to raise the sieges at Tournai in 1340 and at Calais in 1347, Philip was prepared to set up camp in the sight of the Flemings without encountering them in battle. As in those struggles, he would have waited at Cassel until the conflict was solved by diplomacy; he would not have risked what might have resulted in at least a large number of casualties if not a defeat.[54] In this case, the inexperienced Flemings

---

[53] *Chronique Parisienne anonymé*, p. 118: '. . . XXm Flamens ou environ, tous enflambez de batailler, par leur fol hardement, non pourveuz de conseil . . . descendirent aval la montaigne.' Some modern authors have agreed that this ill-advised charge led to the defeat of the Flemings. See Rompaey, p. 123; Lot, I:276; Verbruggen, *Krijgkunst*, pp. 111, 295; and Verbruggen, 'Historiographie,' p. 248.

[54] At the siege of Tournai in 1340 the presence of a large French army within sight of the allied force (English, Flemish, Brabantese and Hainaulter), coupled with the peace efforts made by Jeanne de Valois, eventually caused Jean III, duke of Brabant, to desert his allies and the siege failed. At Calais in 1347 Philip VI was not so lucky. Despite the peacemaking attempts of two papal legates, the English army refused to raise its siege. Unable to fight the large English force, Philip returned to France without

changed the tactics which had afforded them victory at Courtrai. They allowed themselves to be drawn into a battle which they could not win, where cavalry did indeed triumph over infantry.

a victory, and Calais fell to the English. See my 'Contemporary Views of Edward III's Failure at the Siege of Tournai, 1340,' *Nottingham Medieval Studies* (forthcoming) and 'Hunger, Flemish Participation and the Flight of Philip VI: Contemporary Accounts of the Siege of Calais, 1346–47,' *Studies in Medieval and Renaissance History* n.s 12 (1991), 129–81.

IX

THE BATTLES OF DUPPLIN MOOR, 1332, AND HALIDON HILL, 1333

IN JANUARY 1327, after a reign fraught with military defeats, like that at Bannock-burn, and baronial revolution, like that ending at Boroughbridge, Edward II was deposed. He was succeeded by his fourteen year old son, Edward III; but because of the new king's youth, the power in England was held by Edward III's mother, Isabella, and her lover, Roger Mortimer.[1]

For Scotland, the deposition of Edward II presented some problems, but also some opportunities. At the least, it meant that the treaty signed between the deposed king and Robert Bruce in 1323, which recognized Bruce's rule and Scottish sovereignty, was threatened.[2] At the most, it meant a possible invasion of Scotland by an English army. Robert Bruce himself was old and ill. Unwilling to risk his throne or his country, and desiring to take advantage of the confusion caused by the deposition of Edward II and the youth of Edward III, Bruce determined to take the offensive against the English. On February 1, 1327, the day of Edward III's coronation, Bruce's army entered the English border counties of Durham and Northumberland and began besieging Norham Castle and raiding the countryside.[3]

An English army, led by Mortimer and the young king, travelled north to intercept the Scottish force, but the campaign, known as the Weardale Campaign, met with absolute failure. The English troops did cause the Scots to break off their siege of Norham, but they were unable to capture or defeat Bruce's army. In what is recorded as one of the most disastrous military expeditions ever attempted, the heavier English knights were unable either to catch up with their lighter Scottish foes or to provoke them to do battle. The English supply train bogged down in the wet northern countryside, the supplies of bread carried by each English knight became inedible after being soaked with their horses' sweat, and the accompanying Hainaulter mercenary force became agitated and left the campaign. By August the English were forced to return home, fatigued and bankrupt, and without even a minor victory over the Scots to buoy their spirits.[4]

---

1 On the deposition of Edward II see N. Fryde, pp. 195–206; McKisack, pp. 84–94; Michael Packe, *King Edward III* (London, 1983), pp. 23–31; and M.V. Clarke and V.H. Galbraith, 'The Deposition of Edward II,' *Bulletin of the John Rylands Library* 14 (1930), 125–81.
2 See Barrow, pp. 251–52 and Prestwich, *Three Edwards*, p. 57.
3 See Barrow, pp. 251–52 and Nicholson, *Scotland*, p. 118.
4 On the Weardale Campaign see Ranald Nicholson, *Edward III and the Scots: The Formative Years*

To prevent further attacks of the Scots on England, Isabella and Mortimer were forced to negotiate the Treaty of Northampton with Robert Bruce. It was signed in the name of Edward III on March 1, 1328. The 'shameful peace,' as it is now known, acknowledged Bruce's rights as king and arranged the marriage between his very young heir, David, and Edward's sister, Joan. The English renounced all claims over Scotland, and in turn the Scots agreed to pay £20,000 to cover the costs of lost lands and possessions.[5] To the Scots the Treaty of Northampton was the final victorious act in the heroic life of Robert Bruce. To the English the treaty was cowardly and treasonous; Edward III even refused to attend the wedding of his sister and David Bruce.[6]

Robert Bruce died on June 7, 1329. He was succeeded by his son, David. However, David was only five years old, and, as had been the case with Edward III, his minority caused confusion which ultimately led to an attempt to unseat him as king.[7] This was not at the hands of Edward III, however, as he was still 'formally' bound by the Treaty of Northampton. Instead, the threat to David's throne came from a group of men who had unsatisfied claims in Scotland. Known as 'the disinherited,' these men supported the royal claim of Edward Balliol, the son of John Balliol, the Scottish king who had been forced from the throne in 1297. As well as Edward Balliol, they included David of Strathbogie (claimant to the earldom of Atholl), Gilbert Umfraville (claimant to the earldom of Angus), Richard Talbot, Ralph Stafford, Henry Ferrers, Alexander and John Mowbray, and, perhaps most importantly, the rich and powerful Henry of Beaumont (claimant to the earldom of Buchan). Their plan was to take an army into Scotland, to seize their lost lands and titles, and to secure the throne for Balliol.[8]

Although Edward III did not openly support the disinherited, it is clear that their designs presented the English king with a 'no-lose situation.' By being cautious and by withholding his open permission of their expedition, Edward would be honoring the treaty which had been made with Robert Bruce. At the same time, if the disinherited were successful in their military venture, Edward would be willing to accept and to profit from the crowning of Edward Balliol.[9]

By 1332 the disinherited were ready to undertake their conquest. They had raised money for the expedition by leasing their English lands and by obtaining an advance from the Archbishop of York who favored the defeat of David Bruce. They had also raised an army of nearly 1,500 soldiers. With this small force the disinherited set sail for Scotland on July 31. They landed, and after fighting a small battle on the beaches

---

of a Military Campaign (Oxford, 1965), pp. 21–41; Barrow, pp. 252–55; Nicholson, *Scotland*, pp. 118–19; Fryde, pp. 210–13; McKisack, pp. 98–100; Keen, p. 17; and Packe, pp. 34–38.

[5] On the Treaty of Northampton see Nicholson, *Edward III*, pp. 42–56; Barrow, pp. 255–60; Nicholson, *Scotland*, pp. 119–20; McKisack, pp. 98–99; Keen, pp. 77–78, 106; Prestwich, p. 58; and Packe, p. 40.

[6] On the English disapproval of the Treaty of Northampton see Nicholson, *Edward III*, pp. 54–56; Nicholson, *Scotland*, p. 121; and McKisack, p. 115.

[7] On the death of Robert Bruce and the inheritance of David see Barrow, pp. 322–24; Nicholson, *Scotland*, p. 122; McKisack, p. 115; and Keen, p. 107.

[8] On the names of the prominent disinherited and their claims in Scotland see Nicholson, *Edward III*, pp. 57–74; Nicholson, *Scotland*, pp. 124–25; and Packe, pp. 65–66.

[9] See Nicholson, *Edward III*, pp. 75–79 and McKisack, p. 116.

near Kinghorn they proceeded inland towards Perth.[10] On August 11, the disinherited met a much larger Scottish army at Dupplin Moor. The battle was long and bloody, but the disinherited prevailed, chasing the Scots from the field. A few days later they occupied Perth, and on September 24, Edward Balliol was crowned king of Scotland at the traditional coronation site of Scone.[11]

Edward III, who had moved to York to keep an eye on the events occurring in Scotland, was pleased with Balliol's victory.[12] Surprised by the results at the battle of Dupplin Moor, he was nevertheless fully supportive of the new king, receiving his homage in November 1332. However, Balliol's rule at this time was to be short-lived. While he had defeated a large Scottish army at Dupplin Moor, the main Scottish force, under the leadership of Andrew, Earl of Moray, and Sir Archibald Douglas, which supported the kingship of David Bruce, was still active and gathering numbers.[13] Balliol himself was attacked and nearly killed on December 17 and was forced to flee south to York and Edward III's protection.

Edward III was now compelled, by his acceptance of Balliol's homage, to embrace openly the leader of the disinherited. He outfitted Balliol with an English force, and the erstwhile Scottish king travelled north in March 1333 to besiege Berwick Castle, a major Scottish stronghold. Edward III joined him there two months later.[14]

It is clear from the events at Berwick that Edward III did not care about the fall of the castle itself. The English king did not wish to repeat the 1327 campaign in which the elusive Scottish army had continually frustrated English attempts to bring them to the battlefield; he had to force Moray and Douglas to fight his army. He was confident that he could defeat a Scottish force, having learned from Balliol how such a task had been accomplished at Dupplin Moor. Therefore, he negotiated for the surrender of Berwick unless the Scottish army would come to save it by July 11. He even took hostages to ensure that this would occur. However, the Scottish army did not want to come to battle against the English king. They too knew of their fallibility which had been evidenced at Dupplin Moor, and thus they tried another tactic to raise the siege of Berwick: they attacked Northumberland and even laid siege to Bamburgh castle, where Edward's queen, Philippa of Hainault, was in residence. But Edward III refused to be kept from his battle, and he began hanging the hostages on a gallows built outside Berwick, beginning with Thomas Seton, whose father, Sir Alexander Seton, was in command of the castle. In response, the Scottish army marched north to meet the English in battle.[15] It was fought near Berwick, at Halidon

---

[10] See Nicholson, *Edward III*, pp. 79–82.

[11] On the occupation of Perth see Nicholson, *Edward III*, pp. 91–92 and McKisack, p. 116. On the crowning of Balliol at Scone see Nicholson, *Edward III*, pp. 92–94; Nicholson, *Scotland*, pp. 126–27; and McKisack, p. 116.

[12] See McKisack, p. 117 and Keen, p. 108.

[13] On David Bruce's support in Scotland after the battle of Dupplin Moor see Nicholson, *Edward III*, pp. 94–104; Nicholson, *Scotland*, p. 127; McKisack, p. 117; Packe, pp. 68–69; and Jonathan Sumption, *The Hundred Years War: Trial by Battle* (Philadelphia, 1991), pp. 126–28.

[14] See Nicholson, *Edward III*, pp. 119–23; Nicholson, *Scotland*, p. 128; and Packe, p. 69.

[15] On the siege of Berwick see Ranald Nicholson, 'The Siege of Berwick, 1333,' *Scottish Historical Review* 40 (1961), 19–42 and Nicholson, *Edward III*, pp. 123–29. This was, it seems, the same

Hill, on July 19. The result was the same as that at Dupplin Moor: the English soundly defeated their more numerous Scottish foes.

A few days later Berwick surrendered, and Balliol soon had pacified the rest of the kingdom. David Bruce was forced to flee to France with several of his supporters where he was granted asylum by Philip VI, whose allegiance to the defeated king was based solely on his own fear of English invasion. Edward III again accepted Balliol as king, but at the price of a large tract of land in southern Scotland.[16] However, Balliol was an ineffective ruler, and by the end of 1334 Edward III was forced to return to assist his ally. He would return again in 1335, 1336, and 1337.[17]

There are many original sources which discuss the battles of Dupplin Moor and Halidon Hill, and from them a fairly good understanding of what actually occurred on the battlefield can be determined. The English sources include many authors who recorded the battles of Bannockburn and Boroughbridge. And while John Barbour's *Bruce* ends with the death of Robert Bruce, other Scottish chronicles, John Fordun's *Chronica gentis Scotorum*, Andrew of Wyntoun's *The Orygynale Cronykil of Scotland* and the *Liber Pluscardensis*, all written in the late fourteenth and early fifteenth centuries, provide accounts of the battles of Dupplin Moor and Halidon Hill from the Scottish perspective. As well as these sources, there are also two poems written on the battle of Halidon Hill, one by Laurence Minot and the other by an anonymous author, and a letter written on July 22, 1333 by Edward III to William of Melton, the archbishop of York, delineating why the young king felt that they had won the battle of Halidon Hill. However, these last sources contain little about the battle itself, concentrating instead on the role played by God and Scottish pride in the English victory.[18]

Nearly all original sources begin their discussion of the battle of Dupplin Moor with a description of the disinherited army gathered by Edward Balliol. Although the numbers of the troops differ, from a low of five hundred found in the *Liber Pluscardensis* to a high of 3,300 found in Henry Knighton's *Chronicon*,[19] most describe the troops as a united body of confident warriors determined to regain their

---

Alexander Seton who defected from the English to the Scots before the second day of battle at Bannockburn.

[16] See Nicholson, *Edward III*, pp. 139–62; Nicholson, *Scotland*, pp. 129–30; and Prestwich, p. 60.

[17] See Nicholson, *Edward III*, pp. 163–236; Nicholson, *Scotland*, pp. 130–35; and Keen, pp. 109–10.

[18] Laurence Minot's poem is found in Minot, pp. 1–4. The anonymous poem is found in Minot, pp. 95–97 and *The Brut*, I:287–89. Edward III's letter is found in *Gesta Edwardi de Carnarvan*, pp. 116–18 and in Thomas Rymer, ed., *Foedera, conventiones, litterae, et cujuscunque generis acta publica inter reges Angliae et alios quosvis imperatores, reges, pontifices, principes, vel communitates (1101–1654)* (London, 1704–35), II:866.

[19] The numbers for Balliol's army are (from lowest to highest): 500 (*Liber Pluscardensis*, I:264); 1,500 (*Gesta Edwardi de Carnarvan*, p. 106; *Chronicon de Lanercost*, p. 268; Thomas of Burton, II:362; Andrew of Wyntoun, II:382–83; Adam Murimuth, p. 66); 2,500 (Thomas Walsingham, I:193; *The Brut*, I:275; the continuator of Walter of Guisborough, II:303); and 3,300 (Henry Knighton, I:461–62). Modern historians number the force at 1,500. See Oman, II:102 and Nicholson, *Edward III*, pp. 80–81.

lost possessions.[20] They are depicted as a 'confederatyown' by Andrew of Wyntoun[21] and as a 'small army of English soldiers' by the *Chronicon de Lanercost*.[22] On the other hand, the *Anonimalle Chronicle* describes the troops as 'a great army . . . with a great force of Englishmen.'[23] According to Robert of Avesbury, it was an army of 'strong men,' composed of some knights and archers, but mostly simple infantry soldiers.[24] However many were present, the number of disinherited was still quite small in comparison to the number of enemy soldiers which they could expect to encounter in Scotland. As the *Chronicon de Lanercost* exclaims: 'Oh what a small number of soldiers was there for the invasion of a realm then most confident in its strength.'[25]

Without the permission of Edward III, the disinherited sailed for Scotland planning to land at Kinghorn and then to march to Perth.[26] However, the Scots became aware of their intentions and planned to keep them from landing. Their army, led by Duncan, the earl of Fife, and numbering between 4,000 and 24,000, according to the English sources,[27] attempted to stop the disinherited from landing in Scotland. However, Edward Balliol's force prevailed in this small engagement, killing a number of Scots and chasing the rest from the battlefield.[28] This was the first of many unexpected events, one which shamed the earl of Fife who, *The Brut* reports, 'although amazed

---

20 On the disinherited's reasons for going to Scotland see Henry Knighton, I:401; Geoffrey le Baker, p. 49; and Adam Murimuth, p. 66.

21 Andrew of Wyntoun, II:382.

22 *Chronicon de Lanercost*, p. 267.

23 *The Anonimalle Chronicle, 1307 to 1334*, pp. 146–47: '. . . ove grant ost et ove grant poer des Engleis . . .'

24 Robert of Avesbury, p. 296. See also Geoffrey le Baker, p. 49 and *Gesta Edwardi de Carnarvan*, p. 111.

25 *Chronicon de Lanercost*, p. 267: 'O quam parvus numerus bellatorum fuit iste ad invadendum unum regnum de suis viribus plurimum tunc confidens!'

26 On Balliol's trip to Edward III see Robert of Avesbury, p. 296; Thomas of Burton, II:362; Geoffrey le Baker, p. 49; Adam Murimuth, p. 66; and *The Brut*, I:275. All except for *The Brut* insist that Edward III did not grant permission to Balliol for this expedition. The *Anonimalle Chronicle*, while not describing Balliol's trip to Edward, nevertheless insists that it was because 'he did not wish to infringe or disturb the peace arranged between him and those of Scotland' that he refused to allow the disinherited to travel through England to Scotland, thus necessitating their sea travel (pp. 148–49).

27 See *Gesta Edwardi de Carnarvan*, p. 104; Henry Knighton, II:462; Thomas Walsingham, I:193; Thomas of Burton, II:363; Adam Murimuth, p. 66; and Andrew of Wyntoun, II:384. Estimates of Scottish strength at Kinghorn are (from lowest to highest): 4,000 (*Chronicon de Lanercost*, p. 267); 10,000 (*Anonimalle Chronicle*, pp. 148–49; Henry Knighton, II:462; Thomas Walsingham, I:193; the continuator of Walter of Guisborough, II:304; *The Brut*, I:275–76); 14,000 (Thomas of Burton, II:363); and 24,000 (*Gesta Edwardi de Carnarvan*, p. 104). However, the two Scottish sources who mention the fighting at Kinghorn, the *Liber Pluscardensis* (I:265) and John Fordun (I:354), refer to the size of the Scottish army only as a 'few.' Modern historians have avoided making an estimate of this army's size. See Nicholson, *Edward III*, p. 83.

28 Although John Fordun (I:354) insists that only three or four Scots were killed in this engagement, several English chroniclers insist a much larger number were slain there: 90 (the continuator of Walter of Guisborough, II:304); 900 (*Anonimalle Chronicle*, pp. 148–49; Thomas of Burton, II:363); and 1,000 (Thomas of Walsingham, I:193).

Battle of Dupplin Moor

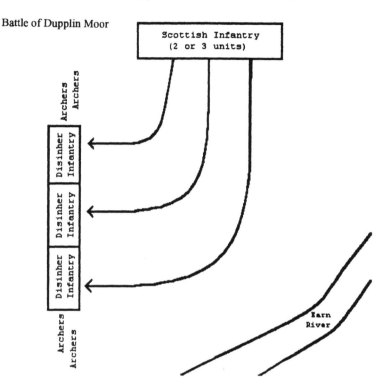

at what had occurred, was sorry and full of shame, because such a small company had defeated him.'[29]

From Kinghorn Balliol marched west to Dumferline where he replenished his food supplies and weapons. Unable to rest for fear of Scottish action against them, the disinherited army quickly continued their march north to Perth.[30] At the Earn river the Scots again tried to stop them, but as at Kinghorn Balliol's force prevailed, and they crossed the river.[31]

As they crossed the Earn, the disinherited army could see a large Scottish army gathered not too far in the distance at Dupplin Moor, an army described by *The Brut* as 'many warriors well outfitted for war.'[32] As the *Anonimalle Chronicle* notes: 'some

---

[29] *The Brut*, I:276: '. . . was þo wonder sory, and ful evel shamede þat so litil company hade him descomfitede.'

[30] See *Anonimalle Chronicle*, pp. 148–49 and *The Brut*, I:276–77.

[31] *Chronicon de Lanercost*, pp. 267–68; Thomas of Burton, II:363; and *Liber Pluscardensis*, I:265–66. The *Liber Pluscardensis* contains a rather curious story of Balliol's army at the Earn river. This anonymous chronicler claims that the disinherited were initially kept from crossing the river by the Scots. However, during the night of August 10–11 Balliol was shown a ford across the river by the lord of Gask, and he was able to cross it, surprise the Scots (who had placed no night sentries to prohibit a night crossing), and fight the battle of Dupplin Moor. The other sources contain no reference to the ford or to the lord of Gask's leading Balliol to it.

[32] *The Brut*, I:277.

of our people were greatly dejected by the small number of their forces.'[33] The Scots had chosen Dupplin Moor as the battlefield, although there appears to have been no particular reason for this choice, and they had gathered there a large army, between 20,000 and 40,000 in number according to contemporary sources, almost all of whom were infantry soldiers.[34] Most contemporary authors maintain that the Scots were prepared for the eventual battle. If nothing else, like the disinherited, they too could see their opponents as they crossed the Earn, and as they observed the smaller force which was coming against them – the disinherited army's numbers had changed very little since their landing at Kinghorn – they grew in confidence because of their own much larger numbers.[35] During the night before the battle, however, the *Anonimalle Chronicle* indicates that the disinherited moved stealthily onto the battlefield, taking over the moor to the left of the Scottish troops. So surprised were the Scots the next morning that they 'marvelled at the manner in which the English had thus taken over the moor.'[36] This may be the origin of the *Liber Pluscardensis*'s belief that the Scots were surprised at the arrival of the disinherited; the anonymous author of this chronicle claims that 'some were asleep, some unarmed, enjoying themselves and playing and drinking and making merry.'[37]

The Scots ordered their army in either two or three divisions.[38] Opposing them was a force which would also fight on foot, except for a contingent of 40–44 German mercenaries who remained on horseback.[39] The disinherited infantry formed three

---

[33] *Anonimalle Chronicle*, pp. 148–49: 'et aucuns de noz gentz furent grantment descounfortez pur la petit quantite des gentz.'

[34] On the Scottish arrival at the battlefield see *Anonimalle Chronicle*, pp. 148–49; Thomas Walsingham, I:194; and the continuator of Walter of Guisborough, II:304. Contemporary chroniclers record the numbers in the Scottish army as: 20,000 (Robert of Avesbury, p. 297); 30,000 (*Chronicon de Lanercost*, p. 267; *Liber Pluscardensis*, I:265; Andrew of Wyntoun, II:385); and 40,000 (*Anonimalle Chronicle*, pp. 148–49; *Gesta Edwardi de Carnarvan*, p. 106; Geoffrey le Baker, p. 49; Henry Knighton, I:462; Thomas of Burton, II:363; Thomas Walsingham, I:193–94; and the continuator of Walter of Guisborough, II:303–04). Because of the disparity of numbers given by the original sources, modern historians do not attempt to give an estimate of the Scottish numbers here. See Oman, II:102 and Nicholson, *Edward III*, pp. 84–85.

[35] On Scottish morale before the battle see *Liber Pluscardensis*, I:265–66. The *Anonimalle Chronicle* insists that the English could easily see the Scottish troops, observing them for an entire day before approaching for battle (pp. 148–49).

[36] *Anonimalle Chronicle*, pp. 148–49: 'Et les Escoz se merveillerent coment les Engleis avoient issint purpris la more.'

[37] *Liber Pluscardensis*, I:266.

[38] The three sources which discuss the Scottish formation at Dupplin Moor all differ on the number of lines in the formation and where they were placed on the battlefield. The *Chronicon de Lanercost* (p. 268) contends that there were two Scottish lines, while *The Brut* (I:277) claims that there were three lines. Both agree that these lines were ordered in front of the disinherited. Andrew of Wyntoun agrees with the Lanercost chronicler on the number of lines, but he believes that one was placed in front of the disinherited army while the other were ordered to the rear, in effect surrounding Balliol's army (II:386).

[39] All chroniclers, English and Scottish, record that the disinherited fought on foot. On the forty mounted German mercenaries see *Anonimalle Chronicle*, pp. 150–51; Henry Knighton, I:462; and the continuator of Walter of Guisborough, II:304. Thomas Walsingham (I:194) also notes the presence of the German mercenaries, but reports their number to be forty-four instead of forty.

solid lines flanked on both sides by a relatively large number of longbowmen.[40] Their morale was also high, despite their obviously smaller numbers. In fact, as Andrew of Wyntoun notes, the disinherited army's morale may have been strong because they were trapped between the river and the Scottish army, 'as fysch in [a] net;' thus unable to flee, they became determined to fight and to win.[41] Their morale also grew with battlefield orations delivered by Edward Balliol and John Burdon who promised them victory.[42]

The Scots made the first charge. Confident in their overwhelming numbers and, claiming, according to the *Liber Pluscardensis*, that 'they would drag the tailed English by the tail and hang them,'[43] they assaulted the disinherited order, rushing past the archers and striking their dismounted opponents. Initially, this charge was effective. The *Chronicon de Lanercost* recounts what occurred: 'Moreover, in the first onset, when the English and Scots were fighting with their spears firmly fixed against each other, the Scots drove back the English some twenty or thirty feet.'[44] However, the English did not flee, but held their position, and spurred on by the encouragement of Ralph Stafford, the earl of Stafford, who shouted 'You English! Turn your shoulders instead of your breasts to the pikes,' the disinherited began to regain their position and to push back the Scots.[45]

The infantry was greatly aided by the archers on their flanks. It seems that most of the Scottish soldiers either wore no helmets or helmets unequipped with visors, and that the disinherited archers, in the words of the *Chronicon de Lanercost*, 'blinded and wounded the faces of the first division of the Scots by an incessant discharge of arrows.'[46] This may have caused little death, but in fact it so disrupted the Scots that their attacks fell on the infantry with disarray and confusion. Thomas of Burton describes this part of the fighting: 'The smaller squadrons, so cut by the archers, were forced to cling to the larger army, and in a short time, the Scots massing together were pressed one into the other.'[47]

The battle lasted from sunrise into the afternoon as the two infantry armies pushed

---

[40] On the formation of the disinherited troops see *The Brut*, I:278. On the ordering of archers along the wings of the infantry see Thomas of Burton, II:364.
[41] Andrew of Wyntoun, II:386.
[42] See Thomas of Burton, II:364 and *The Brut*, I:277–78.
[43] *Liber Pluscardensis*, I:265: '. . . videntes dictum Edwardum tam paucos in exercitu suo habentem, se stolide ex utraque parte in eorum multitudine gloriati sunt, dicentes quod Anglicos caudatos per eorum caudas ad suspendium traherent.'
[44] *Chronicon de Lanercost*, p. 268: 'In primo tamen congressu, quando Anglici et Scotti, fixis in alterutrum lanceis, confligebant, Scotti repellebant Anglicos quasi per viginti pedes vel triginta . . .' See also Thomas of Burton, II:364 and Andrew of Wyntoun, II:388.
[45] *Chronicon de Lanercost*, p. 268: '. . . et tunc clamabat baro de Stafforde, "vos Angli vertatis contra lanceas vestros humeros et non pectus." ' See also Andrew of Wyntoun, II:388 and Thomas of Burton, II:364.
[46] *Chronicon de Lanercost*, p. 268: '. . . victi sunt Scotti maxime per sagittarios Anglicorum, qui primam aciem Scottorum ita excaecaverunt et vulneraverunt in facie continuis ictibus saggitarum quod non poterant se juvare . . .'
[47] See Thomas of Burton, II:364: 'Minores vero turmae, per sagittarios nimium laceratae, adhaerere magno exercitui compelluntur, et in brevi Scotti conglobati alius ab alio premebatur.'

each other back and forth.[48] Eventually, the disinherited soldiers began to dominate their opponents, both because of the unity of their defensive formation and because of their attendant archery fire which continued to harass the flanks and rear of the Scots. Soon the disheartened Scottish leaders, seeing their armies on the verge of defeat, mounted their horses and fled the battlefield.[49] Their troops, for the most part, were unable to follow. Many were so embroiled in the conflict that they continued to fight, but by now the disinherited had begun a steady uniform advance against the disorganized and now leaderless Scots. Ultimately, this ended the battle, as the remaining Scottish soldiers either fled or were killed.[50]

In the words of John Fordun, the Scots 'perished in a no less astounding than unhappy massacre.'[51] The Scottish dead numbered in the thousands, described by most authors as a pile of corpses measuring more than a spear's length high.[52] Many had died not of wounds but of suffocation, having been crushed under the feet of both armies' soldiers. As the anonymous author of the *Liber Pluscardensis* writes: 'more died by being smothered than by the sword, falling one upon another in such numbers that so sad a catastrophe is not recorded to have happened for a very long time.'[53] They were buried in a very large and deep ditch.[54]

The English losses were much smaller, numbering only two knights and thirty-three soldiers, but according to the *Anonimalle Chronicle*, 'no archer nor any footman.'[55] It is recorded that they were buried at Edward III's own expense.

The battle of Dupplin Moor was followed less than a year later by the battle of Halidon Hill. At this battle Edward Balliol and the disinherited were joined by Edward III and the 'official' English army. In considering the battle of Halidon Hill, most sources begin by discussing Edward III's decision to attack Scotland, defending this decision despite the treaty which bound the English king to respect the sovereignty of David Bruce. The treaty with Bruce had been signed when Edward III was a minor and under the control of his domineering mother. Furthermore, Edward Balliol was in fact the just king of Scotland, his father having been forced to relinquish his throne at the point of a sword wielded by two 'Jacobin' friars. Finally,

---

48 Robert of Avesbury (p. 296), Henry of Knighton (I:463), John Fordun (I:354–55), the continuator of Walter of Guisborough (II:304), and the *Liber Pluscardensis* (I:265) all agree that the battle began at dawn and continued for most of the day. However, they all disagree about when in the afternoon it was concluded.
49 See Thomas of Burton, II:364.
50 See Henry Knighton, I:463.
51 John Fordun, I:347: ' . . . non minus morte stupenda, quam infelici perierunt . . .'
52 See *Chronicon de Lanercost*, p. 268; Robert of Avesbury, p. 297; Thomas of Burton, II:364; Thomas Walsingham, I:194; the continuator of Walter of Guisborough, II:304–05; and *The Brut*, I:279. On the numbers of Scots killed at Dupplin Moor see *Anonimalle Chronicle*, pp. 150–51; *Chronicon de Lanercost*, p. 268; Thomas Walsingham, I:194; John Fordun, I:355; and Andrew of Wyntoun, II:388.
53 *Liber Pluscardensis*, I:266: ' . . . plures suffocacione quam gladio interierunt, unus super alium incidentes, in tali multitudine quod tam dolorosus casus a multis retroactis temporibus in cronicis non legitur accidisse.' See also Thomas Walsingham, I:194; the continuator of Walter of Guisborough, II:304–05; and Andrew of Wyntoun, II:388.
54 See Thomas Walsingham, I:194.
55 See *Anonimalle Chronicle*, pp. 150–51; *Chronicon de Lanercost*, p. 269; Henry Knighton, I:463; Thomas of Burton, II:364–65; the continuator of Walter of Guisborough, II:304; and *The Brut*, I:278.

Edward III's northern province of Northumberland had suffered constant raids and invasions by Scottish troops, actions which clearly violated the Anglo-Scottish treaty.[56]

Thus, Edward III traveled north with a large force and began his siege of Berwick. The siege itself is of great interest to most contemporary sources, many of whom outline all of the events which occurred there: the laying of the siege, the stubbornness of the besieged, the continual negotiations for raising the siege, Edward III's taking of hostages, and the eventual execution of Thomas Seton.[57] However, it is clear in these sources that the siege by itself was not important. Edward undoubtedly wished to fight a battle against the Scottish army, and he was using the siege of Berwick only to draw the Scots into a military conflict.[58] He even promised the Scots safe and unhindered passage until they arrived at Berwick to fight with the English.[59] The Scots, on the other hand, did not want to fight against the English King. Instead, they tried to draw Edward from Berwick by raiding Northumberland and besieging the castle at Bamburgh.[60] This tactic did not work, and the Scottish army was soon forced to respond to the English challenge.

The Scots decided not to attack the English at Berwick, determining to fight the battle at nearby Halidon Hill. Their army was large; contemporary sources estimate their numbers to be between 14,629 and 100,000, almost all of whom were infantry.[61] They were led by the most experienced and high-ranking nobles in Scotland, men tactically wise enough to order their troops in several lines on top of the hill.[62] The

---

[56] See *Anonimalle Chronicle*, pp. 156–59; *Chronicon de Lanercost*, p. 273; Thomas Gray, pp. 162–63; Geoffrey le Baker, p. 50; and Adam Murimuth, p. 67.

[57] On the siege of Berwick see *Chronicon de Lanercost*, p. 273; Thomas Gray, pp. 162–63; Henry Knighton, I:459; Geoffrey le Baker, pp. 50–51; *Gesta Edwardi de Carnarvan*, pp. 111–14; *Anonimalle Chronicle*, pp. 156–63; Thomas of Burton, II:367–68; Adam Murimuth, p. 67; Thomas Walsingham, I:195–96; the continuator of Walter of Guisborough, II:306–08; Jean le Bel, I:112–13, 116–17; *The Brut*, I:281–83; and Andrew of Wyntoun, II:399.

[58] See *Anonimalle Chronicle*, pp. 158–59; *The Brut*, I:282; and Andrew of Wyntoun, II:398.

[59] See Thomas Gray, p. 163.

[60] On the trek of the Scots into Northumberland see Robert of Avesbury, p. 298; *Gesta Edwardi de Carnarvan*, p. 113; Geoffrey le Baker, p. 51; Henry Knighton, I:459; Thomas Walsingham, I:196; Thomas of Burton, II:367; and Adam Murimuth, pp. 67–68.

[61] The numbers of Scots are recorded as (from lowest to highest): 14,629 (the continuator of Walter of Guisborough, II:308–09); 30,000+ (*Chronicon de Lanercost*, p. 273); 40,000 (*Gesta Edwardi de Carnarvan*, p. 115); 60,000 (*Liber Pluscardensis*, I:269; Andrew of Wyntoun, II:399); 80,000 (*Anonimalle Chronicle*, pp. 162–63); 90,000 (Thomas of Burton, II:369–70); 100,000+ (*The Brut*, I:285). As well as these calculations, four chroniclers simply report the Scottish army to contain a large number of soldiers without giving a count: Geoffrey le Baker, p. 51; Robert of Avesbury, p. 297; Adam Murimuth, p. 68; and the continuator of Walter of Guisborough, II:308. Finally, the anonymous poet writing on the battle also gives no tally for the number of Scottish soldiers but does claim that they outnumbered the English by a 5:1 ratio (Minot p. 95). On the fact that these were largely infantry troops see Henry Knighton, I:459.

[62] There is disagreement on the number of Scottish lines ordered at Halidon Hill. The *Chronicon de Lanercost* (p. 273), Henry Knighton (p. 459), Geoffrey le Baker (p. 51), Jean le Bel (I:116), and Thomas of Burton (II:370) report a formation of three lines, while the *Anonimalle Chronicle* (pp. 162–63) and the continuator of Walter of Guisborough (II:308–09) records four lines, and *The Brut* (I:384–85) notes five lines of Scottish soldiers. On the leadership of the Scots see *Anonimalle Chronicle*, pp. 164–67 and *The Brut*, I:383.

Scottish morale was high, for they outnumbered their enemy and had the higher ground. This was all explained to them in a speech delivered by Archibald Douglas, who also commanded that no English prisoners were to be taken. Noting the knights present in the English army, Douglas remarked:

> Take comfort my brothers and take up your arms with vigor. Behold, the lords of our enemy are on horseback, so that some of them after being put to flight might more easily arrive at the head of those fleeing. Fortune has led them to this position, as if they were enclosed by boundaries. At their back lies a large town armed with bellicose men. On their right is the spacious and deep ocean. And on their left run the waters of the Tweed River which is filled to overflowing by the tides. Therefore, take spirit, and let your hands kill. Do not allow the English to be ransomed, but let both the lords and the infantry be slain equally on this day.[63]

The English were forewarned of the Scots' advance, and they could see them ordered on the nearby hill.[64] While they marveled at the large number which had gathered for the battle, they did not waver in their resolve to fight. This was, after all, what Edward III had desired, and his troops were prepared for the conflict. Some of the English troops had been left to watch the castle. Those who were to fight at Halidon Hill numbered considerably fewer than their Scottish opponents, although only Thomas of Burton provides a numerical estimate of their strength, at 10,000 soldiers.[65] They were also all expected to fight on foot, despite Geoffrey le Baker claiming that this was 'against the ancient tradition of their fathers.'[66] A large number of archers was also present with the English army.[67]

Edward ordered his army similar to the formation used by the disinherited at Dupplin Moor. He formed three lines of infantry at the base of the hill in the shape of an arc, with the wings composed of archers. It was strictly a defensive formation.[68]

Morale among the English troops seems also to have been quite high. For despite the *Anonimalle Chronicle*'s belief that the English troops were 'very cast down' at

---

[63] Recorded in *Gesta Edwardi de Carnarvan*, p. 115: 'Confortamini, fratres, et arma sumite cum vigore; ecce! duces hostium nostrorum equites sunt effecti, ut ceteris nobis in praedam dimissis fugae praesidium melius consequantur. Nunc alia fortuna tanquam inclusos illos in nostris finibus huc adduxit, hinc, siquidem a tergo, villam optimam viris bellicosis munitam; a dextris vero pelagum spatiosum et altum, a sinistris autem alveum fluminis de Twede cujus intumescens mare riparum marginem jam implevit. Igitur [animos] resumite et manus ad caedendum extendite, nec cuiquam redemptio concedatur, sed principes et pedites pariter pereant isto die.'

[64] See *Chronicon de Lanercost*, pp. 273–74 and Jean le Bel, I:116.

[65] Thomas of Burton, II:367. See also Thomas Walsingham, I:196.

[66] Geoffrey le Baker, p. 51: 'Ibi didicit a Scotis Anglorum generositas dextrarios reservare venacioni fugencium, et, contra antiquatum morem suorum patrum, pedes pugnare.'

[67] See *Chronicon de Lanercost*, p. 274; *Gesta Edwardi de Carnarvan*, p. 114; Henry Knighton, I:459; Thomas of Burton, II:370; and *The Brut*, I:285.

[68] There is another dispute over the number of English lines ordered at Halidon Hill. The *Chronicon de Lanercost* (p. 274), *Gesta Edwardi de Carnarvan* (p. 114) and Thomas of Burton (II:370) all record three lines of formation, while the continuator of Walter of Guisborough (II:309) and *The Brut* (I:285) report four lines. On the formation in an arc see the continuator of Walter of Guisborough, II:309. And, on the archers ordered on the wings see *Gesta Edwardi de Carnarvan*, p. 114, and *The Brut*, I:285.

Battle of Halidon Hill

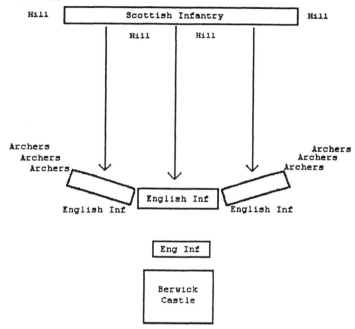

the sight of such a large Scottish relief force,[69] Adam Murimuth writes that they 'were comforted by a strong mood and a brave spirit.'[70] Although being outnumbered by the Scots, Edward III knew that an even more disparate number of Scottish soldiers had been defeated quite handily by the disinherited at Dupplin Moor, and he reckoned that his army could repeat this performance. The English king relayed this message to his soldiers while recalling the recent defeats suffered by the English at the hands of the Scots:

> Consider, my comrades, what kind of people we fight today. For a long time these people have rebelled against our ancestors. It also pains me to remember the subversions and massacres which they have borne against the people and ecclesiastics of our time. For, God willing, the day of vengeance has come, unless you are frightened by their numbers. For, trusting in the leadership of God, we will be at equal strength to them in this battle.[71]

So the two armies stood opposite each other, both ordered in their defensive

---

69 *Anonimalle Chronicle*, pp. 162–63.
70 Adam Murimuth, p. 68: '. . . et omnes bono vultu et audaci animo confortante . . .'
71 As recorded in *Gesta Edwardi de Carnarvan*, p. 115: 'Considerate, commilitones mei, cum quibus gentibus dimicaturi sumus isto die. Diu est quod progenitoribus nostris rebelles extiterunt. Piget itaque referre plebis et religiosorum subversiones et strages quas nostro generi pluries intulerunt. Jam, Deo propitio, dies instat ultionis, nec illorum multitudinem timeatis, quia de Domini praesidio confidentes vobiscum pares erimus in conflictu.' See also *Anonimalle Chronicle*, pp. 162–63; Geoffrey le Baker, pp. 51–52; and Laurence Minot, p. 4.

formations, with neither wishing to break from them. Finally, Geoffrey le Baker reports, the Scots challenged the English to single combat. The situation was, as this English author sees it, similar to that of David and Goliath, with the Scottish army itself playing the Philistine giant. Their combatant is not named, but he is described as using as well as his more conventional weapons a 'certain black dog;' the English chose Robert Benhale, a knight from Norfolk. After receiving the blessing of Edward III, Benhale went against his opponent with sword and shield. He first met the dog, which he killed with his sword, and then, almost as quickly, he slew and decapitated the dog's master.[72]

Still, no battle was being fought. The Scots had chosen the field in order to protect themselves. They had in fact thought that the English would charge them, but Edward's intent was exactly the opposite. He wished to provoke the Scots to charge his lines instead of making his own charge. Ultimately, the stalemate was broken. The Scots, confident in their numbers and perhaps provoked a bit by the loss of their champion in single combat, attacked the English. Trying to take advantage of their larger numbers, they combined their first line into a large mass and charged down the hill into the English formation attempting, in the estimation of the *Chronicon de Lanercost*, to reach Edward Balliol who stood among the troops at the rear of the English army.[73]

It was, according to John Fordun, a 'lachrimabile bellum,' which ended in an extended hand-to-hand fight between two masses of foot soldiers.[74] The Scots attacked 'manfully,' but in the end they were unable to break the English line. The second and third lines of the Scots now also charged into the English infantry, but they met the same fate as their comrades.[75]

The archers again played a role in this defeat. As at Dupplin Moor they attacked the Scots as they rushed onto the infantry lines, and they continued to fire into their flanks and rear as the fight continued. In this, as at Dupplin Moor, they blinded many of the Scots, creating disorder in their ranks and aiding in their slaughter. The Lanercost chronicler writes:

> Now the Scots approaching in the first division were so grievously wounded in the face and blinded by the host of English archery, just as they had been formerly at Glendenmore (Dupplin Moor), that they were helpless, and quickly began to turn away their faces from the arrow flights and to fall.[76]

---

[72] Geoffrey le Baker, p. 51.
[73] *Chronicon de Lanercost*, p. 274.
[74] John Fordun, I:356. See also Adam Murimuth, p. 68.
[75] See *Chronicon de Lanercost*, p. 274; *Gesta Edwardi de Carnarvan*, pp. 115–16; Thomas of Burton, II:370; Geoffrey le Baker, pp. 51–52; and *Liber Pluscardensis*, I:269. Only the *Anonimalle Chronicle* differs with this scenario. This chronicle claims that it was not the Scots who attacked but the English who 'advanced boldly' against their enemy. The Scots 'did not want to fight against the king of England and his forces' because they were waiting for the River Tweed to be at full flood tide, 'that they might drive the king of England and his men into the River Tweed or into the sea to drown them.' However, this rather fanciful strategy did not occur before the English were victorious in this battle (pp. 166–67).
[76] *Chronicon de Lanercost*, p. 273–74: 'Sed Scotti in prima acie venientes ita fuerunt a multitudine saggitariorum Angliae vulnerati in facie et excaecati in hoc bello, sicut in priori apud Gledenmore,

The *Anonimalle Chronicle* uses similar words: 'The English archers destroyed and injured them so that they were in a short time as if choked and blinded, and soon they were thrown into confusion.'[77]

In the end, the English prevailed, 'indubitablely' to quote Thomas Walsingham.[78] The Scots were overcome, and while some who were still embroiled in the battle continued to fight, those able to do so fled from the field. Eventually, all Scots either fled from the field or were killed. *The Brut* describes the victory: 'And thus it happened, as God willed it, that the Scots on that day had no more numbers nor strength to face the English than twenty sheep would have against five wolves.'[79]

The English knights remounted and pursued the fleeing Scots for as many as eight miles. They continued to kill any soldiers they came across, and the Scots who eluded their pursuers did so, claims Adam Murimuth, only with 'much difficulty.'[80]

Dead Scottish soldiers covered the battlefield. *The Brut* describes the scene: 'And there might be seen many Scotsmen thrown dead down to the ground, their banners broken and hacked into pieces, and many a good haubergeon bathed in blood.'[81] The contemporary English chroniclers estimate a death rate between 35,308 and 60,718 with the Scottish historians tallying a lower, although still significant 10,000 total. This number included several notable Scottish leaders including the general in charge, Archibald Douglas.[82] The English death rate was notably smaller, estimated to be under twenty men including only one knight and one man-at-arms.[83]

---

quod se ipsos adjuvare non poterant, et ideo cito faciem saggitarum ictibus avertere et cadere inceperunt.'

[77] *Anonimalle Chronicle*, pp. 166–67: 'les archers Dengleterre les desbaretta et greva, ainsi quils estoient en petite hure auxi come estuffez et envoegles, et tost perdirent lour contenance.' See also Thomas of Burton, II:370 and *The Brut*, I:285. None of these chronicles indicates deaths by archery fire.

[78] Thomas Walsingham, I:196.

[79] *The Brut*, I:285: 'And þus hit bifelle, as God wolde, þat þe Scottis hade þat day no more foisoun ne myght aþeynes þe Englisshe-men, þan xx shepe shulde have a eyns v wolfes.' See also John Fordun, I:356–57 and the anonymous poet in Minot p. 95. That some Scots continued to fight after most had fled see Bridlington, p. 116.

[80] Adam Murimuth, p. 68. See also *Anonimalle Chronicle*, pp. 168–69; *Gesta Edwardi de Carnarvan*, p. 116; Thomas of Burton, II:370; *Liber Pluscardensis*, I:269–70; *The Brut*, I:285; Andrew of Wyntoun, II:401; and the anonymous poet in Minot p. 95.

[81] *The Brut*, I:285: 'And þere might men see meny a Scottisshe-man caste doun vnto þe erthe dede, and hir baneres displaiede, & hackede into pices, and meny a gode habrigoun of stele in hir blode baþede.' See also Andrew of Wyntoun, pp. 401–02.

[82] English chroniclers record the Scottish death total as (from lowest to highest): 30,000+, not including 'valiantz gentz et pedaille' (*Anonimalle Chronicle*, pp. 168–69); 35,308 (Henry Knighton, I:459); 35,712 (*The Brut*, I:286); 36,320+ (*Chronicon de Lanercost*, p. 274); 38,745 (Thomas of Burton, II:370); 40,000 (Robert of Avesbury, p. 298); 50,302 (anonymous poet in Minot p. 96); 60,000 (Geoffrey le Baker, p. 52); and 60,718 (*The French Chronicle of London*, p. 67). As well, Adam Murimuth calculates both the number who died and the number who fled as 80,000 (p. 68). The *Gesta Edwardi de Carnarvan* (p. 116), Thomas Walsingham (I:196), and the continuator of Walter of Guisborough (II:309) all record no death tally, indicating instead only that 'many' were killed at Halidon Hill. As for the Scottish chroniclers, both *Liber Pluscardensis* (I:270) and Andrew of Wyntoun (II:401–02) report 10,000 casualties. On the names of the important Scots killed see Thomas Gray, p. 163 and John Fordun, I:356.

[83] See *Gesta Edwardi de Carnarvan*, p. 116; Henry Knighton, I:459; Thomas of Burton, II:370; and Thomas Walsingham, I:196. The anonymous poet reports only seven English dead (in Minot p. 95).

The war with Scotland seemed at an end. Edward III had travelled north, and he had defeated the largest and best army the Scots could gather. As Adam of Murimuth writes:

> And thus it was publicly reported that war in Scotland was finally at an end, because no one remained in that land who could, knew how to, or wished to gather men for battle, or even if they did, no one knew how to lead those who might be gathered.[84]

This report was, claims Geoffrey le Baker, 'false opinion,' as war would be renewed later with David Bruce himself.[85] Still, the conclusive nature of this battle and that at Dupplin Moor should not be underestimated. These two battles are similar in tactics, strategy, purpose, and result. They represent the character of Edward III's early reign, showing a young king willing to use force to protect the interests of those he favored and to correct the 'injustices' of his father's rule. This was certainly comprehended by the contemporary authors who wrote about the battles, as many original sources pair the two with little discussion of the other historical events which occurred between August 11, 1332 and July 19, 1333.

These battles represent a definite shift in English battlefield tactics. The idea of using dismounted knights in a defensive formation and of using archers on the flanks to provoke an attack, a tactic forced upon the troops at Boroughbridge perhaps because of geographic necessity rather than tactical forethought, appears now to be a 'practice' rather than an 'accident.' It also indicates an army learning from its mistakes; the defeat at Bannockburn in fact had led to military changes.

With the exception of digging ditches on the battlefield, the Scots began both these battles without altering the tactics which had brought them victory at Loudon Hill and Bannockburn. In both battles, they chose the field and seemingly had the better defensive position.[86] They also had the numerical advantage and were fighting to protect their homeland from an English invasion.

Yet none of these usually overwhelming advantages seemed to aid the Scots in these two battles. For, ultimately, it was the tactical changes made by the English armies which determined the outcome of these battles. The English knights dismounting and acting essentially as foot soldiers, ordered in a solid defensive line, was new to and not anticipated by the Scots. They had so influenced their enemy with the victory at Bannockburn that the English changed their tactical formation and now stood awaiting a Scottish charge, just as Robert Bruce had done nearly twenty years before.

The Scots appear not to have learned of this change in English tactics employed

---

84 Adam Murimuth, p. 68: 'Et sic dicebatur publice quod guerra in Scocia fuit finaliter finita et terminata, quia nullus remansit de natione illa, qui posset, sciret, aut vellet homines ad proelium congregare aut regere congregatos.'
85 Geoffrey le Baker, p.52.
86 Richard Lescot, for example, in referring to the Scots' battlefield choice at Halidon Hill determined that it was a wise choice, the Scots having picked the higher ground 'desiring to protect themselves' (p. 32).

so successfully at Boroughbridge, nor do they seem to have realized that the changes which the disinherited used for the victory at Dupplin Moor would be similarly used at Halidon Hill. This certainly seems to be evident in the speech given by Archibald Douglas to his troops before the latter battle, for not only does he maintain that the enemy knights would be on horseback, but he tries to draw a social contrast between those on horseback and those on foot, claiming that the knights were mounted only so that they would be able to flee more easily than those without horses. Thus it appears that the Scots were caught without significant knowledge of how to fight the new tactics of the English army.

Moreover, the English not only changed their tactics by dismounting the knights and fighting on foot, they also changed their tactics by refusing to make an offensive charge against their enemy. This too had been taught them at Loudon Hill and Bannockburn. In both of those battles the English had taken the offensive initiative and had charged unsuccessfully into the Scottish line. At Dupplin Moor and Halidon Hill they reversed this practice, choosing to wait for a Scottish charge rather than initiating combat with their own attack. At Dupplin Moor they did not have to wait too long, for the Scots, who so outnumbered the English that they in no way could anticipate defeat, attacked the disinherited with little delay, despite their tradition of taking a defensive stance and waiting for their opponent's charge. However, at Halidon Hill, the Scots tried to revert to their proven defensive tactics, attempting, at least according to Geoffrey le Baker, to provoke the English into an attack on their solid infantry line.[87] But in this battle, with Berwick castle suffering the hardships of a siege, the Scots could not afford to wait for the possible English charge of their infantry line. Thus, they again put their faith in their numerical advantage and attempted their own, ultimately unsuccessful, attack of the English defensive formation.

It was at this point in the two battles when the archers made their presence felt. Although it may be too much to say, as Jonathan Sumption does, that these battles 'were [both] won by archers,' the archers did play a major role in the battle, although not the one – as a decisive killing machine – which has been bestowed upon them traditionally by scholars.[88] Without having ditches or some other hindrance to control an offensive charge, the English had to do something to narrow the size of the Scottish attack, otherwise the Scots might have outflanked the infantry line and destroyed the advantage of the defensive formation. Therefore, it was the function of the archers, ordered along the infantry flanks, to provide this hindrance and to narrow the Scottish attack. In essence, they performed the same purpose as had the ditches at Courtrai and Loudon Hill, the woods and marshes at Bannockburn, and the bridge at Boroughbridge. In this duty they performed marvelously, so well in fact that this tactic would become standard in all battles fought by the English for the next two hundred years. For even if the archers did not kill many, which seems to be what occurred in these two battles as in most others fought during the fourteenth and

---

[87] Geoffrey le Baker, p. 51.
[88] Sumption, p. 67. Sumption is in error on pp. 125–26 in describing 'some thousands of Scots [dying] of arrow wounds.' There is no record of this in the contemporary battlefield narratives.

fifteenth centuries, they so disrupted and disordered their opponent's charges that when they finally did reach the English line their impetus was slight and the infantry and dismounted knights were more easily able to withstand the attacks.

Perhaps then, Geoffrey le Baker is not simply using rhetorical license in his comparison of the battles of Dupplin Moor and Halidon Hill to that fought between David and Goliath. In both cases it was the larger entity which came forward to attack while the smaller stayed back in defensive anticipation. And, as with the larger Goliath whose weakness caused his defeat at the hands of the smaller David, in these two battles the larger Scottish army was easily defeated by the smaller English force.[89]

[89] Geoffrey le Baker, p. 51.

X

THE BATTLE OF LAUPEN, 1339

WITH THE DISINTEGRATION OF central power in the thirteenth-century Holy Roman Empire there came a desire by many living on the 'frontier' of the Empire to seek independence and self-rule. Of these frontier entities, the most obvious to modern historians are undoubtedly the city-states of northern Italy. By the end of the thirteenth century, Venice, Milan, Florence, and Genoa, to name only the most prominent of these independence-seeking states, had shed their German overlords and begun the process of self-government. To Jacob Burckhardt and his scholarly descendants this was the beginning of the Italian Renaissance, a period which saw constant military confusion coupled with the development of humanistic and artistic excellence.[1]

Nearly forgotten in comparison with the Italian experience is that of Switzerland. Associated with the rest of the Holy Roman Empire since the time of Charlemagne, but different in language, culture, society, and economy, during times of Imperial solidarity, the medieval Swiss had usually remained faithful to the political powers-that-were. But in times of governmental instability, the slightly populated Switzer-land was more likely to be overlooked than concerned with. Swiss towns, far smaller than their German or Italian counterparts, learned to be relatively self-sufficient.[2] To survive they connected with neighboring rural enclaves to form independent political organizations, known as cantons. In 1291, three of these cantons, Uri, Schwyz, and Unterwalden, allied to form a union, the first Swiss Confederation.[3]

While not generating much interest in the Holy Roman Empire as a whole, the Swiss Confederation did concern the Austrian Habsburg family whose holdings

---

[1] Jacob Burckhardt, *The Civilization of the Renaissance in Italy*, trans. L. Geiger and W. Götz, 2 vols. (New York, 1958). See also Eugenio Garin, *Der Italienische Humanismus* (Bern, 1947); Hans Baron, *The Crisis of the Early Italian Renaissance*, 2 vols. (Princeton, 1955); and Denys Hay, *The Italian Renaissance in Its Historical Background* (Cambridge, 1961). For a survey of this concept in Renaissance historiography see Albert Rabil Jr., 'The Significance of "Civic Humanism" in the Interpretation of the Italian Renaissance,' in *Renaissance Humanism: Foundations, Forms, and Legacy*, vol. 1: *Humanism in Italy*, ed. A. Rabil, Jr. (Philadelphia, 1988), pp. 141–74.

[2] Denys Hay, *Europe in the Fourteenth and Fifteenth Centuries*, 2nd ed. (London, 1989), pp. 129–30.

[3] Hay, *Europe in the Fourteenth and Fifteenth Centuries*, p. 130; E. Bonjour, H.S. Offler, and G.R. Potter, *A Short History of Switzerland* (Oxford, 1952), pp. 69–81; W.D. McCrackan, *The Rise of the Swiss Republic*, 2nd ed. (New York, 1901), pp. 83–91; Richard Feller, *Geschichte Berns* (Bern, 1949), I:63–64; and George Holmes, *Europe: Hierarchy and Revolt, 1320–1450* (London, 1975), p. 52. The date of confederation is not known. The first documentary evidence of alliance is August 1291. (A transcription and translation of this document can be found in McCracken, pp. 87–89.)

included those independence-seeking lands. This concern increased further in 1292 when the Confederation united with Zurich and Bern to form an anti-Habsburg league.[4] However, Albrecht I of Austria, deprived, he felt, from his rightful inheritance as Holy Roman Emperor, was tied up for the moment with a political struggle to gain the Imperial throne, and he could not immediately attend to the Swiss independence crisis.[5] Indeed, it would not be until 1315, with Albrecht's sons, Frederick and Leopold, on the throne of the Holy Roman Empire and Austria respectively, that a concerted effort was made by the Habsburgs to break the Confederation. At this time, with the Swiss Confederation supporting a rival candidate to the Imperial throne, Lewis IV of Bavaria, Duke Leopold of Austria mounted a major campaign against his rebelling Swiss lands and their inhabitants. In their 24 years of independence the Swiss had been preparing for an invasion which had never come, but they had not dropped their guard, and when Leopold invaded the geographically isolated Switzerland he found well maintained fortifications barring easily accessible passes and pushing him to journey along more dangerous routes. More importantly, he found a population which was not willing to give up their independence nor willing to fight by conventional means. At Morgarten on November 14, 1315, while the Austrian army traveled through one of these more dangerous passes, the Swiss – primarily men from the Schwyz and Uri cantons – ambushed and massacred them.[6]

The battle of Morgarten was a trumpeting of Swiss independence and military success which has continued to sound until this century.[7] With their unanticipated defeat of the Austrians in that battle, the Swiss Confederation initiated a peace with the Holy Roman Empire and its affiliates which held for much of the following century. However, peace was a relative condition, for while few invading armies proceeded through the alpine passes against Swiss inhabitants, Swiss armies fought frequently among themselves. Much of this was due to the desire for territorial expansion by the larger Swiss towns, few of which had initially supported the Confederation or its aspirations for independence, but all of which now profitted from what had taken place at Morgarten. Among the most active in this regard were Lucerne, Zurich, Freiburg, and Bern.[8]

It is estimated that in the early fourteenth century Bern had a population of only five to six thousand, quite small in comparison to non-Swiss towns, but similar in size to Zurich and twice as large as Lucerne and Freiburg.[9] Bern had joined the Swiss

---

4 Bonjour, Offler, and Potter, pp. 81–85; McCracken, p. 116; and Feller, I:64–65.
5 Feller, I:101–09 and G. Barraclough, *The Origins of Modern Germany*, 2nd ed. (Oxford, 1947), pp. 302–07.
6 Bonjour, Offler, and Potter, pp. 85–86; McCrackan, pp. 117–28; Feller, I:109–10; and Hans Witzig, *Von Mortgarten bis Marignano* (Zurich, 1957), pp. 12–25. For a discussion of the battle of Mortgarten see Appendix.
7 On the endurance of the battle of Mortgarten in Swiss political thought see Holmes, p. 52; Maria Schnitzer, *Die Mortgartenschlacht im werdenden schweizerischen Nationalbewusstsein* (Zurich, 1969); and Fritz Wernli, *Die Entstehung der schweizerischen Eidgenossenschaft* (Zurich, 1972), pp. 277–94.
8 Bonjour, Offler, and Potter, pp. 87–96; McCrackan, pp. 129–46; and Feller, I:110–28.
9 Bonjour, Offler, and Potter, pp. 93–94. Feller's 3,000 inhabitant tally for Bern in 1300 (I:78) seems

anti-Habsburg alliance in 1292 and had always remained friendly with the Swiss Confederation, even signing a mutual assistance pact with it, the treaty of Lungern, in 1323.[10] (Bern would not, however, join the Confederation proper until 1353.)

Bern's friendliness with these Swiss 'rebels' was not approved of by its neighboring town of Freiburg. Eighteen miles from Bern, Freiburg was much more tightly controlled by a noble family, the Kiburgs, which had numerous smaller dynastic attendants and which was also closely allied with the Habsburgs. Since 1315 both Freiburg and Bern had sought to expand their territory beyond earlier boundaries. Weak and unclaimed lands were occupied, and pacts were made with nearby villages. As they were so close to each other, on many occasions the two towns encroached on the other's lands; indeed, trespassing raids were frequent. But it was not until 1339 that open warfare occurred. In that year the Freiburgers, together with their allies and confident in the size and nobility of their army, determined to bring the Bernese to battle. On June 10 they besieged the village of Laupen. Once held by the Kiburg family, Laupen was now firmly under the control of Bern, with more than 600 Bernese soldiers in garrison there. With haste, the Bernese reacted to the siege by mustering a largely infantry army and marching to relieve Laupen; on June 21, less than two miles from the village, they met and defeated the more noble, cavalry-oriented Freiburger troops.[11] The trend had continued: once again an anti-Habsburg, pro-independent Swiss military force had proved victorious on the battlefield.

The battle of Laupen is not recorded in many contemporary historical sources, although what does exist is fairly extensive in its coverage of occurrences on the battlefield. Most important in this regard is the *Conflictus Laupensis*, written in Bern shortly after the battle.[12] Despite being judged as 'unjustifiably famed as an important achievement of military history literature' by Hans Delbrück, who nonetheless uses this narrative as his primary source for the battle of Laupen, the *Conflictus Laupensis* is one of the very few medieval military narratives written within a year or two of what it reports.[13] And while it certainly is written only from the Bernese point of view, its description of the battle is supported by later sources, nearly all of which also support the Bernese postion, but none of which used the *Conflictus Laupensis* for their own narratives. These include: Jean de Winterthur's *Chronica*, written c.1347; Heinrich von Diessenhoven's *Chronicon*, whose short account of the battle was written c.1361; the *Cronica de Berno*, which was completed in 1405 but

---

too small, especially as he later accepts a figure of 1,000–4,000 for the number of Bernese soldiers at the battle of Laupen (I:134–39).

[10] Bonjour, Offler, and Potter, pp. 94–95; McCrackan, pp. 157–59; and Feller, I:116–17.

[11] Bonjour, Offler, and Potter, pp. 93–95; McCrackan, pp. 159–60; and Feller, I:129–34. On the battle of Laupen see Delbrück, III:561–70; Oman (1905), II:242–47; Feller, 1:134–41; Witzig, pp. 27–32; G. Köhler, *Die Entwickelung des Kriegswesens und der Kriegführung in der Ritterzeit von Mitte des 11. Jahrhunderts bis zu den Hussitenkriegen* (Breslau, 1886), II:605–13; and R. von Fischer, *Schweizerkriegsgeschichte*, ed. M. Feldman and H.H.G. Wirz (Bern, 1915), I:9–21.

[12] *Conflictus Laupensis*, in *Die Berner-Chronik des Conrad Justinger*, ed. G. Studer (Bern, 1871), pp. 302–13.

[13] Delbrück, III:562. Delbrück also disagrees with the number of soldiers on both sides reported in the *Conflictus Laupensis*.

with the section on Laupen undoubtedly written earlier; Conrad Justinger's *Berner-Chronik*, written c.1421; and an anonymous *Stadtchronik* of Bern, which was derived from Justinger's chronicle and written in the middle of the fifteenth century.[14]

The *Conflictus Laupensis* begins its narrative with a lengthy discourse on the origin of the conflict between Freiburg and Bern. Simply put, the anonymous author reports,

> it is known that before the time [of battle] discord between Bern and Freiburg and their allies had been seeded for many years and from many causes and on many occasions by both sides.[15]

Ultimately, in 1339, with the Bernese 'working for the common peace and for the conservation of the land,' two nobles associated with Freiburg, Gerhard of Valengin and Peter of Aarburg, increased their malevolent rhetoric and raids on the lands of Bern. The Bernese, frightened by the threats of these nobles, answered with an expedition on May 16 against the fortifications of Aarburg; the expedition failed, as the attackers were unable to draw the counts from the fortifications' protective walls.[16]

This expedition, however, did prompt the Freiburgers to lay siege to Laupen, at least this is the reason given for the siege in the *Conflictus Laupensis*. The other sources do not record the failed assault on Aarburg, indicating rather that the siege of Laupen occurred because the count of Kiburg had a large noble force which he felt could easily defeat the army of Bern.[17]

Whatever the cause, the siege of Laupen took place, with all of the Freiburgers and their allies attacking the town 'with catapults brought on carts by horses.'[18] The date was June 10. The army of Freiburg was large and impressive. Although the *Conflictus'* count of 16,000 infantry and 1,000 cavalry, the *Cronica de Berno's* tally of 24,000, and Conrad Justinger's number of 30,000 soldiers are most certainly exaggerations based on the small population of the town,[19] the presence of the counts of Kiburg, Neuchâtel, Gruyères, Nidau, Valengin, Aarburg, and the lord of Vaud, son

---

[14] Jean de Winterthur, pp. 162–64; Heinrich von Diessenhoven, *Chronicon de Heinricus Truchsess von Diessenhoven*, in *Fontes rerum Germanicarum*, iv, ed. J.F. Bohmer (Stuttgart, 1868), pp. 32–33; *Cronica de Berno*, in *Die Berner-Chronik des Conrad Justinger*, ed. G. Studer (Bern, 1871), pp. 299–300; Conrad Justinger, *Die Berner-Chronik des Conrad Justinger*, ed. G. Studer (Bern, 1871), pp. 72–94; and *Die Anonyme Stadchronik oder der Königshofen-Justinger*, in *Die Berner-Chronik des Conrad Justinger*, ed. G. Studer (Bern, 1871), pp. 352–72.

[15] *Conflictus Laupensis*, p. 302: 'Sciendum est ergo, quod ante tempus prefatum fuit orta discordia inter Bernenses et Friburgenses et adiutores eorundem, que ab annis multis et ex diversis causis et occasionibus hinc inde ab utraque parte fuit seminata.' A discussion of these causes is found on pp. 302–05.

[16] *Conflictus Laupensis*, pp. 305–06.

[17] Jean de Winterthur, p. 162; Conrad Justinger, pp. 74–82; and *Die anonyme Stadtchronik*, pp. 353–56.

[18] *Conflictus Laupensis*, p. 306.

[19] *Conflictus Laupensis*, p. 306; *Cronica de Berno*, p. 300; and Conrad Justinger, p. 82. Hans Delbrück (III:563) believes that these tallies are far from accurate and that in fact the Freiburger army may have been smaller than the Bernese force.

of the count of Savoy, as well as many lesser nobles, with all their retainers, as recorded in the original sources, gives an impression of chivalry that is not present in many other battles of the early fourteenth century: 'They gloried in their multitude and power and in the many decorations of their new and costly vestments.'[20] The *Conflictus Laupensis* and Jean de Winterthur insist also that the besieging army contained a number of Austrians.[21]

Opposing the Freiburg besiegers was a garrison of 600, a number which could not hold out for long against such a siege.[22] Those inside the town could also not hope for any mercy from their attackers; as Laupen had once been part of the Freiburg holdings and now sided with the enemy Bernese, the *Conflictus Laupensis* reports that the Freiburgers were planning to destroy the town and massacre all of its inhabitants.[23]

Thus it was up to the Bernese to enter into the conflict and to assist their confederates. The leaders of the town met in council, but their meeting was brief as they quickly agreed to attempt to raise the siege of Laupen. There was urgency in the matter as the Bernese feared that if they dallied Laupen would fall and its inhabitants would be killed. At the same time, they believed that God was on their side and would aid them in their cause. To them it was a crusade, as their banners, a dark cross on a white background, and the large number of ecclesiastics traveling with the army proved.[24] Six thousand Bernese troops answered the call to arms, including 1,000–1,200 from the three cantons.[25] They were led by an experienced warrior, the knight Rudolf von Erlach.[26]

The Bernese force marched to Laupen, but when they saw 'that the reported large size of their enemy was valid,' the leaders decided not to attack the Freiburgers while they were camped in the steep and forested terrain around the town. Instead, they determined to order their troops, all infantry, as 'a small wedge' – the *Conflictus Laupensis* uses the term 'parvus cuneus' – with troops facing out on all sides on top of a small hill near to the town.[27] Not only would this position give the Bernese the

---

[20] See *Conflictus Laupensis*, p. 306; Jean de Winterthur, p. 162; *Cronica de Berno*, pp. 299–300; and *Die anonyme Stadtchronik*, pp. 354–56. The quotation is from the *Conflictus Laupensis*, p. 306: 'gloriantes de sua multitudine et potentia ac in ornatu vario vestium novarum et pretiosarum.'

[21] *Conflictus Laupensis*, p. 306 and Jean de Winterthur, p. 162.

[22] Conrad Justinger, pp. 82–86.

[23] *Conflictus Laupensis*, p. 307.

[24] *Conflictus Laupensis*, pp. 307–09 and Conrad Justinger, pp. 82–83. The *Conflictus* identifies a number of Bernese leaders including Lord John of Bubenberg, a knight who is identified as the 'senior' of Bern; Burchard of Bennenwyle, the town secretary; Burchard, the master of machines; Rudolf of Muleren, Peter of Balme, Peter Wentzschaz, and John of Herblingen, standard-bearers; John of Seedorf; Berthold of Seedorf; Berthold Glockner; and Peter of Krantzingen.

[25] The *Conflictus Laupensis* (pp. 308–09) counts 1,000 canton soldiers, with the *Cronica de Berno* (p. 300) counting 1,200. Both total the Bernese force at 6,000. This number equals the population of the town and thus appears too high; however, it must also have included troops from throughout the Bernese controlled region of Switzerland.

[26] Only Conrad Justinger (pp. 82–84) names Rudolf von Erlach as leader of the Bernese force. The *Conflictus Laupensis* does not mention a leader of the Bernese. Delbrück's arguments in support of Erlach as leader are convincing (III:564–65).

[27] *Conflictus Laupensis*, p. 309.

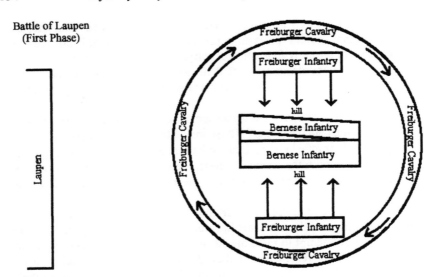

Battle of Laupen
(First Phase)

higher-ground advantage during the battle, but it also allowed them to be warned of the Freiburg approach. As well, Conrad Justinger insists that Rudolf von Erlach wrote to the leaders of the Freiburg army challenging their force to battle; the Freiburgers readily agreed.[28]

This was after all the goal of the Freiburgers, and they quickly prepared for the fight. Their 'new knights' were particularly enthused by the prospect of engaging the Bernese in warfare: they waved their swords in the air in excitement and raced to attack their opponents.[29] Seeing this, some of the Bernese fled from their positions in fright – these numbered some 2,000, according to the *Conflictus Laupensis*. But this still left some 4,000 soldiers, all of whom stood in their formation ready to fight against the oncoming Freiburg army.[30]

The Freiburg cavalry reached the Bernese formation first. The *Conflictus* recounts that they initially rode 'frightfully' around the Bernese formation, waited for an infantry assault to soften the target, and then attacked 'fiercely' the Bernese line themselves. The Bernese reacted by standing solidly in formation against the attacks:

> The Bernese, bursting the chains of all their fear, like Samson, received the assault of the Freiburgers. And they took all of their standards and slew the standard-bearers and many others, all infantry, and the rest they put to a pitiable flight. When those who were circling with their horses charged to their aid, the Bernese without delay either killed all of them or put them to flight.[31]

28 Conrad Justinger, p. 83. See also *Die anonyme Stadtchronik*, pp. 356–58.
29 *Conflictus Laupensis*, p. 309. What constituted a 'new knight' is not explained in the narrative.
30 *Conflictus Laupensis*, p. 309. Conrad Justinger, on the other hand, contends that as these fleeing troops looked back to see their comrades remaining to fight, most regrouped and returned to the formation (p. 89). Delbrück doubts this contention (III:566–67).
31 *Conflictus Laupensis*, p. 309: 'Ipsi Bernenses, more Sampsonis, quasi ruptis vinculis omnis timoris, in se agressos ipsos Friburgenses receperunt, et omnia vexilla eorum protinus abstulerunt, vexilliferis eorum et multis aliis occisis ceterisque peditibus omnibus in fugam miserabilem conversis;

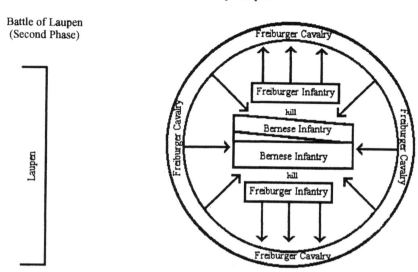

Battle of Laupen
(Second Phase)

In this action, as indicated, large numbers of Freiburgers were killed. Those especially targeted seem to have been the knights among their force; the counts of Nidau and Valengrin were killed, as was the lord of Vaud. All others fled. Among the booty taken by the Bernese were 27 banners and 80 crowned helmets.[32]

The Bernese had not lost as many – an estimated 1,000–1,500 of their force had died[33] – and they did not pursue their fleeing opponents for long. Instead, they returned to Laupen and Bern where a rejoicing population presented honors to the victors and said prayers for the victory.[34] Never again would these towns come to battle, although raids into each others' lands continued for many years.[35]

In comparison with other early fourteenth-century battles the Swiss conflict at Laupen between the armies of the towns of Freiburg and Bern was quite small. Perhaps only the battles of Loudon Hill and Boroughbridge studied here can compare with the few troops which fought on both sides. Yet the tactics used by the Bernese infantry and the outcome they caused against the Freiburger cavalry were very similar to almost all of these other battles.

The Bernese, drawn into the battle by a siege of their allied town, Laupen, were able to muster far fewer troops than those they faced. They were also all infantry, while their opponents had a large number of noble cavalry soldiers. The look of these alone frightened a good number of the Bernese into fleeing from the fight. But those

---

et ad auxilium eorum, qui sub equitibus erant circumdati, se convertentes, ipsi Bernenses sine mora universos aut occiderunt aut in fugam verterunt.' See also Jean de Winterthur, p. 163 and Conrad Justinger, pp. 90–92.

[32] *Conflictus Laupensis*, pp. 309–10; Jean de Winterthur, pp. 163–64; Heinrich von Diessenhoven, pp. 32–33; *Cronica de Berno*, p. 300; Conrad Justinger, pp. 91–93; and *Die anonyme Stadtchronik*, pp. 367–69. The *Cronica de Berno* is the only chronicle which numbers the deceased at 4,000.
[33] Jean de Winterthur (p. 163) claims a death total of 1,000, the *Conflictus Laupensis* (p. 309) 1,500.
[34] *Conflictus Laupensis*, p. 310.
[35] *Conflictus Laupensis*, pp. 310–13.

who remained were able to choose the battlefield, selecting a small hill on which they could order a solid defensive formation. This choice gave them a great advantage against their foes, for although the Bernese troops could not alter the battlefield to narrow the Freiburger charges and were destined ultimately to be surrounded, the Freiburgers had to charge uphill into a 'wedge' of spear-wielding soldiers. This became a task which first the infantry was unable to do and then the cavalry.

Had either the Freiburger cavalry or their infantry broken through the Bernese line, the battle would have been quickly decided and the result would have been quite different. With so few troops, and no reinforcements to fill the opened gaps, as the Bernese stood almost back to back in their wedge, the formation easily would have folded. However, it did not. Indeed, the infantry stood so solidly at Laupen that one must wonder if their formation could ever have been defeated by simply charging into it. At Cassel, fought eleven years earlier in Flanders, the French had chosen not to charge up the hill into the Flemings, but instead to wait until they could draw them out of their defensive formation. Ultimately, it worked, and the French were victorious. The French had faced the Flemings before and knew what to expect; as such, they had to humble the pride of their cavalry in the face of what appeared to be a 'lesser' army. But at Laupen, the Freiburg leadership exulted in their chivalric numbers and saw no need for any other strategy except for an immediate attack on the Bernese infantry. Failure, coupled with large numbers slain, followed.

XI

THE BATTLE OF MORLAIX, 1342

WHILE THE HUNDRED YEARS WAR began with conflicts, largely skirmishes, fought between French and English troops in 1337–1339, it was not until the year 1340 that the war effectively began. At Sluys, on June 24, 1340, a large naval battle was fought and won by England.[1] However, the English king, Edward III, despite having a large army of his own and a gathering of allies – mostly from the Low Countries – unprecedented in the history of the Middle Ages, was unable to take advantage of this victory; his siege of Tournai, undertaken between July and September 1340, was thwarted by financial and political collapse at home and by the disintegration of his alliance in the southern Low Countries.[2] The year ended with a peace treaty, the Treaty of Esplechin, signed on September 25 between Edward and King Philip VI of France, the latter having arrived at Tournai during the siege but having been satisfied to wait out its conclusion without trying to relieve it militarily.[3]

Philip returned to Paris, in somewhat of a celebration, for although his navy was destroyed, he had been able to bring peace to his land without involving his army. Moreover, the Treaty of Esplechin had promised no warfare between England and France for five years, and this would give the French king time to rebuild his fleet, to reform alliances with his Low Countries' Lords, and to prepare his defenses for further assaults.

Edward's return to England was not so happy. Although much of the kingdom's financial crisis could be laid at the king's feet, Edward blamed it, and even the failure at Tournai, on his chancellor, Archbishop John Stratford, and his banker, William de la Pole.[4] Edward's words to Pope Benedict XII on November 18 show his anger: 'I

---

[1] See Kelly DeVries, 'God, Leadership, Flemings, and Archery: Contemporary Perceptions of Victory and Defeat at the Battle of Sluys, 1340,' *American Neptune* 55 (1995), 1–28.

[2] See Kelly DeVries, 'Contemporary Views of Edward III's Failure at the Siege of Tournai, 1340,' *Nottingham Medieval Studies* 39 (1995), 70–105.

[3] Lucas, pp. 420–2 and Sumption, pp. 357–8.

[4] For Edward's money problems at the siege of Tournai see Lucas, p. 418; G.L. Harriss, *King, Parliament, and Public Finance in Medieval England to 1369* (Oxford, 1975), pp. 278–82; T.H. Lloyd, *The English Wool Trade in the Middle Ages* (Cambridge, 1977), pp. 155–56; Nathalie B. Fryde, 'Edward III's Removal of his Ministers and Judges, 1340–1', *Bulletin of the Institute of Historical Research* 48 (1975), 150–3; and E.B. Fryde, *William de la Pole: Merchant and King's Banker (+1366)* (London, 1988), pp. 171–72. E.B. Fryde does insist, however, that 'it would be an exaggeration to put the blame for the failure to capture Tournai solely on a lack of money . . . But Edward would have been in a much stronger position towards his allies if he had been able to pay a large part of the huge subsidies promised to them' (p. 172).

On the financial crisis in England in the years prior to the siege see Harriss, pp. 270–93; E.B. Fryde,

believe that the archbishop meant by lack of money to see me betrayed and killed.'[5] And later to the town of Ghent he wrote:

> Certain of our false councilors and ministers in England have behaved in such a manner towards us that unless we do something about it we shall be unable to sustain the war this season and so we think that, if we do not help ourselves, the aforementioned ministers will quickly put our people to mischief or to disobedience towards us.[6]

On November 30, Edward returned to England. What followed is known to modern historians as the 'Crisis of 1341.'[7] Using the failure at Tournai, the English king eliminated the facets of government hostile to his plans for war against France. This purging of anti-war elements was successful, and by the end of 1341, Edward's finances were under control, and he was again planning an attack on France.[8]

But, 'legally' he could not; at least according to the Treaty of Esplechin, signed a little more than one year previously, Edward had promised not to attack France. His royal counterpart, Philip VI, surely believed that the English would return, but he was counting on the period of peace to prepare for this return. Then, in April 1341, what would have otherwise been only a minor event, changed both kings' plans for pursuing warfare against each other: John III, count of Brittany, died without a male heir. This produced a crisis of inheritance. One claimant to the ducal throne was Joan of Penthièvre, daughter of John III's brother, Guy. A second claimant was John of Montford, step-brother to John III. Naturally, France and England could not both support the same claimant to the leadership of Brittany. Philip VI chose to back Joan, as she was married to the nephew of the French king, Charles, count of Blois; England supported John of Montfort.[9] (Thus occurred the historical irony that had Edward III sustaining his candidate on Salic legal grounds that no noble throne could pass to a woman, a legal principle which he had denied in his own attempt to gain the French kingship. At the same time, Philip VI was disregarding that same Salic Law that had given him the throne in supporting Joan.)

Initially, the war in Brittany remained limited. Edward III was too busy with his problems at home, and Philip VI chose to wait until John of Montford made the first move before sending soldiers to the region. John responded by entering Nantes, the

---

William de la Pole, pp. 135–69; and E.B. Fryde, 'Financial Resources of Edward III in the Netherlands, 1337–40', *Revue Belge de philologie et d'histoire* 45 (1967), 1142–1216.

5 As quoted in Nathalie B. Fryde, 'Edward III' pp. 153–4.

6 In Nathalie B. Fryde, 'Edward III,' p. 154.

7 Probably the best account of the Crisis of 1341 can be found in Roy Martin Haines, *Archbishop John Stratford: Political Revolutionary and Champion of the Liberties of the English Church, ca. 1275/80–1348* (Toronto, 1986), pp. 278–328. See also Nathalie B. Fryde, 'Edward III,' pp. 149–61; W.R. Jones, '*Rex et Ministri*: English Local Government and the Crisis of 1341', *Journal of British Studies* 13 (1973), 1–20; and E. Deprez, *Les préliminaires de la guerre de cent ans* (Paris, 1902), pp. 349–52.

8 See Michael Prestwich, 'English Armies in the Early Stages of the Hundred Years War: a Scheme in 1341', *Bulletin of the Institute of Historical Research* 56 (1983), 102–13.

9 Alfred H. Burne, *The Crecy War* (London, 1955), pp. 66–67 and Henri Denifle, *La guerre de cent ans et la désolation des églises, monastères et hospitaux en France* (Paris, 1899), p. 18.

largest town in the duchy, and then by attacking Joan's allies in the surrounding countryside. Charles of Blois, leading Joan's supporting force, including a French army under the leadership of Philip VI's son, John, countered John's move by attacking and capturing Nantes in November 1341. Montford was captured and imprisoned in Paris where he was to die in 1345.[10]

Before Charles could relish his victory, John's wife, Joan of Flanders, appealed to Edward III for assistance in her husband's claim. Edward responded to her request by sending a small force to Brittany under the leadership of Sir Walter Mauny. But the expedition was delayed by poor weather and did not arrive until May 1342, landing at Hennebout where the countess was under siege. Mauny was immediately successful. The siege at Hennebout was quickly relieved, and in the next few days, Mauny relieved another siege at Auray and then defeated a small Bloisian force at Quimperlé.[11] By July, however, Charles was again victorious; the fortifications of Auray, Vannes, and Guémenée-sur-Scorff fell quickly to him.[12]

Despite these latest setbacks, news of Mauny's victories had reached London, and Edward decided to take advantage of what this small force had done by increasing his numbers in Brittany to more than 3,000.[13] The Hundred Years War continued.

Edward's new army was led by William of Bohun, earl of Northampton, and included Robert of Artois and the earls of Derby and Oxford. All three were experienced generals and had been active participants in the 1340 conflicts in the southern Low Countries. This new force landed at Brest on August 18, 1342. Charles of Blois was then besieging the town, but withdrew at the appearance of the English. Northampton cleared the countryside, arriving outside the town of Morlaix on September 3. Morlaix was in Charles' hands, and Northampton began a siege.[14]

In the meantime, Charles' force had been growing, perhaps to as many as 15,000.[15] He moved to relieve the siege, but outside of the village of Lanmeur, seven miles from Morlaix, he encountered the English army, ordered in a line to receive his attack. The battle of Morlaix was fought on September 30, 1342. Although greatly outnumbered, perhaps as many as four to one, by the end of the day the English had sent the French fleeing from the field. But Northampton, undoubtedly still concerned about his comparatively small numbers, refused to pursue Blois' fleeing troops; he returned to the siege of Morlaix, although the town never did fall to him.[16]

As inconclusive as it was, the battle of Morlaix is less important for the history of the Hundred Years War than for the history of military tactics during the first half of

---

[10] Burne, p. 67 and Denifle, pp. 18–19.
[11] Burne, pp. 67–69 and Denifle, pp. 19–20.
[12] Sumption, p. 398 and Denifle, pp. 20–21.
[13] Burne (pp. 71–72) contends that the total English force numbered fewer than 4,000. Denifle (p. 22) tallies between 4,000–5,000. And Sumption (p. 398), on the other hand, claims a total of 5,500, delivered to Brittany on 440 ships.
[14] Burne, pp. 69–71; Sumption, pp. 400–02; and Denifle, pp. 21–22.
[15] This is Burne's figure, which is in fact much lower than earlier historians had tallied (p. 71). Sumption calculates an even lower number – 3,000 cavalry, 1,500 Genoese mercenary soldiers and sailors, and a 'motley force of Breton infantry' (pp. 401–02).
[16] Modern accounts of the battle of Morlaix include: Burne, pp. 71–76; Sumption, p. 402; and Tout, 'Tactics,' pp. 713–15.

the fifteenth century. Despite Geoffrey le Baker's contention that the soldiers on both sides fought better than their counterparts at Halidon Hill, Crécy, or Poitiers,[17] very few modern accounts of the battle exist, with only T.F. Tout and Colonel Alfred H. Burne giving any more than a paragraph to the conflict in this century. This seems to be little more than a reflection of the lack of original sources for the battle. There is perhaps no battle fought between the forces of England and France during the Hundred Years War that received less comment than did this one. While the English chroniclers Geoffrey le Baker, Henry Knighton, and Adam Murimuth all give accounts of varying lengths of this battle, there is only one short French account, that found in Cuvelier's poetic *Chronique de Bertrand Guesclin*, written 1380–87.[18] Part of this is undoubtedly because there are no contemporary Breton narrative histories; but that Jean le Bel, Jean Froissart, and the author of the *Grandes Chroniques*, all of whom otherwise extensively chronicle the events of the early Hundred Years War, have nothing to report on the battle indicates perhaps its lack of importance, even in the relatively minor Brittany campaign.

But for the history of infantry warfare, especially between 1302 and 1347, the battle of Morlaix is of great importance, even if just to explain why the vastly outnumbered English infantry army was not only able to keep from being annihilated by their French cavalry opponents, but also to cause them to flee in rout from the battlefield. That the earl of Northampton did not pursue the fleeing French, nor later take the town of Morlaix is of little consequence to such a study.

Both Henry Knighton and Adam Murimuth begin their narratives leading to the battle with Walter Mauny's expedition: Knighton recounts that this was because Brittany 'was oppressed by the French king,'[19] while Murimuth writes that Mauny led this expedition, which contained 40 knights and 200 archers, 'with the permission of the king [Edward III].' The latter chronicler also mentions that Mauny was successful, taking three castles and forcing a truce with Charles of Blois, a truce which did not please Edward and was therefore invalid.[20] In response, reports Adam Murimuth, Edward sent more troops, 50 knights and 1000 archers, under the leadership of the earl of Northampton and other leading nobles.[21]

---

[17] Geoffrey le Baker, p. 76: 'Pugnatum est fortiter ex utraque parte, ita quod contigit in illo certamine quod nec in bellis, nec in Halydoneheil nec de Cressi nec de Petter, audivimus contigisse.'
[18] Cuvelier, *Chronique de Bertrand Guesclin*, ed. E. Charrière (Paris, 1839), II:439–45. Geoffrey le Baker and Henry Knighton definitely contain the most extensive account of this battle, with Cuvelier and Adam Murimuth recording much smaller accounts. Robert of Avesbury says nothing about the battle itself, but does comment on the number of English troops in Brittany.
[19] Henry Knighton, p. 23.
[20] Adam Murimuth, p. 125.
[21] Adam Murimuth, p. 125. All English chroniclers award Northampton the supreme leadership of this expedition. Adam Murimuth also mentions the count of Devonshire, the Baron Radulph of Stafford, and William of Killesby in leadership roles (p. 125). Geoffrey le Baker lists Killesby, Hugh Despenser, and Richard Talbot (p. 76). Henry Knighton adds Count Robert of Artois and John D'Arcy to Devonshire and Killesby (whom he calls Gaddesby) (p. 25). And Robert of Avesbury lists the earl of Warwick with Despenser (p. 342).

Northampton, whose army necessitated transport by 14 large ships and many small ones, according to Murimuth, landed at Brest, where the duchess of Brittany and her children were under siege by land and sea by Blois and 'a large force from the French realm.' At this the French army fled from their siegeworks, and Northampton captured and burned most of the besieging fleet.[22]

Few details of Northampton's march to Morlaix are available in the contemporary sources. Henry Knighton simply moves to the siege of Morlaix,[23] with Adam Murimuth reporting that the English 'ran through the country indiscreetly, for the French could find no one who could resist them.'[24] But Geoffrey le Baker, who is the most descriptive chronicler of the events leading to the battle at Morlaix, disagrees with this. He claims that the English 'having gone into Brittany, took land, and, inviting the resistence of their enemies, they had many violent conflicts with them.' Later he adds: 'And they conquered all of the country up to Morlaix, part by surrender and part by destruction.'[25]

Morlaix was not a chance target, declares Adam Murimuth, but one that was chosen after Northampton 'had the counsel of those who knew the country well,' and that he paid these to lead him to the town. There, as he tried to assault the town, he did not fare well; many were hurt, and one knight, Jacob Lovel, was killed. Thus Northampton began a siege, expecting, Murimuth continues, 'aid from the allies of England,' which after fifteen days arrived. The chronicler does not describe further what this aid was.[26]

Also moving towards his position was the army of Charles of Blois. Blois' force was quite large. Henry Knighton numbers his army at 20,000; Adam Murimuth counts 3,000 knights, 1,500 'Janissaries,' and a nonprofessional infantry (Murimuth calls them *populari*) 'without number;' and Geoffrey le Baker refuses to speculate, writing only that the French were 'a huge army.'[27] They came to relieve the siege of Morlaix, and rushed to the site when they realized how few besieging soldiers there were.[28] But, as Henry Knighton reports, the English 'in the complete darkness of night moved to meet their enemy.'[29] They also arrived early enough for Northampton to select his position and to prepare the field where the battle would be fought. Knighton writes:

---

[22] Adam Murimuth, p. 126.

[23] Henry Knighton, p. 25.

[24] Adam Murimuth, pp. 126–27: 'ac discurrentes per patriam indiscrete neminem qui resisteret invenerunt.'

[25] Geoffrey le Baker, p. 76: 'Britanniam itaque profecti, invitis inimicis resistentibus, terram ceperunt, et multos asperos conflictus contra ipsos habuerunt . . . et totam patriam partim redditam et partim destructam sibi submiserunt usque ad villam Morleys.'

[26] Adam Murimuth, p. 127.

[27] Henry Knighton, p. 25; Adam Murimuth, p. 127; and Geoffrey le Baker, p. 76. Another manuscript of Adam Murimuth's *Continuatio chronicarum* (p. 227) mentions only 1,200 'Janissaries,' although the calculation of knights and infantry remain the same.

[28] Henry Knighton, p. 25.

[29] Henry Knighton, p. 25: 'et tota obscura nocte dedit se in occursum inimicorum suorum.'

Battle of Morlaix

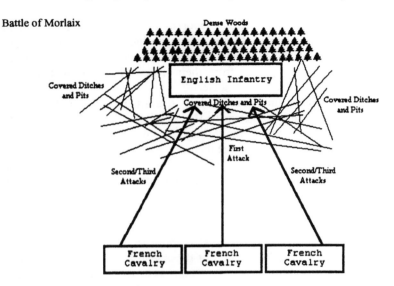

And in the morning they took their position about one league from the enemy in front of a wood, and they dug pits and ditches around them and covered them over with hay and grass. And after the sun rose, they prepared themselves for battle.[30]

Part of this preparation, according to Adam Murimuth, was to dismount the knights and have all the English soldiers fight in one line as infantry.[31]

In response, Blois ordered his troops in three lines. The first, commanded by Geoffrey Charnys (the only named commander besides Blois) and containing many knights, charged into the English line but were, in the words of Henry Knighton, 'Immediately conquered . . . and sent into flight.'[32] The two other lines did not follow, but held their ground. Blois held a quick tactical planning session. But as the French still greatly outnumbered the English, it was decided to attempt another charge, although whether this was to be made by only the second line, as Henry Knighton seems to indicate, or by a combination of the second and third lines, as suggested by Geoffrey le Baker, cannot be determined from the original sources.[33]

In fact, Henry Knighton insists, the French had no thought other than to attack again: 'Seeing the small number of English soldiers, they were taken by an aggressive

---

[30] Henry Knighton, p. 25: 'Et mane ceperunt locum suum quasi per unam leucam ab inimicis prope unum boscum, et foderunt foveas et fossas circa eos, et cooperuerunt eas de feno et herbagio; et post solis ortum paraverunt se ad bellum.' See also Adam Murimuth, pp. 127, 227.

[31] Adam Murimuth, pp. 127, 227.

[32] Only Henry Knighton (p. 26) mentions the formation of Blois' army (although Geoffrey le Baker's claim (p. 77) that Blois fought three times that day may be a reflection of the French order). He is also the only chronicler to report Charnys' failure: 'Et inimici se paraverunt in tres acies divisas. In quarum prima fuit dominus Galfridus Charnys cum multis galletis; qui statim victi sunt ab Anglicis et missi in fugam' (p. 26).

[33] Henry Knighton only mentions two charges of French troops (p. 25), while Geoffrey le Baker, who is far less detailed in his account of the battle, claims that the French charged three times that day (p. 77).

spirit and undertook to overwhelm the English troops.' Furthermore, they were on horses, as cavalry, while they faced only infantry: 'And wishing to trample the infantry under the feet of their very powerful horses, they charged dangerously at them.'[34] However, this attack did not succeed. The French were pushed into the narrow line of English infantry, their charge was halted, and they were driven back into the pits and ditches which surrounded them. Knighton again describes the scene: 'But having been drawn into a narrow cave . . . they fell one on top of the other into the concealed pits which the enemy had made.'[35] Being unable to penetrate the English infantry line and to defeat them, the French retreated from the field. Over fifty French knights had been killed, with many more *populari* also slain, and Geoffrey Charnys and many others were captured – Cuvelier writes that these were 'old and young, great and small.'[36] The English too retreated, 'on account of a [continuing] fear of the large numbers of enemy,' writes Henry Knighton.[37]

It is perhaps easy to dismiss the battle of Morlaix in a study of military history, because of the lack of sources, and because those that do exist are English only. But the similarity of the tactics at Morlaix and those at other battles fought in the beginning of the fourteenth century demonstrates the validity of the narrative here. It also indicates that the battlefield tactical practice of the English, generalship for lack of a better word, was by 1342 known and exercised at every military engagement. As at Boroughbridge, Dupplin Moor, and Halidon Hill, the main tactic of the English troops was to form a solid line or mass of infantry, with even the knights dismounted, and then to force their opponents to charge into it. In this instance, the French chose to make cavalry charges, either two or three of them, and each charge met with failure as it was unable to penetrate the English infantry line or to cause it to rout. Finally, after suffering many losses, and undoubtedly disappointed at their failure to defeat a smaller force, the French fled from the field. The English had won the battle.

However, there is one important difference between this victory and most of the ones which the English won before and after it. While archers played an important role in the battles of Dupplin Moor, Halidon Hill, and Crécy, they do not play the same role at Morlaix. At these other conflicts the archers were positioned along the flanks of the infantry line to urge their opponents into a disorderly charge, to further confuse that charge, to narrow it onto the infantry line, and perhaps, although not entirely necessary, to kill or wound those charging. Although archers seem to have been present at Morlaix, as all chroniclers who mention the numbers in both Mauny's and Northampton's armies indicate a force that included mostly archers,[38] they were

---

[34] Henry Knighton, p. 25: 'Tandem videntes Anglicorum paucitatem et suorum multitudinem, ferocitate animi ducti, opprimere Angliae gentes moliti sunt; et equorum suorum validorum pedibus conculcare volentes capitose irruerunt in eos.'

[35] Henry Knighton, II:25: 'sed antris decepti obturatis, ut praedictum est, ceciderunt quilibet super alium in foveis abinvicem confusi.'

[36] Cuvelier, p. 439. See also Henry Knighton, p. 26; Adam Murimuth, pp. 127, 227; and Geoffrey le Baker, pp. 76–77.

[37] Henry Knighton, p. 26: 'propter metum multitudinis inimicorum.'

[38] See nos. 20 and 21 above.

not positioned as at these other battles. Had Northampton done so, with his small numbers of troops, he would have made his infantry line so thin that the French charges would probably have been successful. So he included the archers among the other troops in the line of infantry, using weapons other than their longbows.

But how could Northampton make up for the loss of flanking archers to narrow and confuse the French charges? In this he resorted to another tactic which was being practiced in battlefield conflicts of the early fourteenth century, although not previously by the English. He arrived first at the battlefield and prepared it for conflict on the next day. He placed his troops with their backs against a dense wood, thus discouraging their flight, and he dug ditches and pits along the flanks of the infantry line and across the battlefield. As the Scots, Flemings, and Swiss – all without the benefit of skilled longbowmen – had found, this tactic was able to narrow and confuse the charge of their opponents so that when they met the infantry lines, they were easily defeated. And so it happened also at Morlaix. Henry Knighton described it nicely; the French were drawn into an 'antrum obturatum,' a 'narrow cave,'[39] a cave in which they met defeat.

---

[39] See no. 35 above.

XII

THE BATTLES OF STAVEREN, 1345, AND VOTTEM, 1346

THE SUCCESS OF THE FLEMINGS in 1302–03 and 1323–27 elicited fear among French nobles that the spirit of rebellion would spread elsewhere in the realm, particularly Bordeaux, Picardy, and Gascony. But with the exception of a small rebellion which broke out in Bordeaux shortly after the battle of Courtrai, France remained relatively calm.[1] The Low Countries did not, however. In the 1330s and 1340s the Low Countries were awash in popular rebellion. In Flanders from 1337 to 1345 a rebellion was led by the Ghentenaar Jacob van Artevelde which succeeded in supplanting Louis of Nevers's comital leadership. In 1344–45 a rebellion was fought by Frisians against their lord, William, count of Hainault, Holland, and Zeeland. And from 1345 to 1347 the town of Liège led neighboring towns, Huy, Dinant, Bouvignes, and Saint-Trond, in a revolt against the Prince-Bishop of Liège, Englebert de la Marck. It is these latter two rebellions which concern us here. For although the Flemings involved themselves in conflicts against the French at Sluys and Tournai in 1340 and would again be found facing the French at Calais in 1346, these engagements were not battles as studied in this work.[2] On the other hand, both the Frisians and the Liègeois faced armies on the battlefield which attempted to put down their rebellions. And in both cases, at Staveren in 1345 and at Vottem in 1346, the rebellious armies, infantry forces, defeated their cavalry-based opponents.

Of all the late medieval Low Countries, Friesland was the most sparsely populated and economically backward. The Frisians even by the early fourteenth century had never really recovered from their harsh conquest by Charlemagne. They were certainly a proud and independent people, but as they were generally quite far from and of little importance to any 'foreign' governmental leaders, Frisian inhabitants were usually left alone without an outlet for their spirit of independence. Indeed, it was not until the beginning of the fourteenth century, with the recognition of and struggle over the rest of the northern Low Countries by France and the Holy Roman Empire, that Friesland also began to seek associations with more powerful European

---

[1] See *Chronographia regum Francorum*, I:119; the first and second continuators of Guillaume de Nangis's *Chronicon*, I:324, 334; and *Chronicon comitum Flandriae*, p. 203.

[2] On the Jacob van Artevelde rebellion see David Nicholas, *Medieval Flanders*, pp. 217–26; Henri Pirenne, *Histoire de Belgique*, II:93–123; Henry Stephen Lucas, pp. 240–528; Hans van Werveke, *Jacques van Artevelde* (Brussels, 1943); and David Nicholas, *The van Arteveldes of Ghent: The Varieties of Vendetta and the Hero in History* (Ithaca, 1988), pp. 1–71.

entities.[3] In 1337 an alliance was agreed to with Philip VI of France, but it brought negligible results. The French king was simply too far distant from this very northern province. Therefore, in 1338, the Frisians turned to a closer ally, placing themselves under the leadership of William III, the governor of the nearby counties of Holland and Zeeland as well as the more southern county of Hainault.[4]

Why the Frisians did this, and in fact who among them had the right to do this, is very much a mystery of medieval history. What is known is that before too long the Frisians began to doubt the wisdom of their choice of governmental leaders. There were some economic benefits, as the connection with Holland and Zeeland increased trade and other commercial contacts, and, at least initially, William left the Frisians alone.[5] But in 1342–44, the count began to rule Friesland with more stringency and immediacy. He became concerned by Hanseatic economic interest in his northern lands, by Frisian ecclesiastical contests, and by what he perceived as a lack of service and loyalty of his subjects there. Against this the Frisians rebelled, and on several occasions William was required to use force and intimidation to pacify them.[6]

By 1345 the situation had deteriorated to such an extent that William decided to mount a major expedition against Friesland. After preparing for this campaign in Amsterdam for more than six months and after besieging Utrecht for more than six weeks (Utrecht was also rebelling against his rule), on September 26 he crossed over the Zuider Zee from Enkhuisen to Staveren, the 'capital' of Friesland. There the Frisian rebels stood ready for battle, a battle which they would win, and which would even cause the death of the count.[7]

In most ways the prince-bishopric of Liège was very different from Friesland. Neither as populous or as economically prosperous as Flanders, Brabant, or Hainault, it was still a powerful entity in the southern Low Countries, holding an important border-position between the French concerns of the region and those of the Holy Roman Empire. Long an ecclesiastical capital, Liège had been governed by a prince-bishop since as early as the tenth century when Bishop Notger was appointed to the position by Emperor Otto II.[8] Since that time the prince-bishops had remained in control of the province by retaining a strong and loyal alliance with the German emperors. Thus, despite a few occasions when the Liégeois were forced to defend their lands against the Brabantese, all of which were successful, the prince-bishopric almost always was at peace with external powers.[9]

But internal peace, especially during the thirteenth, fourteenth, and fifteenth

---

[3] See J.F. Niermeyer, 'Het Sticht Utrecht, Gelre en de Friese landen in de veertiende eeuw,' in *Algemene geschiedenis der Nederlanden*, vol. 3: *De late middeleeuwen, 1305–1477* (Utrecht, 1951), pp. 155–60.

[4] Lucas, p. 505 and Niermeyer, pp. 156–57.

[5] Lucas, p. 506.

[6] See examples given in Lucas, pp. 506–08. On Frisian desires for independence see Niermeyer, pp. 157–59.

[7] Lucas, p. 508 and Jean van Malderghem, *La bataille de Staveren (26 septembre 1345)* (Brussels, 1869).

[8] Pirenne, *Histoire de Belgique*, I, 177–78, II:19 and Godefroid Kurth, *La cité de Liège au moyen-age* (Brussels, 1909), pp. 21–52.

[9] Pirenne, *Histoire de Belgique*, I:207–11; Kurth, I:110–28; and F. Vercauteren, 'Het prinsbisdom

centuries, was almost non-existent. In fact, there may have been no other region in Europe during this period which suffered more popular rebellions, including Flanders. For example, between 1298 and 1347 the major towns of the province were almost continually in rebellion against the prince-bishop.[10]

The specific rebellion which would lead to the battle of Vottem originated at the death of the Prince-Bishop Adolph de la Marck. Adolph de la Marck had not been a favorite of his subjects. His heavy-handed rule was opposed by almost everyone in the province, and he frequently answered this opposition with military force. Examples are numerous: in 1314 he violently put down a rebellion in Saint-Trond, in 1318 in Fosse, also in 1318 in Huy, in 1321 in Ciney, and in 1323 in Tongeren.[11] Ultimately, in 1328 the towns of Liège, Huy, Tongeren, and Saint-Trond decided to oppose the prince-bishop; forming a confederation and mustering an army, the towns fought three battles against Adolph: Erbonne (May 27), Waremme (June 2), and Hoesselt (September 25).[12] Although these battles were by and large inconclusive, the idea of armed rebels opposing his reign frightened the prince-bishop into some constitutional concessions. Reforms of the municipal regime were undertaken in 1330 and 1331. Known either as the *Réformation d'Adolphe* or the *loi de murmure*, the Liégeois were to submit to the authority of the prince-bishop, but in turn they were to see a lessening of local power – 'gouverneurs' were replaced by 'wardeurs' – and an increase in the autonomy of the guilds.[13]

For twelve years there was an extremely tenuous peace between the Liégeois and their prince-bishop. The townspeople took as many privileges as they legitimately could from the new constitutional reforms, and sometimes they took more. Eventually, in 1343, Adolph de la Marck repealed the *loi de murmure* and attempted to return to pre-1330 governance. This might have provoked a new rebellion against the prince-bishop, but before the confederation of towns could again come together, on November 3, 1344, Adolph died.[14] A solution to the problem might have presented itself with the selection of a good new leader, but when the towns found on February 23, 1345 that their new prince-bishop was to be Englebert de la Marck, the nephew of the object of their previous hatred, they immediately gathered an army and prepared for war.[15] Englebert also knew of the feelings of the Liégeois, and he too

Luik tot 1316,' in *Algemene geschiedenis der Nederlanden*, vol. 2: *De volle middeleeuwen, 925–1305* (Utrecht, 1950), pp. 340–41.

[10] Kurth, I:129–51, 179–215, 243–60, II:1–88; Claude Gaier, *Art et organisation militaires dans la principauté de Liège et dans le comté de Looz au Moyen Age* (Brussels, 1968), pp. 262–306; and Fernand Vercauteren, *Luttes sociales à Liège, xiiie et xive siècles* (Brussels, 1946).

[11] Pirenne, *Histoire de Belgique*, II:16–17, 35–37; Kurth, II:1–17; Vercauteren, *Luttes sociales*, pp. 81–85; Vercauteren, 'Het prinsbisdom Luik,' pp. 350–52; and J. Lejeune, 'Het prinsbisdom Luik tot 1390,' in *Algemene geschiedenis der Nederlanden*, vol. 3: *De late middeleeuwen, 1305–1477* (Utrecht, 1951), pp. 177–78.

[12] Lejeune, pp. 179–80; Kurth, II:31–45; and Vercauteren, *Luttes sociales*, pp. 88–89. The best description of these battles is in Gaier, pp. 276–85. I have chosen not to discuss them because of the difficulty in discerning battlefield tactics from the original sources.

[13] Pirenne, *Histoire de Belgique*, II:42–43; Lejeune, p. 180; Kurth, II:38–60; and Vercauteren, *Luttes sociales*, pp. 88–91.

[14] Lejeune, pp. 181–82 and Kurth, II:63–69.

[15] Lejeune, pp. 182–83; Kurth, II:73–74; and Vercauteren, *Luttes sociales*, p. 94.

gathered a force, an army composed of some of the greatest knights in the Holy Roman Empire. The mustering of these two forces took time, and it was not until July 18, 1346 that they faced each other on the battlefield in a northern suburb of Liège known as Vottem. As at Staveren, the rebels prevailed.[16]

Because of the death of Count William, the battle of Staveren is mentioned in several chronicles, among them Jan Beke's *Chronographia*, Jean Froissart's *Chroniques*, the continuation of Richard Lescot's *Chronique*, the *Grandes chroniques de France*, and the *Récits d'un bourgeois de Valenciennes*. But it is only in the *Récits* and Froissart's third redaction that a discussion of tactics on the battlefield can be found.[17]

In 1345 William was in his northern lands for several reasons but primarily to reassert his control over the ecclesiastical capital of the north, Utrecht, and to put down the insurrection in Friesland. Both, of course, required military force. Neither appeared to be an easy task, but the count refused to be apprehensive, and he pressed forward without delay, planning first to attack Utrecht and then Friesland. Utrecht proved to be a difficult target, but after frequently assaulting the town and bombarding its walls with 'many engines' for six weeks, it fell.[18]

Following this victory the count marched his army to Dordrecht, placed his troops on ships, and sailed north to Friesland. The size of this force cannot be known from the original sources. The *Récits d'un bourgeois de Valenciennes* does claim a total of 10,000 men-at-arms and 2,000 'haubergons' at the siege of Utrecht, but it also insists that many stayed there under the command of Jean of Hainault, the count's uncle, and did not go to on Friesland.[19] Instead, the *Récits* and the other original sources all indicate that William's army was quite small in comparison to the Frisian army which was encountered at Staveren. Jean Froissart, for one, claims that the Frisians outnumbered their foes by a twenty to one ratio.[20] It was, however, a force composed of the 'most noble chivalry of Hainault, Holland, Flanders, Brabant, Guelders, Jülich, Namur, and Hesbaye' plus a few others who had either joined him 'on loan' from the king of France or the German emperor. Included was the duke of Guelders, the count of Namur, the count of Salm, the count of Eppenheim, and 35 other knights noble enough to carry their own banners.[21]

The count's ships landed outside of Staveren, and on the morning of September

---

16 Lejeune, pp. 182–83.
17 Jan Beke, pp.301–03; Jean Froissart, IV:324–28 (the third redaction is pp. 326–28); Richard Lescot, p. 68–69; *Grandes chroniques*, IX:257; and *Récits d'un bourgeois de Valenciennes*, pp. 202–05. There is also an anonymous poem on the death of William, but it also contains no details about the battle: 'La mort du conte de Henau,' in *Panégyriques des comtes de Hainaut et de Hollande Guillaume I et Guillaume II*, ed. C. Potvin (Mons, 1863).
18 The most detailed account of the siege of Utrecht is in *Récits d'un bourgeois de Valenciennes*, pp. 196–97, 201–02. See also Jan Beke, p. 301, and Jean Froissart, IV:324–26.
19 *Récits d'un bourgeois de Valenciennes*, p. 197.
20 Jean Froissart, IV:327. See also Jan Beke, p. 301 and *Récits d'un bourgeois de Valenciennes*, p. 203.
21 The quotation comes from Jean Froissart, IV:325. See also Jean Froissart, IV:326; *Récits d'un bourgeois de Valenciennes*, p. 197; and Richard Lescot, pp. 68–69. Some of these may have stayed at Utrecht, as the original sources do not mention any of these at Staveren.

Battle of Staveren

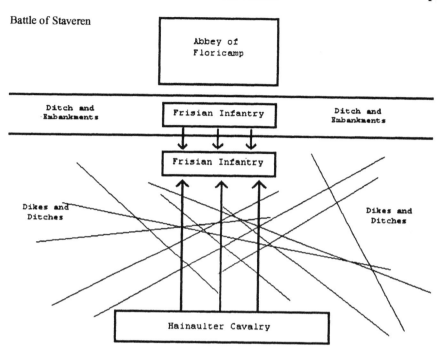

26 the soldiers heard mass and disembarked.[22] William seemed to have known of the presence at Staveren of his Frisian opponents. He may also have known that they outnumbered him. But he did not fear them. Pride, present with almost all fourteenth-century noble forces when facing 'lesser' opponents, also seems to have been common among these knights. Jean Froissart asserts that William 'held little admiration for and did not prize the Frisian power' at Staveren.[23] And the *Récits d'un bourgeois de Valenciennes* writes that William himself led his troops into battle, shouting 'follow me for the honor of God and Saint George.'[24]

On the other side, the Frisians had prepared well for the count's attack. Jean Froissart writes that they had fortified their position, outside of the abbey of Floricamp, while the *Récits d'un bourgeois de Valenciennes* maintains that these fortifications were ditches and embankments.[25] But in seeing the charge of the count's troops the Frisians abandoned their fortified positions and ordered a defensive infantry line in front of them. The reason for this was simple, claims the *Récits*, for the Frisians could see that the oncoming attackers were having difficulty with

---

[22] *Récits d'un bourgeois de Valenciennes*, p. 202.
[23] Jean Froissart, IV:327: 'Chils contes qui fu de grande volonté, hardis et entreprendans oultre mesure, et pour lors en la flour de sa jonèce, et qui petit amiroit et prisoit la poissance des Frisons contre la sienne.'
[24] *Récits d'un bourgeois de Valenciennes*, p. 203: 'Sy me sieve en l'oneur de Dieu et de monseigneur saint George!' See also Jean Froissart, IV:325, 327.
[25] Jean Froissart, IV:326–27 and *Récits d'un bourgeois de Valenciennes*, p. 203.

the dike-filled terrain and were approaching them so quickly that they had lost their ordered composition; they came 'without array, without any order.'[26]

William's soldiers thus charged into this solid infantry formation in disarray, and their attack met with fierce resistance. The Frisians fought well with their 'very large and heavy pikes, their long swords and axes and falchions,' killing all they faced 'without pity and without mercy.'[27] Although the count's troops fought well and also killed many, their lack of numbers eventually proved to be their downfall.[28] Only a very small number were able to flee to the safety of the ships. Most were left dead on the battlefield.[29]

A short time after the battle, and evidently having heard of his nephew's defeat, Jean of Hainault landed another party at the battlefield site. But this group did nothing but collect the bodies of their dead and sail south. The Frisians had the victory.[30]

The battle of Vottem generated far more contemporary commentary than did the battle of Staveren. Lengthy accounts of what occurred can be found in the chronicles of Jean le Bel, Jean d'Outremeuse, and Mathias von Neuenberg, and in the *Récits d'un bourgeois de Valenciennes* and the *Chronique de l'abbaye de Saint-Trond*. Shorter accounts are found in the chronicles of Jean de Winterthur, Jean de Hocsem, Heinrich von Diessenhoven, and Heinrich von Rebdorf, the *Le miroir des nobles de Hesbaye* of Jacques de Hemricourt, and the *Vita Clementis VI* of Werner de Bonn.[31]

An account of the battle of Vottem begins with a discussion on the location of the battlefield. Vottem is a suburb of the town of Liège; in 1346 it was situated just outside the walls of the town, and was selected by the rebels as the place for battle because it lay on the main road into Liège from Tongeren, where Archbishop Englebert de la Marck had set up his court during the rebellion. Thus it was the route which would have to be taken by the archbishop and his troops if they most easily wished to enter Liège.[32] According to the original sources, this was done by the rebels for two reasons: first, they knew that news of the town's insurrection had been

---

[26] *Récits d'un bourgeois de Valenciennes*, p. 203: 'Et quant les Frisons virent qu'il y en eult assés d'issus et qu'ils furent oultre les dicques et qu'ils venoient sy hastivement à grans flottes et sans aroy, ne nul conroy, les Frisons yssirent hors de Stavres et de l'abaye de Flouricamp et partout de leurs embucquemens.'

[27] Quotations are from *Récits d'un bourgeois de Valenciennes*, p. 203. See also Jean Froissart, IV:327.

[28] Jean Froissart, IV:327 and *Récits d'un bourgeois de Valenciennes*, p. 203.

[29] Jean Froissart, IV:327 and *Récits d'un bourgeois de Valenciennes*, pp. 203–04. The *Récits* includes a list of the noble dead.

[30] *Récits d'un bourgeois de Valenciennes*, pp. 204–05 and Jean Froissart, IV:326, 327. The *Récits* claims that there was a small battle fought between Jean and the Frisians but that it was inconclusive.

[31] Jean le Bel, II:140–41; Jean d'Outremeuse, *Chronique abrégée, de 1341 à 1400*, in *Chroniques Liègeoises*, ii, ed. S. Balau and E. Fairon (Brussels, 1931), pp. 165–70; Mathias von Neuenberg, *Chronik*, ed. A. Hofmeister, *MGH nova ser.*, iv (Berlin, 1940), pp. 202–03; *Récits d'un bourgeois de Valenciennes*, pp. 210–13; *Chronique de l'abbaye de Saint-Trond*, II:282–83; Jean de Winterthur, pp. 263–64; Jean de Hocsem, pp. 341–45; Heinrich von Diessenhoven, *Chronicon ab a. 1316–1361*, in *Fontes rerum Germanicarum*, iv, ed. J.F. Boehmer (Stuttgart, 1868), pp. 51–52; Heinrich von Rebdorf, *Annales imperatorum et paparum (1294–1362)*, in *Fontes rerum Germanicarum*, iv, ed. J.F. Boehmer (Stuttgart, 1868), pp. 528–29; Jacques de Hemricourt, *Le miroir des nobles de Hesbaye* in *OEuvres*

Battle of Vottem

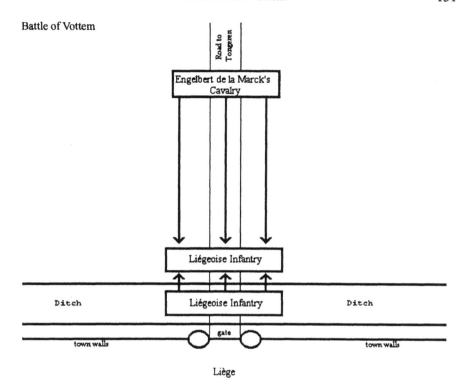

Liège

received by the archbishop, that he had gathered an army, and that he was on his way to the town by the quickest route possible. In the words of Jean de Hocsem: 'the archbishop intended to punish the townspeople of Liège.'[33] Second, the proximity of the battlefield to the town walls boosted the morale of the rebels, as remarked on by Jean de Winterthur, for they knew that if the archbishop got past them, there would be little to prevent him from entering and punishing the town.[34]

It is difficult to know how large the rebel force was at Vottem. Only Mathias von Neuenberg mentions a number for the soldiers, 40,000.[35] What can be determined is that these troops came also from outside of Liège, from Huy, Dinant, and Bouvignes,[36] that they contained very few knights – only Godefroid de Harduemont, Louis d'Agimont, Jean de Borgneval, Walthier de Hautepenne, and Arnoul de

de Jacques de Hemricourt, i, ed. C. de Borman (Brussels, 1910), p. 161; and Werner de Bonn, *Vita Clementis VI*, in *Vitae paparum Avenionensium*, i, ed. S. Baluze-Mollat (Paris, 1914), p. 546.

[32] On the establishment of the archbishop's court in Tongeren see Jean d'Outremeuse, p. 165.

[33] Jean de Hocsem, p. 341: '. . . episcopus intendens se de Leodio vindicare . . .' See also Jean d'Outremeuse, pp. 165–66; Jean le Bel, II:140; Jean de Winterthur, p. 263; and Mathias von Neuenberg, p. 202.

[34] Jean de Winterthur, p. 263. See also Jean d'Outremeuse, pp. 165–66 and Werner de Bonn, p. 546.

[35] Mathias von Neuenberg, p. 203.

[36] Jean d'Outremeuse (p. 168) mentions troops from Huy, while the *Récits d'un bourgeois de Valenciennes* (p. 210) adds Dinant and Bouvignes to Huy as providers of troops to the Liégeois force.

Hautepenne, lord of Villereau and Boilhe and mayor of Liège, are named by the original sources[37] – and that they greatly outnumbered their approaching opponents. Mathias von Neuenberg expresses the latter by numbering Englebert de la Marck's force at 9,000, more than four times smaller than his count for the Liégeois and their allies.[38] Jean le Bel is even more exaggerated in his comparison of the two forces, claiming that the archbishop's army was only one-twentieth the size of the rebels'.[39] It is also known that the approaching army was composed of the 'lords of Germany', including Adolph II, count of La Marck and brother to the archbishop; Adolph VIII, count of Berg; Wilhelm I, count of Namur; John the Blind, king of Bohemia, count of Luxembourg, and father to the emperor; Dietrich of Heinsberg, count of Looz; Wilhelm V, marquis of Jülich; Reinhold III, duke of Guelders; and Dietrich IV, lord of Falkenburg and burgrave of Zeeland.[40] Infantry troops were also included in the archbishop's force.[41]

The rebel army seems to have learned of the archbishop's approach sometime around July 16, as Jean de Hocsem insists that they set up their position at Vottem two days before the battle took place.[42] They also seem to have fortified their position by digging large ditches, not ones like those at Courtrai, made to disrupt a cavalry charge, but like those at Staveren, made to hide in. According to the *Récits d'un bourgeois de Valenciennes*, the ditches were also dug to hinder entry into the town if the archbishop's force was to defeat the rebel army.[43]

On June 18 Englebert de la Marck's army encountered the rebels. Most of these were in the ditches, 'standing well armed and tightly bunched to resist the lords,' writes the anonymous author of the *Chronique de l'abbaye de Saint-Trond*.[44] The archbishop ordered his cavalry in three lines and began to charge the Liégeois positions.[45] 'The bishop and his army proceeded incautiously,' writes Werner de Bonn simply,[46] while the *Chronique de l'abbaye de Saint-Trond* adds a recognition of the pride which carried the horsemen to their task: 'They did not doubt that they would obtain victory, since behold . . . they charged with impetus into the Liégeois.'[47] But in all their enthusiasm, the charge of the cavalry became disordered and

---

[37] Jean d'Outremeuse, pp. 168–69. Other knights are made on the battlefield. For their names see Jean d'Outremeuse, pp. 169–70.

[38] Mathias von Neuenberg, p. 203.

[39] Jean le Bel, II:140.

[40] Jean le Bel (II:140) uses the term 'lords of Germany', while Jean d'Outremeuse (p. 168), Mathias von Neuenberg (pp. 202–03), and *Récits d'un bourgeois de Valenciennes* (p. 210) name some or all of them.

[41] See Jean le Bel, II:141.

[42] Jean de Hocsem, p. 342.

[43] *Récits d'un bourgeois de Valenciennes*, p. 211; Jean le Bel, II:140; Jean d'Outremeuse, p. 168; and *Chronique de l'abbaye de Saint-Trond*, II:282.

[44] *Chronique de l'abbaye de Saint-Trond*, II:282.

[45] Jean d'Outremeuse, p. 168.

[46] Werner de Bonn, p. 546: 'sed episcopo cum suis incaute procedentibus . . .'

[47] *Chronique de l'abbaye de Saint-Trond*, II:282: 'non dubitabant de optinendo triumphum, cum, ecce . . . cum impetu in Leodienses irruit.'

confused.[48] And seeing this, the rebels came out of their ditches, ordered themselves in a solid defensive line, and faced the charging cavalry.[49] As the *Récits d'un bourgeois de Valenciennes* reports:

> It was a great battle, perilous, cruel, and very felonious. The knights were strong and armed with good weapons of iron and steel. So they fought well and shrewdly. And the Liègeois defended themselves with axes and hammers of iron, of lead, of bronze, and of steel, and they killed and knocked down the horses and the knights without pity and without offering ransom.[50]

Defeated, the archbishop's army fled from the field, those on horseback rushing through and past their infantry. The rebels, inspired by the victory, broke from their line and followed the fleeing troops, killing all who hesitated in their flight or straggled behind.[51] Included among these was Dietrich of Falkenburg, whose initial refusal to flee allowed the pursuing Liégeois to pull him from his horse and kill him. His name was added to the fifty-seven 'knights' and more than three hundred other soldiers who also met their end at Vottem.[52]

While entirely different in origin, goals, and participants, the battles with which these two rebellions culminated, and which brought victory to both rebel armies, have many similarities. There is of course the aspect of infantry-based armies facing cavalry-based ones, which is prevalent so often in the early fourteenth century. But these battles differ in the fact that the infantries which won both at Staveren and Vottem greatly outnumbered their cavalry opponents. Could this mean that these victories were acquired then simply because the larger armies overwhelmed the smaller ones? Not if we are to accept what seems to be a fear of these smaller armies by the larger ones. In both battles the rebels chose to construct field fortifications by digging ditches large enough to give them some protection against a cavalry charge. This certainly seems to indicate that they at least feared their smaller numbered foes and refused to trust in the idea that larger numbers alone would bring them victory.

At the same time, it should also be noted that the smaller numbered cavalry-based armies did not fear their larger infantry counterparts. At both the battle of Staveren and the battle of Vottem the noble cavalries charged without hesitation on the rebel

---

[48] See Jean le Bel, II:140; Mathias von Neuenberg, p. 203; and *Récits d'un bourgeois de Valenciennes*, p. 211.

[49] On the Liégeois leaving their ditches see Jean d'Outremeuse, p. 168. On their line see the *Récits d'un bourgeois de Valenciennes*, p. 211 and the *Chronique de l'abbaye de Saint-Trond*, II:282.

[50] *Récits d'un bourgeois de Valenciennes*, p. 212: 'Et là y eult grande bataille périlleuse, cruese et moult félonneuse; car les chevaliers estoient hardis et armés de bonnes armures de fer et d'achier. Sy se combatirent bien et asprement. Et Liégois se deffendoient de haches et de marteaux de fer, de plonc, de laiton, et d'achier, et en tuoient et assommoient ces chevaulx et ces chevalliers sans nulle pité et sans point de renchon.'

[51] Jean le Bel, II:140; Mathias von Neuenberg, p. 203; and *Chronique de l'abbaye de Saint-Trond*, II:282–83.

[52] Jean d'Outremeuse, pp. 169–70; *Récits d'un bourgeois de Valenciennes*, pp. 211–23; Jean de Hocsem, pp. 342–43; *Chronique de l'abbaye de Saint-Trond*, II:282–83; Heinrich von Diessenhoven, p. 52; Heinrich von Rebdorf, pp. 528–29; and Jacques de Hemricourt, p. 161.

infantry positions and without regard for the fortifications in which the rebels hid themselves. In both battles, as with so many other early fourteenth-century examples, the pride of the cavalry forces induced them to ignore the size and defenses of their opponents and provoked them to make unwise and eventually confused charges. Once again this leads to a similarity between these two Low Countries' battles. For seeing the cavalry charges become confused and disordered, both the Frisian and the Liégeois rebel armies left the safety of their field fortifications, formed solid defensive lines, and faced the attacks of the horsemen bearing down on them. Victory was achieved when these charges failed to break the infantry formations and the cavalry soldiers were forced to face more numerous opponents fighting with skill and motivation. The infantry weapons, mentioned prominently in both battles, quickly put an end to the 'more noble' cavalry forces which they faced, and giving no quarter to their opponents, the rebels in both battles killed many.

XIII

THE BATTLE OF CRÉCY, 1346

THE BATTLE OF MORLAIX solved little in the 1342 conflict over Brittany. By the time Edward III arrived at Brest on October 27, with an army numbering several thousand,[1] he found that the province was far from pacified. In response, the English king conducted a chevauchée through the countryside, pillaging and devastating all the land up to the town of Vannes. There, on November 25, he joined his army to that of his renowned lieutenant, Robert of Artois, who had been besieging the important Breton town for nearly a month. (Artois would be fatally wounded outside Vannes before the end of the year.) Within days, English armies also attacked Nantes, Rennes, and Dinan.[2]

A large French army, eventually led by the king, Philip VI, was raised and immediately sent to the war-ridden province. The English army came together in anticipation of a battle. But Philip refused to be drawn into combat, holding his army away from the English for two weeks until papal legates arrived from Pope Clement VI to broker a truce, the Truce of Malestroit. It would last for three years. On February 22, 1343, Edward and his army returned home. The English would not return again to the north of France until 1345.[3]

At the end of the truce, Edward III was again ready to make a claim on his 'rightful' throne of France. English armies attacked French outposts in Brittany and Gascony, fighting there with much success during the next two years.[4] But neither English army had the success of Edward III's main force which sailed to France under the leadership of the king in spring 1346.

It is now apparent, although it may not have been at the time, that the 1345–46 English campaigns in Brittany and Gascony were not to be the main thrusts of Edward's military strategy in France. The armies in those two provinces were there

---

[1] Adam Murimuth claims that Edward's army included 6,000 men-at-arms and 12,000 archers which were transported on more than 400 ships (p. 127).

[2] Burne, pp. 80–84 and Sumption, pp. 403–07. Nantes was beset by the earl of Norfolk, Rennes by the earl of Northampton, and Dinan by the earl of Warwick.

[3] On the signing of the truce see Burne, pp. 84–86 and Sumption, pp. 407–08. On the period of 1343–45 when the truce was in effect see Sumption, pp. 411–54. The truce kept both sides at status quo, with the exception that Vannes became 'neutral' for the duration of the truce.

[4] On the breaking of the truce see Sumption, pp. 447–54 and Jules Viard, 'La campagne de juillet-août 1346 et la bataille de Crécy,' *Le moyen âge*, 2nd ser. 27 (1926), 1. On the war in Brittany before Crécy see Burne, pp. 86–89; Sumption, pp. 471–73, 493–97; and Perroy, pp. 115–16. On Gascony before Crécy see Burne, pp. 100–21; Sumption, pp. 455–59, 463–71, 473–88; Viard, 'Crécy,' pp. 1–3; and Henri de Wailly, *Crécy 1346: Anatomy of a Battle* (Poole, 1987), p. 11.

only as precursors for a larger force which was to land at Normandy, fighting to reclaim that part of France which had once been held by the English crown. Alfred Burne goes one step further. He claims that it was Edward III's plan to bring all three of his armies in France together, 'advancing on three radii, as it were, all directed on Paris, the centre.'[5] However, this may be too speculative on the part of Colonel Burne, for it does not take into account the very large French army which would probably not be inclined to wait around Paris until all the 'radii' of the English plan came to it. Why should the French king not take on the smaller Gascon and/or Breton armies before they could join up with the main English force? This very important question must remain unanswered, however, for original sources do not explain either why the king of England pursued his three-pronged strategy when conventional military wisdom spoke against dividing one's force, or why the king of France chose not to attack the smaller English armies, but instead to do battle with the main force at Crécy-en-Ponthieu.

On April 6, 1346, Edward III ordered a large force to gather at Portsmouth for transportation to the continent. Their destination was not known at the time, with most expecting transit to Gascony or Brittany. The number of troops was large, perhaps as many as 15,000, most of whom were infantry or archers; it is estimated that between 700 and 1,000 ships were needed to transport the force to France.[6] Prepared to set sail immediately, the Channel's weather was foul enough to keep the army in Portsmouth until July 11. On the next day they landed at St. Vaast la Hogue, on the coast of western Normandy.[7]

After a short break for reorganization, the English army proceeded quickly along the coast to begin what some historians describe as a raid or chevauchée and what others call a military campaign.[8] On July 18 it captured Valognes, on July 20 St. Côme-du-Mont, on July 22 Saint-Lô, on July 23 Torigny and Sept-Vents, on July 24

---

[5] Burne, p. 136.

[6] The numbers of English soldiers during the Normandy campaign vary between 7,000–10,000 (Sumption, p. 497) and 30,000 (Viard, 'Crécy,' p. 8). Other tallies include 9,000 (Lot, I:344–47); under 10,000 (Richard Barber, *Edward, Prince of Wales and Aquitaine: A Biography of the Black Prince* (London, 1978), p. 48); 11,000 (Wailly, p. 11); 14,000–15,000 (Andrew Ayton, 'The English Army and the Normandy Campaign of 1346,' in *England and Normandy in the Middle Ages*, ed. D. Bates and A. Curry (London, 1994), pp. 253–68); 15,000 (Burne, pp. 137–38 and Christopher Allmand, *The Hundred Years War: England and France at War, c.1300–c.1450* (Cambridge, 1988), p. 16); and 19,428 (George Wrottesley, *Crecy and Calais from the Original Records in the Public Record Office* (London, 1898), pp. 9–10). For a discussion of English numbers see Burne, pp. 166–68 and Ayton, pp. 253–68. Burne totals the English ships at 700 (pp. 137–38), with Viard counting 1,000 ('Crécy,' p. 8).

[7] Burne, pp. 138–40; Sumption, pp. 500–02; Viard, 'Crécy,' pp. 3–11; Wailly, p. 18; Barber, pp. 47–48; and Perroy, pp. 118–19.

[8] Allmand (p. 15), Wailly (pp. 11–49), and, most recently, Clifford J. Rogers ('Edward III and the Dialectics of Strategy, 1327–1360,' *Transactions of the Royal Historical Society* 6th ser. 4 (1994), 88–102) describe Edward's movements across Normandy as a raid, while Burne (pp. 100–35), Sumption (pp. 471–525), and Viard ('Crécy,' pp. 1–67) all see it as a campaign. There are numerous contemporary letters written by English participants of the campaign. A campaign diary also exists, although only in fragmentary form. These are all most accessibly found in Richard Barber, ed. and trans., *The Life and Campaigns of the Black Prince* (London, 1979), pp. 14–40. For a commentary on these letters see Kenneth A. Fowler, 'News from the Front: Letters and Despatches of the Fourteenth

Torteval, and on July 25 Fontenay-le-Pesnel. Nowhere did they meet much opposition.[9] But at Caen, which was reached on July 26, a French garrison of between 300 and 1500 stood ready to defend their town. The castle of Caen had been built largely by William the Conqueror and his son, Henry I. It was strong and would necessitate siege machines for its fall, machines which Edward III did not have with him. He chose instead to try to lure the castle's garrison from its protective walls by attacking the town it defended. The attack, by both the land and sea, and in sight of the castle, was cruel, but the cries of the beset townspeople finally caused the garrison's surrender; more than 2,500 were massacred.[10]

The speed of march was again impressive. Over the next two weeks, August 1–13, 1346, more than 140 miles were traversed. Once more, there was little opposition to the march, although Edward did come close to the French army – within a dozen miles – which was gathered at Rouen.[11] Several times it appears that he wanted to cross the Seine River, but all of the bridges were destroyed and the narrow crossings were heavily guarded. Only at Poissy was a lightly defended crossing found. The guard was driven off and bridges quickly constructed. Philip VI, expected by Edward to be on the opposite side, was not present, having traveled to Paris instead. He had left a small force behind, but it was insufficient to keep the English army from crossing the river.[12]

On August 15, Edward III crossed the Seine and travelled north, presumably to rendezvous with an allied Flemish army moving southward to meet him.[13] Philip was given little option but to follow and perhaps to stop the English before they and the Flemings could combine forces. (He did have some time before the two armies came together as the Flemings had stopped to besiege Béthune, 125 miles north of Poissy.[14]) Once more the English progress was swift. Edward's army never even

Century,' in *Guerre et société en France, en Angleterre et en Bourgogne, xive–xve siècle*, ed. P. Contamine et al (Lille, 1991), pp. 78–80.
[9] On the first phase of Edward's Norman campaign see Burne, pp. 140–44; Sumption, pp. 502–17; Viard, 'Crécy,' 9–19; Wailly, pp. 19–22; and Barber, pp. 44–53.
[10] On the attack of Caen see Burne, pp. 144–47; Sumption, pp. 507–11; Viard, 'Crécy,' pp. 19–32; Wailly, pp. 20–25; Barber, pp. 53–55; Allmand, p. 15; and Henri Prentout, *La prise de Caen par Edouard III, 1346* (Caen, 1904). Viard claims a garrison of 200 men-at-arms and 100 Genoese crossbowmen ('Crécy,' pp. 20–22); Sumption sees a garrison of between 1,000 and 1,500 (pp. 507–08).
[11] On Philip VI's preparation for battle see Sumption, pp. 513–15, 518–19; Viard, 'Crécy,' pp. 4–6, 36–39; Wailly, pp. 38–41; Barber, pp. 55–56; and Allmand, p. 15.
[12] On the journey from Caen to Poissy see Burne, pp. 148–53; Sumption, pp. 512–18; Viard, 'Crécy,' pp. 32–50; Wailly, pp. 25–27; and Barber, pp. 55–59. Philip may have believed that Edward's destination was to be Paris, lying not far from Poissy, but if so he was gravely mistaken. Attacking Edward during his crossing of the Seine would have been much easier than what occurred: chasing after him until the English king stopped and offered battle.
[13] This is the assertion of Burne (pp. 148–49) and Viard ('Crécy,' p. 33). It may explain why Edward did not stop or attack Paris. At least, according to Jonathan Sumption, the French military leaders believed that this is what Edward planned (p. 524). Against the notion of Edward trying to reach the Flemings see Barber (p. 62) who believes that had the English wished to rendezvous with the Flemings that they could have done so. Oman also claims that Edward did not want to reach the Flemish force, but that he only wished to have the way open for a retreat into Flanders if it was needed ((1905), II:134).
[14] On the movement of the Flemish army see Sumption, p. 519, and Viard, 'Crécy,' pp. 33–37.

paused to pillage or to attack important places, such as Beauvais, although some wished to do so. Moreover, few encounters were fought with the French, so that by August 24, Edward III was ready to ford the Somme River at Blanchetaque. Resistance was minimal; although French numbers were not insignificant and contained several Genoese crossbowmen, the river was crossed with little loss of English life.[15] Shortly thereafter, just north of the Somme in the woods of Crécy, the English army camped and waited for the main French force to reach them.[16]

Why did the English king do this? Alfred Burne supplies an answer:

> . . . three new factors decided [Edward III] to offer battle to his old opponent. In the first place, he now had a fair chance of escape should he be worsted in the battle; for friendly Flanders now lay behind him and so long as he did not allow Philip to outmarch him, his line of retreat was secure. Secondly, he was now in Ponthieu, his grandmother's patrimony, on soil that he considered his own; he would not give up this possession without a struggle. Thirdly, the success of his army in crossing the Somme in the very face of the foe appeared, in that age of faith, to be a miracle; the God of battle was evidently on his side, his cause was a just one in the eyes of the Almighty, who would not allow them to be defeated.[17]

Their faith in God's favor would not be invalidated. On August 26, 1346, the famous battle of Crécy was fought, and the French were soundly defeated, with many killed. Philip VI fled from the field eventually to Paris, there to lick his wounds and attempt to rebound from his defeat. Edward waited for a few days on the battlefield, resting and nursing his soldiers and burying the dead of both sides. From there he traveled to Calais where he besieged the town for the next eleven months.

The battle of Crécy is one of the most famous battles of the Middle Ages. Called decisive by J.F.C. Fuller and Joseph Dahmus,[18] the battle has been highlighted in nearly every medieval military historical survey.[19] Thus it should come as no surprise

---

15 On the English army's movement from the Seine to the Somme see Burne, pp. 153–58; Sumption, pp. 520–23; Viard, 'Crécy,' pp. 51–61; Wailly, pp. 27–31; Barber, pp. 59–61. On crossing the Somme see Burne, pp. 158–62; Sumption, pp. 523–24; Viard, 'Crécy,' pp. 61–66; Wailly, pp. 31–33, 41–46; and Barber, pp. 61–62. Burne's numbers for the French army at the Somme are 500 men-at-arms and 3,000 infantry, including Genoese crossbowmen (p. 158).

16 Burne, p. 162; Sumption, p. 525; Viard, 'Crécy,' pp. 64–67; Wailly, pp. 47–49; and Barber, pp. 62–64.

17 Burne, p. 162. Wailly believes that Edward could not keep up a pace quick enough to reach the Flemings before the French caught up to him (pp. 48–49). Allmand questions whether Edward wanted to come to battle against the French (p. 15).

18 J.F.C. Fuller, *A Military History of the Western World*, vol. 1: *From the Earliest Times to the Battle of Lepanto* (New York, 1954), pp. 444–68 and Joseph Dahmus, *Seven Decisive Battles of the Middle Ages* (Chicago, 1983), pp. 169–96.

19 Delbrück, III:454–62; Oman (1905), II:133–47; Lot, I:340–57; Verbruggen, *Krijgkunst*, pp. 48, 58–59, 204, 529; Contamine, *War*, pp. 140, 155, 198, 257; and Philippe Contamine, 'La guerre de cent ans: Le XIVe siècle. La France au rythme de la guerre,' in *Histoire militaire de la France*, vol. 1: *Des origines à 1715*, ed. P. Contamine (Paris, 1992), pp. 126–29. See also Burne, pp. 169–203; Sumption, pp. 524–34; Barber, pp. 63–70; Perroy, pp. 119–21; Allmand, pp. 15–16; Viard, 'Crécy,' pp. 67–84; Desmond Seward, *The Hundred Years War: The English in France, 1337–1453* (New York, 1978), pp. 63–68; Jean Favier, *La guerre de cent ans* (Paris, 1980), pp. 110–20; Philippe Contamine, 'Crécy (1346) et Azincourt (1415): Une comparison,' in *Divers aspects du moyen age en occident:*

that the battle was also very popular during the fourteenth century, with many contemporary narrative sources detailing what occurred on the battlefield. In this it rivals or even surpasses the battle of Courtrai. Lengthy accounts of the battle can be found in Jean Froissart's *Chroniques*, Jean le Bel's *Chronique*, Gilles li Muisit's *Chronicon*, Jean de Venette's *Chronique*, the *Grandes chroniques*, the *Chronique des quatre premiers Valois*, the *Chronographia regum Francorum*, the *Chronique Normande*, the *Récits d'un bourgeois de Valenciennes*, Geoffrey le Baker's *Chronicon*, *Chronicon de Lanercost*, Thomas of Burton's *Chronica monasterii de Melsa*, the Herald of Chandos' *Life of the Black Prince*, Henry Knighton's *Chronicon*, the *Anonimalle Chronicle*, a later version of Adam Murimuth's *Chronicon*, the *Eulogium historiarum*, the *Chronicon comitum Flandriae*, and Giovanni Villani's *Istorie Fiorentine*, while shorter accounts of the battle are found in the *Chronique de l'abbaye de Saint-Trond*, Richard Lescot's *Chronicon*, Thomas of Walsingham's *Historia Anglicana*, *The Brut*, Jan de Klerk's *Brabantse yeesten*, the *Breve chronicon de Flandriae*, the *Liber Pluscardensis*, Willem van Berchen's *Gelderse Kroniek*, and Jean de Winterthur's *Chronicon*.[20] As well, there remain several letters written by English participants of the battle and three contemporary political poems.[21] What this means is that trying to decide what occurred on the battlefield of Crécy is a process of sifting through and weighing many narrative pieces of evidence in order to try to discover what happened on that August day in 1346, a day which in many ways determined the course of English/French relations for more than one hundred years. The difficulty of such an important task was recognized even by the contemporary authors themselves, with many commenting on the challenge of determining a history of this battle. Gilles li Muisit puts it well, although not succinctly:

1er Congrès Historique des Jeunes Historiens du Calaisis (Calais, 1977), pp. 29–44; and Wailly. (N.B. Wailly's work is so fraught with errors that it is almost worthless for the study of this battle.)

[20] Jean Froissart, V:46–80; Jean le Bel, II:100–09; Gilles li Muisit, pp. 243–46; Jean de Venette, *Chronique*, ed. and trans. R.A. Newhall (New York, 1953), pp. 42–44; *Grandes chroniques*, IX:281–85; *Chronique des quatre premiers Valois*, ed. S. Luce (Paris, 1862), pp. 16–17; *Chronographia regum Francorum*, II:231–34; *Chronique Normande*, pp. 80–82; *Récits d'un bourgeois de Valenciennes*, pp. 229–35; Geoffrey le Baker, pp. 81–86; *Chronicon de Lanercost*, pp. 343–44; Thomas of Burton, II:58–59; Herald of Chandos, *Life of the Black Prince by the Herald of Sir John Chandos*, ed. and trans. M.K. Pope and E.C. Hodge (Oxford, 1910), pp. 7–11; Henry Knighton, II:36–38; *Anonimalle Chronicle*, pp. 22–23; Adam Murimuth, pp. 246–48; *Eulogium historiarum*, III:210–11; *Chronicon comitum Flandriae*, pp. 218–19; Giovanni Villani, *Cronica*, ed. M.L. Ridotta (Florence, 1823), VII:161–73; and Jean de Winterthur, pp. 266–68; *Chronique de l'abbaye de Saint-Trond*, ed. C. de Borman (Liege, 1877), II:283; Richard Lescot, pp. 73–74; Thomas of Walsingham, I:268–69; *The Brut*, II:542–43; Jan de Klerk, II:573–74; *Breve chronicon de Flandriae*, in *Corpus chronicorum Flandriae*, iii, ed. J.J. de Smet (Brussels, 1856), p. 8; the *Liber Pluscardensis*, I:292–93; and Willem van Berchen, *Gelderse kroniek*, ed. A.J. de Mooy (Arnhem, 1950), p. 3.

[21] These letters can be found in Adam Murimuth, pp. 215–17; Robert of Avesbury, pp. 367–72; Froissart, XVIII:289–90; Walter of Hemingburgh, *Chronicon* (London, 1848), II:423–26; and Richard Barber, *The Life and Campaigns of the Black Prince*, pp. 23–25. The poems can be found in Laurence Minot, pp. 21–27; Gilles li Muisit, pp. 246–63; A. Coville, ed., 'Poems historiques du début de la Guerre de Cent Ans,' *Histoire litterature de France* 38 (1949), 282–89; and L. Leger, ed. and trans., 'Un poème Tchèque sur la bataille de Crécy,' *Journal des savants* (1902), 323–31.

Since the events of war are dubious, and as battle is harsh, everyone fighting tends to conquer rather than be conquered; and those fighting cannot consider anything going on away from them, nor are able to judge well even those things which are happening to them. Yet afterwards the events must be judged. Because many people discuss many things and either refer to the conflict from the French side, with some supporting their arguments with things which they could not know with certainty, and others refer to it from the side of the English, with some also supporting their arguments with things which they do not know to be true; therefore, on account of these diverse opinions, I will not write that which I cannot prove. But I will write only those things which I have heard from certain trustworthy persons in order to satisfy the minds of future readers, not however affirming them to be completely what happened.[22]

Hardly any contemporary source separates the battle of Crécy from the military campaign which preceded it. Nor is there a separation between the battle and the siege of Calais which followed it. But for the purposes of this study, it is necessary to focus only on the events of the battle.

Most chroniclers begin their accounts of the battle of Crécy with the arrival of Edward III and his army at the battlefield site. To them there is little doubt that the English king chose with great care where he was to face the French army, and because the battlefield still lies virtually undisturbed, we can agree even today with their determination. It is a relatively flat plain, a 'spacious field' writes Adam Murimuth, which forms a valley in the triangle of roads leading to the villages of Crécy in the west, Wadicourt in the east, and Fontaine in the south. Further to the south is a large, impenetrable forest, and on the west runs the narrow, easily fordable Maye River. Between Crécy and Wadicourt is a small ridge at the highest point of which a windmill stood. North of the ridge grows a small wood, known today as the Bois de Crécy.[23] It was in this wood that Edward set up camp and along the ridge that he ordered his troops; from the windmill he surveyed the battlefield. He did so hoping that there indeed was to be a battle. As the anonymous author of the *Chronicon comitum Flandriae* writes: 'The king of England was anxious for battle, preferring to die gloriously in combat, rather than fleeing from it in shameful disgrace.'[24]

---

22 Gilles li Muisit, pp. 243–44: 'Quoniam eventus belli est dubius, et dum conflictus est acierum, unusquisque bellans intendit plus vincere quam vinci, et non potest quispiam considerare undique confligentes, neque bene de his, quae ibidem eveniunt judicare; sed exitus acta probant, et idcirco quia multi multa dicunt et referunt de conflictu et pro parte regis Franciae, et suorum aliqui sustinent ea, de quibus non potest sciri certitudo; et aliqui pro parte regis Angliae et suorum sustinent etiam illa, quae de vero nesciuntur, et sic propter opiniones diversorum nolo posteris demandare, quod probare non valeram, sed ea quae audivi a quibusdam fide dignis personis proposui hic intellectui futurorum satisfacere, sic esse tamen totaliter non affirmans.'

23 Adam Murimuth, p. 246. See also *Récits d'un bourgeois de Valenciennes*, p. 229. Good modern descriptions of the battlefield can be found in Burne, pp. 169–70 and Oman (1905), II:134–36.

24 *Chronicon comitum Flandriae*, p. 218: 'Sed rex Eduardus Angliae animatis suis ad proelium, malens gloriose mori in proelio, quam cum pudoris verecundia fugere ab eodem.' See also Geoffrey le Baker, p. 82; Jean Froissart, V:21–24; *Grandes chroniques*, IX:282; and Giovanni Villani (ed. Ridotta), VII:163–64.

Murimuth adds that the king even joked with his men on hearing of the approach of the French that his wish for a fight was soon to be fulfilled.[25]

Because the French were still a day's march from the English – ten leagues behind them, reports the *Grandes Chroniques*[26] – Edward first set up his camp and rested for the night. English tents were pitched in the woods, claim most sources, with the wagons and carts which accompanied the troops linked to form a make-shift fortification, just outside and to the east of the woods, reminiscent of that constructed by the Flemings at Mons-en-Pévèle. Within the wagon fortress was placed the English baggage train and the army's horses.[27] Yet this fortification was built, records the *Chronique Normande*, not only to protect the baggage and war horses, but also to keep the French army from attacking the English lines in the rear.[28] The army spent the next several hours repairing their armor, feasting, sleeping, hearing Mass, and preparing for battle.[29]

Only a few authors – Thomas of Burton, Giovanni Villani, Jean le Bel, and Jean Froissart – record the number of English soldiers fighting at Crécy, and none of these agree with another; in fact, in each of Froissart's three redactions different numbers are reported. Thomas of Burton, for example, mentions only a total of 3,000 men-at-arms without indicating a number of other troops. Giovanni Villani notes only the number of archers, 3,000. Jean le Bel tallies 4,000 cavalry, 10,000 archers, and 10,000 Welsh and foot soldiers. Finally, Froissart's first redaction counts 2,000 men-at-arms, 5,200 archers, and 1,000 Welsh infantry. This increases in his second redaction to 4,000 men-at-arms, 11,000 archers and 4,000 infantry. And, in his third redaction, Froissart numbers 3,900 men-at-arms with 15,000 generic infantry, including archers.[30] All of these, as well as several other sources which do not enumerate the English troops, claim that these soldiers were greatly outnumbered by their French opponents.[31]

On the following morning and with English spies and French 'traitors' reporting that Philip's army was quickly approaching the battlefield, Edward ordered his troops in three solid defensive lines.[32] All troops were to fight on foot, the cavalry

---

[25] Adam Murimuth, p. 246.

[26] *Grandes chroniques*, IX:281.

[27] On the English camp see the *Anonimalle Chronicle*, p. 22; Jean le Bel, II:105; Jean Froissart, V:25; Jean de Venette, p. 42; *Grandes chroniques*, IX:281; and *Chronique Normande*, p. 80. Only the *Chronographia regum Francorum* (II:231) contends that the English camp was not in the woods but instead was located in the wagon fortification.

[28] *Chronique Normande*, p. 80.

[29] Jean Froissart, V:25.

[30] Thomas of Burton, II:58; Giovanni Villani (ed. Ridotta), VII:165; Jean le Bel, II:100, 105–06; and Jean Froissart, V:31, 33, 35–36.

[31] See also Herald of Chandos, p. 9 and Giovanni Villani (ed. Ridotta), VII:164.

[32] On Edward's spies see Michael of Northburgh's letter in Barber, *Life and Campaigns of the Black Prince*, p. 24 and Richard Lescot, p. 73. On the three line formation see Geoffrey le Baker, pp. 83–84; Jean le Bel, II:101–02; Jean Froissart, V:31–36; Thomas of Burton, II:58; Adam Murimuth, p. 246; Henry Knighton, II: 37–38; Giovanni Villani (ed. Ridotta), VII:163–64; *Chronique des quatre premiers Valois*, p. 16; *Chronicon comitum Flandriae*, p. 218; and *The Brut*, II:542.

dismounting to stand alongside the rest of the infantry.[33] Even the sixteen-year-old Edward, the Black Prince, who was in command of the first line, was dismounted.[34]

Where the English archers were located in this formation is somewhat of a mystery when one looks at the narrative accounts. Most chroniclers, among them Thomas of Burton, Jean de Venette, and Gilles li Muisit, indicate the ordering of the archers within the English formation, but not where they were placed in that order.[35] Others, Giovanni Villani, Geoffrey le Baker, the *Récits d'un bourgeois de Valenciennes*, and Jean Froissart, are more specific, but not in agreement. Villani, the contemporary Florentine civic official who often visited Flanders and France before his death in 1348, and whose account of Crécy is generally among the most accurate, claims that the archers were unusually placed 'come detto è addietro' or behind the English and Welsh infantry.[36] Baker, writing before 1356, and the *Récits*, written c.1366, maintain the more conventional English archer placement, along the flanks of each line.[37]

But it is Froissart who has most confused modern historians of the battle. Using a word, 'herce' or 'erce,' not used before in conjunction with the ordering of archers, Froissart describes the archers' placement at Crécy.[38] But what does Froissart mean by this term? In an 1895 article in the *English Historical Review*, E.M. Lloyd discussed the many interpretations of 'herce' and concluded that the term must mean either a line of archers formed in front of the English infantry or, more likely, two lines of archers formed along their flanks. In the next issue of the same journal, the views of Lloyd were criticized by Hereford B. George. 'Herce' was defined by George as a 'harrow;' in other words, the archers formed units placed both along the flanks of and as wedges in between the infantry lines. The debate has continued: in 1897, John E. Morris agreed with Hereford George; in 1905, Sir Charles Oman advanced the idea of a flanking formation; in 1923, Hans Delbrück returned to the harrow order; in 1955, Alfred Burne agreed with George, Morris, and Delbrück; in 1976, Robert Hardy also accepted the harrow definition, an interpretation which he repeated in 1986, 1990, and 1992; in 1985, Jim Bradbury returned to Oman's flanking formation; and, finally, in 1990, Jonathan Sumption agreed with Oman and

[33] Giovanni Villani (ed. Ridotta), VII:163–64; Geoffrey le Baker, p. 82; Adam Murimuth, p. 246; Herald of Chandos, p. 10; *Récits d'un bourgeois de Valenciennes*, p. 231; *Chronicon comitum Flandriae*, p. 218; and *Breve chronicon Flandriae*, p. 11.

[34] On the Black Prince's command of the first line see Adam Murimuth, p. 246; Herald of Chandos, pp. 8–10; *Chronographia regum Francorum*, II:232; and *Chronicon comitum Flandriae*, p. 218

[35] Thomas of Burton, II:58; Jean de Venette, p. 43; and Gilles li Muisit, p. 244. See also Jean le Bel, II:102, *Chronographia regum Francorum*, II:231–32; and *Chronique Normande*, pp. 80–81.

[36] Giovanni Villani (ed. Ridotta), VII:165.

[37] Geoffrey le Baker, pp. 83–84: 'Sagittariis eciam sua loca designarunt, ut, non coram armatis, set a lateribus regis exercitus quasi ale astarent, et sic non impedirent armatos neque inimicis occurrerent in front, set in latera sagittas fulminarent.' *Récits d'un bourgeois de Valenciennes*, p. 231: '. . . le roy Édouart d'Engleterre fist et ordonna ossy briefment les siennes, et ne fist que II batailles d'archiers à II costés en la manière d'un escut.'

[38] This is found in only the first and third redactions of Froissart's *Chroniques*. Kervyn de Lettenhove (V:48, 50) and Simeon Luce ((Paris, 1872), III:175, 416) transcribe this as 'herce,' while George Diller, who has only published the second and third redactions of the *Chroniques*, has transcribed it as 'erce' ((Geneva, 1972), pp. 726–27.)

Bradbury, although, in a misreading of the sources, he contended that the archers had surrounded themselves with wagon fortifications.[39]

No doubt the debate over Froissart's meaning of 'herce' will continue. But it certainly should not be an issue at Crécy, as both the more contemporary chronicles of Geoffrey le Baker and the *Récits d'un bourgeois de Valenciennes* claim a formation of archers along the flanks of the infantry. Baker seems most certain in the archers' placement:

> The archers were placed in their order so that they stood not in front of their men-at-arms but on the sides of the king's army like wings. Thus they would not get in the way of their men-at-arms nor be attacked head-on by the enemy, but they would shoot their arrows from the flanks.[40]

And as this was the established formation used by Edward III as seen before at Halidon Hill and later at Neville's Cross and Poitiers – these battle formations asserted also by Froissart – it seems odd to conclude that another formation, identified as a 'herce,' might be used at Crécy. The archers can only have been ordered along the flanks of the infantry lines.

It seems certain that there were also some early gunpowder weapons with the English forces which were used in the battle, although where these were placed in the English formation cannot be determined from the original sources.[41]

The English army stood all day in their lines, 'from dawn to vespers,' claim Geoffrey le Baker and Henry Knighton.[42] They ate a meal,[43] and they listened to a speech from their king. Edward exhorted his troops not to fear the attacks of their enemy, but to put their faith in 'God and the Blessed Virgin,' who would help them to be victorious. He also told them that he wanted to fight the French cavalry and not the infantry, although his reasons for this desire are not recorded. Finally, the king ordered that the English soldiers were not to succumb to greed by taking any prisoners or seeking for booty before the battle was over. If this was done, the English line would be weakened and the battle might be lost.[44]

---

[39] E.M. Lloyd, 'The "Herse" of Archers at Crecy,' *English Historical Review* 10 (1895), 538–41; Hereford B. George, 'The Archers at Crecy,' *English Historical Review* 10 (1895), 733–38; John E. Morris, 'The Archers at Crecy,' *English Historical Review* 12 (1897), 427–36; Oman (1905), II:136–37; Delbrück, III:457–58; Burne, p. 172; Robert Hardy, *Longbow: A Social and Military History*, 3rd ed. (London, 1992), p. 67; Jim Bradbury, *The Medieval Archer* (New York, 1985), pp. 95–105; and Sumption, pp. 526–27. Bradbury's discussion is the most detailed and convincing.

[40] Geoffrey le Baker, pp. 83–84: 'Sagitariis eciam sua loca designarunt, ut, non coram armatis, set a lateribus regis exercitus quasi ale astarent, et sic non impedirent armatos neque inimicis occurrerent in front, set in latera sagittas fulminarent.'

[41] Giovanni Villani (ed. Ridotta), VII:163,165–67; *Grandes chroniques*, IX:282; Jean Froissart, V:46; and *Istorie Pistolensi* in *Scriptores rerum Italicarum*, xi, ed. L. Muratori (Rome, 1728), p. 516. For a discussion of the gunpowder weapons at Crécy see Burne, pp. 193–203 and T.F. Tout, 'Firearms in England in the Fourteenth Century,' *English Historical Review* 26 (1911), 671–73. Even with such seemingly undeniable proof for the existence of guns at Crécy, there are still some who doubt that they were there. See Oman (1905), II:142n2 and Wailly, p. 91.

[42] Geoffrey le Baker, p. 83 and Henry Knighton, II:37.

[43] Jean le Bel, II:106; Richard Lescot, p. 73; and *Récits d'un bourgeois de Valenciennes*, p. 232.

[44] On Edward's speech see Jean le Bel, II:106–07; Geoffrey le Baker, p. 82; Adam Murimuth, p. 246;

During their wait for the battle to begin, the English also dug ditches in the battlefield, if Geoffrey le Baker is to be trusted. He writes:

> the English . . . quickly dug many holes in the earth in front of the first line, one foot deep and one foot wide, so that if it happened that the French cavalry were able to attack them, the horses might stagger because of the holes.[45]

Perhaps most importantly, the English troops watched as the French soldiers continued to arrive. Ultimately, they saw a large force composed of numerous knights in the most expensive and impressive military attire, large numbers of Genoese crossbowmen, and a seemingly unending multitude of other infantry.[46] Philip VI had been ardently following the English army, realizing, Jean de Venette insists, that 'he had been duped and tricked and was sorrowful therefore.' He may also have hoped that such a fervent pursuit of the English might cause them to flee from France without coming to battle, at least this is the assessment of the *Chronicon comitum Flandriae*.[47] But if this was the French king's hope, it must have been shattered when he learned from his scouts that Edward III's army had stopped at Crécy and was preparing for battle.[48] Nevertheless, he prepared his own troops for battle.

The French army was, by most medieval standards, massive, greatly outnumbering the English troops.[49] Contemporary estimations of French cavalry run from 12,000 to 30,000, with more than 60,000 foot frequently reported.[50] Other sources simply note the imposing sight of such a large force of armed men; 'whoever saw the strength and power of the king of France could only describe it as a great marvel,' writes the Herald of Chandos.[51] Among the French troops was also a large number of Italian mercenary crossbowmen, 2,000–12,000 according to contemporary sources.[52]

---

and *Chronique Normande*, p. 80. The *Chronique Normande* is alone in insisting that Edward wanted to fight the French cavalry, and Jean le Bel is alone in claiming that Edward ordered the taking of no prisoners or booty before the battle's end.

[45] Geoffrey le Baker, p. 83: 'Anglici . . . effodierunt in parvo tempore multa foramina in terra coram acie prima, profunditatem unius pedis et eandem latitudinem habente quolibet illorum, ut, si, quod abfuit, equites Gallicorum ipsos nimis fuissent insecuti, equi ad foramina titubassent.'

[46] Geoffrey le Baker, p. 82.

[47] Jean de Venette, p. 42 and *Chronicon comitum Flandriae*, p. 218. See also Gilles li Muisit, p. 244; Jean le Bel, II:100; Richard Lescot, p. 73; *Grandes chroniques*, IX:281; *Chronique des quatre premiers Valois*, p. 16; and Thomas Walsingham, I:268.

[48] Jean le Bel (II:101) and Jean Froissart (V:28–30) both claim that Philip sent two parties of scouts to spy on the English position. The first reported that the English had stopped at Crécy, while the second reported the English formation.

[49] The *Breve chronicon de Flandriae* (p. 11) claims that the French army outnumbered the English either 40 or 20 to 1. *The Brut* (II:542) declares that the French had more in one of their four lines than the English had in their whole army. Both probably exaggerate the French to English ratio but give the contemporary impression of an English victory over incredible odds.

[50] The following numbers are given: 12,000 cavalry and 60,000 infantry (Richard Wynkeley in Barber, *The Life and Campaigns of the Black Prince*, pp. 19–20 and Adam Murimuth, p. 246); 20,000 cavalry (*Chronicon comitum Flandriae*, p. 218 and *Anonimalle Chronicle*, p. 22); 20,000 cavalry and 100,000+ foot (Jean le Bel, II:100); and 30,000 cavalry (Thomas of Burton, II:58).

[51] Herald of Chandos, p. 9: 'Qe veist venir la puissance / Et la poair du Roy de ffrance / Graunt meruaille serroit a dire.' See also Geoffrey le Baker, p. 82; Henry Knighton, II:37; *Récits d'un bourgeois de Valenciennes*, p. 230; *Eulogium historiarum*, III:210; and Willem van Berchen, p. 3.

[52] The following numbers of Genoese crossbowmen are found in contemporary sources: 2,000

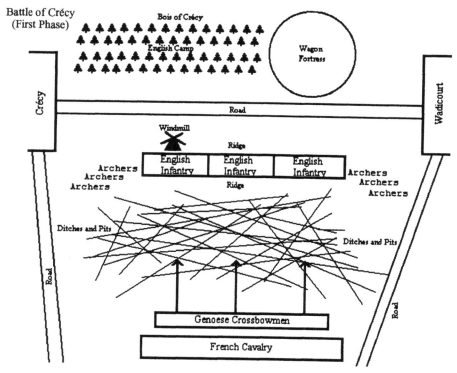

Known as Genoese crossbowmen, it is doubtful that they all came from that northern Italian town. These would play a very important part in the battle. All of these troops were led by the French king, his constable and marshals, and many other great lords and knights of France, with some others, most notably the kings of Bohemia and Majorca, coming to fight with the French as well.

As Philip VI approached the field he called his councilors together. The French king told his nobles what he had learned from his scouts, that the English had stopped at Crécy, and that they had ordered their troops in a defensive formation, one which they were unlikely to break in order to attack the French army. The French councilors advised the king to attack the enemy lines forcefully with his cavalry, but that this attack should not take place until the following morning. The final part of this recommendation was not heeded.[53]

To counter the English formation, Philip VI also ordered his troops for battle, although the contemporary sources seem unclear as to how many lines he formed with these troops. Between four and nine lines are mentioned by the chroniclers.[54]

(*Chronographia regum Francorum*, II:231); 10,000 (Gilles li Muisit, p. 244); and 12,000 (Jean le Bel, II:100). See also Jean de Venette, pp. 42–43.

[53] On Philip's war council see Jean le Bel, II:101–02; *Récits d'un bourgeois de Valenciennes*, p. 230; Jean Froissart, V:38–56; and Richard Lescot, p. 74.

[54] The following numbers of lines are noted by contemporary sources: 4 (*The Brut*, II:542); 5 (*Récits d'un bourgeois de Valenciennes*, pp. 230–31); 8 (*Eulogium historiarum*, III:210); and 9 (Geoffrey le

Philip placed himself in the rear line, according to the *Récits d'un bourgeois de Valenciennes*, in the vanguard, according to Richard Wynkeley.[55] As the course of battle will show, the *Récits* is undoubtedly correct. Next to the king, the oriflamme was unfurled. This was done, Geoffrey le Baker writes, so that 'it was not lawful for anyone, on penalty of death, to take any prisoners.'[56]

The pride of the French cavalry is noted directly or indirectly by almost all contemporary authors. Two stories in particular stand out as examples of this pride. The first comes from Geoffrey le Baker who insists that the French leaders were so confident in their victory that they chose who they would be allowed to take as prisoners:

> So secure were the leaders of the French in the multitude of their army, that they asked for specific Englishmen to be given to them as prisoners. The king of Majorca asked that the king of England be given to him; others sought the prince, others the earl of Northampton, and others other leaders, according to their noble rank.[57]

The second is recorded by Jean Froissart. He reports that after receiving the recommendation of his councilors to wait until morning for battle, Philip VI commanded his army to discontinue their advance. But while those in the front of his army halted their march, those behind them refused to do so, continuing their move forward. It soon became a question of honor. When those who had halted saw that their comrades had pressed on, they took up the march again, wishing to prove their own courage:

> And thus a great pride and arrogance governed the events, because each wished to surpass his companion . . . Neither the king nor his marshals were able to stop their troops, for there was such a great number of soldiers and such a large number of great lords, each of whom wished to demonstrate his power. They rode on in this way, without formation and without order, until they approached the enemy and saw that they were in their presence.[58]

Baker, p. 82 – Baker also mentions 8 lines of order later in his chronicle, p. 83). See also Gilles li Muisit, p. 244; Giovanni Villani (ed. Ridotta), pp. 164–65; and *Chronique Normande*, p. 80.

[55] *Récits d'un bourgeois de Valenciennes*, p. 231 and Richard Wynkeley in Barber, *The Life and Campaigns of the Black Prince*, pp. 19–20.

[56] Geoffrey le Baker, p. 82: 'Set tirannus . . . iussit explicari suum vexilium quod vocatur Oliflammum, quo erecto, non licuit sub pena capitis aliquem capere ad vitam reservandum.' See also Gilles li Muisit, p. 244.

[57] Geoffrey le Baker, p. 82: 'Tantum securi fuerunt in multitudine sui exercitus heroes Francorum, quod singuli pecierunt singulas personas Anglicas suis carceribus mancipandas. Rex Malogrie peciit regem Anglorum sibi dari, alii principem, alii comitem Norhamptonie, alii alios, secundum quod videbantur nobiliores.'

[58] Jean Froissart, V:42: 'Si chevaucièrent si doi mareschal, li uns devant, et li aultres derrière, en disant et commandant as baneres: "Arrestés, banières, de par le roy, ou nom de Dieu et de monsigneur saint Denis." Cil qui estoient premier, à ceste ordenance s'arrestèrent, et li darrainier point, mès chevauçoient toutdis avant, et disoient que il ne s'arresteroient point jusques adont que il seroient ossi avant que li premier estoient; et quant li premier veoient que il les approçoient, il chevauçoient avant. Ensi et par grant orgueil et boubant fu demenée ceste cose, car cascuns voloit sourpasser son compagnon . . . Ne ossi li rois, ne si mareschal ne peurent adont estre mestre de leurs gens, car il y

Forced in confusion and disarray by their pride into a battle situation, the French army could not effectively regroup or recover from their disorder before beginning the battle. Nor could they keep from beginning the battle immediately.[59]

One other matter must also be discussed before looking at the battle of Crécy proper. Sometime during the last phases of the French march to the battlefield, and while the English army stood in their formations, there fell a heavy rain shower, complete with thunder and lightening. Although it seems from the original sources that this rain had dissipated by the beginning of the battle, it also seems certain that it made the field of action muddy – it had not rained previously for more than six weeks, according to Thomas of Burton.[60] There may also have been other effects of the rain, in particular on the bowstrings of the Genoese crossbowmen. Both Jean de Venette and the *Grandes chroniques* note that 'the strings of the Genoese crossbow-men ... were soaked by the rain and shrank, so that when it was time for them to be drawn against the English, they were, woe is me! useless.' The same effect was not felt by the English longbowmen, however, as 'they had quickly protected their bows by putting the bowstrings on their heads under the helmets.'[61]

The battle began with the sound of trumpets, drums, and other French musical instruments. These were sounded, claims the *Récits d'un bourgeois de Valenciennes*, 'to cause fear' among the enemy.[62] But as a scare tactic they were ineffective, especially as the English were able to answer back with their own noise-makers, their cannons, which were discharged also at the beginning of the battle.[63] Through it all, Edward III's soldiers stood solidly in their formation.

Immediately upon hearing the sound of the instruments, the Genoese crossbow-men began their approach towards the English formation. As seen in the battle of Courtrai, this was a standard French tactic: the crossbowmen were to get within range of the enemy's line, let loose at least one volley (or perhaps more if they had the time and ability to reload), and in this way cause confusion and possibly flight among their opponent's force. Ultimately it was hoped, and had often been proved, that this tactic would enable the main part of the French army, the vaunted cavalry, to charge

---

avoit si grant nombre de gens et si grant nombre de grans signeurs, que cascuns par envie voloit là monstrer sa poissance. Si chavaucièrent en cel estat, sans arroy et sans ordenance, si avantque il approcièrent les ennemis et que il les veirent en leur présence.' See also Jean Froissart, V:45 and Jean le Bel, II:102.

[59] Others describing the French pride at Crécy include: Richard Lescot, p. 74; Jean Froissart, V:39–40; and Giovanni Villani (ed. Ridotta), VII:163.

[60] Thomas of Burton, II:58; Henry Knighton, II:37; Jean de Venette, p. 43; *Récits d'un bourgeois de Valenciennes*, p. 232; *Grandes Chroniques*, IX:282; and Jean Froissart, V:48–49.

[61] Jean de Venette, p. 43 and *Grandes chroniques*, IX:282. Both of these sources record the shrinking of the Genoese crossbow strings, but only Jean de Venette records the English protection of their strings. While some modern historians of the battle have either disregarded or determined that the story of the wet and dry bow strings was merely an excuse for later Genoese inaction (Oman (1905), II:141–42; Delbrück, III:458; Wailly, pp. 66–67; Barber, p. 66; Bradbury, pp. 106–07), the relative difficulty of stringing a crossbow in comparison to the stringing and unstringing of a longbow would give the English a quicker solution to the problem of rainfall than it would the Genoese.

[62] *Récits d'un bourgeois de Valenciennes*, p. 232 and Henry Knighton, II:37.

[63] Giovanni Villani (ed. Ridotta), VII:163, 165–67; *Grandes chroniques*, IX:282; Jean Froissart, V:46; and *Istorie Pistolensi*, p. 516.

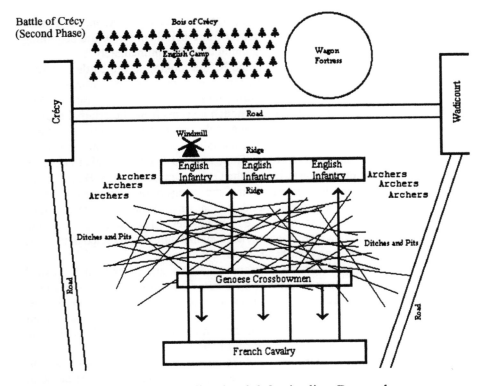

on and defeat the confused and disordered defensive line. But, as the anonymous author of the *Chronographia regum Francorum* succinctly puts it, 'sed aliter evenit – something else happened.'[64] Jean Froissart describes the archery exchange:

> When the Genoese had all been brought together and put in order, and after they had begun to approach their enemy, they started to shout as loud as they could to frighten the English. But the English remained quiet and did not move. Thus the Genoese shouted again and moved a bit closer, but the English still remained silent and did not move. The Genoese again shouted, very loud and very clear, and shortly thereafter they raised their crossbows and began to fire. The English archers, when they saw this formation, took one step forward and let their arrows fly in such large numbers that they fell on the Genoese so evenly that it seemed like snow. The Genoese, who had not earlier faced such archers as those of the English, when they saw that the arrows had pierced their arms, heads, and faces, became so confused that they cut their bowstrings and threw away their crossbows. Then they turned and fled.[65]

---

64 *Chronographia regum Francorum*, II:231.

65 Jean Froissart, V:49: 'Quant li Génevois furent tout recueilliet et mis ensamble, et li deurent approcier leurs ennemis, il commencièrent à juper très-haut que ce fu merveilles, et le fisent pour esbahir les Englès, mès li Englès se tinrent tout quois, ne onques n'en fisent nul samblant. Secondement encores jupèrent ensi, et puis alèrent un petit avant, et les Englès retoient tout quoi, sans yaus mouvoir de leur pas. Tiercement encores jupèrent moult hault et moult cler, et passèrent avant et

The Genoese were fatigued after already having marched for more than six leagues that day, notes Jean Froissart; and their advance was too hasty, causing them to be disordered and confused, insists Jean de Venette.[66] Most importantly, claims Gilles li Muisit, the Genoese could not withstand the English archery onslaught as they had no armor and carried no shields.[67] This led to large numbers of Genoese casualties lying on the battlefield.[68] The rest quickly fled from the massacre.

Seeing what was occurring in the archery exchange, the French constable and marshals approached Philip VI and complained that their Genoese mercenaries were unable to compete against the English troops and were now in flight.[69] Philip responded by commanding his cavalry to ride forward and kill the fleeing Genoese. At least this is the contention of Gilles li Muisit, Jean de Venette, Jean Froissart, the *Grandes chroniques*, and the *Chronographia regum Francorum*. Again Froissart tells the story:

> Between them [the Genoese] and the French there was a large body of men-at-arms, mounted and richly armed, who saw the failure of the Genoese, and made it so they could not retreat. Because the king of France, greatly angered when he had seen their disorder and then their defeat, commanded the men-at-arms and said: 'Listen! Kill all that rabble: They hold us back and block the road without reason!' Then the aforesaid men-at-arms rode among them and attacked them, and many were cast down and fell, unable to save themselves.[70]

Jean le Bel, on the other hand, does not blame the king for this lethal plan. Instead, he writes that the knights were simply so excited to enter the battle, being 'envious' of the archers who had been able to make the first strike against the English, that

---

tendirent leurs arbalestres et commencièrent à traire. Et cil arcier d'Engleterre, quant il veirent ceste ordenance, passèrent un pas avant, et puis fisent voler ces saïettes, de grant façon, qui entrèrent et descendirent si ouniement sus ces Génevois que ce sambloit nège. Les Génevois qui n'avoient point apris à trouver tels arciers que sont cil d'Engleterre, quant il sentirent ces saïettes qui leur perçoient bras, tiestes et banlèvres, furent tantos desconfi, et copèrent li pluiseur d'yaus les cordes de leurs ars, et li aucun les jettoient jus: si se misent ensi au retour.' See also Jean Froissart, V:46–49, 51–53; Jean le Bel, II:102; Gilles li Muisit, pp. 244–45; Jean de Venette, p. 43; Geoffrey le Baker, p. 83; *Grandes chroniques*, IX:282; *Chronique Normande*, pp. 80–81; *Chronographia regum Francorum*, II:231–32; and Giovanni Villani (ed. Ridotta), VII:165–66. There are a few variations to Froissart's story: Gilles li Muisit insists that the French foot also made this attack; Jean de Venette claims that the crossbowmen were unable to fire any bolts; and the *Grandes chroniques* believes that the English cannons were what frightened the Genoese from the battlefield.

[66] Jean Froissart, V:48 and Jean de Venette, p. 43.

[67] Gilles li Muisit, p. 244.

[68] *Chronographia regum Francorum*, II:232.

[69] Gilles li Muisit, p. 245.

[70] Jean Froissart, V:49: 'Entre yaus et les François avoit une grande haie de gens d'armes, montés et parés moult richement, qui regardoient le convenant des Génevois, sique quant il cuidièrent retourner, il ne peurent; car li rois de France, par grant mautalent, quant il vei leur povre arroi et que il se desconfisoient ensi, commanda et dist: "Or tos, or tos! tués toute ceste ribaudaille: il nous ensonnient et tiennent le voie sans raison." Là veissiés gens d'armes entoueilliés entre yaus férir et fraper sus yaus, et les pluiseurs trébuchier et chéir parmi yaus, qui onques puis ne se relevèrent.' See also Jean Froissart, V:52; Gilles li Muisit, p. 245; Jean de Venette, p. 43; *Grandes chroniques*, IX:283; and *Chronographia regum Francorum*, II:232.

they 'accidentally' rode down the Genoese crossbowmen.[71] Whoever was to blame, this maneuver, which the *Chronique Normande* insists killed many of the crossbowmen, raised the English morale and caused confusion and disorder among the French cavalry.[72]

After the slaughter of Genoese crossbowmen or, if Jean le Bel is to be believed, concurrent with it, the French cavalry charged forward to attack the front line of English infantry. Although the archery exchange had proved a defeat for the French army, its main body, the cavalry, armed with lance and sword, was still an impressive and formidable force, which in the past with its ordered charges had often caused infantry foes to flee in panic before even encountering them. This had not, however, happened at Courtrai, Arques, Mons-en-Pévèle, or Morlaix; nor would it happen at Crécy. In fact, it seems that while several charges were made during the battle, none could be called 'ordered', and this may be the cause of their ultimate failure.

The initial charging cavalry were first disrupted by the fleeing, dead, and wounded crossbowmen over and through whom they were forced to ride.[73] This was followed by an archery onslaught from the English longbowmen who, flushed with confidence by their success against the Genoese, continued to fire their arrows at the oncoming troops. What was the result of this? Most contemporary battle commentators report that the arrows of the English longbows caused the death of many men and horses. Indeed, the *Chronicon comitum Flandriae* claims that the whole line of French cavalry, which he numbers at 2,000, was 'entirely destroyed' by this tactic.[74] However, others, namely Geoffrey le Baker, the *Grandes chroniques*, and the *Chronographia regum Francorum*, report only the wounding and slaying of horses during this part of the attack. So many horses were wounded by arrows, asserts the author of the *Grandes chroniques*, that 'it is pitiful and sad to record it.'[75] No matter which account is accepted, the effect on the charge was the same: increased disruption and confusion. As Jean le Bel puts it:

> On their side the archers fired so skillfully that some of those on horses, feeling the barbed arrows, did not wish to advance, while others charged forward as planned; some resisted them tirelessly, while others turned their backs on the enemy.[76]

---

71 Jean le Bel, II:102–03. See also Richard Lescot, p. 74.

72 *Chronique Normande*, p. 81. See also Jean de Venette, p. 43.

73 Geoffrey le Baker, p. 84.

74 *Chronicon comitum Flandriae*, pp. 218–19: '. . . atque cum suis in Gallicos irruens ex una parte cum gladiis et lanceis, et suis sagittariis cum sagittis equos et homines transverbantibus, illam omnino devicit aciem.' See also Adam Murimuth, p. 247; *Eulogium historiarum*, III:211; Jean Froissart, V:47, 49–50, 52–53; *Récits d'un bourgeois de Valenciennes*, p. 233; *Chronique des quatre premiers Valois*, p. 16; and Laurence Minot, p. 24.

75 *Grandes chroniques*, IX:283; Geoffrey le Baker, p. 84; and *Chronographia regum Francorum*, II:232.

76 Jean le Bel, II:103: 'Et d'aultre part les archiers tiroient si merveilleusement que ceulx à cheval, sentans ces flesches barbelées [qui] faisoient merveilles, l'ung ne vouloit avant aler, l'aultre sailloit contremont si comme arragié, l'aultre regimboit hydeusement, l'aultre retournoit le cul par devers les anemis.' See also the *Chronographia regum Francorum*, II:232.

Thus by the time that the French cavalry actually encountered the English line they were in complete disorder and their impetus had been lost. They simply had 'no assembly,' reports the *Chronique Normande*.[77] The opposite was true on the English side. Jean le Bel writes that the English soldiers held their infantry line with strength and solidarity, and that this was 'so wise and so intelligent that fortune turned to them.'[78] Geoffrey le Baker describes the action:

When fighting with the English men-at-arms, the French were beaten down by axes, lances, and swords. And in the middle of the army, many French soldiers were crushed to death by the weight of numbers without being wounded.[79]

It was a brutal fight, described by the bourgeois of Valenciennes as 'very perilous, murderous, without pity, cruel, and very horrible.'[80] The Herald of Chandos agrees: 'That day was there battle so horrible that never was there a man so bold that would not be abashed thereby.'[81] The French cavalry made a number of attacks on the English line, but how many can not be determined by the original sources: two attacks were repulsed claims Adam Murimuth; while, according to Richard Wynkeley, three attacks were turned back; finally, Geoffrey le Baker asserts that 'at this time the French three times shouted hostilely at our troops, and fifteen times they charged them.'[82] Geoffrey le Baker adds further that those French horsemen 'killed, wounded, or fatigued' were quickly replaced by 'fresh troops,' which continually kept the English line engaged in combat.[83]

With the archers on the flanks, the French charges became directed at the center of the English front line, the section commanded by the Black Prince. Indeed, the Prince himself became the target of many direct attacks, and despite on one occasion being 'compelled to fight on his knees,' the Prince and his men held their position strongly against the continual onslaughts of French cavalry charges.[84]

Many feats of arms are also reported on the other side of the conflict. This was not a battle where one side's army fought with less courage than the other.[85] For the

---

[77] *Chronique Normande*, p. 81. See also *Grandes chroniques*, IX:283 and Adam Murimuth, p. 246.

[78] Jean le Bel, II:106: 'Et attendirent tant que les Françoys vinrent, et firent si sagement et sy à point que la fortune tourna pour eulx.'

[79] Geoffrey le Baker, p. 84: 'Cum Anglicis armatis confligentes securibus, lanceis, et gladiis proternuntur, et in medio exercitu Francorum multi compressi a multitudine honerosa sine winere opprimuntur.' See also Thomas Walsingham, I:268–69 and Laurence Minot, p. 23.

[80] *Récits d'un bourgeois de Valenciennes*, p. 232: 'et dura la bataille moult périlleuse, murdrière, sans pité, creuse et trèsorrible . . .'

[81] Herald of Chandos, p. 9: 'Celuy iour ot il bataille / Si orible qe tout sanz faille / Unqes ne fuist corps si hardis / Qe nen poeit estre esbahis.' See also Michael Northburgh's letter in Barber, *Life and Campaigns of the Black Prince*, p. 24 and Willem van Berchen, p. 3.

[82] Adam Murimuth, p. 246; Richard Wynkeley in Barber, *Life and Campaigns of the Black Prince*, p. 20; and Geoffrey le Baker, p. 84: 'in quanto tempore ter Gallici nostros exclamaverunt hostiliter, quindecies nostris insultum dederunt.'

[83] Geoffrey le Baker, p. 84.

[84] The quote is from Geoffrey le Baker, p. 84. See also *Récits d'un bourgeois de Valenciennes*, p. 233 and *Anonimalle Chronicle*, p. 22.

[85] On French military prowess see Jean Froissart, V:54–55 and Thomas Walsingham, I:268.

French, both Philip VI and John, the king of Bohemia, are particularly singled out for their fighting prowess. The former, the *Chronique Normande* records, had two horses killed from under him during the battle,[86] while the latter, blind, is reported by Jean Froissart to have asked his knights to take him into the middle of the fight: 'Lords, you are my men, my friends, and my companions. Today I would ask and require you to take me forward enough that I am able to strike a blow with my sword.' They did so, having first tied their horses together so that the blind king would not get lost in the chaos of fighting.[87] Other French soldiers cited for their boldness on the battlefield include the counts of Alençon, Flanders, Saint-Pol, and Blois, and the duke of Lorraine.[88] But valor and fighting prowess alone could not bring victory.

'Thus from sunset to the third quarter of the night was shown the horrid face of Mars.' So wrote Geoffrey le Baker about the length of the battle of Crécy.[89] Perhaps Jean Froissart is correct in concluding that 'it was very late when the battle began,' and that this hurt the French military cause 'for many men-at-arms, knights, and squires lost their lords and leaders during the night; so they wandered the field and did not know where to go.'[90] On the other hand, the approaching darkness had little to do with the fact that the English line had held so long against many serious French cavalry attacks. More importantly, as darkness drew on, Philip VI chose to leave the battlefield. Why he did this cannot be determined from the original sources. Thomas of Burton and Gilles li Muisit claim that he fled after assessing that his army could not defeat the English.[91] Several English chroniclers, following the lead of Richard Wynkeley's letter, maintain that Philip was wounded by an arrow which had struck his jaw, but no French source confirms this.[92] Wynkeley also asserts that the English troops had come close enough to the French king to kill his standard-bearer and shred his standard.[93] Other sources report that Philip had been taken from the field by Jean

[86] *Chronique Normande*, p. 81. See also *Chronographia regum Francorum*, II:233; *Chronique des quatre premiers Valois*, p. 16; Adam Murimuth, p. 247; and Thomas Walsingham, I:269. The *Grandes chroniques* (IX:283) claims that Philip wanted to fight Edward III at Crécy and searched everywhere for him, but he could not find the English king.

[87] Jean Froissart, V:53–54, 55–56: 'Signeur, vous estes mi homme et mi ami et mi compagnon à le journée d'ui; je vous pri et requier très-espécialment que vous me menés si avant que je puisse férir un cop d'espée.' On John of Bohemia see Walther Rose, 'König Johann der Blinde von Böhmen und die Schlacht bei Crécy (1346),' *Zeitschrift für historisches Waffenkunde* 7 (1915–17), 37–60.

[88] Jean Froissart, V:63.

[89] Geoffrey le Baker, p. 84: 'Sic a solis occasu usque ad terciam noctis quadrantem fuerat vicissim orrida Martis facies ostensa.' See also Jean le Bel, II:103, 106; Gilles li Muisit, p. 245; *Grandes chroniques*, IX:283; and Thomas of Burton, II:58.

[90] Jean Froissart, V:68: 'car, quant la bataille commença , il estoit jà moult tart, et ce greva plus les François que aultre cose, car pluisseurs gens d'armes, chevaliers et esquiers, sus la nuit, perdirent lors signeurs et lors mestres. Si vaucroient par les camps et ne savoient où il aloient.' See also Jean Froissart, V:61.

[91] Thomas of Burton, II:58–59 and Gilles li Muisit, p. 245.

[92] Richard Wynkeley in Barber, *Life and Campaigns of the Black Prince*, p. 20; Thomas of Burton, II:58; Adam Murimuth, p. 247; Henry Knighton, II:38; and *Eulogium historiarum*, III:210–11.

[93] Richard Wynkeley in Barber, *Life and Campaigns of the Black Prince*, p. 20.

of Hainault, who was worried about the king's safety.[94] What is known for certain is that the king and his party fled first to La Broye and then to Amiens.[95]

As their king fled, so too did the rest of the French army. The English, obviously fatigued by the heavy fighting that had occurred during the day, did not pursue the fleeing troops. Instead, they simply camped where they had fought, trying to get some sleep in anticipation of more fighting that night or on the following day.[96] But there was to be no continuation of the battle. On the next day a few French troops were found, principally by the earls of Northampton and Norfolk, although who and how many they were is difficult to determine from the original sources. Jean le Bel calls them 'common soldiers' who had no leaders, while Geoffrey le Baker and *The Brut* declare them to be a large force – four divisions claims Baker. Giovanni Villani gives them a number, 3,000 cavalry and 4,000 infantry. And Jean Froissart writes that these were new troops, from the towns of Rouen and Beauvais, who 'did not know about the defeat which had occurred on the previous day.' All agree, however, that whoever and how many they were, they were quickly killed or routed.[97]

The English had won the battle of Crécy. Although they had taken few prisoners and little booty, and although they had not pursued the fleeing French forces, there was no question of their victory.[98] After praising God and holding a celebratory mass on the battlefield, Edward III commended his soldiers and awarded some with knighthood.[99] The dead of both sides were then buried in pits near where they had fallen. The French dead were particularly numerous and are commented on by every contemporary source. Among these were several notables, nine princes, more than

---

[94] Jean Froissart, V:57–58; *Chronographia regum Francorum*, II:233; and *Chronique Normande*, pp. 81–82.

[95] Richard Wynkeley in Barber, *Life and Campaigns of the Black Prince*, p. 20; Giovanni Villani (ed. Ridotta), VII:168; Gilles li Muisit, p. 245; Jean le Bel, II:103–04; Jean Froissart, V:57–59, 64; *Chronographia regum Francorum*, II:232–34; *Chronique Normande*, pp. 81–82; *Chronique des quatre premiers Valois*, p. 17; *Breve chronicon Flandriae*, p. 11; Willem van Berchen, p. 3; Thomas of Burton, II:58; Adam Murimuth, p. 247; Henry Knighton, II:38; *Anonimalle Chronicle*, p. 23; *Eulogium historiarum*, III:210–11; *Chronicon de Lanercost*, p. 344; Thomas Walsingham, I:269; and Laurence Minot, p. 24.

[96] Michael Northburgh in Barber, *Life and Campaigns of the Black Prince*, p. 25; Jean le Bel, II:107; Giovanni Villani (ed. Ridotta), VII:168; *Récits d'un bourgeois de Valenciennes*, pp. 233–34; *Grandes chroniques*, IX:284; Thomas of Burton, II:58; Henry Knighton, II:38; and *Anonimalle Chronicle*, p. 23. Thomas of Burton (II:58) also writes that during the night the English feasted on the food supplies of the French and burned their captured weapons.

[97] Jean le Bel, II:107; Geoffrey le Baker, p. 85; *The Brut*, II:542–43; Giovanni Villani (ed. Ridotta), VII:168; Jean Froissart, V:71: 'Ce dimence au matin s'estoient parti de Abbeville et de Saint-Rikier-en-Pontieu les communautés de Roem et de Biauvais, qui riens ne savoient de le desconfiture qui avoit esté faite le samedi.' See also Michael Northburgh in Barber, *Life and Campaigns of the Black Prince*, p. 24; *Grandes chroniques*, IX:284; and Adam Murimuth, pp. 247–48. Thomas of Burton (II:59) and Henry Knighton (II:38) both claim that the French troops encountered by the English were prepared to fight but fled in the face of superior numbers.

[98] Jean le Bel (II:106–07) claims that there were no prisoners or booty taken, as they had been so commanded by Edward III, but both the *Grandes chroniques* (IX:284–85) and the *Récits d'un bourgeois de Valenciennes* (p. 235) claim that the English did capture some booty.

[99] On the English mass after the battle see Jean le Bel, II:107; Giovanni Villani (ed. Ridotta), VII:169; Geoffrey le Baker, p. 85; and Adam Murimuth, p. 248. On Edward's making of knights see *Chronographia regum Francorum*, II:234.

1,200 knights, and between 15,000 and 16,000 others, according to Jean le Bel; included among these numbers were the counts of Alençon, Flanders, Blois, Harcourt, Auxerre, Aumale, Savoy, Moreuil, Nevers, and Grandpré, the duke of Lorraine, the archbishop of Xanten, and the bishop of Noyon.[100] Perhaps the most celebrated death was that of the king of Bohemia, whose body was found among the slain. His blindness was known by the English, and his participation in the battle, seen as bravery rather than foolishness, as well as his royal status accorded his corpse special treatment. Brought to Edward III, Geoffrey le Baker writes that the body was washed, wrapped in clean linen, placed on a horse-drawn litter, and returned to Germany; with the English king and his earls present, the bishop of Durham, celebrated the office of the dead over the corpse.[101] The number of English soldiers killed was far smaller.[102]

Because of the numerous excellent original sources on the battle, the tactics of Crécy are simple to discern. So too are the causes of victory for the English and defeat for the French.

Edward III chose the battlefield with an eye to its defensibility. He found a ridge between two woods on which to order his troops. The woods would protect his flanks; to protect his rear he had a wagon fortress constructed. He also may have ordered the digging of ditches to add further to the security of his position. (The rain which fell just prior to the battle helped as well.) Edward's soldiers, fewer in number than their French opponents, were ordered as infantry in a solid defensive formation on this high ground. Finally, lines of archers were positioned along the flanks of the English formation.

Edward knew what he wanted to happen at the battle of Crécy. He told his troops that he wished to fight the French cavalry. He wanted to provoke them to charge uphill, through the hindrances of a constant archery deluge and over ditches – which would cause disorder among those charging – into his solid infantry formation.

Philip VI also knew what the English king desired. He recognized his opponent's formation and understood its purpose. He could see it ordered on the ridge at Crécy, and in 1328 he had encountered a similar formation at Cassel. Finally, his armies

---

[100] Jean Froissart, V:73–77; Jean le Bel, II:108; Gilles li Muisit, pp. 245–46; Jean de Venette, pp. 43–44; *Grandes chroniques*, IX:283–84; *Chronique des quatre premiers Valois* p. 16; *Chronographia regum Francorum*, II:233; *Chronique Normande*, p. 82; *Récits d'un bourgeois de Valenciennes*, pp. 233; Geoffrey le Baker, p. 85; *Chronicon de Lanercost*, p. 344; Thomas of Burton, II:59; Herald of Chandos, p. 11; Henry Knighton, II:38; *Anonimalle Chronicle*, p. 23; Adam Murimuth, pp. 247; *Eulogium historiarum*, III:210; *Chronicon comitum Flandriae*, p. 219; Giovanni Villani (ed. Ridotta), VII:167–68; and Jean de Winterthur, p. 267; *Chronique de l'abbaye de Saint-Trond*, II:283; Richard Lescot, p. 74; Thomas of Walsingham, I:268; *The Brut*, II:542–43; Jan de Klerk, II:574; *Breve chronicon de Flandriae*, p. 11; the *Liber Pluscardensis*, I:293; and Willem van Berchen, p. 3. Numbers vary as to how many French soldiers were killed.

[101] Geoffrey le Baker, p. 85. See also Jean le Bel, II:108; Giovanni Villani (ed. Ridotta), VII:169; Jean de Venette, p. 44; *Chronographia regum Francorum*, II:234; *Récits d'un bourgeois de Valenciennes*, p. 235; Herald of Chandos, p. 10; Minot, p. 24; and Jean de Winterthur, p. 267.

[102] Only three sources mention the number of English notables dead: 3 (Adam Murimuth, p. 247); 40 (Geoffrey le Baker, p. 85); and 300 (Jean le Bel, II:108–09). No original source mentions numbers of non-notable English dead. See also Gilles li Muisit, p. 246; Jean de Venette, p. 44; and Michael Northburgh in Barber, *Life and Campaigns of the Black Prince*, p. 24.

had also faced the English using this same formation at Morlaix. At Cassel, the French king had won by following a policy of patience, by waiting until the Flemish rebels could be induced to leave their defensive positions on the hill-top. (A similar policy outside of the besieged town of Tournai in 1340 had also brought victory.) Should he have tried patience at Crécy? Gilles li Muisit, for one, believes that he should have.[103]

But at Crécy, Philip could not follow this policy. The destruction of surrounding lands – a significant factor in provoking the Flemish troops from their Cassel positions – would incite no similar feeling among the English. Moreover, the king had also to consider the possible arrival of Flemings from the north to reinforce the English. Therefore, patience was not an option. Instead of patience, Philip had as a tactical advantage a large contingent of Genoese crossbowmen, whose intensive and deadly fire into the English lines he reckoned should cause them either to break into rout or to become so disordered that a cavalry charge could be effective against them.

To this point the French king and his soldiers had not done anything that could be considered incautious. (To some it may seem that he should not have attacked on the evening of August 26, but even that could not be considered incautious in that if Philip's tactics had worked, the battle would have been over long before dark.) But the attack of the Genoese crossbowmen failed miserably, as these archers were completely stopped in their approach by a counter-attack of English longbowmen; some sources indicate that the Genoese were unable to discharge even one shot. Once this attack failed, Philip had lost his tactical advantage. What followed were errors compounded by pride. The Genoese retreated, but were not allowed back to their lines as Philip VI, perceiving their flight to be treasonous, ordered their destruction by his own cavalry. This order was accepted with enthusiasm by the French cavalry, but all it ultimately did was to add further hindrances to the many cavalry charges which followed against the English infantry lines. Although the fighting was intense, these lines received the disordered French charges without breaking, and eventually, as darkness fell, Philip VI left the battlefield followed by his army.

It is perhaps no mistake that both Jean le Bel and Giovanni Villani compare the battle of Crécy to the battle of Courtrai.[104] There are certainly many similarities between the two battles: Edward III choosing the battlefield, utilizing the natural terrain to protect his flanks, and placing his troops, fewer in number than their French opponents, in a solid defensive formation. There are also several differences, the most notable of which was the participation on both sides of large numbers of archers. But the similarity which impressed Le Bel and Villani was the way the two armies finally met in combat, one a charging cavalry and the other a solid defensive line of infantry. As at Courtrai, the infantry soldiers stood in unity, without giving way to their attackers. It was a great victory, one which would eventually supersede in importance not only the battle of Courtrai but almost all other medieval battles.

---

[103] Gilles li Muisit, p. 245.
[104] Jean le Bel, II:109 and Giovanni Villani (ed. Ridotta), VII:167.

XIV

THE BATTLE OF NEVILLE'S CROSS, 1346

FROM THE SUCCESSFUL battlefield of Crécy, Edward III moved to besiege the town of Calais. This seems to have been part of the 'grand strategy' of the English king, to follow a victory over an opponent with a siege of one of that same opponent's major towns:[1] Edward had acted similarly in 1333 by following Balliol's victory at Dupplin Moor with the siege of the town of Berwick, in 1340 by following the victory at Sluys with the siege of Tournai, and he would do so again in 1356 by following the battle of Poitiers with the siege of Rennes. This did two things for the king of England: first, it allowed him to capitalize on his victory by acquiring territory, something that the battlefield victory alone did not necessarily achieve. At Berwick, Calais, and Rennes, he was successful in this strategy, while at Tournai he was unsuccessful. Second, by besieging an important location in his enemy's lands, he was generally able to draw to him another of his opponent's armies in an attempt to relieve the siege; this produced the possibility of a more decisive victory. At Halidon Hill, he defeated the Scottish army which had come to relieve the siege of Berwick, but at Tournai, Calais, and Rennes, he failed to bring the French force to battle. Some modern historians, such as Alfred H. Burne, have criticized this as short-sighted, but Edward seems never to have wavered from this strategy.[2]

The siege of Calais was an impressive affair, with few medieval equivalents. Planning for the siege to be extremely long in duration, the English destroyed the town's suburbs and quickly constructed an intricate series of siegeworks, which included an elaborate city known as Ville-à-Neuve complete with a market place and towers built around the harbor.[3] This allowed Edward's army, numbering around 32,000 men – the largest army of the century, according to J.F. Verbruggen – relatively comfortable surroundings, often duplicating more a garrison in England than a siege in northern France.[4] Indeed, Thomas of Burton claims that so many prostitutes were in Ville-à-Neuve during the siege that God cursed the English troops with dysentery, effectively halving the English force there.[5]

---

[1]   See my 'Hunger, Flemish Participation and the Flight of Philip VI: Contemporary Accounts of the Siege of Calais, 1346–47,' *Studies in Medieval and Renaissance History* n.s 12 (1991), 129.
[2]   For example, Burne believes that Edward should have sought the capture of Paris after his victory at Crécy (pp. 206–07).
[3]   See DeVries, 'Calais,' p. 133 and Jules Viard, 'Le siege de Calais,' *Le moyen âge* 40 (1929), 178.
[4]   On the numbers at Calais see J.F. Verbruggen, 'La tactique de la chevalerie française de 1340 à 1415,' *Publications de l'université de l'état à Elisabethville* 1 (1961), 42 and Henneman, pp. 218–19.
[5]   Thomas of Burton, II:65.

With so many troops in France, and with all of Edward's logistical powers being used to supply these troops, what was still left in England? In fact, would this not *entice* the Scots, who had been defeated only thirteen years before, to reassert their independence, especially if urged to do so by the French king, who would desire such a revolt at least to weaken the English effort and even perhaps to break the siege at Calais? The first question is rhetorical, the answer to the second is yes.

Since their defeat at Halidon Hill the Scots had been anything but quiet. It was true that there had been a loss of many high-ranking nobles in the battle, some killed and some taken into custody. And, at least initially, there was the solid establishment of Edward Balliol and the other disinherited in the ranks of Scottish government: Balliol served as king; Hugh Beaumont became Earl of Moray and Buchan; Richard Talbot became Lord of Mar; and David of Strathbogie, earl of Atholl, became Steward of Scotland. By February 1334, Balliol was even able to hold a parliament at Holyrood, which, although dominated by the disinherited, brought together many other Scottish secular and ecclesiastical lords, all of whom gave him homage as their ruler.[6] Finally, the ten-year-old David Bruce, whose reign in Scotland had been supported by the force defeated at Halidon Hill, had even taken refuge in France, invited to exile there by Philip VI.[7]

But there were still many Scottish military leaders who were unwilling to be governed by the English, in the person of Edward Balliol or Edward III. By the summer of 1334, John Randolph, who before Halidon Hill was the Earl of Moray, had united the remnants of the Bruce party and had begun to invade Balliol's territory; before the English could mobilize their forces, in November, Randolph, with the assistance of Sir Andrew Moray, William Douglas, and Alexander Ramsey, had recaptured much of Scotland. For the next three years, Scottish and English troops often invaded each other's territory. Raids, with their inherent pillaging and destruction, were constant, with few clashes between troops taking place. Truces, pacifications, and peace settlements frequently were made and just as frequently broken.[8] Even a large expedition mounted by Edward III in 1335 failed to bring the Scottish army to battle and thus failed to recapture the territory which he and Balliol had held in 1333.[9]

Finally, in 1337, as war with France became imminent, Edward III began to lose interest in his northern enemy. He turned command of his troops there – probably numbering no more than 3,500 – over to Thomas Beauchamp, earl of Warwick, and settled down to plan an invasion of France.[10] For the next few years, Warwick

[6] For the most complete discussion of this period see Nicholson, *Edward III and the Scots*, pp. 139–62. See also Nicholson, *Scotland*, p. 129 and Packe, pp. 69–70.

[7] Nicholson, *Edward III and the Scots*, p. 157; Nicholson, *Scotland*, p. 130; and McKisack, p. 117.

[8] The most complete discussion of this is Nicholson, *Edward III and the Scots*, pp. 163–202. See also Nicholson, *Scotland*, pp. 130–36; Packe, p. 70; and Bruce Webster, 'Scotland Without a King, 1329–1341,' in *Medieval Scotland: Crown, Lordship and Community: Essays Presented to G.W.S. Barrow*, ed. A. Grant and K.J. Stringer (Edinburgh, 1993), pp. 224–30.

[9] Nicholson, *Edward III and the Scots*, pp. 203–36 and Packe, pp. 70–71.

[10] Nicholson, *Scotland*, p. 136 and Packe, p. 71.

continued to defend the Balliol claims in Scotland, but mostly without success; the power of the English in Scotland had begun to dissolve.[11]

Edward had found success at Sluys in 1340, but this had been followed by defeat at Tournai, and by the beginning of 1341 he was back home, anxious to find a new reason to attack France. He again paid no attention to Scotland. Scottish leaders took advantage of this situation, and a new offensive was launched. On April 16, Edinburgh Castle had been recaptured, and by the end of May, the kingdom was secure to its old borders, with Balliol forced to retreat to England. This gave impetus to the return of David Bruce, who landed in Scotland on June 2. Still Edward III did little.[12]

From 1341 to 1346 an unsure truce persisted between the two old enemies. The English troops along the Scottish border did not travel north, despite the wishes of their commander, Edward Balliol, who had been given the lead of this force in 1344, but neither did the Scots cross their southern border. However, when Edward III set sail for France again on July 12, 1346, a new opportunity for Scottish invasion was presented. It would take place during the King's lengthy siege of Calais.[13]

While Edward III had paid no attention to Scotland during the 1340s, Philip VI of France had taken a great interest in Scottish affairs. His hosting of David Bruce from 1333 to 1341 had been active, and since Bruce's return to Scotland, the French king had supported his reinstatement on the throne with funds, friendship, and encouragement.[14] In 1346, after his defeat at Crécy, Philip stood in need of repayment of these favors. Naturally, he did not expect military intervention in France, and he obviously recognized the extreme poverty of a state whose finances almost entirely went to supporting a defense of its borders. On the other hand, an attack of Scottish troops into the poorly guarded north of England could perhaps draw at least some of the English troops home, and such a weakened force might allow the French king to relieve the siege of Calais.[15]

The Scots responded with fervor. On October 6, 1346, the Scottish army mustered at Perth. All noble leaders but two were present, as was King David Bruce. The invading army's progress to the south was swift – Cumberland and Westmorland put up little opposition – and by October 16, the Scottish force was encamped within sight of the Durham Cathedral.[16] But the English were not going to stand by and allow the Scots easy access into their northern lands. Knowing early of the Scottish intentions, perhaps even before the army had left Scotland, Lords William La Zouche, the archbishop of York, Henry Percy, and Ralph Neville had recruited as many troops as they could. It was not a very large number with so many English

---

11 Nicholson, *Scotland*, pp. 136–38; Webster, pp. 230–35; and Packe, pp. 71–74.

12 Nicholson, *Scotland*, pp. 139–44 and Packe, p. 72.

13 Nicholson, *Scotland*, pp. 144–45.

14 Prestwich, *Three Edwards*, pp. 167–68; McKisack, pp. 118–19; W.M. Ormrod, *The Reign of Edward III: Crown and Political Society in England, 1327–1377* (New Haven, 1990), p. 9; and Scott L. Waugh, *England in the Reign of Edward III* (Cambridge, 1991), p. 14.

15 Nicholson, *Scotland*, p. 145.

16 Nicholson, *Scotland*, p. 146.

soldiers serving in France, but its appearance and morale surprised the Scots. On October 17, 1346, at Neville's Cross, outside the walls of Durham, the Scots were soundly defeated. Almost the entire army was killed or captured, including David Bruce, whose next residence was the Tower of London.[17] Calais fell to Edward less than ten months later.

There are several contemporary or near-contemporary accounts of the battle of Neville's Cross. Many are quite lengthy and detailed. These include: the English chronicles of Geoffrey le Baker, Thomas of Burton, Henry Knighton, John of Reading, Robert of Avesbury, and the *Anonimalle Chronicle*; the Scottish chronicle of the *Liber Pluscardensis*; and the 'foreign' chronicles of Jean le Bel, Jean Froissart, and Giovanni Villani.[18] Three poems, two anonymous and one by Laurence Minot, also deal with the battle.[19] Finally, an important, but unusual source for what occurred on the battlefield is a letter written by Thomas Samson, a clerk of the archdiocese of York.[20]

The contemporary commentators of this battle set the conflict at Neville's Cross in the wider context of the English involvement at the siege of Calais. Jean le Bel exemplifies this. He begins his account of the battle:

> At the time when the noble King Edward was away on his good campaign against the king of France, a short time after Crécy while he was besieging Calais, King David of Scotland assembled a large number of men-at-arms to pillage and waste England, because he knew well that King Edward was not there.[21]

David believed that 'the whole strength of arms were with King Edward,' declares Adam Murimuth, leaving only 'farmers, herders, and chaplains, imbeciles and the decrepit,' writes Henry Knighton; 'only the ecclesiastics and rustics, women and children had been left behind,' claims John of Reading.[22]

Most chroniclers also report Philip VI's complicity in the Scottish invasion. To them the French king was certainly guilty of encouraging David Bruce in the affair,

---

[17] Sumption, pp. 550–53; Oman (1905), II:149–51; Burne, pp. 218–19; Nicholson, *Scotland*, pp. 146–47; and Packe, p. 166.

[18] Geoffrey le Baker, pp. 86–88; Thomas of Burton, II:60–67; Henry Knighton, II:41–45; John of Reading, pp. 102–04; Robert of Avesbury, pp. 376–77; *Anonimalle Chronicle*, pp. 23–28; *Liber Pluscardensis*, I:292–95; Jean le Bel, II:125–30; Jean Froissart, V:118–33; and Giovanni Villani (ed. Ridotta), VII:186–87.

[19] All three are published in Joseph Hall's edition of Minot's poems, pp. 30–33, 110–20.

[20] Found in *Oeuvres de Froissart*, ed. Kervyn de Lettenhove (Brussels, 1869), V:489–92.

[21] Jean le Bel, II:125–26: 'En celluy temps que le noble roy Edowart avoit eu celle belle avanture contre le roy de France assez prez de Cressy, et au'il avoit assiegié Calaiz, assembla le roy David d'Escoce grand nombre de gens d'armes pour venir gaster et exillier Angleterre, car il sçavoit bien que le roy Edowart n'y estoit pas.' See also Jean Froissart, V:119, 122, 129; Robert of Avesbury, p. 376; Adam Murimuth, p. 218; Henry Knighton, II:42–43; John of Reading, p. 102; Giovanni Villani (ed. Ridotta), VII:186; and *Liber Pluscardensis*, I:292.

[22] *Chronicon de Lanercost*, pp. 348–49; Adam Murimuth, p. 218; Henry Knighton, II:42; John of Reading, p. 102; and *The Brut*, II:299, 543.

hoping to take pressure off of Calais, if not actually driving the English king back to his kingdom.[23] Geoffrey le Baker and Giovanni Villani also insist that Philip sent troops and money to the Scots, but their claims seem to be unsubstantiated; at least no French are recorded to have been killed or captured after the battle of Neville's Cross.[24]

The *Liber Pluscardensis* asserts that some Scottish nobles, 'trusty men,' suggested that David not take the advice of the French king, but that the Scottish king was 'inflamed by youthful counsels,' and thus entered England.[25] However, none of the more contemporary chronicles concur with this account, and, indeed, the large number of Scottish troops and nobles which joined with David in his invasion, casts doubt on what the *Liber* proclaims. The *Chronique Normande* reports the Scottish numbers at 6,000. The *Chronicon de Lanercost* numbers the Scots at more than 2,000 knights and men-at-arms, 20,000 'drawn from the villages, called "hobelars",' and more than 10,000 foot soldiers and archers. Jean Froissart records the number of invading Scottish troops at 3,000 knights and 30,000 other soldiers, a tally which includes all of the major Scottish nobles. While Jean le Bel agrees with the former number but increases the latter to 43,000. Thomas Samson claims a number of 2,000 men-at-arms, 20,000 other professional soldiers, and 40,000 'comunes,' non-professional milita 'which use lances, axes, and bows. Finally, the *Récits d'un bourgeois de Valenciennes* reports a count of 80,000 soldiers.[26] These six are alone in noting Scottish numbers, and all but the *Chronique Normande*'s are surely exaggerations, but the existence of a large and powerful force seems certain as it is mentioned by all commentators. It was 'a very strong and excited army,' writes Henry Knighton.[27]

But it was not an army without opposition, as David Bruce had hoped. The English had learned of the Scottish invasion early, maybe even before it left Scotland. Perhaps they were also expecting it, for Giovanni Villani insists that Edward had left some of his barons behind in England 'to guard his realm.'[28] If the invasion was not expected by the English, their speed of assembly was extremely impressive, for the

---

[23] For example, Jean Froissart, V:120 and Giovanni Villani (ed. Ridotta), VII:186. See also Robert of Avesbury, p. 376; Adam Murimuth, p. 218; Geoffrey le Baker, p. 86; the Anonymous of Canterbury, p. 192; *Liber Pluscardensis*, I:292; Andrew of Wyntoun, II:470–71; and the *Chronique Normande*. Also, Laurence Minot's poem on Neville's Cross, as well as an anonymous companion piece, both accuse Philip VI of a strong involvement in the campaign that would lead to David Bruce's failure (Minot, pp. 30–33, 110–12).

[24] Geoffrey le Baker, p. 86 and Giovanni Villani (ed. Ridotta), VII:186.

[25] *Liber Pluscardensis*, I:293. Andrew of Wyntoun agrees somewhat with this; however, he only names William Douglas as the advisor believing that it was unwise to attack England (II:472–73).

[26] *Chronique Normande*, p. 87; *Chronicon de Lanercost*, pp. 344–45; Jean Froissart, V:120, 123; Jean le Bel, II:126; Thomas Samson in Froissart, V:489–90, 492; and *Récits d'un bourgeois de Valenciennes*, p. 241. *The Brut* (II:543) does not number the Scots, but does indicate that they outnumbered the English 3 to 1. See also *Chronographia regum Francorum*, II:242 and *Chronique Normande*, p. 87. The *Récits d'un bourgeois de Valenciennes* also claims that the Scottish numbers include archers (p. 241); no other source mentions archers among the Scottish ranks.

[27] Henry Knighton, II: 42. See also Robert of Avesbury, p. 376; Adam Murimuth, p. 218; John of Reading, pp. 102–03; the Anonymous of Canterbury, p. 192; and Andrew of Wyntoun, II:472.

[28] Giovanni Villani (ed. Ridotta), VII:186.

Scots had gained little ground before they encountered a sizeable enemy army. But who was responsible for such a reaction to the invasion? Contemporary chroniclers seem somewhat uncertain. Most credit Archbishop William La Zouche of York with raising the alarm and also the defending troops. As well, these all name Henry Percy and Ralph Neville as instrumental in the battle.[29] On the other hand, Jean Froissart, Jean le Bel, and the Bourgeois of Valenciennes give their patron, Philippa, Edward's queen, credit for the quick initiative against the Scots, claiming that she went so far as to travel to Newcastle to urge on the English troops; then she even traveled with the army to the battlefield itself. All came to fight the Scots, Jean Froissart writes, 'out of love for their good queen, their lady.'[30]

The English army was not as large as its opponent's, perhaps numbering no more than 8,000. But it did include cavalry, infantry, and archers; some had also fought at Crécy.[31] Morale was high, and those preparing to fight were devoted to the defense of their kingdom, with Henry Knighton noting that 'all unanimously agreed to be prepared to give life or death for the salvation of the realm.'[32] They also hoped by swift action to save the town of Durham from attack.

The campaign of the Scots before Neville's Cross was quick and largely unopposed. Only at Liddel did an English force try to resist their invasion, and this conflict, really a siege of the town, is recorded by Thomas Samson, the *Chronicon de Lanercost*, Robert of Avesbury, Geoffrey le Baker, the *Anonimalle Chronicle*, Andrew of Wyntoun, and an anonymous poet. They claim that it was short – lasting only five or six days and brought to an end by siege machines – and relatively bloodless – although it did cost the life of Walter of Selby, 'a warrior of great honor,'

---

[29] See Thomas Samson in Froissart, V:490; *Chronicon de Lanercost*, p. 347; Robert of Avesbury, p. 376; Henry Knighton, II:42; Geoffrey le Baker, p. 87; Adam Murimuth, p. 218; Thomas of Burton, II:61; Laurence Minot, p. 31; the Anonymous of Canterbury, p. 192; *Anonimalle Chronicle*, p. 24; *Chronographia regum Francorum*, II:242; and Andrew of Wyntoun, II:474.

[30] Jean Froissart, V:122, 126–27. Froissart's first redaction mentions Philippa's presence on the battlefield until asked to leave for fear of her capture. Reluctantly she returned to Newcastle. See also Froissart, V:119–31; Jean le Bel, II:126; and *Récits d'un bourgeois de Valenciennes*, p. 241.

[31] Several sources record the English numbers at Neville's Cross. Giovanni Villani ((ed. Ridotta), VII:186–87) counts only a total of 1,000 soldiers, while Jean Froissart in his second redaction numbers 8,000 soldiers (V:124). In his first redaction, Froissart divides and increases his second redaction's total: 1,200 cavalry, 3,000 archers, and 5,000 infantry (V:126). The *Chronique Normande* (p. 87) and Andrew of Wyntoun's (II:472) total of 1,400 men-at-arms and 20,000 archers should be disregarded as unsubstantiated by more contemporary chronicles. Also suspicious is Thomas of Burton's 900 men-at-arms and 9,000 archers (II:61), although these are almost the same as the 800 men-at-arms and 10,000 archers found in the *Anonimalle Chronicle* (p. 25). (Such an inordinate ratio of archers to men-at-arms seems unwarranted from the description of fighting found in all contemporary sources.) Finally, the *Récits d'un bourgeois de Valenciennes* claim an outlandish total of 70,000 English soldiers (p. 241). Other authors who mention the different types of troops include Robert of Avesbury, p. 376 and Jean le Bel, II:126–27. On those experienced at Crécy see *Anonimalle Chronicle*, p. 26.

[32] Henry Knighton, II:42: 'omnes unanimi assensu parati vivere et mori pro salvatione regni convenerunt.'

and other defenders.[33] All other chroniclers mention only the large amount of destruction caused by the Scots both on their journey to and around Durham.[34]

But if there had been little resistance before Durham, thus confirming David Bruce and Philip VI's prediction of all the English soldiers being in France, at Durham the Scots found a relatively large English army which had traveled south from Newcastle to stop their invasion. Did this surprise the Scots? Not according to John of Reading, who holds that the time and place of the battle had been set before the actual fighting.[35] Nor according to Jean Froissart, who contends that the Scots had heard of the gathering and movement of the English but had refused to believe it.[36] Finally, the author of the *Anonimalle Chronicle* does not believe that the English presence surprised the Scots, reporting that prior to the appearance of the defensive force two monks from Durham Cathedral had tried to persuade the Scottish troops not to destroy their lands. While not accusing these monks of reporting the English advance, the author of this work does claim that David Bruce thought that this was a ploy to draw his army into an ambush by the English force, thus counselling his army to avoid Durham. But the Scots disregarded their king's advice, claiming that they were ready to fight.[37]

Only the *Chronicon de Lanercost* and the *Liber Pluscardensis* claim that the English surprised the Scots at Neville's Cross. The anonymous authors of these works report that while camping near Durham, the Scots 'being unaware of the approach of the English,' had sent out a raiding party under the command of William Douglas to pillage the nearby countryside. Instead, Douglas 'suddenly found himself unawares almost in the middle of the English army' all ordered and ready for combat. This party 'hastily' returned to the main force and reported the incident.[38]

The only facet of this account which may be true is that the English were the first to reach Durham and therefore had the opportunity to select a defensible battlefield site at Neville's Cross. Although no contemporary author refers to the prudence of

---

[33] Thomas Samson in Froissart, V:490; *Chronicon de Lanercost*, pp. 345–46; Robert of Avesbury, p. 376; Geoffrey le Baker, pp. 86–87; *Anonimalle Chronicle*, pp. 23–24; Thomas of Burton, II:61; Andrew of Wyntoun, II:472–73; and Poem IV in Laurence Minot, p. 113. On Walter of Selby see Edward Miller, *War in the North: The Anglo-Scottish Wars of the Middle Ages* (Hull, 1960), pp. 13–14. On the devastation of the Scots in north England see *Chronicon de Lanercost*, pp. 344–47. Lanercost was one of the priories sacked by the Scots in 1346, and the monks writing this chronicle appear to have been eyewitnesses to this devastation.

[34] Jean Froissart, V:121, 124, 125; Jean le Bel, II:127; Geoffrey le Baker, p. 87; Adam Murimuth, p. 218; *Anonimalle Chronicle*, pp. 24–25; *The Brut*, II:299; Anonymous of Canterbury, p. 192; *Récits d'un bourgeois de Valenciennes*, p. 241; *Chronographia regum Francorum*, II:242; *Chronique Normande*, p. 87; and *Liber Pluscardensis*, I:293.

[35] John of Reading, p. 102: 'Assignatisque loco et die belli . . .'

[36] Jean Froissart, V:130. However, this appears only in Froissart's final redaction which was written c.1400.

[37] *Anonimalle Chronicle*, p. 26. The *Chronicon de Lanercost* (pp. 348–49) gives a different time, purpose, and result for the visit of the Durham monks.

[38] *Chronicon de Lanercost*, pp. 348–49 and *Liber Pluscardensis*, I:294: 'Willelmus vero de Douglas de mane, de appropinquacione Anglorum inscius, cum suo agmine, prout de sero ordinatum est, ad depraedandum devastandum patriam se festinando, confestim quasi in medio exercitus Anglorum ignoranter cecidit. Quod percipientes primitivi equestres inimicos eorum in tribus aciebus belli ordinatos, paratos ad pugnam, reversi sunt festinanter ad regem David, exponentes ei modum.'

Battle of Neville's Cross

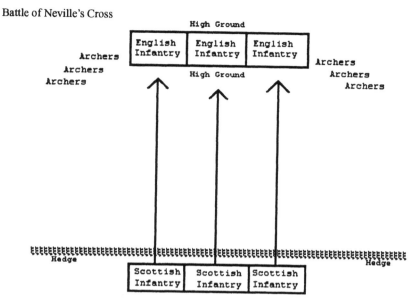

this choice, maps showing the physical features of the battlefield reveal the existence of a high ground on which the English lines formed, their backs to the hill on which Durham is located.[39] Thomas of Burton confirms this when he reports that the Scots 'ascended' in their march towards the English.[40] According to Jean Froissart and Andrew of Wyntoun, there was also a hedge or dike which separated the Scots from the English. To attack these lines, the Scots would have had to pass through this impediment and charge uphill.[41] On this site the English leaders ordered their army as infantry in three lines.[42] (Jean le Bel and one of Jean Froissart's redactions count four lines.[43]) Each line was commanded by one baron and one ecclesiastical prelate. According to Jean Froissart and Thomas of Burton, the archers were placed along the sides and somewhat in front of the infantry lines.[44]

---

[39] See, for example, the eighteenth-century map reprinted in Frank Graham, *Famous Northern Battles* (Rothbury, 1988), p. 13.

[40] Thomas of Burton, II:61.

[41] Jean Froissart (V:132) uses the Old French word 'haie' and Andrew of Wyntoun (II:475) uses the Middle English 'dykis'.

[42] For a three line formation see Thomas Samson in Froissart, V:491; *Chronicon de Lanercost*, pp. 350–51; *Anonimalle Chronicle*, pp. 26–27; Thomas of Burton, II:61; Froissart, V:124; *Liber Pluscardensis*, I:294; and an anonymous poem, Poem IV, found in Minot, p. 115. The *Anonimalle Chronicle* also insists that the Scots ordered in three lines first, with the English responding with their own three line formation, but no other source corroborates this view. For four lines see Jean le Bel, II:127 and Jean Froissart, V:126. This is found in the first redaction of Froissart; the second redaction reduces the number to three lines; and the final redaction does not mention the number of lines in the English formation.

[43] Jean Froissart, V:126 and Jean le Bel, II:127. The first line was commanded by Percy and the bishop of Durham, the second by Neville and the archbishop of York, the third by Mowbray and the bishop of Lincoln, and the fourth by Edward Balliol and the archbishop of Canterbury.

[44] Jean Froissart, V:124, 130 and Thomas of Burton, II:61.

The Scots arrived on the battlefield and also ordered themselves in three lines.[45] They were confident in their numbers which were far greater than those opposing them, and Giovanni Villani maintains that they wanted to attack the English immediately.[46] But, according to Froissart and an anonymous contemporary poet, David Bruce and William Douglas decided to hold off their attack in order to meet in council and to speak to their troops.[47] The Scottish leaders may also have wanted to take advantage of the growing fatigue of the English army, which by that time, noon, had stood in its lines for several hours.[48] The English leaders too met in council, but their mood was decidedly different from the confidence shown by the Scots. According to Jean Froissart, they considered that the battle would not be fought until the next morning, and thus they urged attentiveness throughout the night, reckoning that the Scots, 'a great people,' could cause much damage. The English might even lose if the Scots 'came suddenly upon them.'[49] They then 'placed their faith in God' and prepared for battle.[50]

Undoubtedly, the English leaders also laid out their tactical plan for the battle, although by this time it was well known and, at least since 1322, well practiced. They were to stand in a defensive formation, as solid lines of infantry, awaiting the Scottish charge. As Robert of Avesbury reports: 'They were to stand in the way of the Scots, then they were to fight with them strongly.'[51] The archers were to fire at the oncoming troops, provoking, disorienting and slowing their charge.

As it was laid out so it happened. The Scots did or perhaps could not wait for the night to pass. (Thomas of Burton claims that 500 archers provoked the attack by firing arrows into the Scots while they waited to attack the English, but he is alone in this assertion.[52]) They armed themselves, and whoever had them mounted their horses;[53] at three o'clock Scottish horns sounded, signalling to their own troops that

---

45 *Chronicon de Lanercost*, pp. 349–50; Henry Knighton, II:42; *Anonimalle Chronicle*, p. 26; Jean Froissart, V:128; *Liber Pluscardensis*, I:229; and Andrew of Wyntoun, II:475.

46 Giovanni Villani (ed. Ridotta), VII:187. On Scottish confidence see Froissart, V:126, 128–29, 130.

47 Jean Froissart, V:130 and Poem IV in Laurence Minot, pp. 115–16.

48 Jean Froissart, V:130.

49 Jean Froissart, V:131: 'Li signeur et li prélat se remissent ensamble en consel, et dissent chil liquel estoient le plus usé d'armes: "Se nous atendons jusques à la nuit, ces Escoçois, qui sont grans gens, nous poront venir courir sus et porter trop grant damage. Si seroit bon que nous envoions viers euls jusques à cinq cens lances pour euls atraire hors de lors logeis et que li nostre se facent cachier, tout au lonch de celle haie, là où nostre archier seront mis et aresté, et se les Escos viennent soudainement après nos gens, ensi que il sont bien taillet de ce faire (car il sont chaut, boullant et orguilleus, et tant que pour l'heure il prisent moult petit nostre affaire), nostres archiers qui sont frès et nouveauls, trairont sus euls et entre euls, et nous aussi, gens d'armes, les requellerons ensi comme il apertient à faire. Par ce parti porons-nous bien avoir bonne aventure, et se il se voellent tenir là où il sont, il donront à entendre que il nous vodront venir courir sus de nuit; mais nous nos départirons avant et nous retrairons dedens le Noef-Chastiel, car pas ne nous seroit proufitable à chi atendre et logier le nuit." '

50 Henry Knighton, II:42 and *Anonimalle Chronicle*, p. 26.

51 Robert of Avesbury, p. 377: '. . . obviam sibi dantes, cum eodem fortiter proeliarunt.'

52 Thomas of Burton, II:61.

53 Jean Froissart, V:131.

a charge was to commence, but also warning the English of that same charge;[54] and, with a war cry, they moved, 'fortified in their number by their polished helmets and shields,' towards the infantry defensive formation.[55] A 'grave and large' battle followed.[56]

It was 'very cruel and very marvelous,' writes the Bourgeois of Valenciennes, and Jean le Bel compares it to that fought by Roland and Oliver at Roncevalles.[57] As the Scottish troops passed through the hedge and progressed up the incline towards the English army, they first encountered the arrows of the longbowmen. Jean Froissart describes the action:

> And when the Scots came through the hedge, the English archers commenced to fire very strongly and at a great distance. And they impaled men and horses and caused a great disruption.

Later he adds that the archers 'gave a great comfort to their men-at-arms and great pain to the Scots.'[58]

Still, the 'great pain' given by the archers neither stopped the charge nor, at least according to Geoffrey le Baker, did it seem to have been as effective at disordering it as Froissart claims. Baker uses the verb 'frustrare' to describe this ineffectiveness: 'The Scots . . . frustrated the English archers at the beginning of the battle.'[59] What this means is difficult to determine from this account alone. However, a solution may be found in Thomas Samson's letter, as he writes that the charge of the Scots caused the archers and non-professional militia to retreat twice from the battlefield, 'but our men-at-arms fought well and lasted until the archers and 'communes' reassembled.'[60] Geoffrey le Baker may be saying the same thing when he adds that 'the first line of [English] soldiers greeted the enemy with deadly spears.'[61]

The Scottish soldiers, as a dense formation itself, hit the English lines with power and strength; both sides fought well – as 'rabid lions' records one contemporary

---

[54] Henry Knighton, II:42; Jean Froissart, V:129; and Poem IV in Laurence Minot, p. 117. The time of the charge is recorded by Jean le Bel, II:127.

[55] The quote is from Geoffrey le Baker, p. 88: '. . . cassidibus politis et umbonibus numero firmatis . . .' On the Scottish war cry, see Jean Froissart, V:131. See also Henry Knighton, II:42; *Anonimalle Chronicle*, p. 27; Thomas of Burton, II:61; and Jean Froissart, V:131. The *Liber Pluscardensis* (I:294) contends that the English were the first to attack at Neville's Cross, but none of the more contemporary writers corroborate this statement.

[56] Jean Froissart, V:132.

[57] *Récits d'un bourgeois de Valenciennes*, p. 241 and Jean le Bel, II:127–28. See also Adam Murimuth, p. 218 and Jean Froissart, V:124, 127.

[58] Jean Froissart, V:132: 'et quant les Escos furent venu à celle haie, les archiers englois commenchièrent à traire moult fort et moult roit et à enpaller hommes et cervaus et à mettre à grant meschief . . . et donnèrent moult grant confort as gens d'armes de lor costé et grant painne as Escoçois.' This description exists only in Froissart's final redaction. The account of his first redaction is much shorter and does not describe any damage done by the archers (V:126–27). See also Poem IV in Laurence Minot, pp. 115, 117.

[59] Geoffrey le Baker, p. 88: 'Nacio Scotia . . . sagittas Anglicorum in primordio belli frustravit.'

[60] Thomas Samson in Froissart, V:490–91: 'Deux foits se retraièrent les archers et comunes de nostre part; mais nos gents d'armes se combatièrent et se continuèrent durment bien tant qe les archers et communes reassemblèrent.' My thanks to Cliff Rogers for pointing me to this interpretation.

[61] Geoffrey le Baker, p. 88: 'Set armatorum acies prima ictubus letalibus hostes salutavit.'

commentator – with many displays of bravery.[62] The *Anonimalle Chronicle* is almost poetic in its description: 'In this conflict lances were broken, swords destroyed, armor pierced, helmets and bascinets smashed, and shields split.'[63] Although Thomas of Burton claims that the English first line was initially pushed back, ultimately, the defending force held against the Scottish onslaught, even, according to the *Anonimalle Chronicle*, through a second and third charge.[64] As the number of dead rose, the Scots began to lose heart.[65] Some of their nobles fled, and soon so did many of the others.[66] At the end, Geoffrey le Baker reports, only forty nobles remained, standing in a circle around their king and prepared to fight to the death.[67] David Bruce, who was wounded at least once in the face by an arrow during the battle, chose not to be killed.[68] The English victory was greeted from the Cathedral tower by prayers and shouts from monks who had watched the battle; their exhilaration was heard by the troops below.[69] When news of the victory reached Calais, the English forces there echoed the Durham monks' cheers.[70]

Jean Froissart sums up the battle of Neville's Cross:

> That day, as in that conflict which the king of England and his troops fought at the battle of Crécy at which only fifty thousand men had defeated one hundred

---

[62] The quotation is from Poem IV in Laurence Minot, p. 117. See also Henry Knighton, II:42; Geoffrey le Baker, p. 88; Thomas of Burton, II:61–62; Jean Froissart, V:124, 127, 132; and Andrew of Wyntoun, II:476.

[63] *Anonimalle Chronicle*, p. 27: 'En quele conflykte launces furrent frussez, espeis debrisez, haubergeouns desmaillez, helmes et bacynetz availlez et escues desquarterez.'

[64] Thomas of Burton, II:61–62 and *Anonimalle Chronicle*, p. 27. Andrew of Wyntoun reports two Scottish attacks (II:475–76).

[65] Only five sources record the number of Scots killed with the latter four obvious exaggerations: *Chronique Normande*, p. 87 – 2,000; Adam Murimuth, p. 218 – 12,000; Thomas Samson in Froissart, V:491 – 540 knights and 12,000 others; Henry Knighton, II:43 – 100 knights and 20,000 others; and *Récits d'un bourgeois de Valenciennes*, p. 241 – 40,000. See also Robert of Avesbury, p. 377; Geoffrey le Baker, pp. 88–89; *Anonimalle Chronicle*, p. 27; Thomas of Burton, II:62; John of Reading, p. 103; *The Brut*, II:299; the Anonymous of Canterbury, p. 192; Jean Froissart, V:125, 127; *Chronographia regum Francorum*, II:242; *Chronique Normande*, p. 87; Poem IV in Laurence Minot, p. 118; *Liber Pluscardensis*, I:294–95; and Andrew of Wyntoun, II:476–77.

[66] *Chronicon de Lanercost*, p. 351; Henry Knighton, II:43; Geoffrey le Baker, p. 88; *Anonimalle Chronicle*, p. 27; *The Brut*, II:543; Poem IV in Laurence Minot, p. 119; and John Fordun, I:367.

[67] Geoffrey le Baker, p. 88.

[68] That David was wounded see Thomas Samson in Froissart, V:491; Henry Knighton, II:44; Adam Murimuth, p. 219; Thomas of Burton, II:62; Anonymous of Canterbury, p. 192; *The Brut*, II:543; *Chronique Normande*, p. 87; and *Liber Pluscardensis*, I:294. (The *Chronique Normande* claims that David Bruce was wounded twice in the face with arrows, with one arrowhead remaining in his face for four years and the other for nine years before being removed.) On the Scots captured see Thomas Samson in Froissart, V:491–92; Robert of Avesbury, p. 377; Henry Knighton, II:43–44; Geoffrey le Baker, p. 88; Adam Murimuth, pp. 218–19; *Anonimalle Chronicle*, p. 28; John of Reading, p. 103; *The Brut*, II:299–300; Anonymous of Canterbury, p. 192; Poem III in Laurence Minot, pp. 110–12; Poem IV in Minot, p. 119; Jean Froissart, V:125, 128, 133; Jean le Bel, II:128; *Récits d'un bourgeois de Valenciennes*, p. 241; *Chronographia regum Francorum*, II:242; John Fordun, I:358; and Andrew of Wyntoun, II:476–77. A list of the Scottish leaders captured at Neville's Cross and interred in the Tower of London is found in Rymer, *Foedera*, III.1:95.

[69] Henry Knighton, II:42–43.

[70] *Anonimalle Chronicle*, p. 28 and Jean le Bel, II:129–30.

thousand, equally in the battle which I have just presented to you, a small force of English were met by the Scots and defeated their enemy.[71]

Thus Froissart made the comparison between the two 1346 English victories. The Hainaulter chronicler, never one to let subtlety be his guide, was perhaps claiming too much, especially when we consider the disparity in sizes of the English and opposing armies, the leadership differences, and the purposes for fighting – one defensive and the other offensive.

But there are several similarities apparent between the two battles. Most of these deal with the tactics employed by the English on the field. The English chose the battlefield: at Neville's Cross the choice of a high, defensible ground was significant in the victory; the hedge through which the Scots were forced to pass also must have caused some confusion and disruption among those charging towards the English lines. Their leaders chose to dismount the cavalry: indeed, in none of the chronicles is cavalry even mentioned outside of the categorization of them in an initial tally of soldiers fighting for the English. The infantry was ordered in a formation of three or four solid lines: these were to take on the charges of the Scottish troops, and it was their ability to hold against these attacks that ultimately brought victory. And the archers were set up along the sides of the infantry lines to provide disrupting firepower: this narrowed the Scottish charge so that it struck the strength of the English defensive formation, the infantry lines.

The archers proved very capable in narrowing the charge of the Scottish force, as no contemporary commentator reports any flanking maneuver attempted by those attacking the English line. However, unless Froissart's account is accepted over those of the more contemporary Geoffrey le Baker and Thomas Samson, the archers were unsuccessful in disordering the charge of the Scots so that it fell onto the English infantry lines in an almost completely intact order.[72] Yet that the archers were unsuccessful in confusing and disrupting the charge of the Scots as they had done against the French at Crécy and against the Scots at Halidon Hill proved of little significance to the outcome of the battle. The English infantry at Neville's Cross simply had to fight as the Flemings, Bernese, Catalan Company, Frisians, Liégeois, and even Scots had since the beginning of the fourteenth century, with little or no disordering confusion caused by archery. They found, as those other armies did in their victories, that the role of anyone, including archers, was secondary to that of the infantry soldier standing solidly in line against the attack of his foes. If the infantry lines held, the charge could be, and at Neville's Cross was, defeated.

---

[71] Jean Froissart, V:132: 'Che jour, ensi que de la belle aventure que li rois d'Engleterre et ses gens orent de la bataille de Créchi et que euls quinze mille hommes en tout en desconfirent cent mille, parellement en la bataille dont je vous parole présentement, un petit de gens que les Englois estoient ou regart des Escos, desconfirent lors ennemis.'

[72] Even Sir Charles Oman ((1905) II:150) must reluctantly admit that 'the matter was not entirely settled by archery, as the masses of spearmen were seriously engaged for some time at close quarters.' . But Jonathan Sumption accepts Froissart's account without considering what Geoffrey le Baker has to say (p. 553). Finally, Nicholson believes that it was the English archery which caused the Scottish army to attack, although they 'wished to remain on the defensive' (*Scotland*, p. 147), but I can find nowhere in the original sources when this is suggested.

APPENDIX

Three Infantry Ambushes: The Battles of Morgarten, 1315, Auberoche, 1345, and La Roche-Derrien, 1347

By only discussing those battles which began as 'two armies entirely assembled and ordered against each other', three early fourteenth-century infantry victories by definition have been excluded. The battle of Morgarten, where the Swiss defeated the Austrians in 1315, and the battles of Auberoche and La Roche-Derrien, where the English defeated the French in 1345 and 1347 respectively, all were fought by one army, in each case the victorious one, surprising their opponents, and by using this surprise, defeating them.

The battle of Morgarten followed the invasion of the rebellious Switzerland by Duke Leopold of Austria.[1] The Austrian army, composed largely of knightly cavalry and numbering between 2,000 and 3,000, moved through Switzerland with what seemed to them to be little difficulty. But in reality, by blocking more accessible passes, the Swiss had directed the march of the Austrians over precipitous terrain and through dangerous passes. In one of these, the pass of Morgarten, along the east bank of the Aegeri Lake, a force of between 3,000 and 4,000 peasants lay in ambush.[2]

The narrowness of the pass road required the Austrians to reduce the size of their cavalry column, but even after doing so, the vanguard of the column became compressed and congested. At this point, the Swiss moved from their hiding spots, high on the steep slopes of the pass, and sent large stones and logs down on the surprised Austrians. Smaller stones and arrows also were showered onto the cavalry column. This completely confused the Austrians, who tried vainly to get out of the way of these disruptive devices. However, before they could regain their order, the Swiss infantry charged down the hill into the confused column. Using their famed

---

1 Contemporary and near contemporary sources on the battle of Morgarten can be found in the *Chronicon Aulae Regiae*, Rudolf von Radegg's *Capella heremitana*, Johann von Bictring's *Chronik*, Jean de Winterthur's *Chronicon*, the *Chronik* of Mathias von Neuenberg, the *Oesterreichische Chronik*, Jakob Twinger von Königshofen's *Chronik*, Konrad Justinger's *Berner Chronik*, the *Bürcher Chronik von 1428*, and numerous other smaller historical works. All of these original sources are edited in Theodor von Liebenau, 'Berichte über die Schlacht am Morgarten,' *Mitteilungen des historischen Vereins des Kantons Schwyz* 3 (1884), 1–85. Modern accounts of Morgarten can be found in Delbrück, pp. 551–60; Oman (1905), II:238–41; Wernli, pp. 277–94; McCrackan, pp. 123–28; Bruno Meyer, 'Die Schlacht am Morgarten: Verlauf der Schlacht und Absichten der Parteien,' *Revue Suisse d'histoire* 16 (1966), 129–79; and Robert Durrer, *Schweizer Kriegsgeschichte*, ed. M. Feldmann and H.H.G. Wirz (Bern, 1915), I:74–90.

2 These numbers and those of the Austrians are from Hans Delbrück, pp. 553–54; they are much smaller than those given in the original sources.

'halberds', the Swiss easily cut down most of the knights from their horses, killing them as they lay helpless on the ground. Those who could, and they were few, fled out of the pass. Soon they encountered the rear-guard of the Austrian army, causing them also to flee. Deaths were numerous, with Duke Leopold himself barely able to flee.

The battle of Auberoche was fought on October 21, 1345 during the earl of Derby's invasion of the Périgord region of Gascony.[3] Derby, an experienced leader who had been with the English army in Flanders in 1340, was sent to Gascony in June 1345 by Edward III to defend those Gascon nobles who had remained loyal to the English throne and thus were threatened by French incursions into their territory. He may also have been sent there to keep Philip VI preoccupied while the main English force prepared to attack Normandy.

The earl of Derby moved first against the French-controlled town of Bergerac which, after a concerted defense by Bertrand, the count de l'Isle, fell to the English leader. From there he proceeded north to Périgueux, the capital of the region, but found it too strongly defended for his small army to attack. Thus he moved east to the castle and village of Auberoche. The French army, made aware of the English progression by, among others, the count de l'Isle, who had been able to escape from Bergerac, gathered at La Réole and marched quickly to Auberoche. However, their approach was seen by the English, who numbered no more than 1,200, and they were able to successfully hide in nearby woods. The French army, numbering between 7,000 and 10,000, but not realizing the proximity of the English, camped very close to them.[4]

Derby, knowing that his army's supplies would not last long, decided that they should break out of their hiding place and attack the French camp during the evening meal. The timing of the English attack was perfect; with trumpets blaring and banners unfurled, the English troops, under the cover of a constant archery barrage, charged from the woods and reached the French camp, some 200–300 yards away, without opposition. The French troops were completely surprised and utterly confused by the English onslaught. Few were able even to grab their weapons let alone don their armor. Casualties were extremely high, as both arrows and swords easily cut down the unprotected French soldiers. A few French leaders were able to regroup, and they attempted to restore some defensive order. But eventually they could do nothing but retreat from the battlefield, saving their own lives. For the most part, the French army in Gascony lay dead among their tents.

Nearly two years later, on June 20, 1347, the battle of La Roche-Derrien was fought in Brittany between two secondary armies of the French and English, the main

---

[3] Original sources on the battle of Auberoche include: Adam Murimuth, pp. 189–90; Henry Knighton, II:31–32; Robert of Avesbury, pp. 356–57; *Anonimalle Chronicle*, p. 18; Jean Froissart, IV:252–73; *Grandes chroniques*, IX:258–59; *Chronique Normande*, pp. 65–66; *Récits d'un bourgeois de Valenciennes*, pp. 194–95; Villani (ed. Muratori), col. 927; and *Chronicon Vazatense*, in *Archives historiques du département de la Gironde*, xv (Bordeaux, 1874), pp. 43–44. Secondary sources which recount the battle include: Burne, *Crecy War*, pp. 107–14 and Sumption, pp. 468–69.
[4] These numbers are from Burne, *Crecy War*, pp. 107–08.

forces of both kingdoms gathered at the siege of Calais.[5] The leader of the French force was Charles of Blois, the count of Brittany, and the leader of the English army was Sir Thomas Dagworth. Both leaders were very experienced in warfare. In fact, they had faced each other almost constantly since May 1345 when Dagworth first landed with the earl of Northampton's army in France; Thomas Dagworth had also led the English force at the small battle of St. Pol de Léon, fought on June 9, 1346, where Charles of Blois had been defeated.

By spring 1347 Charles was ready to fight again. Hoping to avenge the recent defeats of the French, including that at Crécy, and perhaps also hoping to raise the siege of Calais by defeating an English force in Brittany, Charles gathered an army and in May besieged the English-controlled town of La Roche-Derrien. Charles was patient at La Roche-Derrien. He had time to take the town by hunger and thus did not press for an attack on its walls. At the same time, he undoubtedly wanted to bring Dagworth, whose army was much smaller than the count of Blois', to battle – the English force had no more than 1,000 soldiers, including 300 men-at-arms and 400 archers.[6]

Sir Thomas Dagworth delayed his relief attack until June. Perhaps this delay lulled Blois into believing that no relief force would come to La Roche-Derrien. If not, he had unwisely determined that Dagworth's approach would come only along the western bank of the Jaudi River. Dagworth came instead along the more dangerous east bank, which necessitated a night march through woods and harsh country. Just before dawn on June 20, Dagworth's army charged into the sleeping French camp. The attack was completely unexpected – sentries had not even been posted – and in the dark the French soldiers were easily cut down by the English who knew each other only by a secret password. Some French did recover from the surprise and were able to make a couple of counter-attacks, one of which wounded Dagworth, but ultimately the English gained the field. Charles of Blois, unable to don his armor, was also wounded during the fight; taken by Dagworth's troops, he was sent to England and imprisoned with David Bruce in the Tower of London. Large numbers of French soldiers had been killed and many more captured, but part of the French army, in itself larger than the English force, had remained inactive during the battle, besieging the town on the opposite side of the river from the main French camp. Demoralized by the victory over their general, they left the siege without further combat.

---

[5] Original sources on the battle of La Roche-Derrien include: Henry Knighton, II:48–49; Robert of Avesbury, pp. 388–90; John of Reading, p. 104; Jean le Bel, II:145–49; Jean Froissart, V:164–77; *Grandes chroniques*, IX:298–309; *Chronique Normande*, pp. 90–91; and *Récits d'un bourgeois de Valenciennes*, pp. 254–56. There also exists a letter from Thomas Dagworth to the chancellor of England which discusses the battle of La Roche-Derrien. It is recorded in Robert of Avesbury, pp. 388–90 and in Froissart, XVIII:299–300. Secondary sources on the battle include: Oman (1905), II:254–55; Burne, *Crecy War*, pp. 89–99; and Sumption, pp. 572–75.

[6] The numbers are Burne's (*Crecy War*, pp. 91–92). See also pp. 96–97.

CONCLUSIONS

THERE IS BUT ONE main conclusion to this study: infantry armies fought battles during the early fourteenth century using distinctive, and in most cases, decisive tactics. This occurred not just in Flanders or in France or in Scotland, as some historians have insisted, but throughout Europe. The number of battles fought in such a short period of the Middle Ages is a historical fact. The constancy of infantry victories may surprise some, but no less surprising should be the uniformity in tactics used by all these infantry armies throughout such a large geographical region.

To begin to explain the constancy and uniformity of infantry tactics during the early fourteenth century, we must start by characterizing the troops which won and lost these battles. While each had different social backgrounds, military experience, and motives for fighting, the only consistent characteristic of those armies described here as infantry armies is that they primarily, and in most cases entirely, fought on foot. The Flemings at Courtrai, Arques, Mons-en-Pévèle, and Cassel, the Scots at Loudon Hill and Bannockburn, the Catalan Company at Kephissos, Andrew Harclay's force at Boroughbridge, the disinherited at Dupplin Moor, the Bernese at Laupen, the Frisians at Staveren, and the Liégeois at Vottem all fought using, as far as the original sources are concerned, only infantry soldiers. Robert Bruce even went so far, according to John of Trokelowe and Thomas Walsingham, to insist that his army at Bannockburn only fight as infantry, so that they would not suffer a similar defeat as that at the battle of Falkirk.

When cavalry also are reported to be present, as at Courtrai and at Kephissos, they are said to be dismounted and fighting as infantry. So too were the English troops at the battles of Halidon Hill, Morlaix, Crécy, and Neville's Cross, induced to dismount the cavalry and order as infantry after suffering defeat against the Scots at Bannock-burn, or, if we are to agree with T.F. Tout and J.E. Morris, influenced by Harclay's victorious 'Scottish' infantry tactics at Boroughbridge.[1] Whatever the initial cause of their dismounting, it was, as Geoffrey le Baker claims in his description of the battle of Halidon Hill, 'against the ancient tradition of their fathers.'[2] Soon, however, that ancient tradition was completely supplanted by the new, victorious tactics of the English army.

The troops these armies faced in battle were often, although not in every case, cavalry-based forces. That is not to say that each of these armies was exclusively cavalry; on the contrary, in the battles discussed here the cavalry did not stand alone, but was joined by non-cavalry soldiers: for example, infantry, as with the Freiburger cavalry at Laupen; archers, as with the French at Crécy; or infantry and archers, as

[1] Tout, 'Tactics,' 711–13 and Morris, 'Mounted Infantry,' 86–91.
[2] Geoffrey le Baker, p. 51: 'Ibi didicit a Scotis Anglorum generositas dextrarios reservare venacioni fugencium, et, contra antiquatum morem suorum patrum, pedes pugnare.'

with the French at Courtrai or the English at Bannockburn. But it was, in almost every battle, the cavalry of these armies charging against infantry opponents which led directly to their defeat. Only at Dupplin Moor, Halidon Hill, and Neville's Cross was it an infantry charge against infantry opponents which was the climactic point of the battle, and in each of these conflicts the defensive infantry formation was able to withstand the attacking infantry troops. As well, both at Courtrai and Laupen infantry attacks were resisted before receiving cavalry charges. Finally, at Mons-en-Pévèle and Cassel, the only indisputable defeats suffered by infantry armies studied here, it was the attacks made by the defending troops which ultimately led to their defeats. At Mons-en-Pévèle, this came late in the battle, after the Flemings had successfully withstood many French cavalry charges, even reaching the French camp and threatening Philip IV before being turned back. At Cassel, no cavalry charges were made against the position of the Flemish force on top of the hill; instead, Philip VI harassed the Flemings into a charge down the hill by artillery fire and by burning the countryside around the battlefield. This attack also reached the French camp and threatened the king before a counter-attack stopped the Flemings, killing those who did not take flight.

Another characteristic of the troops which is similar in most of the battles described here is that these infantry armies were usually smaller in number than their opponents. Only at Arques, Mons-en-Pévèle, Staveren, and Vottem are the defending troops reported to be larger in number than those attacking them, and only at Staveren and Vottem does this size advantage aid in achieving victory. At Mons-en-Pévèle, the larger Flemish numbers could not help them from being defeated. And at Arques, while their larger numbers may have kept this later Flemish army from defeat, they lost far more soldiers than their opponents in the battle and thus were forced to retreat from the field without being able to take the town of St. Omer, their motive for fighting the battle.

The next point in understanding the constancy and uniformity of infantry tactics in the battles of the early fourteenth century is to identify what was done by these armies to prepare to fight these battles. In all but four battles, Arques, Mons-en-Pévèle, Dupplin Moor, and Halidon Hill, the infantry armies chose the site of the battle. At Courtrai, the battlefield was chosen because of its proximity to the Lys River, which not only filled agricultural ditches cutting across the field but also served as a non-penetrable shield for the Flemish lines through which no one could attack and no one could flee. At Loudon Hill, Robert Bruce found a flat, dry plain flanked on one side by a deep and wide morass on which to order his troops, and at Bannockburn he gathered his army at New Park, also a flat plain, but this time bordered on three sides by impenetrable trees and marshes. At Kephissos, the Catalan Company placed themselves on a dry plain surrounded by marsh and river. At Boroughbridge, Andrew Harclay ordered his troops to block the bridge and ford across the Ouse River. Had Thomas of Lancaster tried to move to another river crossing he would have encountered the main English army. At Cassel, the Flemings ordered their soldiers on the top of a hill. Similarly, at Laupen, the Bernese were allowed to march past the Freiburgers besieging the town and place themselves on high ground nearby. At Morlaix, the English ordered themselves in front of a wood.

At Staveren and at Vottem, the Frisians and Liégeois chose to fight outside of the largest town of the respective region, using the town itself as a protection against attack from the rear. At Crécy, Edward III ordered his troops along a small ridge north of which stood the Bois de Crécy. And at Neville's Cross, the English positioned their lines on a high ground outside of Durham.

But choosing a good battlefield site was not the only important aspect of pre-battle preparation for these armies. Arriving early on the battlefield gave them on several occasions the opportunity further to ready the site for conflict. The most frequent means of doing this was by digging ditches and pits, either along the flanks or in front of the soldiers. Although these seem to have been a feature of battlefields since at least the early Middle Ages, never were ditches more effective than during this period. In all cases, they either disrupted a cavalry charge or narrowed its length preventing any flanking of a defending line. They were constructed at Courtrai, where most were filled with water and some were covered over with dirt and branches; even though their position was known to the French they would prove to be disruptive to their charge. They were also dug at Loudon Hill, where Robert Bruce had three large and deep trenches made across the field leaving only small gaps for the English horses to charge through. At Bannockburn, ditches and pits were dug in front of the Scottish lines, a tactic which obviously impressed the English, as Geoffrey le Baker insists that Edward III did the exact same thing at Crécy. (The muddiness of the battlefield of Crécy resulting from the pre-battle rainfall must have made these especially treacherous, although no contemporary writer confirms this.) And at Morlaix, the earl of Northampton dug pits and ditches both on the flanks and in front of the infantry which, when combined with the woods behind them, created what Henry Knighton described as a 'narrow cave'.[3] At Staveren and Vottem ditches were dug by the infantry armies, but not for the purpose of disrupting or narrowing cavalry charges. Instead, they were constructed as trenches for the defending army to hide in. In neither case, however, did these troops remain in their trenches.

Another battlefield preparation was the construction of wagon fortresses at Mons-en-Pévèle and Crécy. As described by the *Annales Gandenses*, at the battle of Mons-en-Pévèle this fortress was built by circling the wagons and carts, removing one wheel from each, and attaching them all together. The baggage train and horses were placed inside to protect them, but the fortifications also served to guard the rear of the troops. As well, if we are to believe the word of Jean de Paris, the Flemings built their wagon fortress at Mons-en-Pévèle so that if needed they might be able to retreat there 'to make a stand and fight inside such a circle.'[4] No similar purpose for the fortress at Crécy is mentioned.

Finally, at Kephissos, the site of battle was prepared for fighting when the Catalan Company cut ditches into the banks of the river and flooded the already marshy field.

In many of these early fourteenth-century battles the selection of the site and the

---

[3] Henry Knighton, II:25.
[4] Jean de Paris, p. 643: 'Flandrenses autem astute fecerant quasi munitionem de suis curribus et quadrigis, magnum terrae spatium hujus modi vehiculis circumdantes, ut infra talem circuitum possent in necessitate consistere et pugnare.'

preparing of the field meant that opponents had only one course of attack: a frontal assault. At Loudon Hill, Kephissos, Boroughbridge, Morlaix, and Crécy, the charging troops had no means of attacking from the flanks or the rear. The same was true for the second day's battle at Bannockburn. At Mons-en-Pévèle, a French flank attack was stopped by the Flemish wagon fortress. And at Courtrai, only the French garrison in the castle could attack the Flemish troops from the rear. But the Flemings had planned for such an action, and when it did occur, late in the battle, it was quickly countered by a contingent placed there to stop such an attack. At other battles during the early fourteenth century, there seems to have been the ability of the charging troops to attack from the rear and flanks. However, in these conflicts either the attacking forces chose, for several different reasons, only to make frontal assaults – at Dupplin Moor, Halidon Hill, Staveren, Vottem, Neville's Cross, and the first two phases of the battle of Arques – or the defenders altered their tactics and thus compensated for any flanking and rear attacks – at Laupen, the first day's battle at Bannockburn, and the final phase of the battle of Arques.

The English in these battles had in the longbow a technological advantage which no one else had, and they used this weapon not as 'a killing machine', as some historians have contended, but instead to narrow their opponents' charges and to protect against flank attacks. Indeed, using their archers as the English did, ordered along and protruding out from the flanks of the infantry lines, as shown at the battles of Halidon Hill, Crécy, Neville's Cross, and to a lesser extent at Bannockburn, Boroughbridge, and Dupplin Moor, there was little need for the longbowmen to kill many of their opponents. Their purpose was simply to narrow and confuse the attacker's charge so that when it fell onto the infantry troops, it did so in a disrupted and relatively impotent manner. (The English cannons at Crécy seem to have been used in the same way.) The perfect staging of this may have occurred at Halidon Hill, where Thomas of Burton describes what happened to the Scottish charge after encountering the English longbow fire: 'The smaller squadrons, so cut by the archers, were forced to cling to the larger army, and in a short time, the Scots massing together were pressed one into the other.'[5] And at Crécy, Jean le Bel notes:

> On their side the archers fired so skillfully that some of those on horses, feeling the barbed arrows, did not wish to advance, while others charged forward as planned; some resisted them tirelessly, while others turned their backs on the enemy.[6]

Any deaths of men and horses which occurred would obviously have added to the disruption of the charge. Finally, if the archers found themselves in range of the opposing troops before the attack, their fire could hasten a charge which was being

---

[5] See Thomas of Burton, II:364: 'Minores vero turmae, per sagittarios nimium laceratae, adhaerere magno exercitui compelluntur, et in brevi Scotti conglobati alius ab alio premebatur.'

[6] Jean le Bel, II:103: 'Et d'aultre part les archiers tiroient si merveilleusement que ceulx à cheval, sentans ces flesches barbelées [qui] faisoient merveilles, l'ung ne vouloit avant aler, l'aultre sailloit contremont si comme arragié, l'aultre regimboit hydeusement, l'aultre retournoit le cul par devers les anemis.'

formed, again effectively disrupting it; this occurred, if we are to trust Thomas of Burton, at Neville's Cross.[7] The longbowmen also proved themselves very effective against the attack of the Genoese crossbowmen at Crécy, completely defeating their archery counterparts before the Genoese could fire even one shot in reply.

After all pre-battle preparations had been undertaken and as the battle was about to commence, the infantry soldiers were ordered in their defensive formation. This was undoubtedly the most important tactic of every early fourteenth-century battle studied here. The infantry and dismounted cavalry were to form one or more solid lines. Sometimes there was a rearguard, and in other battles only a single solid line was ordered. Most often the line was straight and thick, while at the ford at Boroughbridge and at Halidon Hill it was slightly curved like an arc. At Courtrai, Mons-en-Pévèle, Loudon Hill, Kephissos, the second day of Bannockburn, Boroughbridge, Cassel, Morlaix, and Crécy, the infantry line was formed to accept and endure at least one and perhaps more than one frontal cavalry charge. (The Frisians at Staveren and the Liégeois at Vottem would also form a solid infantry lines, but these were ordered only after seeing that the cavalry charges being made against the trenches where these troops were hidden had become confused and disrupted in their attack.) At Dupplin Moor, Halidon Hill, and Neville's Cross, it was to be an infantry charge.

At the third phase of Arques, the first day of Bannockburn, and Laupen, the charges were made by cavalry, or, as at Laupen, by both cavalry and infantry, but they differed from other early fourteenth-century battles as these charges came from all sides. In these conflicts a different type of infantry line was ordered. At Arques, the *Annales Gandenses* describes the formation as 'a circle like a bowl or a crown.'[8] At Bannockburn, John Barbour writes that the Scots set up 'back to back with their spear points outward.'[9] And at Laupen, the *Conflictus Laupensis* depicts the formation as a 'small wedge'.[10] All authors report basically the same formation, a solid mass of soldiers who faced out in all directions, so that there was no front or rear and no flanks. Sometimes called a 'hedgehog', this infantry formation had the same function and, at least in these battles, the same result as the infantry line which faced only one direction.

The solid defensive infantry line was not only the most important tactic used by infantry armies in these early fourteenth-century battles, but it may also have been the most difficult tactic to achieve. While failing in only two battles, at Mons-en-Pévèle and Cassel where the infantry forces forgot their defensive purpose and attempted offensive attacks, the ability to form and then to keep an infantry line well ordered seems to have been a difficult task and certainly denotes some adept generalship. The tactic itself may not have been very intricate or elaborate, but the discipline needed to make it successful must have taxed both leaders and men, especially in the case when the soldiers charging down on them were 'the flower of

---

[7] Thomas of Burton, II:61.
[8] *Annales Gandenses*, p. 40.
[9] John Barbour, II:280.
[10] *Conflictus Laupensis*, p. 309.

French chivalry', as the Flemings faced in so many battles, or those English knights who were so 'brightly' armed that 'they appeared to be angels of a heavenly kingdom', as faced by the Scots at Loudon Hill and Bannockburn. Similar descriptions accompany the knights at Boroughbridge, Laupen, Staveren, and Vottem. Even when dismounted English warriors faced equals in their battles against the French or 'lesser soldiers' as against the Scots, the discipline required to succeed in this tactic, especially as it was so new to English military practice, is impressive.

Perhaps this is why so many battle commentators acknowledge the importance of the leaders of these armies, even when the leadership is vague or is not named. At Courtrai it was John of Renesse and William of Jülich who rose to great leadership; at Arques it was William of Jülich again; at Loudon Hill and Bannockburn, Robert Bruce led his army to victory; at Boroughbridge, it was Andrew Harclay; at Dupplin Moor, Edward Balliol defeated the Scots; at Halidon Hill and Crécy, the king of England, Edward III, showed great generalship; at Laupen, Rudolf von Erlach led the Bernese; at Morlaix, it was the earl of Northampton whose leadership is singled out; and at Neville's Cross, it was either William of La Zouche, the archbishop of York, Henry Percy, or Ralph Neville, who provided the leadership which achieved victory.

Often these leaders inspired their troops with battle orations. At Courtrai, John of Renesse urged his troops to fight strongly, attacking horses and riders with their weapons and pushing them into the ditches. He promises the Flemings that if they would 'fight strongly for their wives and their children, for the laws and liberty of their homeland,' that God 'would be merciful to those who were humble, giving consolation and victory to them.'[11] It was a speech which would be given, in differing words, by Robert Bruce at Loudon Hill and Bannockburn, by Nikolaas Zannekin at Cassel, by Edward III at Halidon Hill and Crécy, and by the English generals at Neville's Cross. While the accuracy of their words may be questioned, it must be concluded, as John R.E. Bliese has done in his study of battle orations from the central Middle Ages:

> The speeches, of course, are not verbatim reports of what the commanders actually said; they are the rhetorical products of the chroniclers themselves. However, the speeches are not mere flights of fancy. The tradition of rhetorical historiography in which the chroniclers were writing demanded that devices of amplification and ornamentation such as speeches had to be plausible. Battle orations thus contain much useful information because they are a recurrent rhetorical form that concentrates the authors' conceptions of motivation and morale in war.[12]

---

11 *Chronicon comitum Flandriae*, p. 168.
12 This quote comes from John R.E. Bliese, 'When Knightly Courage May Fail: Battle Orations in Medieval Europe,' *Historian* 53 (1991), 491. See also his 'Rhetoric and Morale: A Study of Battle Orations from the Central Middle Ages,' *Journal of Medieval History* 15 (1989), 201–26; 'Aelred of Rievaulx's Rhetoric and Morale at the Battle of the Standard, 1138,' *Albion* 20 (1988), 543–56; 'The Battle Rhetoric of Aelred of Rielvaulx,' *Haskins Society Journal* 1 (1989), 99–107; 'The Courage of the Normans. A Comparative Study of Battle Rhetoric,' *Nottingham Medieval Studies* 35 (1991), 1–26; and 'Leadership, Rhetoric, and Morale in the Norman Conquest of England,' *Military Affairs* 52 (1988), 23–28.

By speaking to their troops, outnumbered and ordered as infantry against cavalry, the leaders of these armies prepared the soldiers for combat, filling them with an enthusiasm and a belief that they could win against anyone they faced. They became, as Jean de Brusthem describes the Flemings at Courtrai, 'rejoicing and excited, roaring in the manner of lions.'[13] Ceremonies, especially religious and patriotic rites, also boosted the enthusiasm of those about to be attacked.

On came the charges, mean and ferocious, led by proud warriors who believed that they could not lose. As planned, the charges in every battle quickly became disordered and confused. The impetus was lost, and the soldiers, cavalry and infantry, hit their target with little force. Horses would not penetrate the infantry lines, and infantry could not penetrate them. They had become like a 'hare' caught in a 'trap', as the Middle English poem describes the French cavalry at Courtrai.[14] Knights were pulled from their horses and infantry soldiers were knocked down. There they became vulnerable to attacks from their opponents' weapons; lances, spears, swords, axes, halberds and godedags proved effective against all they faced, no matter who they were or how well they were armored. Future charges, if there were any, also failed. The number of dead rose and was always impressive to all contemporary writers. As Guillaume Guiart, an eyewitness to the battle of Mons-en-Pévèle, recalled later, 'death and blood dwelt there.'[15]

---

[13] Jean de Brusthem, p. 60:

[14] There are several editions of this poem. The one I have used is edited by Rossell Hope Robbins in his collection, *Historical Poems of the XIVth and XVth Centuries* (New York, 1959), pp. 9–13. Other editions can be found in *Political Songs of England*, Camden Society, vi, ed. T. Wright (London, 1839), pp. 187–195 and *Chants historique de la Flandre, 400–1650*, ed. L. de Baecker (Lille, 1855), pp. 161–72. The above reference can be found in Robbins, pp. 192–93.

[15] Guillaume Guiart, p. 293.

BIBLIOGRAPHY

Primary Sources

Ancienne chronique de Flandre. In *RHF*, xxii. Ed. Guignant and de Wailly. Paris, n.d.

Annales Gandenses. Ed. Hilda Johnstone. London, 1951.

Annales Paulini. In *Chronicles of the Reigns of Edward I and Edward II*. Vol. 1. Ed. W. Stubbs. RS. London, 1883.

Annales St. Jacobi Leodensis. In *MGH, SS*, xvi. Ed. G.H. Pertz. Hannover, 1850.

Annales Tielenses. In *MGH, SS*, xvi. Ed. G.H. Pertz. Hannover, 1879.

Anonimalle Chronicle, 1307 to 1334, The. Ed. W.R. Childs and J. Taylor. Leeds, 1991.

Anonimalle Chronicle, 1333–81, The. Ed. V.H. Galbraith. Manchester, 1927.

Anonyme Stadchronik oder der Königshofen-Justinger, Die. In *Die Berner-Chronik des Conrad Justinger*. Ed. G. Studer. Bern, 1871.

Avesbury, Robert of. *De gestis mirabilibus Edwardi III*. Ed. E.M. Thompson. RS. London, 1889.

Baker, Geoffrey le. *Chronicon*. Ed. E.M. Thompson. Oxford, 1889.

Barber, Richard, ed. and trans. *The Life and Campaigns of the Black Prince*. London, 1979.

Barbour, John. *The Bruce, or the Book of Robert de Broyss, King of Scots (1286–1332)*. Ed. W.W. Skeat. 4 vols. EETS. 1870–77; rpt. Oxford, 1968.

Beke, Jan. *Chronographia Johannis de Beke*. Ed. H. Bruch. 's Gravenhage, 1973.

Bel, Jean le. *Chroniques de Jean le Bel*. Ed. J. Viard and E. Duprez. 2 vols. SHF. Paris, 1904–05.

Berchen, Willem van. *Gelderse kroniek*. Ed. A.J. de Mooy. WUVG, xxiv. Arnhem, 1950.

Bonn, Werner de. *Vita Clementis VI*. In *Vitae paparum Avenionensium*, i. Ed. S. Baluze-Mollat. Paris, 1914.

Bower, Walter. *Scotichronicon*. Ed. D.E.R. Watt. 8 vols. Aberdeen, 000.

Breve chronicon de Flandriae. In *CCF*, iii. Ed. J.J. de Smet. Brussels, 1856.

Bridlington, Auctor of. *Gesta Edwardi de Carnarvan*. In *Chronicles of the Reigns of Edward I and Edward II*. Vol. 2. Ed. W. Stubbs. RS. London, 1883.

Brut, The, or the Chronicles of England. Ed. F.W.D. Brie. 2 vols. EETS. London, 1906–08.

Budt, Adrien de. *Chronicon Flandriae*. In *CCF*, i. Ed. J.J. de Smet. Brussels, 1837.

Burton, Thomas of. *Chronica monasterii de Melsa a fundatione usque ad annum 1396*. Ed. E.A. Bonds. 3 vols. RS. London, 1866–68.

Brusthem, Jean de. *Chronique*. In *CL*, ii. Ed. C.S. Balau. Liège, 1931.

Calendar of Documents Relating to Scotland. Ed. J. Bain. 4 vols. Edinburgh, 1883.

Canterbury, Anonymous of. *Chronicon*. Ed. J. Tait. Manchester, 1914.

Chandos, Herald of. *Life of the Black Prince by the Herald of Sir John Chandos*. Ed. and trans. M.K. Pope and E.C. Hodge. Oxford, 1910.

Chants historique de la Flandre, 400–1650. Ed. L. de Baecker. Lille, 1855.

'Chronicle of the Civil Wars of Edward II, A.' Ed. G.L. Haskins. In *Speculum* 14 (1939), 73–81.

Chronicon comitum Flandriae. In *CCF*, i. Ed. J.J. de Smet. Brussels, 1837.

Chronicon de Lanercost. Ed. J. Stevenson. Edinburgh, 1839.

Chronicon Rotomagensi. In *RHF*, xxiii. Ed. de Wailly, Delisle and Jourdain. Paris, n.d.
Chronicon Vazatense. In *AHDG*, xv. Bordeaux, 1874.
Chronique anonymé Française finissant en MCCCLVI. In *RHF*, xxi. Ed. Guignant and de Wailly. Paris, 1855.
Chronique Artésienne et chronique Tournaisienne. Ed. F. Funck-Brentano. Paris, 1898.
Chronique de Flandre. In *Istore et croniques de Flandres*. Ed. Kervyn de Lettenhove. 5 vols. Brussels, 1879–80.
Chronique de l'abbaye de Saint-Trond. Ed. C. de Borman. 2 vols. Liège, 1877.
Chronique des Pays-Bas, de France, d'Angleterre et de Tournai. In *CCF*, iii. Ed. J.J. de Smet. Brussels, 1856.
Chronique des quatre premiers Valois. Ed. S. Luce. SHF. Paris, 1862.
Chronique Liegeoise de 1402, La. Ed. E. Bacha. Brussels, 1900.
Chronique Normande de xiv siècle. Ed. A. and E. Molinier. SHF. Paris, 1882.
Chronique Parisienne anonymé de 1316 à 1339. Ed. A. Hellot. In *Mémoires de la société de l'histoire de Paris* 11 (1895), 1–181.
'Chronique Valenciennoise inedité, une.' Ed. Etienne Delcambre. In *Bulletin de la commission royale d'histoire de Belgique* 94 (1930).
Chronographia regum Francorum. Ed. H. Moranville. 2 vols. SHF. Paris, 1891–97.
Codex diplomaticus Flandriae. Ed. Thierry de Limburg-Stirum. 2 vols. Bruges, 1879.
Conflictus Laupensis. In *Die Berner-Chronik des Conrad Justinger*. Ed. G. Studer. Bern, 1871, pp. 302–13.
Coville, A., ed. 'Poems historiques du début de la Guerre de Cent Ans,' *Histoire litterature de France* 38 (1949).
Cronica de Berno. In *Die Berner-Chronik des Conrad Justinger*. Ed. G. Studer. Bern, 1871.
Cuvelier. *Chronique de Bertrand Guesclin*. Ed. E. Charrière. 2 vols. Paris, 1839.
Desnouelles, Jean. *Chronique*. In *RHF*, xxi. Ed. Guignant and de Wailly. Paris, 1855.
Diessenhoven, Heinrich von. *Chronicon ab a. 1316–1361*. In *FRG*, iv. Ed. J.F. Boehmer. Stuttgart, 1868.
Eulogium historiarum sive temporis. Ed. F.S. Haydon. 3 vols. RS. London, 1858–63.
ffoulkes, Charles. 'A Carved Flemish Chest at New College, Oxford,' *Archaeologia* 2nd ser. 15 (1914), 113–28.
Fordun, John. *Chronica gentis Scotorum*. Ed. W.F. Skene. 2 vols. HS. Edinburgh, 1871.
Franchet, Guillaume de. *Chronicon et continuationes*. In *RHF*, xx. Ed. Guignant and de Wailly. Paris, 1840.
French Chronicle of London, The. Ed. G.J. Augnier. CS. London, 1844.
Froissart, Jean. *Chroniques*. In *Oeuvres de Froissart*. Ed. Kervyn de Lettenhove. 29 vols. Brussels, 1867–77.
———. *Chroniques*. 15 vols. Ed. S. Luce *et al*. SHF. Paris, 1869–1975.
———. *Chroniques: Début du premier livre. Edition du manuscrit de Rome Reg. lat. 869*. Ed. G.T. Diller. Geneva, 1972.
Gallia christiana. Paris, 1744.
Gesta abbatum St. Trudoniensum. In *MGH, SS*, x. Ed. G.H. Pertz. Hannover, 1851.
Grandes chroniques de France, Les. Ed. J. Viard. 10 vols. SHF. Paris, 1920–53.
Gray, Thomas. *Scalachronica*. Ed. J. Stevenson. Edinburgh, 1836. Trans. H. Maxwell. Glasgow, 1907.
Gregoras, Nikephoros. *Byzantina historia*. In *PG*, 148. Ed. J.-P. Migne. Paris, 1865.
Gui, Bernard. *Flos chronicorum necnon e chronico regum Francorum*. In *RHF*, xxi. Ed. Guignant and de Wailly. Paris, 1855.

Guiart, Guillaume. *Branche des royaux lignages*. In *RHF*, xxii. Ed. Guignant and de Wailly. Paris, n.d.

Guisborough, Walter of. *Chronicon*. Ed. H. Rothwell. CS. London, 1957.

Hemingburgh, Walter of. *Chronicon*. 2 vols. EHS. London, 1848.

Hemricourt, Jacques de. *Le miroir des nobles de Hesbaye*. In *OEuvres de Jacques de Hemricourt*. Ed. C. de Borman. 3 vols. Brussels, 1910.

Historical Poems of the XIVth and XVth Centuries. Ed. R. H. Robbins. New York, 1959.

Hocsem, Jean de. *La chronique de Jean de Hocsem*. Ed. G. Kurth. Brussels, 1927.

Istorie Pistolensi. In *SRI*, xi. Ed. L. Muratori. Rome, 1728.

Ives. *Pars ultima chronicon*. In *RHF*, xxi. Ed. Guignant and de Wailly. Paris, 1855.

Justinger, Conrad. *Die Berner-Chronik des Conrad Justinger*. Ed. G. Studer. Bern, 1871.

Klerk, Jan de. *Brabantse yeesten of rijmkroniek van Braband*. Ed. J.F. Willems and J.H. Bormans. 2 vols. Brussels, 1839.

Knighton, Henry. *Chronicon*. Ed. J.R. Lumby. 2 vols. RS. London, 1889–95.

Kronyk van Vlaenderen van 580 tot 1467. Ed. P. Blommaert and C.P. Serrière. 2 vols. Ghent, 1839.

Leger, L., ed. and trans., 'Un poème Tchèque sur la bataille de Crécy,' *Journal des savants* (1902), 323–31.

Lescot, Richard. *Chronique*. Ed. J. Lemoine. SHF. Paris, 1896.

Lettres de Jean XXII (1316–1334). In *Analecta Vaticano-Belgica*, 2. Ed. Fayan. Rome, 1908.

Liber Pluscardensis. Ed. F.J.H. Skene. 2 vols. HS. Edinburgh, 1877.

Libro de los fechos et conquistas del principado de la Morea compilado por comandamiento de Don Johan Ferrandez de Heredia. Ed. A. Morel-Fatio. Geneva, 1885.

Macray, W.D., ed. 'Robert Baston's Poem on the Battle of Bannockburn,' *English Historical Review* 19 (1904), 507–08.

Minot, Laurence. *Poems*. Ed. J. Hall. Oxford, 1897.

'Mort du conte de Henau, La.' In *Panégyriques des comtes de Hainaut et de Hollande Guillaume I et Guillaume II*. Ed. C. Potvin. Mons, 1863.

Muisit, Gilles li. *Chronicon*. In *CCF*, ii. Ed. J.J. de Smet. Brussels, 1841.

Muntaner, Ramón. *Crònica*. Trans. H.M. Goodenough. 2 vols. London, 1920–21.

Murimuth, Adam. *Continuatio chronicorum*. Ed. E.M. Thompson. RS. London, 1889.

Nangis, Guillaume de. *Chronicon et continuationes*. Ed. H. Geraud. 2 vols. SHF. Paris, 1843.

Neuenberg, Mathias von. *Chronik*. Ed. A. Hofmeister. *MGH, SS* (nova series), iv. Berlin, 1940.

Outremeuse, Jean d'. *Chronique abrégée, de 1341 à 1400*. In *CL*, ii. Ed. S. Balau and E. Fairon. Brussels, 1931.

Paris, Geoffroi de. *Chronique rimée*. In *RHF*, xxii. Ed. Guignant and de Wailly. Paris, n.d.

Paris, Jean de. *Memoriale temporum*. In *RHF*, xxi. Ed. Guignant and de Wailly. Paris, 1855.

Passio Francorum secundum Flemingos. In *Die Parodie im Mittelalter*. Ed. Paul Lehmann. Stuttgart, 1963, pp. 30–31.

Political Songs of England. Ed. T. Wright. CS. London, 1839.

Procurator, Willem. *Chronicon*. Ed. Pijnacker Hardwijk. WHGU, 3rd ser., 20. Amsterdam, 1904.

Reading, John of. *Chronicon*. Ed. J. Tait. Manchester, 1914.

Rebdorf, Heinrich von. *Annales imperatorum et paparum (1294–1362)*. In *FRG*, iv. Ed. J.F. Boehmer. Stuttgart, 1868.

Récits d'un bourgeois de Valenciennes. Ed. Kervyn de Lettenhove. Brussels, 1877.

Rijmkroniek van Vlaenderen. In *CCF*, iv. Ed. J.J. de Smet. Brussels, 1865.

Rymer, Thomas, ed. *Foedera, conventiones, litterae, et cujuscunque generis acta publica inter reges Angliae et alios quosvis imperatores, reges, pontifices, principes, vel communitates (1101–1654).* 20 vols. London, 1704–35.

Soulèvement de la Flandre maritime de 1323–1328, Le. Ed. H. Pirenne. Brussels, 1900.

Stiermarken, Otto von. *Oesterreichische reimkroniek.* In *MGH, Deutschen Chroniken,* v. Ed. J. Seemuller. Hannover, 1893.

Stoke, Melis. *Rijmkroniek van Holland.* Ed. W.G. Brill. 2 vols. WHGU, n.s. xl and xlii. Utrecht, 1885.

Thilrode, Johannes. *Chronicon.* In *MGH, SS,* xxv. Ed. G.H. Pertz. Hannover, 1880.

Trokelowe, John of. *Annales.* Ed. H.T. Riley. RS. London, 1866.

Velthem, Lodewijk van. *Voortzetting van de Spiegel historiael (1284–1316).* Ed. H. Vander Linden et al. Brussels, 1922.

Venette, Jean de. *Chronique.* Ed. and trans. R.A. Newhall. New York, 1953.

Villani, Giovanni. *Istorie Fiorentine.* In *SRI,* xiii. Ed. L. Muratori. Rome, 1728.

———. *Cronica.* Ed. M.L. Ridotta. 7 vols. Florence, 1823.

Vita Edwardi secundi. Ed. and trans. N. Denholm-Young. London, 1957.

Vita et mors Edwardi secundi. In *Chronicles of the Reigns of Edward I and Edward II.* Vol. 2. Ed. W. Stubbs. RS. London, 1883.

Walsingham, Thomas. *Historia anglicana.* Ed. H.T. Riley. 2 vols. London, 1863–64.

Winterthur, Jean de. *Chronicon.* In *MGH, SS* (nova series), iii. Ed. F. Baethegen. Hannover, 1924.

Wrottesley, George, ed. *Crecy and Calais from the Original Records in the Public Record Office.* London, 1898.

Wyntoun, Andrew of. *Brevis Chronica.* HS. Edinburgh, 1879.

———. *Orygynale Cronykil of Scotland.* 3 Vols. HS. Edinburgh, 1872, 1873, 1879.

Secondary Sources

Abels, Richard P. *Lordship and Military Obligation in Anglo-Saxon England.* Berkeley, 1988.

Allmand, Christopher. *Henry V.* Berkeley, 1992.

———. *The Hundred Years War: England and France at War, c.1300–c.1450.* Cambridge, 1988.

Ayton, Andrew. 'The English Army and the Normandy Campaign of 1346.' In *England and Normandy in the Middle Ages.* Ed. D. Bates and A. Curry. London, 1994, pp. 253–68.

———. *Knights and Warhorses: Military Service and the English Aristocracy under Edward III.* Woodbridge, 1994.

Bachrach, Bernard S. *Fulk Nerra, the Neo-Roman Consul, 987–1040.* Berkeley, 1993.

Barber, Malcolm. *The New Knighthood: A History of the Order of the Temple.* Cambridge, 1994.

Barber, Richard. *Edward, Prince of Wales and Aquitaine: A Biography of the Black Prince.* London, 1978.

Barker, Juliet R.V. *The Tournament in England, 1100–1400.* Woodbridge, 1986.

Barlow, Frank. *William I and the Norman Conquest.* New York, 1965.

Baron, Hans. *The Crisis of the Early Italian Renaissance*. 2 vols. Princeton, 1955.

Barraclough, G. *The Origins of Modern Germany*. 2nd ed. Oxford, 1947.

Barron, Evan M. *The Scottish War of Independence: A Critical Study*. 2nd ed. Inverness, 1934.

Barrow. G.W.S. *Robert Bruce and the Community of the Realm of Scotland*. 3rd ed. Edinburgh, 1988.

Bartlett, Robert. 'Military Technology and Political Power.' In *The Making of Europe: Conquest, Colonization and Cultural Change, 950–1350* (Princeton, 1993), pp. 60–84.

Bartusis, Mark C. *The Late Byzantine Army: Arms and Society, 1204–1453*. Philadelphia, 1992.

Beeler, John. 'Towards a Re-Evaluation of Medieval English Leadership,' *Journal of British Studies* 3 (1963), 1–10.

———. *Warfare in England, 1066–1189*. Ithaca, 1966.

———. *Warfare in Feudal Europe, 730–1200*. Ithaca, 1971.

Bellamy, J.G. *The Law of Treason in England in the Late Middle Ages*. Cambridge, 1970.

Bliese, John R.E. 'Aelred of Rievaulx's Rhetoric and Morale at the Battle of the Standard, 1138,' *Albion* 20 (1988), 543–56.

———. 'The Battle Rhetoric of Aelred of Rielvaulx,' *Haskins Society Journal* 1 (1989), 99–107.

———. 'The Courage of the Normans. A Comparative Study of Battle Rhetoric,' *Nottingham Medieval Studies* 35 (1991), 1–26.

———. 'Leadership, Rhetoric, and Morale in the Norman Conquest of England,' *Military Affairs* 52 (1988), 23–28.

———. 'Rhetoric and Morale: A Study of Battle Orations from the Central Middle Ages,' *Journal of Medieval History* 15 (1989), 201–26.

———. 'When Knightly Courage May Fail: Battle Orations in Medieval Europe,' *Historian* 53 (1991), 489–504.

Bonaparte, Louis-Napoleon and I. Favé. *Du passé et l'avenir de l'artillerie*. 6 vols. Paris, 1856.

Bonjour, E., H.S. Offler, and G.R. Potter. *A Short History of Swizterland*. Oxford, 1952.

Bovesse, J. 'Le Comte de Namur Jean Ier et les événements du comté de Flandre en 1325–1326,' *Bulletin de la commission royale d'histoire* 131 (1965), 385–454.

Bradbury, Jim. *The Medieval Archer*. New York, 1985.

———. *The Medieval Siege*. Woodbridge, 1992.

Burckhardt, Jacob. *The Civilization of the Renaissance in Italy*. Trans. L. Geiger and W. Götz. 2 vols. New York, 1958.

Burne, Alfred H. *The Agincourt War: A Military History of the Latter Part of the Hundred Years War from 1369 to 1453*. London, 1956.

———. *The Crecy War: A Military History of the Hundred Years War from 1337 to the Peace of Bretigny, 1360*. London, 1955.

Burns, R. Ignatius. 'The Catalan Company and the European Powers, 1305–1311,' *Speculum* 29 (1954), 751–71.

Chaplais, Pierre. *Piers Gaveston: Edward II's Adoptive Brother*. Oxford, 1994.

Cheetham, Nicolas. *Mediaeval Greece*. New Haven, 1981.

Chickering, Howell, and Thomas H. Seiler, eds. *The Study of Chivalry: Resources and Approaches*. Kalamazoo, 1988.

Clarke M.V. and V.H. Galbraith. 'The Deposition of Edward II,' *Bulletin of the John Rylands Library* 14 (1930), 125–81.

Contamine, Philippe. 'Crécy (1346) et Azincourt (1415): Une comparison.' In *Divers aspects du moyen âge en occident: 1er Congrès Historique des Jeunes Historiens du Calaisis*. Calais, 1977, pp. 29–44.

———. 'La guerre de cent ans: Le XIVe siècle. La France au rythme de la guerre.' In *Histoire militaire de la France*, vol. 1: *Des origines à 1715*. Ed. P. Contamine. Paris, 1992.

———. *L'oriflamme de Saint-Denis aux XIVe et XVe siècles*. Nancy, 1975.

———. *War in the Middle Ages*. Trans. M. Jones. London, 1984.

Corfis, Ivy A. and Michael Wolfe, eds. *The Medieval City Under Siege*. Woodbridge, 1995.

Creasy, Sir Edward. *The Fifteen Decisive Battles of the World*. 36th ed. London, 1894.

Crouch, David. *William Marshal*. London, 1994.

Curry, Anne. *The Hundred Years War*. Houndmills, 1993.

Dahmus, Joseph. *Seven Decisive Battles of the Middle Ages*. Chicago, 1983.

Daniels, E. *Geschichte des Kriegswesens*. Vol. II: *Das mittelalterliche Kriegswesen*. 2nd ed. Berlin, 1927.

Davies, James Conway. *The Baronial Opposition to Edward II: Its Character and Policy*. London, 1918.

Davis, R.H.C. *The Medieval Warhorse*. London, 1989.

Delbrück, Hans. *History of the Art of War Within the Framework of Political History*. Vol. III: *Medieval Warfare*. Trans. W.J. Renfroe, Jr. Westport, 1984 – originally *Geschichte der Kriegskunst im Rahmen des Politischen Geschichte*. Vol. III: *Mittelalter*. 2nd ed. Berlin, 1923.

Denifle, Henri. *La guerre de cent ans et la désolation des églises, monastères et hospitaux en France*. Paris, 1899.

Deprez, E. *Les préliminaires de la guerre de cent ans*. Paris, 1902.

Devic, C. and J. Vaissette. *Histoire générale de Languedoc*. Toulouse, 1872.

DeVries, Kelly. 'Contemporary Views of Edward III's Failure at the Siege of Tournai, 1340,' *Nottingham Medieval Studies* 39 (1995), 70–105.

———. 'God, Leadership, Flemings, and Archery: Contemporary Perceptions of Victory and Defeat at the Battle of Sluys, 1340,' *American Neptune* 55 (1995), 1–28.

———. 'Hunger, Flemish Participation and the Flight of Philip VI: Contemporary Accounts of the Siege of Calais, 1346–47,' *Studies in Medieval and Renaissance History* n.s 12 (1991), 129–81.

———. *Medieval Military Technology*. Peterborough, 1992.

Digard, Georges. *Philippe le Bel et le Saint Siège de 1285 à 1304*. 2 vols. Paris, 1936.

Douglas, David C. *William the Conqueror: The Norman Impact upon England*. Berkeley, 1964.

Du Boulay, Caesar Egassio. *Historia universitatis Parisiensis*. 1668; rpt. Frankfurt, 1966.

Duby, Georges. *William Marshal: The Flower of Chivalry*. Trans. R. Howard. New York, 1985.

Duncan, A.A.M. 'The War of the Scots, 1306–23,' *Transactions of the Royal Historical Society* 6th series, 2 (1992), 125–51.

Durrer, Robert. *Schweizer Kriegsgeschichte*. Ed. M. Feldmann and H.H.G. Wirz. 2 vols. Bern, 1915.

Erben, W. *Kriegsgeschichte des Mittelalters*. Berlin, 1929.

Favier, Jean. *La guerre de cent ans*. Paris, 1980.

Felbien, Michel. *Histoire de l'abbaye royale de Saint-Denis en France*. 1707; rpt. Paris, 1973.

Feller, Richard. *Geschichte Berns.* 3 vols. Bern, 1949.

Fischer, R. von. *Schweizerkriegsgeschichte.* Ed. M. Feldman and H.H.G. Wirz. Vol. 1. Bern, 1915.

Fisher, Andrew. 'Wallace and Bruce: Scotland's Uneasy Heroes,' *History Today* 39 (February 1989), 18–23.

Fletcher, Richard. *The Quest for El Cid.* Oxford, 1989.

Forey, Alan. *The Military Orders: From the Twelfth to the Fourteenth Century.* Toronto, 1992.

Fowler, Kenneth A. 'News from the Front: Letters and Despatches of the Fourteenth Century.' In *Guerre et société en France, en Angleterre et en Bourgogne, xive–xve siècle.* Ed. P. Contamine et al. Lille, 1991, pp. 63–92.

Fryde, E.B. 'Financial Resources of Edward III in the Netherlands, 1337–40,' *Revue Belge de philologie et d'histoire* 45 (1967), 1142–1216.

———. *William de la Pole: Merchant and King's Banker (+1366).* London, 1988.

Fryde, Natalie B. 'Edward III's Removal of his Ministers and Judges, 1340–1,' *Bulletin of the Institute of Historical Research* 48 (1975), 149–63.

———. *The Tyranny and Fall of Edward II, 1321–1327.* Cambridge, 1979.

Fuller, J.F.C. *The Decisive Battles of the Western World and their Influence upon History.* 2nd ed. 2 vols. London, 1970.

———. *A Military History of the Western World.* Vol. 1: *From the Earliest Times to the Battle of Lepanto.* New York, 1954.

Funck-Brentano, Frantz. *Mémoire sur la bataille de Courtrai (1302, 11 juillet) et les chroniqueurs qui en ont traité, pour servir à l'historiographie du règne de Philippe le Bel.* Paris, 1981.

———. *Philippe le Bel en Flandre: Les origines de la guerre de cent ans.* Paris, 1896.

———. 'Le traité de Marquette (Septembre 1304).' In *Melanges Julien Havet.* 1895; rpt. Geneva, 1972, pp. 749–58.

Gaier, Claude. *Art et organisation militaires dans la principauté de Liège et dans le comté de Looz au Moyen Age.* Brussels, 1968.

———. 'La cavalerie lourde en Europe occidentale du XIIe au XVIe siècle,' *Revue internationale d'histoire militaire* 31 (1971), 385–96.

———. 'L'invincibilité anglaise et le grande arc après la guerre de cent ans: un mythe tenace,' *Tijdschrift voor gescheidenis* 91 (1978), 378–85.

Garin, Eugenio. *Der Italienische Humanismus.* Bern, 1947.

George, Hereford B. 'The Archers at Crecy,' *English Historical Review* 10 (1895), 733–38.

Gillingham, John. *Richard the Lionheart.* London, 1978.

Graham, Frank. *Famous Northern Battles.* Rothbury, 1988.

Haines, Roy Martin. *Archbishop John Stratford: Political Revolutionary and Champion of the Liberties of the English Church, ca. 1275/80-1348.* Toronto, 1986.

Hamilton, J.S. *Piers Gaveston, Earl of Cornwall, 1307–1312: Politics and Patronage in the Reign of Edward II.* Detroit, 1988.

Hardy, Robert. *Longbow: A Social and Military History.* 3rd ed. London, 1992.

———. 'The Longbow.' In *Arms, Armies and Fortifications in the Hundred Years War.* Ed. A. Curry and M. Hughes. Woodbridge, 1994, pp. 161–82

Harriss, G.L. *King, Parliament, and Public Finance in Medieval England to 1369.* Oxford, 1975.

Haskins, George L. 'Judicial Proceedings Against a Traitor after Boroughbridge, 1322,' *Speculum* 12 (1937), 509–11.

Hay, Denys. *Europe in the Fourteenth and Fifteenth Centuries.* 2nd ed. London, 1989.

———. *The Italian Renaissance in Its Historical Background.* Cambridge, 1961.

Head, Thomas and Richard Landes, eds. *The Peace of God: Social Violence and Religious Response in France around the Year 1000.* Ithaca, 1992.

Henneman, John Bell. *Royal Taxation in Fourteenth-Century France: The Development of War Financing, 1322–1356.* Princeton, 1971.

Holmes, George. *Europe: Hierarchy and Revolt, 1320–1450.* London, 1975.

Housley, Norman. *The Later Crusades, 1274–1580: From Lyons to Alcazar.* Oxford, 1992.

Howard, Michael. *War in European History.* Oxford, 1976.

Hugenholtz, F.W.N. *Drie boerenopstanden uit de viertiende eeuw.* 's Gravenhage, 1978.

Jacoby, David. 'La "compagnie catalane" et l'état catalan de Grèce. Quelques aspects de leur histoire,' *Journal des savants* (1966), 78–103.

Jones, Archer. *The Art of War in the Western World.* Oxford, 1989.

Jones, W.R. '*Rex et Ministri*: English Local Government and the Crisis of 1341,' *Journal of British Studies* 13 (1973), 1–20.

Keegan, John. *The Face of Battle.* Harmondsworth, 1978.

Keen, M.H. *Chivalry.* New Haven, 1984.

———. *England in the Later Middle Ages: A Political History.* London, 1973.

Kenyon, John R. *Medieval Fortifications.* New York, 1990.

Köhler, G. *Die Entwickelung des Kriegswesens und der Kriegführung in der Ritterzeit von Mitte des 11. Jahrhunderts bis zu den Hussitenkriegen.* 3 vols. Breslau, 1886.

Kurth, Godefroid. *La cité de Liège au moyen-age.* 3 vols. Brussels, 1909–11.

Leclerq, Jean. 'Un sermon prononcé pendant la guerre de Flandre sous Philippe le Bel,' *Revue du moyen âge latin* 1 (1945), 165–72.

Lejeune, J. 'Het prinsbisdom Luik tot 1390.' In *Algemene geschiedenis der Nederlanden.* Vol. 3: *De late middeleeuwen, 1305–1477.* Utrecht, 1951, pp. 175–89.

Liddell Hart, B.H. *Strategy: The Indirect Approach.* New York, 1954.

Liebenau, Theodor von. 'Berichte über die Schlacht am Morgarten,' *Mitteilungen des historischen Vereins des Kantons Schwyz* 3 (1884), 1–85.

Lloyd, E.M. 'The "Herse" of Archers at Crecy,' *English Historical Review* 10 (1895), 538–41.

Lloyd, T.H. *The English Wool Trade in the Middle Ages.* Cambridge, 1977.

Longnon, J. 'The Frankish States in Greece, 1204–1311.' In *A History of The Crusades.* Ed. K.M. Setton. Vol. II: *The Later Crusades.* Ed. R. L. Wolff and H.W. Hazard. Madison, 1969), pp. 235–74.

Lot, Ferdinand. *L'art militaire et les armées au moyen âge en Europe et dans le proche orient.* 2 vols. Paris, 1946.

Lucas, Henry Stephen. *The Low Countries and the Hundred Years' War, 1326–1347.* Ann Arbor, 1929.

Lyon, Bryce. 'The Role of Cavalry in Medieval Warfare: Horses, Horses All Around and Not a One to Use,' *Mededelingen van de Koninklijke Academie voor Wetenschappen, Letteren en Schone Kunsten van België* 49 (1987), 77–90.

Lyons, Malcolm Cameron and D.E.P. Jackson. *Saladin: The Politics of the Holy War.* Cambridge, 1982.

Mackenzie, W.M. *The Battle of Bannockburn: A Study in Mediaeval Warfare*. Glasgow, 1913.

Maddicott, J.R. *Thomas of Lancaster, 1307–1322: A Study in the Reign of Edward II*. Oxford, 1970.

Malderghem, Jean van. *La bataille de Staveren (26 septembre 1345)*. Brussels, 1869.

Marshall, Christopher. *Warfare in the Latin East, 1192–1291*. Cambridge, 1992.

McCrackan, W.D. *The Rise of the Swiss Republic*. 2nd ed. New York, 1901.

McGuffie, T.H. 'The Long-bow as a Decisive Weapon,' *History Today* 5 (1955), 737–41.

McKisack, May. *The Fourteenth Century*. Oxford History of England. Oxford, 1959.

Mertens, Jacques. 'De boerenopstand onder Zannekin.' In *Nikolaas Zannekin en de slag bij Kassel 1328–1978*. Dixmude, 1978, pp. 96–103.

———. 'La confiscations dans la Chatellenie du Franc de Bruges après la bataille de Cassel,' *Bulletin de la commission royale d'histoire de Belgique* 134 (1968), 239–84.

———. 'De economische en sociale toestand van de opstandelingen uit het Brugse Vrije, wier goederen na de slag bij Cassel (1328) verbeurd verklaard werden,' *Revue Belge de philologie et d'histoire* 47 (1969), 1131–53.

———. 'Zannekin of de evolutie van het beeld van een volksheld,' *De Frans Nederlanden. Les Pays-Bas Français* (1978), 24–37.

Meyer, Bruno. 'Die Schlacht am Morgarten: Verlauf der Schlacht und Absichten der Parteien,' *Revue Suisse d'histoire* 16 (1966), 129–79.

Miller, Edward. *War in the North: The Anglo-Scottish Wars of the Middle Ages*. Hull, 1960.

Moncado, Francisco de. *Expedición de los Catalanes y Aragoneses contra Turcos y Griegos*. Madrid, 1941. Translation: *The Catalan Chronicle of Francisco de Moncado*. Trans. F. Hernández. Ed. J.M. Sharp. El Paso, 1975.

Morillo, Stephen. *Warfare under the Anglo-Norman Kings, 1066–1135*. Woodbridge, 1994.

Morris, John E. 'The Archers at Crecy,' *English Historical Review* 12 (1897), 427–36.

———. *Bannockburn*. Cambridge, 1914.

———. 'Mounted Infantry in Mediaeval Warfare,' *Transactions of the Royal Historical Society* 3rd ser. 8 (1914), 77–102.

———. *The Welsh Wars of Edward I*. Oxford, 1901.

Neilson, George. *John Barbour, Poet and Translator*. London, 1900.

Nicholas, David. *Medieval Flanders*. London, 1992

———. *Town and Countryside: Social, Economic and Political Tensions in Fourteenth-Century Flanders*. Bruges, 1971.

———. *The van Arteveldes of Ghent: The Varieties of Vendetta and the Hero in History*. Ithaca, 1988.

Nicholson, Helen. *Templars, Hospitallers and Teutonic Knights: Images of the Military Orders, 1128–1291*. Leicester, 1995.

Nicholson, Ranald. *Edward III and the Scots: The Formative Years of a Military Campaign*. Oxford, 1965.

———. *Scotland: The Later Middle Ages*. Edinburgh, 1974.

———. 'The Siege of Berwick, 1333,' *Scottish Historical Review* 40 (1961), 19–42.

Niermeyer, J.F. 'Het Sticht Utrecht, Gelre en de Friese landen in de veertiende eeuw.' In *Algemene geschiedenis der Nederlanden*. Vol. 3: *De late middeleeuwen, 1305–1477*. Utrecht, 1951, pp. 125–60.

Nowé, Henri. *La bataille des éperons d'or*. Brussels, 1945.

Oman, Charles. *The Art of War in the Middle Ages A.D. 378–1515*. Ed. J.H. Beeler. Ithaca, 1953.

———. *A History of the Art of War: The Middle Ages from the Fourth to the Fourteenth Century*. London, 1898.

———. *A History of the Art of War in the Middle Ages*. 2 vols. London, 1905.

Ormrod, W.M. *The Reign of Edward III: Crown and Political Society in England, 1327–1377*. New Haven, 1990.

Packe, Michael. *King Edward III*. London, 1983.

Partner, Peter. *The Knights Templar and their Myth*. Oxford, 1981.

Pascot, Jep. *Les almugavares: Mercenaires catalans du moyen age (1302–1388)*. Brussels, 1971.

Pernoud, Reginé. *Joan of Arc: By Herself and Her Witnesses*. Trans. E. Hyams. New York, 1964.

Perroy, Edouard. *The Hundred Years War*. Trans. W.B. Wells. London, 1951.

Phillips, J.R.S. *Aymer de Valence, Earl of Pembroke, 1307–1324: Baronial Politics in the Reign of Edward II*. Oxford, 1972.

Pirenne, Henri. 'Documents relatifs à l'histoire de la Flandre pendant la première moitié du XIVe siècle,' *Bulletin de la commission royale d'histoire* 7 (1897), 477–93

———. *Early Democracies in the Low Countries: Urban Society and Political Conflict in the Middle Ages and the Renaissance*. Trans. J.V. Saunders. New York, 1971.

———. *Histoire de Belgique*. Vol. 1: *Des origines du commencement du XIVe siècle*. Brussels, 1903.

———. *Histoire de Belgique*. Vol. 2: *Du commencement du XIVe siècle à la mort de Charles le Téméraire*. Brussels, 1903.

———. 'Un mémoire de Robert de Cassel sur sa participation à la révolte de la Flandre maritime en 1324–1325,' *Revue du nord* 1 (1910), 45–50.

———. 'La version flamande et la version française de la bataille de Courtrai, note historiographie de XIVe siècle,' *Bulletin de la commission royale d'histoire* 4th ser., 17 (1890), 11–50; 'Note supplémentaire,' *Bulletin de la commission royale d'histoire* 5th ser., 2 (1892), 85–123.

Pollard, A.J. *John Talbot and the War in France, 1427–1453*. London, 1983.

Pounds, N.J.G. *The Medieval Castle in England and Wales: A Social and Political History*. Cambridge, 1990.

Powers, James F. *A Society Organized for War: The Iberian Municipal Militias in the Central Middle Ages, 1000–1284*. Berkeley, 1988.

Powicke, F.M. *The Thirteenth Century, 1216–1307*. Oxford History of England. Oxford, 1953.

Powicke, M.R. 'Edward II and Military Obligation,' *Speculum* 39 (1956), 92–119.

Prentout, Henri. *La prise de Caen par Edouard III, 1346*. Caen, 1904.

Preston, Richard A., Alex Roland, and Sydney F. Wise. *Men at Arms*. 5th ed. Fort Worth, 1991.

Prestwich, Michael. *Edward I*. London, 1988.

———. 'England and Scotland during the Wars of Independence.' In *England and Her Neighbours, 1066–1453: Essays in Honour of Pierre Chaplais*. Ed. M. Jones and M. Vale. Woodbridge, 1989, pp. 181–97.

———. 'English Armies in the Early Stages of the Hundred Years War: a Scheme in 1341,' *Bulletin of the Institute of Historical Research* 56 (1983), 102–13.

———. *The Three Edwards: War and State in England, 1272–1377*. London, 1980.

Pryor, John H. *Geography, Technology, and War: Studies in the Maritime History of the Mediterranean, 649–1571.* Cambridge, 1988.

Rabil, Albert, Jr. 'The Significance of "Civic Humanism" in the Interpretation of the Italian Renaissance.' In *Renaissance Humanism: Foundations, Forms, and Legacy.* Vol. 1: *Humanism in Italy.* Ed. A. Rabil, Jr. Philadelphia, 1988, pp. 141–74.

Rees, Gareth. 'The Longbow's Deadly Secrets,' *New Scientist* 138 (June 5, 1993), 24–25.

Rogers, Clifford J. 'Edward III and the Dialectics of Strategy, 1327–1360,' *Transactions of the Royal Historical Society* 6th ser. 4 (1994), 88–102.

———. 'The Military Revolutions of the Hundred Years War,' *Journal of Military History* 57 (1993), 249–51.

Rogers, R. *Latin Siege Warfare in the Twelfth Century.* Oxford, 1992.

Rompaey, Jan van. 'De opstand in het vlaamse kustland van 1323 tot 1328 en de figuur van Nikolaas Zannekin.' In *Nikolaas Zannekin en de slag bij Kassel 1328–1978.* Dixmude, 1978, pp. 104–32.

Rose, Walther. 'König Johann der Blinde von Böhmen und die Schlacht bei Crécy (1346),' *Zeitschrift für historisches Waffenkunde* 7 (1915–17), 37–60.

Sabbe, Jacques. *Vlaanderen in opstand, 1323–1328: Nikolaas Zannekin, Zeger Janszone en Willem de Deken.* Bruges, 1992.

Sayles, George. 'The Formal Judgments on the Traitors of 1322,' *Speculum* 16 (1941), 57–63.

Scammell, Jean. 'Robert I and the North of England,' *English Historical Review* 73 (1958), 385–403.

Schnitzer, Maria. *Die Morgartenschlacht im werdenden schweizerischen National-bewusstsein.* Zurich, 1969.

Setton, Kenneth M. *Catalan Domination of Athens, 1311–1388.* Cambridge, 1948.

———. 'The Catalans in Greece, 1311–1380.' In *A History of The Crusades.* Ed. K.M. Setton. Vol. III: *The Fourteenth and Fifteenth Centuries.* Ed. H.W. Hazard. Madison, 1975, pp. 167–224.

Smallwood, T.M. 'An Unpublished Early Account of Bruce's Murder of Comyn,' *Scottish Historical Review* 54 (1975), 1–10.

Scott, Ronald McNair. *Robert the Bruce: King of Scots.* New York, 1982.

Seward, Desmond. *The Hundred Years War: The English in France, 1337–1453.* New York, 1978.

Showalter, Dennis E. 'Caste, Skill, and Training: The Evolution of Cohesion in European Armies from the Middle Ages to the Sixteenth Century,' *Journal of Military History* 57 (1993), 407–30.

Smail, R.C. *Crusading Warfare, 1097–1193.* Cambridge, 1956.

Smet, J.M. de. 'Passio francorum secundum flemyngos,' *De leiegouw* (1977), 289–319.

Smet, Joseph de. 'Les effectifs Brugeois à la bataille de Courtrai en 1302,' *Revue Belge de philologie et d'histoire* 12 (1933), 631–36.

Strayer, Joseph. *The Reign of Philip the Fair.* Princeton, 1980.

Sumption, Jonathan. *The Hundred Years War: Trial by Battle.* Philadelphia, 1991.

Talbot, Hugh. *The English Achilles: The Life and Campaigns of John Talbot, 1st Earl of Shrewsbury.* London, 1981.

TeBrake, William H. *A Plague of Insurrection: Popular Politics and Peasant Revolt in Flanders, 1323–1328.* Philadelphia, 1993.

Thompson, M.W. *The Decline of the Castle.* Cambridge, 1987.

———. *The Rise of the Castle.* Cambridge, 1991.

Tout, T.F. 'Firearms in England in the Fourteenth Century,' *English Historical Review* 26 (1911), 666–702.

———. *The Place of the Reign of Edward II in English History*. 2nd ed. Manchester, 1936.

———. 'The Tactics of the Battles of Boroughbridge and Morlaix,' *English Historical Review* 19 (1904), 711–15.

Tuck, J.A. 'War and Society in the Medieval North,' *Northern History* 21 (1985), 33–52.

Vale, M.G.A. *Charles VII*. Berkeley, 1974.

van Creveld, Martin. *Command in War*. Cambridge, 1985.

Verbruggen, J.F. *The Art of Warfare in Western Europe during the Middle Ages: From the Eighth Century to 1340*. Trans. S. Willard and S.C.M. Southern. Amsterdam, 1977.

———. 'De goededag,' *Militaria Belgica* 1977, 65–70.

———. 'De historiografie van de guldensporenslag,' *De leiegouw* (1977), 245–72.

———. *De krijgkunst in west-europa in de middeleeuwen (IXe tot XIVe eeuw)*. Brussels, 1954.

———. 'De rol van de ruiterij in de middeleeuwse oorlogvoering,' *Revue Belge d'histoire militaire* 30 (1994), 389–418.

———. *De slag der guldensporen, bijdrage tot de gescheidenis van Vlaanderens vrijheidsoorlog, 1297–1305*. Antwerp, 1952.

———. 'La tactique de la chevalerie française de 1340 à 1415,' *Publications de l'université de l'état à Elisabethville* 1 (1961), 39–48.

———. 'La tactique militaire des armées de chevaliers,' *Revue du nord* 29 (1947), 161–80.

Vercauteren, Fernand. *Luttes sociales à Liège, xiiie et xive siècles*. Brussels, 1946.

———. 'Het prinsbisdom Luik tot 1316.' *Algemene geschiedenis der Nederlanden*. Vol. 2: *De volle middeleeuwen, 925–1305*. Utrecht, 1950, pp. 338–52.

Viard, Jules. 'La campagne de juillet-août 1346 et la bataille de Crécy,' *Le moyen âge* 2nd ser. 27 (1926), 1–84.

———. 'La guerre de Flandre (1328),' *Bibliothèque de l'ecole de chartes* 83 (1922).

———. 'Le siege de Calais,' *Le moyen âge* 40 (1929), 129–89.

Wailly, Henri de. *Crécy 1346: Anatomy of a Battle*. Poole, 1987.

Warner, Marina. *Joan of Arc: The Image of Female Heroism*. Harmondsworth, 1981.

Waugh, Scott. L. *England in the Reign of Edward III*. Cambridge, 1991.

———. 'For King, Country and Patron: The Despensers and Local Administration,' *Journal of British Studies* 22 (1983), 23–45.

———. 'The Profits of Violence: The Minor Gentry in the Rebellion of 1321–22 in Gloucestershire and Herefordshire,' *Speculum* 52 (1977), 843–69.

Webster, Bruce. 'Scotland Without a King, 1329–1341.' In *Medieval Scotland: Crown, Lordship and Community: Essays Presented to G.W.S. Barrow*. Ed. A. Grant and K.J. Stringer. Edinburgh, 1993, pp. 224–38.

Wernli, Fritz. *Die Entstehung der schweizerischen Eidgenossenschaft*. Zurich, 1972.

Werveke, Hans van. 'Les charges financières de traité d'Athis (1305),' *Revue du Nord* 22 (1950), 81–93.

———. *Jacques van Artevelde*. Brussels, 1943.

Witzig, Hans. *Von Morgarten bis Marignano*. Zurich, 1957.

INDEX

Lightning Source UK Ltd.
Milton Keynes UK
UKHW021126210721
387528UK00004B/157